Monstrous Deviations in I

At the Interface

Series Editors
Dr Robert Fisher
Dr Daniel Riha

Advisory Board

Dr Alejandro Cervantes-Carson
Professor Margaret Chatterjee
Dr Wayne Cristaudo
Mira Crouch
Dr Phil Fitzsimmons
Professor Asa Kasher
Owen Kelly

Dr Peter Mario Kreuter
Martin McGoldrick
Revd Stephen Morris
Professor John Parry
Dr Paul Reynolds
Professor Peter Twohig
Professor S Ram Vemuri

Revd Dr Kenneth Wilson, O.B.E

An *At the Interface* research and publications project.
http://www.inter-disciplinary.net/at-the-interface/

The Evil Hub
'Monsters and the Monstrous'

2011

Monstrous Deviations in Literature and the Arts

Edited by

Cristina Santos & Adriana Spahr

Inter-Disciplinary Press

Oxford, United Kingdom

© Inter-Disciplinary Press 2011
http://www.inter-disciplinary.net/publishing/id-press/

The *Inter-Disciplinary Press* is part of *Inter-Disciplinary.Net* – a global network for research and publishing. The *Inter-Disciplinary Press* aims to promote and encourage the kind of work which is collaborative, innovative, imaginative, and which provides an exemplar for inter-disciplinary and multi-disciplinary publishing.

All rights reserved. No part of this publication may be reproduced, stored in a retrieval system, or transmitted in any form or by any means without the prior permission of Inter-Disciplinary Press.

Inter-Disciplinary Press, Priory House, 149B Wroslyn Road, Freeland, Oxfordshire. OX29 8HR, United Kingdom.
+44 (0)1993 882087

British Library Cataloguing in Publication Data. A catalogue record for this book is available from the British Library.

ISBN: 978-1-84888-049-8
First published in the United Kingdom in paperback in 2011. First edition.

Printed in Great Britain by Marston Book Services Limited, Oxford.

Cover design by Peter Day.

Table of Contents

Acknowledgements   vii

Introduction   ix
Cristina Santos & Adriana Spahr

PART 1   All that is Different is not Monstrous?

Divine Monsters in the Guarani Aboriginal Culture   3
Adriana Spahr

From Monster to Deviant: European Conceptions of New World Peoples in Early Colonial Peru   21
Felipe E. Ruan

Protest and Pretence: Depicting the Monstrous Immigrant Body in *How the Other Half Lives* and *The Jungle*   43
Shelley Galliah

PART 2   Monstrous Transgressions in the Socio-Cultural and Political Imaginaries

Social Deviants and Freakish Misfits in the Short Stories of Annie Vivanti   63
Anne Urbancic

The Zombie's Great Escape in René Depestre's *Hadriana dans tous mes rêves*   81
Tamara El-Hoss

The Labyrinth, Lustrate and Liminal in *Requiem for a Beast*: The Monster Resurrected as Multi-Modality   95
Phil Fitzsimmons

Barbarians at the Gate in Tom Clancy's *Ghost Recon: Advanced Warfighter* Series   111
Tracy Crowe Morey

PART 3   Mad Women (and not Necessarily Just in the Attic)

Monstrous Minds, Boundless Bodies: Madness, the Monstrous Feminine and the Victorian Imagination   131
Elizabeth Hollis Berry

	Offended Readers and Monstrous Texts: Theorising Monstrosity and Narrative *Jonathan A. Allan*	157
	Vampire, Witch, Serial Killer or All of the Above? The Bloody Countess Elizabeth Bathory *Cristina Santos*	177
	Giovanna Rivero's 'Contraluna': Meeting the Monstrous Lilith *Verónica H. Saunero-Ward*	193
PART 4	**The Mechanics of Monsterisation**	
	A Three-Eyed Monster: The Picture of a Photographer in World Literature *Joanna Madloch*	213
	Unmasking Mary Shelley's *Frankenstein* in Patrick Süskind's *Das Parfum* *Samantha Michele Riley*	229
	Mutants, Mice and Monstrosities: Dystopia in *Kys'* by Tatyana Tolstaya *Cristina Ruiz Serrano*	251
	The Distorted Mirror: The Monstrosity of Artificial Beings *Jesús Eduardo Oliva Abarca*	269
	Notes on Contributors	285

Acknowledgements

The editors would like to thank the authors of the chapters in this book for their time and efforts and for sharing their important work. They would also like to thank the support of the following people: Colin Bailey, Eugenio Bolongaro, Pamela Farvolden, Corrado Federici, Suzanne Hayman, Natalia Pylypiuk, and Sherryl Vint.

The editors would also like to extend a special acknowledgement of thanks to Mario J. Valdés and Linda Hutcheon in recognition of their continual mentorship and for the invaluable experience of having worked with them as graduate student research assistants. Those years of guidance on true interdisciplinary and collaborative work became fundamental to the development of their collaborative projects.

Cristina Santos would like to thank the Humanities Research Institute at Brock University for the funding of the artwork by Rudy Ramos and the Brock University BSIG Grant that also assisted financially in the completion of this project. She would also like to thank Jonathan A. Allan, her research assistant that also worked on this project in proofreading and formatting. Finally, she would like to thank Martin, Joseph and Lucas Walkes and her family, as always, for their unlimited understanding, love and support.

Adriana Spahr would like to thank the Supplemental Professional Development Fund and Grant MacEwan Research, Scholarly Activity and Creative Achievement Fund, both at Grant MacEwan University, for contributing to the funding of this project. She would like also to thank her family: especially Hugo De Marinis and her nieces and nephews, for their unconditional love and support; and her friends, especially Cristina, for her infinite encouragement, help and support.

Introduction

Cristina Santos & Adriana Spahr

> We are both very good at imagining things. Let's look at this rationally, though. We both know too much nonsense. [Elizabeth] Bathory is a monster in the popular imagination. It's not hard to imagine her wickedness ... but the popular imagination may be more monstrous than the real person. It is the popular imagination that allows monsters and heroes to appear.[1]

Each historical period has always created its own monsters and has interpreted them as either a deformation or deviation of the norm based on the prevailing socio-cultural values of the era. The patriarchy has, through morality, politics, religion and other governing institutions, culturally determined the parameters that have delineated and (re)configured these 'monstrous' deviances.

That which is 'monstrous' has been used to identify and/or describe disorder, chaos, discontent and other expressions of non-conformity or deception that have been perceived as threatening the status quo. For example, the liminal Other (woman, indigenous, homosexual, the conqueror/conquered, to name a few) has been depicted as monstrous for various reasons, ranging from preconceived notions of sexuality as well as social and racial prejudgments.

In recent years, deviance and monstrosity have been the subjects of a wide variety of representations in various fields: world literatures, visual arts, film, philosophy, social science, history and psychology (to name a few). It is within this scope that we have undertaken this project to explore, through a multi- and inter-disciplinary approach, the monstrous deviations in the cultural imaginary as examples of universally recognized reflections of human existence and interchange with their socio-cultural environment.

Post-modernism has allowed for the concept of a fluctuating and even challenging form of identification in which the 'self' is in constant flux. Paul Ricoeur's process of mimesis[2] has often been applied to the reading and writing process but it can also be applied to this post-modern identity construction. Mimesis, or the prefigurative, can be interpreted as the basis for identification: our social, cultural and familial environment into which we are born. Mimesis, or the configurative, could be seen as the lived experience; and finally, mimesis, or the refigurative, is the new 'self' constructed after each lived experience. Therefore, identity in flux is seen as ever changing because within mimesis the refiguration is, intrinsically, ever changing and giving birth to a new prefigurative or foundation of the 'I'. In this study, we shall see that this very 'flux' in identity construction is the very part of the anxiety of the Other and why that which escapes a fixed definition is imagined as the monstrous.

The 'monster' becomes, as we shall see, humanity's fear and/or anxiety of what escapes a fixed meaning or is not entirely explainable or that which is different. However this relationship of 'self' and 'Other' is not stable since it is based on the equation of the 'I' being the social normative and the 'not I' as the different, and at times deviant. It is the constant binary opposition of normal vs. abnormal, natural vs. unnatural and even human vs. inhuman. If we are to maintain our postmodernist context, it would allow for a more fluid and ever-changing construction without the aforementioned anxiety but instead with the endeavour to understand the Other and therefore moving away from anxiety and towards what can be shaped into a form of acceptance. If we are to take this a step further, to know, understand and possibly accept the Other intrinsically involves the recognizing and acceptance of all that the 'self' embodies.

The problematic of the 'monster' and of 'monstrosity' lies in understanding the Other in all its complexities and that it is entirely possible that we may actually recognize in the 'monstrous' Other the very characteristic we deny in our selves. In denying the Other, one is also denying the self and continues to hide the secrets that it holds. Margrit Shildrik, in *Embodying the Monster: Encounters with the Vulnerable Self*, extrapolates the transgressivity of the self and the monstrous Other in that 'what we see mirrored in the monster are the leaks and flows, the vulnerabilities in our embodied being'.[3] It is this very fluidity, or flux as previously alluded to, that raises the problematic in the discussion of monstrosity. Social and cultural institutions have historically functioned as normative powers that have systematically placed all that is non-normative as a liminal existence. Nevertheless, it will become obvious throughout this study that there is never a clear definition of the monster and that, at times, that which is physically monstrous is not necessarily the 'real' monster but that which is most human-looking that is the 'real' monster.

Not only do participants in this volume come from different parts of the world but also from varying disciplines of study and with different cultural experiences. Furthermore, they have had different lived realities and, as a result, have diverse views of the world. Within the academia, their interests vary in their area of expertise thereby embodying, not only the multidisciplinary approach to the topic at hand, but also the broader definition of 'monsters' and 'monstrosity'. However, they are united by their love of literature and their serious desire to reveal and study what is considered a 'monster' or an embodiment of 'monstrosity' and its implication within a given society. The collaborators agreed that the institutionalisation of the term represented and continues to represent a mechanism of cultural discourse. In the hands of the powerful, this discourse led to the marginalisation of either a social group and/or the symbolic castration of a human being to satisfy the 'normal' function of a society.

Owing to the nature of this collection, readers will be disappointed if they expect sections to be divided into periods, countries or even continents. The diversity of the meaning of the notions of 'monsters' and 'monstrosity' created in a single period by any society would be possible only by grouping them in an encyclopaedia.[4] Due to the nature of 'monster,' which is proposed here as a cultural invention, it is impossible to classify it within a tidy and all encompassing definition. Moreover, owing to the elusive definition of what it is,[5] readers will find a grouping of chapters in this study that reflect a common dialogic link as insinuated by the title of each section.

The first section, entitled 'All that is Different is not Monstrous' presents three chapters which allow us to have a vital vision and evolution or 'involution' of the term 'monstrosity'. It covers a period from a pre-Colombian era to the twentieth century in America. *Adriana Spahr*'s chapter situates us in the world of the Guarani people before the arrival of the Spanish in South America; *Felipe E. Ruan* investigates the reality of the *mestizo* within the early colonial period in Peru; and *Shelley Galliah* deals with the figure of the immigrant in the United States in the early twentieth century.

Adriana Spahr's, 'Divine Monsters in Guarani Aboriginal Culture', leads the reader to the mystical and ancient world of the Guarani people. These people occupied, for an unaccounted number of years, the south-central part of South America in an area that covers Paraguay, part of Bolivia, the south of Brazil, and Argentina. Spahr's chapter focuses on the survival of these people's beliefs in Argentina after the Spanish colonization. For the Guaranis the concept of monstrosity is an integral part in the formation of their deities. Contrary to our conception of the world in binary terms (good/evil; angels/witches; gods and demons), for the Guaranis these oppositional terms are united in their deities. As a reflection of human beings, they are capable of doing good and lovely things at one moment and being revengeful and cruel at another. The Guaranis' deities, some of them with physical deformations, cohabitated with society. In a single deity both good and evil could be found and it is safe to say that these deities remain among them today because they are the true reflection of mankind's own likeness and imperfections.

As with other ancient cultures, monsters, as Bettina Bildhauer and Robert Mills state, 'were closer to home'; they lived, somewhat harmoniously, in what was considered 'normal'. This notion of the world changed in Europe during the late Middle Ages and for some scholars this change was an expression of an early colonialist mentality that needed to create distinctions between territories and people. As a result, European conception of monster moved to extreme geographical location such as the Far East, India, Antipodean zones and Ethiopia.[6] This idea is the starting point of 'From Monster to Deviant: European Conceptions of New World Peoples in Early Colonial Peru' by *Felipe E. Ruan*. In one of the letters of Christopher Columbus to Luis de Santangel, finance minister to Ferdinand II, Columbus expresses his surprise when neither he nor other conquerors found 'monster men' in the New World. Monster-men and monster-women were created later by the *conquistadors* when they needed to conquer and dominate the Amerindians and to impose on them the European vision of the world. Amerindians became the 'other', the 'barbarian,' the imperfect being which had to be dominated or exterminated. The focus of Ruan's chapter is on Peruvian society in which the physical deformity of the monsters imagined by the Spanish, was transformed into a moral deviance attributed to the Amerindians and in particular, to the *mestizo*. They were marginalized and discriminated against for being 'ill inclined' and deformed, to give two examples. By showing that only the native cultures were deviant, the Spanish stated that indigenous people inherited their deviance from their mothers since, as the indigenous contribution to the child's *mestizo* heritage she was the corruptive element of the 'pure blood' of the Spanish father. The situation of the Amerindian in general, and of the *mestizos* in particular, worsened in the seventeenth century when their numbers increased and they rebelled against the Spanish. They constituted the 'other', 'the monster' 'the unruly' because they represented a threat to the authority of the Spanish.

The following centuries failed to diminish divisions and the racial and socio-cultural classification of people. Human beings continued to not accept difference amongst them or to acknowledge the dark side of the human psyche. Therefore, monsters kept revealing themselves, mutating according to the historical moments in which they were engendered. The reader will see this in 'Protest and Pretence: Depicting the Monstrous Immigrant Body in *How the Other Half Lives* and *The Jungle*', by *Shelley Galliah*.

Similar to the first years after the conquest where the Spanish considered the inhabitants of the New World to be integrated within the specific hierarchy of their newly defined community - in the history of the United States, immigrants were warmly accepted. In the late eighteenth century immigrants were glorified for their contributions to the creation of a great country. By the early nineteenth century, this changed: some groups, for example, saw the Catholics as the representation of evil, seeking to replace their government with the Papacy. Later, when another crisis hit the country and the rate of unemployment rose, different 'monsters' emerged. Unlike the moral monstrosity attributed to Amerindian and other groups in Latin America, the monstrosity attributed to the new immigrants in the U.S. was physical. The newer waves of immigrants from poorer countries in Europe were labelled as 'semi-barbarians' because they lived in filthy and crowded conditions. They became targets of criticism and blame in the late nineteenth century when the economic situation deteriorated for many. Poverty became a disease and, as a mechanism of self-protection, the 'ill people' had to be kept away. This new 'other' was seen as the carrier of physical, moral and political diseases. Even writers, such as Jacob Riis, concerned about poverty in his country, perpetuated this idea: Typhus fever and smallpox as diseases were brought over from across the sea by the large immigration populace, as stated by Galliah. For Riis, Italians were pigs, Chinese secretive and cat-like, Arabs '[a]dirty stain' and Jews 'monstrous, leaking bodies, both physically contaminated and morally suspect.' For his part,

Upton Sinclair, with a more progressive view than that of Riis, depicted the poor as depraved animals. The three chapters, which cover almost four hundred years in the Americas, clearly ratify that monsters, as a cultural body, are created to satisfy the needs of a particular cultural group, and at times are embodiments of their own (sub)conscious fears and concerns.

In section two 'Monstrous Transgressions in the Socio-Cultural and Political Imaginaries' we have a collection of essays that revolve around the ever-present question of the racial/social Other as monstrous. Each chapter differs markedly from the others in the section but all are inextricably linked by an innate fear and/or anxiety of the Other that is either racially or socially dissimilar. *Anne Urbancic*'s study of Annie Vivanti presents Vivanti's social deviance as a deliberate ostracism from her socio-cultural surroundings while *Tamara El-Hoss*' investigation of Hadriana in Despestre's novel equates the female protagonist's zombification to represent Haiti's own political state of zombification. With *Phil Fitzsimmons* and *Tracy Crowe Morey*'s contributions there are explorations of the 'monstrous' other in different modalities: the graphic novella and the computer game.

In *Urbancic*'s chapter, Vivanti's cultural and linguistic hybridity results in no fixed identity that in turn becomes problematic to an audience that is accustomed to a more traditional personification of the individual. This unconventional identity differs from her socio-cultural norm and sets the stage for her perception as the 'social misfit and freak' because she chooses not to follow the social rules and norms that govern her society. Her beauty becomes the veneer masking the 'ugliness' that lies underneath in how she treats and abandons her lovers. Urbancic ultimately links Vivanti's examples of psychosocial deviance in her characters as a metaphorical mirror that she holds us to reflect society's own fears and phobias and how deviance and monstrosity are, in due course, 'socially sanctioned constructions.'

The following chapters in this section pick up on the concept of deviance and monstrosity as a 'socially sanctioned construction' as indicated by Urbancic. This discussion is furthered with respect to the question of the racial Other at times based on a post-colonial reaction to the eroticised Other (El-Hoss) or the misunderstood, or even demeaned, Other (Fitzsimmons and Crowe Morey). *El-Hoss* explores the character of Hadriana in *Hadriana dans tous mes rêves* as representative of the complexities of the differing cultures where the 'colonized' culture is seen as monstrous because it is more linked to a wild nature and there is a 'need' to 'tame' it by Western standards. Myth and reality co-exist in Hadriana where she becomes the virginal sacrifice that embodies not only the religious beliefs behind zombification but also the metaphorical rendition of an historical and political zombification of the country itself. At one point, Hadriana thought to be dead, lies in her casket watching 'history' happening all around her but paralysed and powerless to react to what is occurring around her. This 'taming' of

Hadriana can also be interpreted as the colonizer's need to feel 'at home' in the new land and the attempt to control the unknown and one's deep insecurities vis-à-vis the embodiment of the Other.

A similar argument of colonizer/colonized is intimated in *Fitzsimmons*' essay on the Australian award-winning graphic novel *Requiem for a Beast*. In this example the text becomes 'monstrous' because it delineates a non-typical childhood and, similar to Vivanti, because of the mixing of cultural codes and the need to suppress the 'monster within' in order for the social self to be able to belong as per the status quo. Fitzsimmons also develops the idea of the sense of disconnectedness from one's environment since it does not represent a reality that is true to one's self thereby setting up the paradigm of the self as monstrous since it lacks a connection to a cultural and familial prefigurative that all others seem to share. As in El-Hoss' chapter this essay also reflects on a racial and post-colonial historical and social monstrosity where feelings of abandonment transform the self into the beast (or zombie). Yet, both the texts examined by El-Hoss and Fitzsimmons hold the promise of a new beginning for the perceived monster who was never really the true monster – the 'real monsters' were the racial and cultural conventions of colonialism and post-colonialism.

Tracy Crowe Morey takes our discussion of the racial and cultural paradigms of monstrosity to the present in which gameplay is used to represent the socio-cultural context of the current political environment regarding border relations between Mexico and the US. She reminds us of the cliché of the Mexican *bandido* as the embodiment of the fear of the Other at the border at close proximity that in post 9/11 becomes a fear of terrorism of being over-taken by the Other. In examining the *Ghost Recon* games Crowe Morey discusses that the perception of the Other as inferior continues to be propagated where the Mexican is still seen as the 'barbarian at the gates' ready to invade not necessarily as the historical *bandido* but now as the *narcotrafficker*. But the threat to governability remains and fear is punctuated now since the enemy 'looks like us', which begs to question 'Who is the true monster here?'

The third section of our edited volume is organised under the title 'Mad Women (And Not Necessarily Just in the Attic)'. The underlying focus in the chapters included here is on the concept of madness in women as doubly monstrous since, historically, women have already been viewed as liminal and the added element of hysteria makes them doubly monstrous. One will note however, that said madness is not limited to the madwoman but can be contagious to the reader, as insinuated by *Jonathan A. Allan*, or even to the normative male scientist as in *Saunero Ward*'s contribution. Ultimately, it is not only madness in women that has the innate possibilities of contagion but, most importantly, the threat of non-normative female sexuality on the male sensibilities characteristic of the patriarchal code.

Elizabeth Hollis Berry's 'Monstrous Minds, Boundless Bodies: Madness, the Monstrous Feminine and the Victorian Imagination', sets the stage for this section's investigation of the fear of the unknown of female sexuality and the patriarchy's self-preserving need to label non-normative female sexual behaviour as expressions of madness, insanity or hysteria. Within her Victorian setting Hollis Berry examines society's fear of the feminine that exists outside of cultural propriety as not only transgressive but as threatening contagion to others. Nevertheless, these protagonists find themselves unable to fulfill the roles predefined for them and consequently results in a depression and/or psychological breakdown for the self. Similar to Elizabeth Bathory (as discussed by Allan and Santos) these women also become incarcerated, but unlike these Victorian protagonists, Bathory had both the money and socio-political power to protect herself and hide her madness for a longer time period but, as we know, also ended her life walled in her bedroom of one of her castles – returning the madwoman not to the attic, but to the bedroom.

As we have seen thus far in this collection there is no one neat definition of 'monster' or 'monstrous'. In his study, *Jonathan A. Allan* furthers this statement to include the narrative construction of monstrosity vis-à-vis the configurative reading experience. He takes up the case of the Bloody Countess Elizabeth Bathory and provides a hermeneutical dissection of the Penrose and Pizarnik texts about this historical figure. Allan proposes that the construction of monstrosity is achieved through a process of distanciation so that the Other could not possibly be anything like the 'I'. In order to do so he argues that there is a metaphorisation of Elizabeth Bathory as a psychopath, demon, sociopath and lesbian (to name a few) that not only distances her from the historical facts around this person but also monsterises her through dehumanisation. Implicit also to the metaphorisation of Bathory is the hyperbolisation of her cruelty and ultimate imaginary construction of the 'Bloody Countess'.

Santos' study of the Countess Elizabeth Bathory in 'Vampire, Witch, Serial Killer or All of the Above? The Bloody Countess Elizabeth Bathory' approaches the topic of the monsterisation of the historical figure of Elizabeth Bathory from a complementary, yet differing perspective from Allan. Santos explores, through the use of both fictional and (purportedly) non-fictional texts, how the historical figure of Bathory has passed the pages of historicity to popular culture icon as vampire, witch and serial killer. Similar to the Victorian protagonists in Berry's essay Bathory's downfall here can be attributed to her monstrous hybridity: beautiful yet a sadistic murderer. Here, as well as in the other essays in this section, one comes to note that the monstrous-feminine is a disruptive power to the status quo and each woman that transgresses the norm are only able to escape being incarcerated in the metaphorical 'attic' for a limited time only. Like Bathory, they are either imprisoned physically for their crimes against others or incarcerated figuratively in the demented confines of their monstrous and tortured minds.

Saunero-Ward's analysis of Giovanna Rivero's short story 'Contraluna' links the male fear of the female sexual body to the Hebrew myth of Lilith in which Lilith represents what men fear (because they do not understand) about women's sexuality and sexual aggressivity. Rivero's text provides us with a different perspective on the theme of madness in this section – in this example it is the male scientist traveling into the jungles of Brazil looking for the 'cure' against female pheromones that ultimately goes mad. His obsession with the exotic female other - a mulatta - leads to his self-destruction because of his inability to come to terms with his own impotency in the presence of sexually aggressive women. In his madness he perceives the female other as Lilith-like: as demons with vagina dentate that must be destroyed. Interestingly Rivero ends her story with the scientist's own suicide - bringing one to question is science dead when it comes to understanding the psycho-emotional intricacies of women's sexual identity?

In the last section 'The Mechanics of Monsterisation', the four chapters are related to writers' concern that scientific and technological advances result in a new creation of monsters. *Joanna Madloch* contemplates in her chapter the monstrous figure of the photographer in literary works from the nineteenth-century to the present day; *Samantha Michele Riley* compares the creature in Mary Shelley's *Frankenstein, or the Modern Prometheus* to the Grenouille in Patrick Süskind's *Das Parfum Die Geschichte eines Mörders* (1984); *Cristina Ruiz Serrano* centres her study on the effect of the nuclear bomb in *Kys* (2000) by Tatyana Tolstoya and *Jesús Eduardo Oliva Abarca* looks at the elucidation of artificial beings in a selection of literary works.

The first chapter of this last section, *Joanna Madloch*'s 'A Three-Eyed Monster: The Picture of a Photographer in World Literature', provides the reader with a tour of the literary figure of the photographer. When cameras were first invented, photographers were seen as an object of derision. Later, with the technological advances these monstrous figures began to instil feelings of revulsion and terror. Madloch, a photographer herself, further elaborates that the descriptions of the photographer in works of fiction are diverse: some are dirty and ugly, badly deformed, hydrocephalic semi-dwarfs, demons looking for souls and even depraved creatures. Specifically, in *The Ogre* (1970) by Michel Tournier, the photographer, with his camera, is depicted as having a Cyclopean eye, an enormous sexual organ or even a weapon. From the point of view of the reader, photographers become the 'other' because of their physical defectiveness, psychological shortcoming, and their lack of social adaptation. Madloch also proposes that photographers represented in literature certain socio-culturally rejected norms since they tended to live in isolated lives detached emotionally from their family, if they had one. The question that arises from the chapter is: what makes the photographer a monster? The answer is: their psychotic obsession to get a picture. In order to do that, they differentiate themselves from society by breaking its rules. As monsters they 'pollute' the establishment,[7] creating chaos when they express their insensitivity towards their models' feelings when they push them to reproduce scenes of violence. The photographers' inability to love, also makes them a hybrid creature, a machine, who uses the camera as a shield, to distance themselves from the world. Madloch argues that it is not the photographers themselves who cause horror but their ability to disengage themselves from scenes of horror so that they may capture these images through their camera lens. Further advances in technology, such as digital photography, in developing pictures and the manipulation of picture through Photoshop (popular high-end image editor) photographers (professional and amateur) will continue their metamorphisation as monsters.

In the second chapter, 'Unmasking Mary Shelley's *Frankenstein* and Patrick Süskind's *Das Perfum*', *Samantha Michele Riley* compares the main characters of each novel in the attempt to define the monster as a cultural artefact; the concept is elusive and ever-changing. The unnamed Creature created by Dr. Frankenstein, like photographers, suffers rejection on two levels: from those around him on account of his enormous proportion and, from the readers because his body is created from pieces of dead bodies. However, the Creature is perceived as a monster by all, including his creator, when he commits a human act of revenge. In an act of passion he kills members of his creator's family and friend when Frankenstein 'kills' his future wife, thereby denying him the possibility of being loved and of having his own family - crucial elements to being considered an integrated member of any society. On the other hand, Riley also presents the case of Grenouille, who is considered to be a monster due to his lack of smell. Contrary to Frankenstein's Creature, Grenouille shows no interest in becoming a part of society. His monstrosity lies in his obsession in making the perfect perfume from the body parts of the numerous young girls he murders. Unlike Frankenstein's creation, who is always seen as the monstrous other, since he is never accepted by society despite his efforts and attempts to integrate himself into it, Grenouille, despite his psychopathic behaviour, succeeds in becoming integrated into his society. By using his own perfect perfume society sees and fully accepts him. However, his is ritualized at the end: he is ultimately devoured by people and is no longer considered a monster since he 'becomes, at last, as Riley expresses, 'society incarnate'.

Cristina Ruiz Serrano's chapter 'Mutants, Mice and Monstrosities: Dystopia in *Kys*' by Tatyana Tolstaya', presents the catastrophic consequences in Russia of the arms race that led to mass destruction. Ruiz Serrano bases her chapter on Foucault's notions of power and the definition of monsters as created artefacts to be interpreted as identified by J. J. Cohen. Ruiz Serrano analyses the authoritarianism and the fate of Russian culture in the last century in that the fictional totalitarian society depicted in the novel dominates people by keeping them in ignorance, hunger and fear. Owing to the effect of the blast, everyone born after the blast has mutated: some have tails, extra limbs, gills, cockscombs sprouting from eyelids and other deformities. Moreover, the degree of mutation varies depending on people's proximity to those in political power further emphasizes that monstrosity, as shown in previous chapters, can be determined by social structures. Here, the poor not only present a higher degree of mutation but also have to hunt mice in order to survive. The real monster, however, is not the latter but rather the powerful that, in their hunger for power, condemn the population to the lowest level of poverty, both intellectually and physically. Like a reflection in the mirror, Ruiz Serrano's text raises the question of power and once again, reflects the nature of humanity who, in its hunger for power, continues to repeat its actions, creating monsters to marginalize people without seeing its own monstrosity.

We close this section with *Jesús Eduardo Oliva Abarca*'s 'The Distorted Mirror: The Monstrosity of Artificial Beings'. Oliva Abarca uses the literary works of E.T.A. Hoffman, Mary Shelley, Auguste Villiers de L'Isle-Adam, Edgar Allan Poe, Phillips K. Dick, and Čapek to investigate the eternal quest of human beings to reveal the secret of life. Guided by this concept, society begins to create artificial beings (automatons, robots and androids), made in their image and likeness. Most interestingly, and contrary to previous discussions on monstrosity, these artificial beings are seen as monstrous because they so closely resemble humans. Consequently, the more self-awareness the artificial beings develop, the more they are seen as 'the other', that like a reflection in a mirror, questions the very existence of their human creators and are thusly perceived as a threat. This can be seen, amongst other examples, in Victor Frankenstein's creation. The scientist is not horrified that his creation is made from parts of dead bodies, but when the Creature expresses the same need as his creator of having a family, this raises in Frankenstein the fear of a new race of inhabitants on earth: '[a] roots of devils'[8] that threatens the very existence of humanity and therefore questions the concept of humanity and the 'other'. The latter is made clear in the world created by Čapek, in this world, the great advances in technology break down the barrier between the mechanical and the human since scientists here have created androids that serve society better than humans. They do not only physically resemble humans but also have their own identity in so much that the android Luba Luft questions the concept of humanity, claiming it as her own. In this chapter, the 'other', like a mirror, reflects humanity's own image: the image of its own fear, its own shortcomings, what humanity does not want to see in itself and that names it as 'monstrosities' in others.

Chapters compiled here, are an attempt to begin to redefine (re)presentation of monstrosity and the monster within a multi- and inter-disciplinary approach that implicitly seeks to widen the spectrum through new interpretations and points of view. It has been the intention of the collaborators of this edited volume to bring to the fore discussions on monsters and the monstrous by unmasking racial, cultural and social paradigms hidden behind the concept of 'others', applied, indistinctly, to individual and/or groups of people. The idea that those who deviate from the socio-cultural perception of the norm are perceived as inferior, both physically or mentally, because they differ from a particular predefined lifestyle or conviction. These 'others' are then the monstrous deviations that are perceived not only as liminal but as threatening to the status quo's 'sense' of security. The problematic of this concept, as we have seen throughout this edited volume, is that 'monster and monstrosity' are cultural representations and as such, function as mirror reflections of humanity's anxieties and fears.

As the editors, we agree with the postmodern idea that 'self' is in constant flux and hope that in the process of the reconfiguration of these readings, in the strictest sense of Ricoeurian hermeneutics, we contribute to the understanding and identification of what is represented as 'monster' within our cultural imagination. Perhaps, if we recognize our own demons within as our ancestors did, we will become less intransigent to others and, more importantly, we will have a better understanding of ourselves. Then the next step will be, to learn how to keep our monsters in check toward a more just society.

Notes

[1] A. Codrescu, *The Blood Countess: A Novel*, Simon & Schuster, New York, 1995, p. 212.
[2] P. Ricouer, *Time and Narrative*, Vol. I., trans. K. McLaughlin & D. Pellauer, University of Chicago Press, Chicago, 1984.
[3] M. Shildrik, *Embodying the Monster: Encounters with the Vulnerable Self*, Sage Publications, London, 2002, p. 4.
[4] B. Bidhauer & R. Mills, *The Monstrous Middle Ages*, University of Toronto Press, Toronto, 2003, p. 6.
[5] J.J. Cohen (ed), *Monster Theory: Reading Culture*, University of Minnesota Press, Minneapolis, 1996, pp. 4-6.
[6] B. Bildhauer & R. Mills, p. 8.
[7] Cohen, p. 7.
[8] M. Shelley, *Frankenstein or The Modern Prometheus*, Pocket Books, First Washington Square Press, New York, 1995, p. 178.

Bibliography

Bidhauer, B. & Mills, R., *The Monstrous Middle Ages*. University of Toronto Press, Toronto, 2003.

Codrescu, A., *The Blood Countess: A Novel*. Simon & Schuster, New York, 1995.

Cohen, J.J. (ed), *Monster Theory: Reading Culture*. University of Minnesota Press, Minneapolis, 1996.

Ricouer, P., *Time and Narrative.* Vol. I, trans. McLaughlin, K. & Pellauer, D., University of Chicago Press, Chicago, 1984.

Shelley, M., *Frankenstein or The Modern Prometheus*. Pocket Books, First Washington Square Press, New York, 1995.

Shildrik, M., *Embodying the Monster: Encounters with the Vulnerable Self.* Sage Publications, London, 2002.

PART 1

All that is Different is not Monstrous

Divine Monsters in Guarani Aboriginal Culture

Adriana Spahr

Abstract
The Enlightenment profoundly changed the way in which human beings perceived the world, rejecting what could not be scientifically or rationally proven. From this new perspective, the monsters which had populated the cultural imagination since ancient and medieval times were simply classified as proof of the backwardness of those cultures which lacked an 'objective', analytical mind. Despite the tenacious efforts of rationalism, however, this magic world continued to surround human beings under the respectful protection of the most vulnerable and, condescension and often ambivalence of the majority. In the Latin American context, the abundance of myths derived from the indigenous cultures are still alive today despite the vicissitudes of the Spanish conquest of the fifteenth century and continues to attract our attention. In this cosmovision, the Guarani people are an example worthy of attention. These people suffered doubly from the 'missionary' pressure to which they were subjected: on one hand the political and religious pressure which came from the Spanish Crown and, on the other hand, the strictly religious pressure embodied by the Jesuit missionaries with whom the Guaranis lived for approximately one-hundred-fifty years. In spite of this double subjugation, the Guaranis continue to show respect to its primitive gods. Like in other pre-Christian cultures, these mythological gods are represented as monstrous yet positive figures in the Guarani cultural imaginary.

Key Words: Guaranis, monster, pre-Christian culture, seven monsters, Latin America, deity, *Caá Yarí*.

*****

> The earth, as if infused with new life, rotated harmoniously. Its face offered a powerful and sublime spectacle, but something was missing to complete this marvellous spectrum of the Creation and so *Tupá* decided to create the first human couple.[1]

> The myth of Genesis, which describes God as the One who begins in the darkness and creates light, asserts that man is made in the image of God.[2]

The triumph of the Scientific Revolution profoundly changed the way human beings perceived the world, rejecting all that could not be proven in a rational manner. From this new perspective, the monsters that had populated the cultural imaginary since ancient and medieval times, were simply classified as proof of the backwardness of those cultures which lacked an 'objective' analytical mind. Despite the tenacious efforts of Rationalism, however, this magic world continued to surround human beings, under the respectful protection of the most vulnerable despite the incredulity, condescension and often ambivalence of the majority. The persistent survival of this magic was due to the fact that Positivism was incapable of eradicating the ancestral fears of all humans, fears caused, for the most part, by hunger, war and death.[3]

In the Latin American context, the abundance of myths derived from the indigenous cultures that survived despite the vicissitudes of the Spanish conquest of the fifteenth century, still attracts our critical attention and will be the focus of this study. The choice of this particular indigenous group is based on the double 'missionary' pressure to which they were subjected: on the one hand the political and religious pressure which came from the Spanish Crown and, on the other hand, the strictly religious pressure embodied by the Jesuit missionaries with whom the Guarani lived for approximately one-hundred-fifty years. In spite of this sustained foreign influence Guarani culture continues to show respect to its primitive gods. As in other pre-Christian cultures, these gods are represented as monstrous, but are also positive and reflect basic human behaviour. We will limit our study to the Guarani culture existing fundamentally in the northwest Argentina. It is understood that such a division is arbitrary and that the Guarani culture extends into part of Bolivia, Brazil and Paraguay, ignoring the arbitrary division of geographical borders imposed at the beginning of the nineteenth century.[4]

The Guarani belong to the linguistic group of the *Tupí-Guaranies* who left the Amazon region and travelled southwards in approximately 200 B.C. The *Tupí* settled in Brazil, together with other groups that inhabited that area, and the Guarani settled in those areas which bordered the Paraná, Paraguay and Uruguay rivers and their tributaries - the present-day territories of Argentina, Paraguay, and Bolivia.[5] According to their beliefs, their ancestors inhabited a beautiful land created near five palm trees that they had to leave because evil had taken over it. Hence came the search for the 'land without evil' - a search for a lost paradise - a crucial belief that, together with other elements from Guarani culture facilitated their acceptance of the preachings of the Jesuits.[6]

For the purpose of evangelisation in South America, in 1604 the Papal Bull created the province of Paraguay for the Jesuits. By 1610 the Jesuit missions in Guarani territory were already established.[7] The evangelical campaign and the type of organization that the Jesuits implemented, were admired by some and disdained by others,[8] generally respected the economic, political and social structures of the Guarani. This allowed the mission settlements to function and to finance themselves.[9] From a mythical point of view, the Guarani believed in the importance of the spoken word and the practice of prayer, which was carried out principally by shaman during long ritualistic dances.[10] Although the practice of prayer coincided with the preachings of the followers of Francisco de Loyola

(1491-1556), it was also a point of friction and rivalry since it concerned who would lead the Guarani people: the shamans searching for 'the land without evil' or the Jesuit with his search for 'Paradise.'[11] The Guarani, caught in the plundering of European expansion, received protection from the Jesuits from the Portuguese who were looking for slaves for their Brazilian plantations and also from the Spaniards who forced them to work in the *encomiendas*.[12] Despite the long period of cohabitation - forced or consented to - where the two cultures met, the Guarani adapted Catholic myths, while also maintaining their own traditions that are still present today.

Monstrosity is in general depicted as an integral part in the formation of their deities to whom the Guarani turn for help in interpreting their reality.[13] Our world is conceived in binary categories and monstrosity is represented as one of those poles

> the monstrous is constitutive, producing the contours of both bodies that matter (humans, Christians, saints, historical figures, gendered subjects and Christ) and, ostensibly, bodies that do not animals, non-Christians, demons, fantastical figures and portentous freaks.[14]

This fragmented concept of good and evil (God/Devil; saints/sinners; angels/witches) was introduced by Catholicism in Latin America. Today, as in history, this binary is not limited to Latin America but has universal applicability. The conception rules human behaviour and makes us believe in 'a Other' to blame for negative and horrifying actions. This invented Other serves as a scapegoat to stigmatize those individuals or groups that think or act differently. The monster we have to destroy exists so that we can deny its human nature or, to put it differently, the monster is the darkness of humanity denying its own monstrosity.

For the Guaranis both principles are united in the deity

> The ideals of goodness and purity ... are expressed in benign deities who mix with the bad ones sketching the destiny of the world. ... although at times the struggle remains a merciless fight, both sides tending to complement one another, since any prolonged conflict creates dependents and, weaves solid nets that mix the contenders in a same system.... Evil needs Good to define itself and what would Good become without the existence of Evil? The game becomes a ritual. [But] the war can no longer be a war until death, since both parties are of the same spirit, of one nature.[15]

Ñamanduré also known as Ñandeyara, Tunpaete, Tunpaete Vaé y Yanderú Tunpa is the god (*Tupã*) of the Guarani. He is a being who is in the *Tunparentá* (sky). He is venerated as the creator of all good things, visible and invisible. He makes it rain; he makes the carob beans, the corn and the rest of the edible plants, grow and ripen; he gave the human race the seeds and tools necessary to live. Suddenly, however, he decided to annihilate humanity, because *Araparigua* (the first man whom *Tupã* rescued from the first flood) asked him to do so. Subsequently, when the few survivors multiply, *Araparigua* returned to earth to enjoy sexual pleasures. The Guarani tried to kill *Araparigua* for abusing women, but, *Tupã* saved him, this time from the anger of the men of the earth, by taking him to his dwelling. The god acquiesced to *Araparigua*'s demand for vengeance and destroyed the earth. Subsequently, *Tupã* created the earth for the third time because he felt alone.[16]

Although in the beginning, the god, *Tupã*, seems to be categorizable within the binary principles to which we are accustomed; in the end what triumphs is what we know as plausible: not the perfection of the morally righteous, but rather the bad, what we conceive as monstrous. *Tupã*'s behaviour is no different from that of a father who is not able to see the pain caused by his son. He is deaf to the accusations of others regarding his own flesh and blood. To protect his first son, there must be no proof of his misbehaviour and pain that he causes, therefore, without consideration, *Tupã* destroys the human race to hide these faults. Without regret or sorrow, once again he recreates the earth, simply so that he will not feel alone.

The notions of good and evil that are shown in *Tupã* are consciously transmitted to the human race. Good and evil were present from the moment of conception itself and from the moment of the formation of the first human beings. Firstly, the father of the universe and his wife *Arasy* (mother of the sky) together gave life to all that exists on earth, the stars and all the beings of the universe. Then they mixed with clay the entire mixture of ka'aruvcha[17] (plant), blood of the *yuyja'u* (a bird), leaves and an *ambu'a* (myriapod). They threw water on him and from that they created two statues in his likeness and left them in the sun to dry. Thus the first couple was created - *Sypave* (father of the people) and *Rupvaé* (mother of the people). From the start, we see that the newly-created beings inherit not only their physical appearance from their ancestors, but other traits such as egotism and dissatisfaction (as we saw in Tupã); they behave like capricious children and everything they receive seems little to them. Tupã, as a father, tries to please them; *Arasy*, as a mother, tries to impose limits. Finally, overburdened with abundance, the god gives them *Tau* (evil spirit) and *Angatupyry* (benign spirit) as companions

-'Why do you give us Tau as a companion?' whined fearful *Sypavé*.

-'His presence is necessary among you!' replied *Tupã*. If fear did not exist, you would be very unfortunate ... if all that you gained were effortless, you would not know the value of things ... The curative power of herbs would not be known if illnesses did not exist; neither would you know pleasure if you did not know pain... You would wander, suffering, without being able to die, and I would not want you to live denying life, full of envy and blasphemy ... If something bad happens to you, it is because Tau is testing you and thus begins the battle between him and *Angatupyry*. This will be the eternal battle between Good and Evil. If you regain your health, it is because Tau has abandoned the fight, defeated, and it is *Angatupyry*, on the other hand, who is the victor ... Do not let yourselves fall into the temptation to rob ... Do not rob life from your kinfolk.[18]

Just as humans were the playthings in the disagreements among the inhabitants of Olympus, for the Guarani the struggle between good and evil affects the fate of the individual. *Tupã* advises the first humans to perform good actions. After explaining to the couple how to make use of and take care of Nature the god and goddess disappeared. The couple lived happily without hunger, anguish or want.[19]

From this union came seven children: four females and four males. *Porasy*, the goddess of beauty; *Guarasyáva*, the mistress of the rivers and seas; *Yrasem*, the goddess of music and *Tupinambá* (of incomparable physical strength) mother of the of the *Tupí* tribe. The three men were: *Marangatú*, a virtuous and good man; *Tumé Arandu*, a prophet and father of knowledge; and *Japeausá*, who kills his sister *Yrasema*. Unlike Cain who kills Abel to get the attention of the Creator, *Japeusá*'s attitude is a result of his innate nature of doing nothing right. When his mother sends him to look for herbs to cure his mute sister, he brings her the wrong ones, which causes her death. With the anger and pain of the *Japeusá* people against him, he commits suicide by hanging himself. Like many of the first humans *Japaeusá* resuscitated. In his case, he returns to earth as a crab, thereby condemning the entire crab community to walking backwards.[20]

These deities had other mishaps. *Tau*, the evil spirit, captured the beautiful *Keraná*, the daughter of *Marangatú* when he discovered that his love was not reciprocated. *Keraná*'s grandmother, *Arasy*, angered by *Tau*'s attitude, condemns all his offspring: *Tejú-Jagua, Mboi-tu'I, Moñai, Jasy Jatere, Kurupi, Aó-Aó* and *Huichó*, to be monsters. They were frightening not only because of their physical deformities, but also because of their evil. From infancy, the seven monsters found pleasure in creating confusion and terror. Townspeople accused one another of robberies, fires and rapes caused by them. P*orasy*, the goddess of beauty, together with her wise brother *Tumé Andú* and certain local authorities - at the request of *Tupã* - decide to end the discord by burning the seven monsters with a simple but well-designed plan.

Figure 1. *Crab-man* by Rudy Ramos

Using her beauty, *Porasy* claimed to be in love with *Moñai* (the monster with a serpent's body and gilded horns) and asked him to marry her. To celebrate Moñai's happiness, the brothers start drinking and soon become inebriated. This is the opportunity for *Porasy* to escape while *Tumé Andú* set fire to the cave. Unfortunately, her husband discovers the trick and prevents her departure. Nevertheless, she shouts to her brother to continue with the plan. At the conclusion everyone in the cave dies. According to the Guarani mythology all of them become stars: *Porasy* into the star of the dawn, while the brothers become the constellation of the seven goats.[21]

In accordance with the Guarani cosmovision, the conclusion of this story could not be different: Good and Evil are integrated and form part of the same identity and neither part must be neglected. *Porasy* is shown as a saviour of the town but also capable of deceit and murder. The behaviour of the goddess corresponds to the supreme god *Tupã* who taught the first human beings *Sypave* and *Rupave* and is able to destroy humans at *Araparigua*'s request. The Guarani like many ancients civilization, create their deities as reflections of the human beings, capable of doing good things as well as terrible ones. These characteristics remained within Guarani culture, despite of the arrivals of the European conquerors, Christianity and the passage of the time.

Figure 2. *Porasy Conquers Heart of Moñai* by Rudy Ramos.

The Guarani did not adore statues before the arrival of Christianity.[22] Despite this, seven divine monsters had well-defined characteristics handed down to each generation through the oral tradition. If *Moñai*, for example was a snake deformed by horns, *Teju jagua* melded in his body into the form of an iguana and various dog heads. Like his brothers, his appearances remained throughout time despite the imperfect nature of the oral tradition and the changes in the culture that had given birth to them.

In daily life, these imaginary beings created by popular imagination are shadows, whistles, loud or subtle noises that are difficult to identify and which occur at any give time of the day, suggesting the presence of someone or something.[23] In Western culture we are accustomed to relating these noises to the presence of good or bad ghosts, depending on who perceives it, attributing their presence to some 'unfinished business' on the part of the dead person. Some of us, displaying our scepticism or 'objectivity,' condescendingly explain that, at the best, these 'presences' are useful to satisfy the emotional needs of the person who claims to have seen it. But in any culture there exists a community that agrees on giving a name to these 'presences' and, more importantly, when these forms are seen, heard or interpreted by a group of people constitute a shared communal reality. Time and repetition of these stories in the oral traditions of the group fix these images in the collective imagination of the community.[24] These 'presences', as Holly Baumgartner and Roger Davis effectively show, are not lacking in substance, but, on the contrary, they reveal a certain social order.[25] That statement is proved to be true within the Guarani culture in the presence of the seven divine monsters. We will stop to consider the two most popular: *Jasy-Jateré* and *Kurupi*.

Jasy-Jateré is the middle son of Tau and *Kerana* and the only one of his siblings who does not have any physical deformities. According to some scholars, the talents of their mother permitted her children to develop good characteristics, thus diminishing *Arasy*'s curse on the descendants of *Tau*.[26] *Jasy-Jateré* is the onomatopoeic name of the sound he emits to signal his presence. It is similar a bird song. The name in Guarani means a sliver of moon or a waning moon, despite the fact the figure usually makes his appearance at midday or at *siesta* time. Present day descriptions of *Jasy-Jateré* vary: for some people he is small, good-looking with blue eyes and a youthful-looking appearance; for others he is a handsome dwarf, with the same light eyes, but sporting a beard. He is agile and muscular and looks like a six-year old child. Some attribute to him characteristics that belong to his brother *Kurupi*, who has feet facing backwards and the legs of a dog. Everybody agrees on his nakedness - the way the Guarani lived before the arrival of the missionaries. He travels across the countryside with a straw hat and a golden walking stick in his hand - some believe is a cane - where his power is concentrated, allowing him to make himself invisible and to change the course of nature. On the upper part of this walking stick he has a whistle that produces a spine-chilling call that frightens women at night. He is also said to protect the bees and the forest (the former domain of his brother *Kurupi*) and resides in tree trunks.

When *Jasy-Jateré* appears he attracts children with games and takes them to his dwelling, either to carry on playing with them or to teach them to rob other children. When he tires of them he leaves them in the woods, sometimes tied to trees and some claim he even drowns them. The children who are returned by *Jasy-Jateré* suffer psychological problems, which prevent them from remembering the past. In a few cases he has been accused of the abduction of women to satisfy his sexual appetite. If the women become pregnant, he will arrange for the child to receive honey to nourish it, thus assuming his role as father.

In his dominions *Jasy-Jateré* punishes those who mistreat Nature. For this reason he is feared by the woodcutters and the harvesters of *yerba mate*[27] and by all those who plunder nature. On the other hand, he guides those who get lost in the forest. Since one of his weaknesses is tobacco, some people feed his vice by leaving him tobacco leaves or other objects that he likes in the place where it is believed he frequents. In this case, he will appear to the person who seeks his friendship and help him/her to get what s/he wants. If, however, s/he forgets the gift, he will become his/her enemy. In his better moments *Jasy-Jateré* can be a good companion to both adults and children. As a monster, he highlights the dangers of wandering in the woods and forest or of accepting the company and invitation of strangers. His story thereby helps to regulate the behaviour of children. By telling this story to their children parents are able to keep their children inside their homes during the suffocating heat of mid-afternoon and keep them away from dangerous areas.

In his introduction to *Monster Theory* Jeffrey Jerome Cohen explains that the monster regulates sexual desire by opposition, since it represents our forbidden fantasies that only can be realized through the monster's body.[28] In this sense, *Kurupi*, the younger brother of *Jasy-Jateré* is the example that sums up these fantasies. Kurupi or Curupi is usually represented as a strong being, of small stature, with an oval-shaped face and a moustache. There are some people who say that he walks with his feet backwards, with great strength in his hands, but at the same time that he is clumsy, uncoordinated and easy to break free from as he cannot swim, nor can he climb trees. He is distinguished by a big 'member' that can penetrate a sleeping woman without having to enter her house. He also uses his penis to trap women. The trapped person can free herself by cutting his penis with a knife, thus leaving him defenceless. He mainly pursues women, but sometimes also children.[29] Within nature, he protects the forests and the animals.[30] If, as Fariña Nuñez claims, this myth originated to warn women of the dangers of the forest.[31] Its dominion has increased to the point that nobody is exempt from the Kurupi's attacks. On account of his sexual characteristics, this monster is the acknowledged father of unwanted pregnancies in the community.

The other five brothers are frightening in appearance, being a mix of local animals. As well, they emit horrifying sounds and cries. They are *Tejú-Jagau*, a lizard with seven dogs' heads who protects the cavern and the fruits, horrible to look at, with ferocious-looking eyes, but calm and inoffensive. *Mboo-tu'i*, a snake with a parrot's head and a head covered with feathers, with a gaze like his shrill cry that terrifies people, protects amphibians, the dew, flowers and moisture. *Moñai*, with the body of a snake and golden horns likes to playfully torment humans by moving and making things disappear in their homes. He is the guardian of the fields and air, and the protector of villains and thieves. *Aó-Aó* is the fairy of fertility. His dominions are the hills and mountains. The last one is *Huichó*, master of the night and companion of death, and as such, his power is found in cemeteries.[32]

Two basic elements have permitted these deities to remain alive: oral tradition and a culture that continues to need monstrous involvement to interpret its reality. *Yasi Yateré*, on account of his prevailing importance and of his physical description, appears in time with variations of his name (*Yasi Yateré, Yasy Yateré, Jasy-Jateré*). Thus he is often confused or melded with his brother *Kurip*, also known as *Curupi*, and with *Pombero*, a small, ugly wood spirit. In the present day, the three of them share the same Dionysian qualities and are said to be the parents of unwanted children.[33]

The seven monsters with both their positive and negative qualities offer endless services to the community. In their positive characteristics they act and promote examples to follow, like the need to protect and care for nature. As monsters, they are scapegoats for those actions that disturb the normal functioning of the social group. Thus, if a child disappears, if a house is broken into, if a woman is raped or there is a sexual indiscretion, the seven deities are a means to purge the evil. Anticipating modern psychological studies, the Guarani community named and clearly identified its monsters in order to dominate them: *Moñai* steals and takes things from a house; *Tejú-Jagua, Mboi-tu'i, Huichó* scare us; and *Kurupi* is the abuser. Once the culprit is identified, order can be re-established and peace return to the community. In other words and as Cohen states, through these monsters the community expiates its sins.

Contrary to what Cohen claims about modern monsters, however, that '[t]hey can only be pushed to the farthest margins of geography and discourse, hidden away at the edges of the world and in the forbidden recesses of our mind, but they always return'[34] the Guarani monsters do not live in faraway and unknown territories but rather delimit spaces –both physical and geographical - in the Guarani culture that not only nurtures them but also changes them, sometimes even leading to their destruction.

This process is contradictory. It is interesting to note that it was not the evangelical process that destroyed and continues to put an end to these mythological beings but rather the advance of science.[35] It was not religious education that made them abandon their gods, but the destruction that the industrialization brought with it - the slow but constant destruction of nature. Thus, the divine monster, created to defend nature and punish human beings who do not respect nature, is destroyed by another monster, one that is much more ferocious: the industrialized human being. The human race's excessive ambition that brings about the destruction of the environment and kills what he has created in order to survive. For example *Zapam-zucum*, is a deity who within the present-day Guarani belief system, but who serves to explain the disappearance of ancient deities.

Zapam-zucum is the onomatopoeic name for the sound that her large and voluminous breasts make when she walks up the mountain where she lives. This female deity with her large dark eyes, white hands and black hair, like the seven brothers, has positive and negative traits. During the day she looks after children whose mothers leave them in the shade of the carob trees. She suckles them and keeps the campfire going at night so that the carob pickers can find it. Another name for *Zapam-zucum* is *Capansucana* or *Capasucana*, an onomatopoeic name for the sound that she produces when she interrupts men's parties. She throws herself on those who do not manage to escape and covers them with her breasts. Her voluptuous breasts - which symbolize her breastfeeding mission and sexual fantasies for men - transform themselves at night into suffocating pincers that trap men and choke them. The monstrous side of the deity that surfaces at night acts a regulator of men's moral behaviour. This myth remains only in a few areas of northwestern Argentina because the carob tree woods where she used to dwell have been deforested, thus reducing her presence as a local goddess.[36]

Another feminine deity deeply rooted in the Guarani culture and who has also suffered modifications during the era of the Jesuit missions when *yerba mate* plantations were reduced, is the young and beautiful *Caá Yarí*. She was transformed into this plant by *Tupã* to assure her immortality, and thus became the protector of the mate plantations and helped the men in their work. But her help is not of a disinterested nature. To gain her assistance it is necessary for the man to promise on a bunch of mate that he will not cheat on her with another woman. In order for the deal to be sealed the man must also leave a piece of paper with his name and the time when he will return to see her. At the given hour, the man will be attacked by vipers, tigers, toads and other mountain animals. If he does not become scared and remains there, the goddess in her form as a beautiful, blonde young woman will appear to him.

As with the other imaginary beings, only the person who makes the promise will see her and must renew his vow in the presence of *Caá Yarí*. From this moment onwards, every time the man goes to the mate plantation he will fall into a deep, peaceful sleep while she will take his place in picking yerba mate (just as the Guarani woman did even before the Conquest).[37] But, if he is unfaithful to her, she will kill him, showing her vindictive and thus monstrous side. It is believed that every man who turns up dead in the mate plantations has betrayed this goddess.[38] *Caá Yarí* still has the cultural and moral values of yesteryear within the Guarani tribe where death is the price that any man or woman had to pay for committing adultery. This was a punishment from which only some shaman were exempt, since, for them, extra-marital sex was not considered adultery. Rather having more than one woman was a sign of prestige.[39]

The gods of the Guaraní world correspond to a primitive world where the monstrous - the physical, psychic/evil and/or moral and good - are part of the same entity. This concept is shared by other ancient cultures and traces of it can also be seen in medieval Catholicism. The most well-known examples are the image of Christ with a bird's head and the representation of the Holy Trinity with a head and three bodies or a body with three heads. The arrival of the Counter-Reformation with the Council of Trent (1545-1563) classified these art expressions as the product of uneducated minds. In 1628 Pope Urban VIII ordered that these types of representations be burnt as they constituted heretical practices.[40] A binary concept of the world was imposed (good/evil; saint/devil; devils/Christ). By the eighteenth century, rationalist trends introduced a great skepticism with regard to the imaginary world. Reason, hand in hand with Christianity, branded the exponents of the imaginary world as superstitious and ignorant. The Guaraní gods, like other deities, sought refuge in their own people, partly because the capitalist system of production pushed them into the background. Also, because created in the people's own likeness, the former reflects not only Guaranis' people goodness but most important their imperfections, their evil part. The Guaranis gods reveal (as the word *monstum* epistemologically signifies) the hidden part of the human being: their weakness, their fears, their desires and their perversions: the monster that lives inside any human beings.

Translators: Kathleen MacDermott & Dominique Russell

Notes

[1] N. Colmán, *Nuestros antepasados*, *(Ñande Ypy Kuéra)*, Biblioteca del Paraguay, 1998, p. 5. All translations from Spanish to English are the author's responsibility unless otherwise indicated: 'La tierra, como infundida de nueva vida, giraba armoniosamente y toda su faz ofrecía un espectáculo portentoso y sublime, pero faltaba algo para completar la gama maravillosa de todo lo creado y entonces Tupã se propuso crear la primera pareja humana'.

[2] M. Novak, *The Experience of Nothingness*, Harper & Row, New York, 1971, p. 50.

[3] E. Fromm states that: [T]here is the need to overcome this feeling of separateness. The gift of reason makes him aware of himself as a separate entity.... of this one short life span, of the fact that without his will he is born and against his will he dies, that he will die before those whom he loves, or they before him.... Of his aloneness and separateness of his helplessness before the forces of nature and society. *The Art of Loving*, Perennial Library, New York, 1986, p. 8.

[4] It is interesting to note that in Paraguay the Guarani language has been recognized as an official language since 1992.

[5] B.A. Gansón, *Guarani Under Spanish Rule in the Rio de la Plata*, Stanford University Press, Palo Alto, 2003, pp. 17-18.

[6] P.A. Trento, *Reducciones jesuíticas: El paraíso en el Paraguay*, Parroquia San Rafael, Asunción, 2003, pp. 15-17.

[7] The Jesuits had settled in Brazil in 1549, in Peru from 1568 and in Mexico from 1572. The Province of Paraguay extended from the east of Bolivia, Argentina, southwest Brazil, Uruguay and Chile (separated in 1625). Present-day Argentina comprised the neurological point [0]of the ecclesiastical province. The majority of

the institutions were found in the provinces of Córdoba, Catamarca, Buenos Aires, Corrientes, La Rioja, Salta Tucumán, Sante Fé and Santiago del Estero. There were founded schools where theology and technology were taught.

[8] The Jesuits in Paraguay were the focus of attention and much controversy: in *Candide* (1759) Voltaire portrays the missions as a place of richness and independence from European crowns. Meanwhile, a popular book of the century *The History of Nicolas I, King of Paraguay and Emperor of the Mamelukes* (Dresden, 1756) accused the Jesuits of establishing an empire and amassing enormous fortunes by armed force. N. Cushner, *Why Have You Come Here? The Jesuits and the First Evangelization of Native America*, Oxford University Press, Oxford, 2006, p. 102. This dispute continues today. For many people the mission was the place where utopia became reality. For others, it was an area of exploitation, see J. Crocitti, 'The Internal Economic Organization of The Jesuit Missions Among The Guarani', *International Social Science Review*, Vol. 77, N.1-2, 2003, pp. 3-15; B. Melía, *El Guarani conquistador y reducido: ensayos de etnohistoria*, Vol. 5, Biblioteca Paraguaya de Antropología, Centro de Estudios Antropológicos, Universidad Católica, Asunción, 1988, pp. 181-202; Cushner, op.cit., pp. 102-27. A. Gansón sees the Guarani as practical individuals who knew how to negotiate and to adapt to the circumstances in which they had to live. From the missionaries the Guarani learnt new trades and productive techniques introduced by the Jesuits They also formed an army to defend themselves against Portuguese attacks. This army favoured the interests of the Spanish crown because it impeded Portuguese expansion, repressed internal conflicts, but defended the rights to remain in its territories. (op.cit., pp. 47-50 and pp. 136-63).

[9] To satisfy the needs of the community and to make it self-sufficient, the Guarani became highly-skilled craftsmen, carpenters, blacksmiths, shoemakers, hat-makers, dyers, leather workers, sculptors, makers of musical instruments, and became printers, amongst other specialized work (Ibid., p. 58 and p. 68).

[10] Melía, op.cit., p. 202.

[11] B. Gansón, op.cit., p. 37.

[12] The *encomienda* was an institution that already existed in Europe. The Spanish crown implemented its in America with the aim/objective of pleasing those who had expanded the Crown's dominion. In order to do so, the Crown gave these individuals a certain number of Indians to work for them for two lives' worth. As the Crown wanted to convert the Indians, the *encomenderos* were obliged to treat the Indians well and to educate them. In practice, these obligations were ignored and the *encomienda* ended up as forced labour to the benefit of the *encomandero*.

[13] O. Mendieta, 'Seres mitológicos Guaranies de ayer y de hoy', C. Santos & A. Spahr (eds), *Defiant Deviance: The Irreality of Reality in the Cultural Imaginary*, Peter Lang, New York, 2006, pp. 53-63.

[14] H.L. Baumgartner & R. Davis (eds), *Hosting the Monster*, Rodopi, 2008, p. 2.

[15] C. Colombres, *Seres sobrenaturales de la cultura popular argentina*, Ediciones del Sol, Buenos Aires, pp. 10-11. Los ideales de bondad y pureza... se expresan en deidades benignas que se integran con las del mal, dibujando el destino del mundo. ... aunque a veces la lucha parezca sin cuartel, ambos principios tienden a complementarse, en la medida que todo conflicto prolongado crea dependencias, teje redes solidarias que integran a los contendientes en un mismo sistema. Es que sin oposición no hay identidad. El mal necesita del bien para perfilarse ¿y que sería del bien sino existiera el mal? El juego se vuelve ritual. [Pero] la guerra no puede ser a muerte, desde que ambas partes comulgan en un mismo espíritu, en una naturaleza única.

[16] C. Colombres, *Seres mitológicos argentinos*, Emece, Buenos Aires, 2000, pp. 36-37 and pp. 256-57.

[17] *Ka'aruvicha* is the name of the herb (a plant that is found among the vegetables of Paraguay) and whose juice mixed with blood of the *yujia'u* bird becomes a *paye* (leader/conductor). *Ka'aruvicha*, combined with the sap of other bushes gives the 'elixir of life' the remedy to immortality, which is confirmed by the philosopher's stone of the Guarani (Colman, op.cit., p. 77, explanatory note number 5).

[18] Ibid., p. 8. ¿Para qué nos dais por compañero a Taû? –gimió medrosa, Sypavê. ¡Su presencia es necesaria entre vosotros! –replicole Tupã. Si el miedo no existiese, serías muy desdichados ..., si todo lo obtuvieseis sin esfuerzo alguno, no sabríais el valor de las cosas.... No llegarían a conocerse las virtudes curativas de las hierbas si no existieran las enfermedades; tampoco experimentarías placer si no conocieras el dolor...Vagaríais errantes, padeciendo, sino pudierais morir, y yo no quisiera que vivierais renegando de la vida, cargados de hastío y de blasfemias.... Si os afecta algún mal es porque Taû os somete a prueba y comienza entonces el combate entre él y Angatupyry. Esta será la eterna lucha del bien con el mal. Si llegáis a recobrar la salud, es porque Taû abandona la lid, derrotado, y es Angatupyry, en cambio, el que queda triunfante.... No os dejéis llevar jamás por la tentación de robar ... No arrebatéis jamás la vida de vuestros semejantes.

[19] Ibid., p. 10.

[20] Ibid., pp. 11-14.

[21] Ibid., pp. 17-18, pp. 22-24. Also, the death of the seven brothers marks the beginning of a war that ends with the destruction of the first generation of men.

[22] Melia, op.cit., p. 202.

[23] Colombres, *Seres Sobrenaturales*, op.cit., p. 12.

[24] In his study on the role of witches in the Spanish community, C. Baroja shows that they existed merely because society believed in them (*Las brujas y su mundo*, Alianza, Madrid, 1973, pp. 10-11).

[25] H. Baumgartner & D. Roger, op.cit., p. 1.

[26] Mendieta, op.cit., p. 54. On the Jasy-Jateré see M. Blaché, *Structural Analysis of Guarani: Memorates and Anecdotes*, Diss. University of Pensylvania, 1977, p. 75;

Colman, op.cit., p. 7; A. Colombres, *Seres Sobrenaturales*, op.cit., pp. 281-82; A. Colombres, *Seres Mitológicos*, op.cit., p. 102; and O Mendieta, op.cit., pp. 55-58.

[27] *Yerba mate* was used by the shaman in their religious ceremonies. It was the principal source of income in the missions from where it was exported to other areas of the viceroyalty of the River Plate region and to Chile (Crocitti op.cit., pp. 6-9). The benefits that this commerce engendered was another area of conflict with the *criollos* who wanted to take over this business (Gansón op.cit., pp. 56-64). In Brazil, Uruguay, Chile and Peru it was used as a herbal drink and is still used as a herbal drink, either hot or cold, instead of tea or coffee. But, unlike the latter, where in each gathering, each person has his/her own cup of tea or coffee, the *mate* (the bowl in which it is served and is also the name of the drink) is drunk from - most of the time - a metal straw that everybody shares. Present day *yerba mate* is exported to other countries on account of its digestive qualities. Moreover, though a caffeinated drink, it is considered more benign than coffee.

[28] J.J. Cohen (ed), *Monster Theory: Reading Culture*, Minnesota University Press Minnesota, 1996, p. 14.

[29] Colombres, *Seres Mitológicos*, op.cit., pp. 62-63.

[30] Colmán, op.cit., p. 17.

[31] Fariña Nuñez cited by Colombres, *Seres Sobrenaturales*, op.cit., p. 50.

[32] Mendieta, op.cit., pp. 54-55 and Colmán, op.cit., p. 16.

[33] Blaché, op.cit., p. 75 and Mendieta, op.cit., p. 59. While Narciso Colmán (1878-1954) calls them Jasi Jatere and Kurip, the other authors who were most recently consulted show the changes undergone by Colmán.

[34] Cohen, op.cit., p. 20.

[35] The fact that the Guarani Indians have preserved pre-Colombian cults has not prevented them from adopting Christianity and practicing its rituals. The deities of both religions are part of its cosmology. It is interesting to note that in their healing practices, the shaman still mix their centuries-old knowledge with Catholic prayers (O. Mendieta & A. Spahr, 'La fuerza curativa y el poder de las hierbas', *Defiant Deviance: The Irreality of Reality in the Cultural Imaginary*, C. Santos & A. Spahr (eds), Peter Lang, New York, 2006, pp. 15-22 and pp. 17-18.

[36] Colombres, *Seres Mitológicos*, op.cit., p. 288.

[37] Gansón, op.cit., p. 24.

[38] Colombres, *Seres Mitológicos*, op.cit., p. 52.

[39] Gansón, op.cit., p.19 and p. 23. Curiously, death as punishment for a man who breaks his word to a woman can be seen in two Japanese stories popular stories. These stories *Black Hair* and *The Woman of the Snow* (Yuki-Onna) were included in the film *Kwaidan* (1965) of Masaki Kobyashi. In *The Woman of the Snow* the story is not about fidelity, as in *Black Hair*, but is rather about the importance that a man knows how to keep a secret when a woman asks him to do so. Both stories are adaptations from the collection of short stories about Japanese folklore.

L. Hearn, *Kwaidan: Stories and Studies of Strange Things*, Houghton, Mifflin and Co, Boston, 1904. VViewed on 11 May 2009, <http://www.sacredtexts.com/shi/kwaidan/index.htm>.
[40] R. Mills, 'Jesus as a Monster', B. Bildhauer & R. Mills (eds), *The Monstrous Middle Age*, Toronto University Press, Toronto, 2003, p. 40 and p. 48.

Bibliography

Abou, S., *The Jesuit 'Republic'of the Guaranis (1609-1768) and Its Heritage*. (trans) Johnson, L.J., The Crossroad Publishing Company/UNESCO Publishing, New York, 1997.

Bartomeu, M., El guaraní conquistador y reducido: ensayos de etnohistoria. Vol. 5, Biblioteca Paraguaya de Antropología, Centro de Estudios Antropológicos, Universidad Católica, Asunción, 1988.

Baumgartner, H.L. & Davis, R. (eds), *Hosting the Monster*. Rodopi, Amsterdam, 2008.

Blaché, M.T., *Structural Analysis of Guarani, Memorates and Anecdotes*. Diss. University of Pennsylvania, 1977.

Cadogán, L., *Ayvu Rpyta. Textos míticos de los Mbyá-Guaraní del Guairá*. Facultad de Filosofía, Ciencias y Letras de la Universidad de São Paulo, São Paulo, 1992.

Caro-Baroja, J., *Las brujas y su mundo*. Alianza, Madrid, 1973.

Cohen, J.J. (ed), *Monster Theory: Reading Culture*. Minnesota University Press, Minnesota, 1996.

Colmán, N.R., *Nuestros antepasados (Ñande Ypy Kuéra)*, Biblioteca Virtual del Paraguay, 5 May. 2009.

Colombres, A., *Seres mitológicos argentinos*, Emece, Buenos Aires, 2000.

——, *Seres sobrenaturales de la cultura popular argentina*. Ediciones del Sol, Buenos Aires, 2003.

Crocitti, J., 'The Internal Economic Organization of The Jesuit Missions among The Guaraní'. *International Social Science Review*. Vol. 77, 1-2, 2002, pp. 3-15.

Cushner, N.P., *Why Have You Come Here? The Jesuits and the First Evangelization of Native America.* Oxford University Press, Oxford, 2006.

Fromm, E., *The Art of Loving.* Perennial Library, New York, 1986.

Gansón, B.A., *Guarani Under Spanish Rule in the Rio de la Plata.* Stanford University Press Palo Alto, 2003.

Hearn, L., *Kwaidan: Stories and Studies of Strange Things.* Houghton, Mifflin and Co, Boston, 1904. Viewed on 11 May 2009, <http://www.sacredtexts.com/shi/kwaidan/index.htm>.

Melía, B., *El guaraní conquistador y reducido: ensayos de etnohistoria.* Vol. 5, Biblioteca Paraguaya de Antropología, Centro de Estudios Antropológicos, Universidad Católica, Asunción, 1988.

Mills, R., 'Jesus as a Monster'. *The Monstrous Middle Ages.* Bildhauer, B. & Mills, R. (eds), Toronto University Press, Toronto, 2003.

Mendieta, O., 'Seres mitológicos guaraníes de ayer y de hoy'. *Defiant Deviance: The Irreality of Reality in the Cultural Imaginary.* Santos, C. & Spahr, A.(eds), Peter Lang, New York, 2006.

____, & Spahr, A., 'La fuerza curativa y el poder de las hierbas'. *Defiant Deviance: The Irreality of Reality in the Cultural Imaginary.* Santos, C. & Spahr, A. (eds), Peter Lang, New York, 2006.

Novak, M., *The Experience of Nothingness.* Harper & Row, New York, 1971.

Trento, P.A., *Reducciones jesuíticas: El paraíso en el Paraguay.* Parroquia San Rafael, Asunción, 2003.

From Monster to Deviant: European Conceptions of New World Peoples in Early Colonial Peru

Felipe E. Ruan

Abstract
In Christopher Columbus's First Voyage letter of 1493, the Genoese explorer writes that he did not find 'the human monsters which many people expected' to see in the New World. While Columbus notes that no monsters were found among the inhabitants of the newly discovered lands, in European conceptions of New World peoples the idea of the monstrous persisted, was reworked and recast into that which is morally deviant, deformed or corrupt. This reformulation of deviance extended to other New World peoples and in particular to the *mestizo*, the product of the biological mix of European and Amerindian. This chapter focuses on the process through which the *mestizo* is refashioned as morally deviant and is ultimately conceived as a potential threat to colonial interests and authority in sixteenth-century colonial Peru. The moral deviance attributed to the *mestizo* and *mestiza* is said to be transmitted through his/her Indian mother, thus the process of marginalisation of the *mestizo* is closely related to Spanish conceptions of the Amerindian, and, more generally, to European attitudes toward the non-European in the history of colonialism from the sixteenth century onwards.

Key Words: *Mestizo/a*, Amerindian, monsters, deviance, colonialism, Peru, New World, Spain.

*****

In Christopher Columbus's 1493 letter to Luis de Santangel, the Genoese explorer writes,

> 'no he hallado ombres mostrudos, como muchos pensavan.... Así que mostruos no he hallado ni noticia, salvo de una isla...que es poblada de una iente que tienen en todas las islas por muy ferozes, los cualles comen carne umana.'[1]

While Columbus writes that no monsters are found in the newly discovered lands, his reference to 'monstrous men' speaks to European conceptions of those peoples who were thought to inhabit the peripheral regions of the known world, and as a result were remote and hence conceived as different from Europeans. Nearly eighty years later, in a 1572 letter to the king about the increasing number of *mestizos* in colonial Peru, Fray Juan de Vivero writes, 'Hay otro mal en este reino... [que] nacen gran copia de mestizos de los cuales muchos salen aviesos por no les favorecer la mezcla.'[2] Columbus's description stands at the initial phase of colonization in Spanish America, while Vivero's account is produced during the early stages of colonial society in the Viceroyalty of Peru. Both documents, however, are deeply enmeshed in colonial discourse in terms of European conceptions of New World peoples[3]. Columbus's letter may be viewed as anticipating debates on the very nature of the indigenous peoples of America. It anticipates, in particular, Fray Antonio de Montesinos (d. 1545) challenge of 1511, 'Are these [Indians] not also men?' an utterance that bespeaks the depreciated status of the Amerindian at the early stages of colonization.[4] Vivero's letter also refers to the nature of non-European peoples, emphasizing in particular the potential corruption or deviance racial mixing may bring to colonial society.[5]

In what follows I argue that while Columbus's reference to 'human monsters' is characterized by the absence of such creatures in the New World, the physical deformity and deviance of the monsters that Europeans expected to find in America was recast, redeployed and attributed to New World peoples in terms of moral and behavioural deformity and deviance.[6] This reshaping of deviance extended to other New World peoples and in particular to the *mestizo*, the product of the racial mix of European and Amerindian. My interest lies in the ways in which, because of his/her proximity to the Amerindian world, the *mestizo* is refashioned as morally deviant and is ultimately conceived as a potential threat to colonial interests and authority in sixteenth-century colonial Peru. The *mestizo*'s moral deviance is attributed to his/her proximity to indigenous peoples, thus the *mestizo*'s *Indianization* is closely related to Spanish conceptions of the Amerindian, and, more generally, to European attitudes toward the non-European in the context of the history of colonialism from the sixteenth century onwards.

Writing on colonial discourse Ania Loomba reminds us that, '[k]nowledge is not innocent but profoundly connected with the operations of power.'[7] Knowledge-power relationships account not only for ways of seeing the world but also of controlling it. The monsters that Columbus expected to find in the New World correspond to European conceptions of otherness whose history can be traced back to antiquity. As Loomba aptly notes, 'the Greek and Roman periods ... provide abiding templates for subsequent European images of 'barbarians' and 'outsiders.''[8] These images 'were reworked in medieval and early modern Europe, where Christianity became 'the prism through which all knowledge of the world was refracted.''[9] This is perhaps most apparent in Christian European cartographic representations of the world, such as the well-know medieval T-O maps, which located Jerusalem at the centre of the world, and which remained in vogue well into the sixteenth century. T-O maps are circles (hence the O) in which bodies of water forming a T divide the orb into the main three land masses: Asia in the upper half, Europe in the lower left and Africa in the lower right. One such T-O map was used to illustrate the *Etymologies* by Isidore of Seville, a seventh-century Spanish bishop whose work aimed to analyze and present the world through language.[10] As Walter Mignolo explains,

> [t]he map, oriented toward the east, contains the names of the three continents and identifies each with one of Noah's sons: Asia with Shem, Europe with Japheth, and Africa with Ham (spelled Cham).[11]

In this conception of the known world, 'Europe and Asia were thought to be the homes of the descendants of Noah's good sons, Japheth and Shem.'[12] Ham, on the other hand, and as Augustine (354-430 AD) had suggested in his *City of God*, was Noah's bad son, and was associated with the forces of evil.[13] Moreover, it was thought that as the evil son, Ham had fathered the monsters of the world.[14]

A second medieval *mappa mundi* offers what Mignolo calls, 'a paradigmatic illustration of territorial representation in Christian cosmology.'[15] The Ebstorf Map dates from the thirteenth century and is organized in a variation of the 'T-O-scheme.' It incorporates the body of Christ as a reference point for the four directions, the top oriented toward the East. Africa, however, extends along the right side of the circle, together with a peripheral zone full of monsters.[16] Tellingly, most of the monstrous races may be found on Christ's left hand, the sinister side of the body.[17] As John B. Friedman explains,

> ...monstrous men are symbolically the farthest from Christ of anything in creation, and are represented in a narrow band at the edge of the world, as far as possible from Jerusalem, the center of Christianity.[18]

Medieval Europeans sought to understand the world in every detail as a creation of God, including that which is deviant. Like Augustine, Isidore of Seville attempted a Christian taxonomy and etymology of the monstrous and relied on classical learning for that purpose. As Palencia-Roth explains, Aristotle wrote in *The Generation of Animals* that 'the first characteristic of the monster is to be different' and that 'the monster is a kind of deformity.'[19] Aristotle labels 'terata' or monsters any deviation from type in the natural world.[20] In the first century AD, Pliny the elder catalogued in his *Natural History* the monsters that were thought to inhabit the earth. Pliny's work became the source material on the monstrous for most medieval writers.[21] The monsters included in Pliny's *Natural History*, were recounted again slightly more than a century before Columbus set sail for the Americas in the *Travels of Sir John Mandeville* (c. 1356), a work repeatedly printed in Europe and one that was likely known to Columbus.[22]

As Columbus sailed west to reach the east, we should wonder what type of monsters his late medieval European world-view stowed. His obsession with anthropophagi or 'men who eat flesh' we know.[23] Other monstrous creatures may have included such diverse and fantastic beings as Cynocephali (dog-headed people), giants, horned men, pygmies, Panotii (long-eared people) and Acephali (people with their faces on their chests), beings that together have come to be known as the 'Plinian races.' These monsters, which in most cases have recognizable human characteristics, were thought to inhabit the margins of the known world.

Monstrosity represented a way in which Europeans speculated about the nature of the unknown, and, more importantly for our purposes, how they thought about the 'other' in distant and unknown regions of the world. Above all, however, the cartographic, pictorial and textual examples that I have referred to represent regimes of knowledge-power, in terms of viewing, understanding and classifying the world. These regimes were redeployed and mobilized in the New World as a means of incorporating, dominating, and simultaneously marginalizing Amerindians and other New World peoples such as *mestizos*. On encountering Native Americans, Europeans began to impose their vision and division of the world upon them (figure 1).[24] This imposition involved a dehumanization of the Amerindian, the simplest method of dealing with all that is culturally unfamiliar. As Anthony Pagden has noted, to members of a community or 'insiders,' 'outsiders' can appear as members of another species.[25] Europeans tended to view Amerindians as humanoids or imperfect beings, and described them as "not men with rational souls but wild men of the woods."[26] Some, such as Juan Ginés de Sepulveda (c.1490-1573), referred to Amerindians as *homunculi*, 'those 'unnatural' and 'monstrous' beings that, according to medieval medicine, were created by magic or by other nefarious means.'[27] Others argued that Amerindians 'were like the Ethiopians, 'black' and slavish, the cursed descendants of Ham.'[28] As Europeans shifted their attention to the discoveries in the New World, interest in monstrous races gradually declined but did not disappear, it transformed instead.[29] 'The monstrous men of antiquity,' writes Friedman, 'were reduced to a single figure, the hairy wild man' and eventually this figure 'became conflated with the aboriginal peoples found in the New World.'[30] For Europeans, Native Americans became 'barbarians,' a term that implied that any creature so described was somehow an imperfect human being. The term 'barbarian' was deployed as a powerful form of domination and generally functioned as a signifier that, like the term monster, represented surplus alterity.[31]

As applied to Native Americans, 'barbarian' came so signify an anomaly of nature; a 'natural slave;' a half-man creature; irrational and deviant behaviour such as cannibalism, paganism and heresy associated with Satan. Colonial discourse toward Amerindians was not monolithic, however.

There were attempts to understand the indigenous peoples of America and to modify European conceptions of them. Most notably, the views of Bartolomé de las Casas (1484-1566) and that of the Jesuit José de Acosta (1539-1600) who argued that Native Americans were rational beings, as well as proto ethnographic approaches such as that of Bernardino de Sahagún (c.1500-1590) in Mexico.[32] For the most part, however, negative views toward indigenous peoples prevailed and intensified, particularly as colonialism's economic, political and religious objectives confronted resistance and opposition.

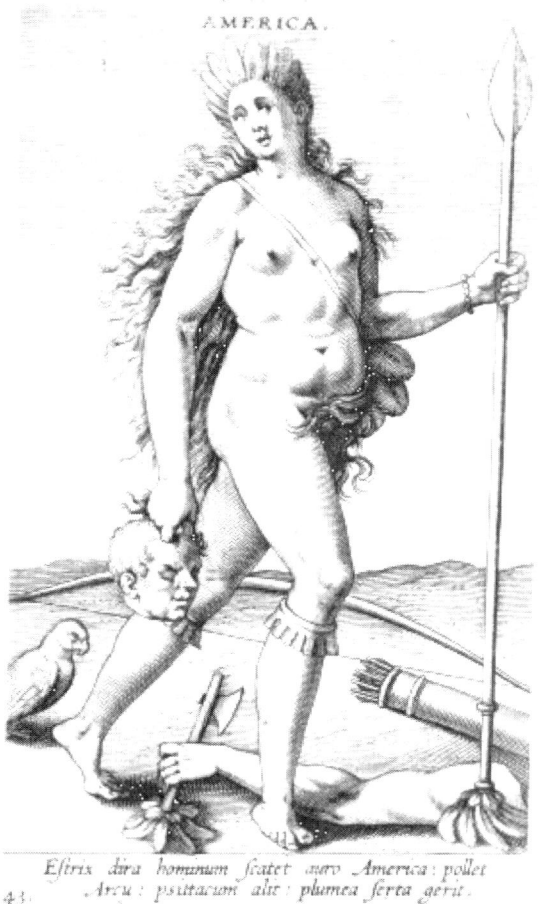

Figure 1. Philippe Galle, 'America' from a work entitled *Prosopographia* (1579-1600). The Latin inscription below the image identifies 'America' with cannibalism: 'America, an ogress who devours men, who is rich in gold, and who is skilled and powerful in use of her bow […].' (Courtesy of the New-York Historical Society, Negative no. 38936).

The deviance, inferiority and corruption attributed to the indigenous people of America extended to *mestizos*. The *mestizos* and *mestizas* I study belong to the first post-conquest *mestizo* generation of sixteenth-century Peru. The term *mestizo* emerges as a distinct classification in the second half of the sixteenth century. As a descriptive category the term begins to coalesce as the first post-conquest *mestizo* generation was coming of age, and as the varied social group known as *castas* or mixed bloods (which included *mestizos*) was experiencing significant demographic growth.[33] As far as the conception of colonial society in terms of a 'republic of Spaniards' and a 'republic of Indians,' *mestizos* were initially viewed as belonging to the community of Spaniards, but as their numbers grew, they began to be cast as suspicious social subjects of ambivalent political loyalty.[34]

Referring to the growing number of *mestizos* and their association with mixed bloods, in a 1572 letter to Philip II Friar Juan de Vivero writes,

> Hay otro mal en este reino y que como la tierra es tan ocasionada para que los hombres se den al vicio de la sensualidad, nacen gran copia de mestizos de los cuales muchos salen aviesos por no les favorecer la mezcla o por criarse entre mulatos e indios.[35]

Although the word 'avieso' means 'ill inclined,' it also connotes 'crookedness,' a type of moral deformity. This deformity or deviance of nature is believed to be the product of the racial mixing with indigenous women, and it is also thought to be the result of the *mestizo*'s close proximity to Indians and other mixed-bloods such as mulattos. Moreover, the degenerative American environment appears to influence the lascivious behaviour of Spaniards ('because the environment is such that men give themselves to the vice of sensuality').[36] Other Spanish views, however, attribute such wantonness mainly to the lax sexual behaviour of indigenous women. Colonial authorities partly blamed Spaniards for having Indian women as concubines, but a large part of the blame was attributed to the immoral sexual conduct of indigenous women. Sexual relations between Spaniards and Indian women were framed in terms of a vice that had to be checked. Indian women were characterized as 'bad women' ('malas mujeres') or 'easy women' ('las indias son fáciles'). As the Franciscan Bernardino de Cárdenas writes in a royal report circa 1632,

> hay muchísimos [mestizos] porque el pecado de mesclarse los españoles con las indias es generalísimo y muy frecuentado porque las indias son fáciles y el hábito que traen muy la(s)civo y deshonesto [descubiertos los braços y los pies].[37]

Clearly, here both colonial and early modern gender discourses intersect. The indigenous woman is the reason for the Spaniards sins and, moreover, she is the source of a moral corruption that is transmitted to *mestizo* children through her blood and through her milk.³⁸

The 'bad' or corrupt behaviour of the indigenous woman turns the milk that is meant to nourish her children into 'bad milk,' so that flaws and deviance are passed on as the *mestizo* child drinks the Indian mother's milk. But the transmission of bad character through 'bad Indian milk' extends beyond the *mestizos* to the creoles of America. In colonial texts there are references to Indian women serving as wet nurses of creole children, the children of Spaniards born in America. In his *Descripción breve de toda la tierra del Perú* (1605), the Dominican Reginaldo de Lizarraga writes that the sons of Spaniards in colonial Peru are reared by Indian women.³⁹ These creole children are said to be ill inclined because they suckled the 'bad milk' of their wet nurses: 'El que mama la leche mentirosa, mentiroso; el que borracha, borracho; el que ladrona, ladrón.'⁴⁰ The deviant behaviour transmitted through the 'bad Indian milk,' however, is also transmitted culturally. Creoles and *mestizos* are reared by Indian women and therefore learn their language and their culture. For Europeans, the proximity of creoles to Indians and to those of mixed origins came to be interpreted as a sign of degeneration, one that lowered the status of American-born 'Spaniards.'⁴¹ Classifications of distinction could be manipulated in a variety of ways, so that even those of European descent (creoles) may be seen as sharing the deviance and degeneration attributed to Indians. Even in the backlands of the Viceroyalty of Peru such views were common. Governor Diego Rodriguez de Valdés, who arrived in Paraguay in the 1590s, wrote that 'in the creoles one can put little trust and in the *mestizos*, none.'⁴²

Mestizas are also a source of corruption. In the textual material they are said to learn immoral female behavior form their Indian mother. The *mestiza*'s alluring beauty represented an even greater temptation for Spanish men. *Mestiza*'s are cast as the 'Devil's bait' and are said to be the reason that Spanish men commit 'millions of sins'.

> Son hermosas y traen con esto hábito muy deshonesto, lascivo y libre, porque andan con el hábito de indias, que es deshonestísimo...y con la libertad que tienen, sin honra y obligación, traen los hombres locos y causan innumerables pecados, y las hijas que nacen destas van causando otros muchos.⁴³

The proposed solution is to separate *mestizas* from their Indian mother so that they may be raised by prominent Spanish women and educated in Spanish ways.⁴⁴ Here the tacit implication is that if *mestizas* were to be reared according to Spanish customs, they would grow up to be more 'civilized' and perhaps even come to marry a Spaniard.

Conceptions of the *mestizo* as a morally deviant and corrupt social subject are grounded on his or her biological and cultural proximity to Amerindians. These conceptions are early attempts at shaping notions of difference in terms 'race,' a socially constructed category that would come to be regarded as inherited through blood. From the initial stages of Spanish colonization, the non-European is subjected to European valuative and classificatory discursive categories that conceive him or her as 'inferior' and that in turn underscore European 'superiority.' Social structures based on rank, however, subsumed issues of miscegenation. In colonial Peru, *mestizos* were absorbed into colonial Spanish society in accordance to their social status, so that *mestizos* of higher social rank, and whom their Spanish father recognized, were considered creoles. In other words, social rank (class) and identification with Spanish culture trumped 'race.'[45] As for some *mestizas*, they often married prominent colonial Spaniards, their indigenous lineage often drifting from baptism register to marriage register so that they ultimately 'absorbed' the Spanish social characteristics of their husbands.[46] Lower ranking *mestizos* and *mestizas* were generally absorbed into the indigenous population. Some became domestic servants, others engaged in artisanal and commercial activities. While middle ranking *mestizos* held ecclesiastical positions or were officials in the colonial administration.[47] Although some *mestizos* did integrate into 'Spanish' social sectors, during the early stages of colonial society *mestizos* were also subject to exclusionary attitudes and practices.[48]

The anxiety toward the *mestizo* that is evident in testimonies of early colonial Peru can be largely attributed to demographic, historical and political factors. *Mestizos* had grown to large numbers and this population growth combined with *mestizo* rebellions in Cuzco (1567) and then later in Quito (1583), made colonial authorities suspicious of their loyalty.[49] Viewed as an unruly and ill inclined group, *mestizos* began to be cast less so as members of colonial Spanish society and more so as 'outsiders.'[50] Moreover, *mestizos* began to be associated with other mixed-bloods that made up the *castas*. Particularly opprobrious was the *mestizo*'s proximity to the 'increasing presence of Africans and their descendents among the *castas*.'[51] The Jesuit José de Teruel, Rector of the Jesuit College at Cuzco, was among those who in the 1580s expressed anxiety about the growing number of peoples of mixed origin, grouping, perhaps not unwittingly, *mestizos* with blacks and mulattos: 'En todo este reino es mucha la gente que hay de negros, mulatos, mestizos y otras misturas de gentes y cada día crece más el número de estos.'[52] In his 1585 letter to the king, Teruel notes that he is writing 'for the good of the Spanish republic' ('por el bien de la república hispana'), to warn about the potential danger of rebellion that, in his view, the *castas* or mixed-bloods represent. In Teruel's text there is the implication that those of mixed origins do not belong to his conception of a Christian *república hispana*:

> Esta gente se cría en grandes vicios y libertades, sin trabajar ni tener oficio, comen y beben sin orden y críanse con los indios y indias y hállanse en sus borracheras y hechicerías, no oyen misa ni sermón en todo el año, sino alguno muy raro, y así no saben de la ley de Dios, nuestro criador, ni parece en ellos rastro della.[53]

Grouped with Indians and mixed-bloods, *mestizos* are conceived as a corrupt and deviant social group. Moreover, most salient is the *mestizo*'s and, more generally, the *castas*'s association with Amerindians ('críanse con los indios y indias').[54] Like the Amerindian, for Europeans the *mestizo* is prone to vice, he is lazy and eats and drinks without moderation; he is inclined to drink, and perhaps more damaging still, his practice of witchcraft makes him into heretic, a person who challenges the social order and authority of the Christian community. Teruel's letter also groups blacks alongside *mestizos*, mulattoes and Indians. While the Jesuit may be simply reporting on the demographic growth of the *castas*, it is useful to bear in mind that, as Kuznesof underscores, colonial documents 'constitute a coded text, in which racial categories were manipulated' in a variety of ways.[55] In Spanish America, Africans were associated with slave status and were 'almost universally depreciated.'[56] Lumping *mestizos* with Africans, mulattoes and Indians effectively devalued the *mestizo*'s status in sixteenth-century colonial Peru.

The *Indianization* of the *mestizo* aimed to reassert the original, neat spatial order that divided the colonial world into a 'republic of Spaniards' and a 'republic of Indians.' This bipartite division was reproduced in the spatial configuration of Spanish colonial cities, where a number of square blocks in the centre of the city was the area reserved for Spanish occupancy, while the region surrounding that area was earmarked for Indian residence.[57] Like in earlier Christian cartographic representations, the marginalisation of the *mestizo* constituted an attempt to place on the outer or peripheral regions of the world those conceived as unruly and deviant. The growing number of people of mixed origins and their gradual insertion into colonial society, however, would ensure ongoing negotiations aimed at re-writing and re-configuring the colonial map.

Every age has its 'monsters.' The idea of the monster is present in the first European descriptions of New World peoples. Even if it is the monster's absence that Columbus emphasizes ('no he hallado ni noticia [de monstruos]'), 'monsters' are potentially there, in other yet to be explored New World regions: 'salvo en una isla que es Carib,...que es poblada de una iente que tienen en todas las islas por muy ferozes, los cualles comen carne umana.'[58] Palencia-Roth has argued that 'the Western tradition of the monster, or teratology'[59] with its Classical and Christian roots, became enmeshed in the process and discourse of European conquest and colonization. People who eat flesh or cannibals that Columbus refers to in his letter, reappear in Hernán Cortés's Second Letter to the king:

> for in addition to [the natives] having killed the aforementioned Spaniards and rebelled against Your Highness's service, they are all cannibals, of which I send Your Majesty no evidence because it is so infamous.[60]

In this and other instances, 'Europeans found it expedient to describe indigenous peoples as cannibals to justify their enslavement.'[61] The charge of anthropophagy became a powerful marker of 'monstrous' behaviour, deployed to fashion 'barbarian' and corrupt indigenous peoples. This and other European conceptions of the New World 'otherness' were reworked and transformed to cast the *mestizo* as deviant, corrupt and inferior.

In colonial Peru, from about the 1560s, *mestizos* began to be viewed as the 'other' who 'lurked uncomfortably nearer home,' and who as a result needed to be refashioned symbolically as the social element to be excluded from the community of Spaniards.[62] The symbolic violence that was deployed to recast the *mestizo* as a threatening other was grounded on previous and ongoing attitudes that tended to depreciate and dehumanize indigenous peoples. Amerindians were associated with monstrous practices such as cannibalism in the early phases of the colonization, while later they came to be linked to corruption and deviance such as promiscuity, laziness, drunkenness, witchcraft, idolatry and paganism. The *mestizo*'s biological and cultural ties to indigenous peoples became a powerful source for attitudes and discursive practices that assigned moral deformity and waywardness to *mestizos*. While not the 'monsters' that early colonial discourse had made of some Amerindians, *mestizos* were nonetheless recast as morally deformed subjects of the colonial world. The *mestizo* was thus symbolically transformed into a 'monstrous' or deviant being of early colonial Peru.*

Notes

[1] 'I have not found the human monsters which many people expected.... Not only have I found no monsters but I have had no reports of any except [of those on an island]...which is inhabited by a people who are...extremely fierce and who eat human flesh'. J.M. Cohen, (ed and trans), *The Four Voyages of Christopher Columbus*, Penguin Books, Harmondsworth, 1969, p. 121. Spanish language citations are from C. Varela (ed), *Cristóbal Colón. Textos y documentos completos, relaciones de viajes, cartas y memoriales*, 2nd ed, Alianza Editorial, Madrid, 1984, pp. 144-145. M. Zamora notes that 'Columbus' use of "monster" denotes someone who does not conform either in appearance or behavior to the European norm' in, *Reading Columbus*, University of California Press, Los Angeles, 1993, p. 171. The letter of 15 February 1493 is addressed to Luis de Santangel, *escribano de ración* of the Catholic Monarchs, Varela, op cit., p. 139.

[2] 'There is another ill in this kingdom...[that] a great number of mestizos are born, many of which are ill inclined because the racial mix does not benefit them.' (Carta de Fray Juan de Vivero; Cuzco, 24 de enero de 1572; [AGI, Lima 314, fl. 3r.]) All translations are my own unless otherwise indicated.

[3] In *Marvelous Possessions* Stephen Greenblatt examines the discourse of wonder in the writings of Columbus, among others, and how it serves to mediate the ways in which Europeans represented non-European peoples. Wonder and possession are closely related, as Greenblatt underscores by noting that '[t]he claim of possession is grounded in the power of wonder' in *Marvelous Possessions: The Wonder of the New World*, University of Chicago Press, Chicago, 1991, p. 80. In a more recent study, Rolena Adorno aptly notes that 'the polemics of possession' are 'central to the Latin American literary tradition,' beginning with the writings of the early Spanish colonial period, *The Polemics of Possession in Spanish American Narrative*, Yale University Press, New Haven & London, 2007, p. 4. The Spanish representation of *mestizos* that I analyse also engages the 'polemics of possession' in that it addresses key issues such as who belongs to colonial society, and by extension to whom does that society belong.

[4] 'Estos, ¿no son hombres? ¿No tienen ánimas racionales?', B. de las Casas, *Historia de las Indias. 1527-1559*, [ed.], A.M. Carlo, 3 Vols., Mexico City, Fondo de Cultura Económico, 1951, Vol. 2, pp. 441-442. P. Seed examines the controversy surrounding the Indians' humanity in 'Are These Not Also Men?: The Indians' Humanity and Capacity for Spanish Civilisation', *Journal of Latin American Studies*, Vol. 25, October 1993, pp. 629-652.

[5] S.B. Schwartz & F. Solomon note that in Spanish America *mestizaje* (miscegenation) was viewed 'as a social evil,' however, 'although early colonial Iberians ideologically deplored miscegenation, they also connived at it in pursuit of tangible interests', 'New Peoples and New Kinds of People: Adaptation, Readjustment, and Ethnogenesis in South American Indigenous Societies (Colonial Era)', *The Cambridge History of the Native Peoples of the Americas*, S.B. Schwartz & F. Solomon (eds), Vol. 3, Pt. 2, Cambridge University Press, Cambridge & New York, 1996-2000, pp. 444 & 483. As P. Bakewell writes, 'during the founding phase of the mainland empire' 'intermarriage of Spaniards and natives...became normal policy' in *A History of Latin America*, Blackwell, Oxford, 2004, p. 85. Intermarrying or taking on as concubines the daughters of local Indian elites represented a way to forge strategic alliances with indigenous groups and to consolidate power in K.J. Andrien, 'The Spanish Atlantic System', J. P. Greene & P.D. Morgan (eds), *Atlantic History: A Critical Appraisal*, Oxford University Press, Oxford, 2009, p. 58. The pioneering study on race mixture in Latin American history is M. Mörner, *Race Mixture in the History of Latin America*, Little, Brown and Company, Boston, 1967.

[6] The formulation of my own argument benefits from Palencia-Roth's view that '[w]hen Native Americans turned out not to have the monstrous or inhuman features, monstrous or inhuman behavior was attributed to them by Europeans' in 'Enemies of God: Monsters and the Theology of Conquest', *Monsters, Tricksters, and Sacred Cows: Animal Tales and American Identities*, A.J Arnold (ed), University Press of Virginia, Charlottesville and London, 1996, p. 24. The emphasis of my argument, however, differs from Palencia-Roth's in that it focuses on how deviance is attributed to the first, post-conquest *mestizo* generation of colonial Peru.

[7] A. Loomba, *Colonialism/Postcolonialism*, 2nd ed, Routledge, London/New York, 2005, p. 42.

[8] Ibid., p. 92. This is most apparent in Juan Ginés de Sepúlveda's deployment of Aristotle's theory of natural slavery in order to cast the Indians as non civil beings whose deviant behaviour such as cannibalism and human sacrifice violated the law of nature in A. Pagden, 'Dispossessing the Barbarian: The Language of Spanish Thomism and the Debate over the Property Rights of the American Indians', *Theories of Empire. 1450-1800*, D. Armitage (ed), Ashgate, Aldershot, 1998, pp. 170-72. Elsewhere, Pagden notes that '[i]t was, above all, Rome which provided the ideologues of the colonial systems of Spain, Britain and France with the language and political models required'. See A. Pagden, *Lords of all The World: Ideologies of Empire in Spain, Britain and France c.1500-c.1800*, Yale University Press, New Haven, 1995, p. 11.

[9] Ibid., p. 92. Loomba cites R. Miles, *Racism*, Routledge, London, 1989, p. 16.

[10] Palencia-Roth op. cit. p. 28; and W. Mignolo, 'The Movable Center: Geographical Discourses and Territoriality During the Expansion of the Spanish Empire', *The Latin American Cultural Studies Reader*, A. del Sarto, A. Ríos & A. Trigo (eds), Duke University Press, Durham, N.C., 2004, pp. 270-71.

[11] Mignolo op. cit., p. 270.

[12] Palencia-Roth op. cit., p. 28.

[13] Ibid., pp. 26-28; Loomba, op. cit., p. 92.

[14] Palencia-Roth, op. cit., p. 28. On Noah's curse and European colonialism and racism see B. Braude, 'The Sons of Noah and the Construction of Ethnic and Geographical Identities in Medieval and Early Modern Periods', *William and Mary Quarterly*, Vol. 53, October 1997, pp. 103-142.

[15] Mignolo, op. cit., p. 270.

[16] B. Bildhauer, 'Blood, Jews and Monsters in Medieval Culture', *The Monstrous Middle Ages*, B. Bildhauer. & R. Mills (eds), University of Wales Press, Cardiff, 2003, p. 77.

[17] Palencia-Roth, op. cit., p. 33.

[18] J.B. Friedman, *The Monstrous Races in Medieval Art and Thought*, Harvard University Press, Cambridge, 1981, p. 37.

[19] Palencia-Roth, op. cit., p. 24.
[20] E. Sober, 'Evolution, Population Thinking, and Essentialism', *Philosophy of Science: An Anthology*, M. Lange (ed), Wiley-Blackwell, London, 2006, p. 394.
[21] Pliny's *Natural History* was influential in describing the natural world of America. When writing his *General and Natural History of the Indies*, Gonzalo Fernández de Oviedo (1478-1557) styled himself as a 'Pliny of the New World'. See M. de Asúa & R. French, *A New World of Animals: Early Modern Europeans on the Creatures of Iberian America*, Ashgate, Aldershot, 2005, p. 62.
[22] J.M. Wright, 'True Peoples and Their Monsters: Speculations on the Other in the Age of Exploration', *Terrae Incognitae*, Vol. 37, 2005, p. 3. R. Tzanaki notes that Columbus 'may very well have owned or at least read a copy of [Mandeville's book], though this cannot be proved.' Nonetheless, Tzanaki underscores that even in the sixteenth century 'Mandeville was being read as a geographical authority of some standing.' Columbus certainly owned Pliny's *Natural History*. R. Tzanaki, *Mandeville's Medieval Audiences: A Study on the Reception of the Book of Sir John Mandeville (1371-1550)*, Ashgate, Aldershot, 2003, p. 120. Zamora offers an overview of the 'cartographic tradition that informed Columbian geography,' noting that both *mappa mundi* and portolan charts (written coastline descriptions) were part of this tradition; Zamora, op. cit., p. 107 & pp. 102-117.
[23] Pagden explains that 'the European interest in man-eating amounts to almost an obsession,' and that 'anthropophagi, as they were known before the discovery of America, have played their role in the description of non-European cultures ever since the Greeks ventured out into the western Mediterranean'. See A. Pagden, *The Fall of Natural Man: The American Indian and the Origins of Comparative Ethnology*, Cambridge University Press, Cambridge, 1986, pp. 80-81.
[24] Indigenous peoples, however, were not mere passive subjects. Wright explains that 'many native communities resorted to telling fabulous tales to manipulate the movements of Europeans both in and out of their territories.' Some of these tales included 'stories of monsters.' Wright notes that for the same reasons as Europeans, Native Americans also believed in the existence of monsters, and accounted for them in their own cosmologies; Wright, op. cit., pp. 5 & 8.
[25] Pagden, op. cit., p. 17.
[26] Cited in Pagden, Ibid., p. 23.
[27] Palencia-Roth, op. cit., p. 40.
[28] J. Cañizares Esguerra, 'New World, New Stars: Patriotic Astrology and the Invention of Indian and Creole Bodies in Colonial Spanish America', *American Historical Review*, Vol. 104, February 1999, p. 34.
[29] References to monsters in America are found well into the seventeenth century. Patricia Seed writes that in his influential *Disputationem de Indiarum jure* (Madrid, 1629), Juan de Solorzano Pereira offers 'a summary discussion of Augustine's monsters and their relation to Spanish categories of dominion. He concludes (lib. 2,

cap. 9) that no such monsters have been found (p. 340)'; Seed, op. cit., p. 634. Solorzano Pereira later produced a Spanish adaptation of the *Disputationem* entitled *Política indiana* (1648).

[30] Friedman, op. cit., p. 197.

[31] Bildhauer, op. cit., p. 80.

[32] Pagden notes that José de Acosta's *Historia natural y moral de las Indias* (1590) was 'a work that for the latter part of the sixteenth century and for most of the seventeenth century dominated speculations on Amerindians and their culture'; Pagden, op. cit., p. 146. José de Acosta spent nearly 15 years in colonial Peru; ibid., p. 148. R. Adorno explains that las Casas' *Apologética historia*, although unpublished during the author's lifetime, was however read by individuals such as Jerónimo de Román y Zamora who incorporated it into his own works, such as *Repúblicas del mundo* (1575, 1595). See *The Polemics of Possession in Spanish American Narrative*, Yale University Press, New Haven, 2007, p. 94.

[33] B. Ares Queija notes that the social classification of *mestizos* becomes an issue in the 1560s when a generation of *mestizos* born after the civil wars and Indian rebellion of the 1530s were in their early twenties ("Un borracho de chicha y vino.' La construcción social del mestizo [Perú, siglo XVI]', in *Mezclado y sospechoso. Movilidad e identidades, España y América [siglos XVI-XVIII]. Coloquio internacional [29-31 de mayo de 2000]. Actas reunidas y presentadas por Gregorio Salinero*, Casa de Velázquez, Madrid, 2005, p. 134). The history of Peruvian miscegenation, however, antedates the conquest. Ares Queija notes that there were a number of black female slaves and Indian women that the conquistadors brought to Peru from other regions of Spanish America; ibid., p. 123. Lockhart writes that 'mestizos and Spanish children were born in Peru from 1533 on', however, it was the following generation of mestizos, those born after the Indian rebellion of 1537, who came of age in the 1560s. J. Lockhart, *Spanish Peru, 1532-1560: A Social History*, 2nd ed, University of Wisconsin Press, Madison, 1994, p. 186.

[34] Spanish American society was composed of a 'three-category ethnic scheme of Spaniard, Black, and Indian'; S. B. Schwartz & J. Lockhart, *Early Latin America: A History of Colonial Spanish America and Brazil*, Cambridge University Press, Cambridge, 1988, p. 129. As P. Bakewell notes, an additional element, the result of the mixture of Indian, Spanish and black, 'was rising in numbers to occupy, or better, perhaps, to create a social space between Europeans and natives'; op. cit., p. 173. This element of mixed bloods was referred to as *las castas*, a genetically and culturally varied group that included *mestizos*, mulattoes (black and Spanish), *zambos* (black and Indian), and other mixed bloods. For a comprehensive discussion on *castas* see S.B. Schwartz, 'Colonial Identities and the *sociedad de castas*'. *Colonial Latin American Review*, Vol. 4, No. 1, 1995, pp. 185-201.

[35] 'There is another ill in this kingdom, because the environment is such that men give themselves to the vice of sensuality, a great number of *mestizos* are born, many of who are ill inclined because the racial mix does not benefit them, or because they are reared among mulattos and Indians.' Carta de Fray Juan de Vivero; Cuzco, 24 de enero de 1572, (AGI, Lima 314, fl. 3r.).

[36] As J. Cañizares Esguerra explains, basing their claims on Hippocratic-Galenic physiology and astrology, Europeans attributed negative climatological and astrological characteristics to the New World. The American environment was viewed as having degenerative effects on both natives and Spaniards, Cañizares Esguerra, op. cit., pp. 36-49. Some believed that the Indies produced only degenerative humans. Juan de la Puente argued in 1612 that 'the heavens in America induce inconstancy, lasciviousness and lies, vices characteristic of the Indians and which the constellations make characteristic of the Spaniards who are born and bred there'; cited in J. Cañizares Esguerra, p. 14.

[37] 'There are many [mestizos] because the sin of Spaniards mixing with Indian women is very common, and Indian women are easy and their dress lascivious and dishonest [their arms and feet go uncovered].' Cited in B. Ares Queija, 'Mancebas de españoles, madres de mestizos: Imágenes de la mujer indígena en el Perú colonial temprano', *Las mujeres en la construcción de las sociedades iberoamericanas*, P.G. Aizpuru & B. Ares Queija, coordinators, CSIC/Colegio de México, Sevilla/México, 2004, p. 29. The original source is Bernardino de Cárdenas, *Memorial y relación de las cosas muy graves y muy importantes el remedio y aumento de el reino del Perú y al consuelo de la conciencia del rey* (c. 1632), fl. 64v. Biblioteca Nacional de Madrid, Manuscritos, no. 3198.

[38] On the relationship of race and gender in colonial Spanish America with a specific emphasis on *mestizos* and *mestizas*, see E.A. Kuznesof, 'Ethnic and Gender Influences on 'Spanish' Creole Identity in Colonial Spanish America', *Colonial Latin American Review*, Vol. 4, No. 1, 1995, pp. 153-176. For more recent research on the topic see N. Jaffary (ed), *Gender, Race and Religion in the Colonization of the Americas*, Ashgate, Aldershot, 2007.

[39] 'Nacido el pobre muchacho lo entregan a una india o negra borracha que le crió sucia, mentirosa…y críase, ya grandecillo, con indiezuelos' ['Once born, the poor child is given to a drunkard Indian or black woman who rears him in filth and lies…and once older, he is reared among Indians']; R. de Lizarraga, , *Descripción breve de toda la tierra del Perú, Tucumán: Río de la Plata y Chile,* in *Biblioteca de Autores Españoles*, Vol. 216, Atlas Ediciones, Madrid, 1968, p. 101. It is noteworthy that black women are also viewed as having a corrupting influence.

[40] 'He who suckles liar's milk, will be a liar; drunkard's milk, a drunkard; a thief's milk, a thief.' Lizarraga, op. cit., p. 101.

[41] On the topic of the 'Spanishness' of colonial society see Kuznesof, op. cit., pp. 153-170.

[42] Cited in Schwartz, 'Colonial Identities and the *Sociedad de Castas*', op. cit., p. 193.

[43] 'They are beautiful and they don dress that is dishonest, lascivious and free because they wear Indian garb which is very dishonest ... and with the freedom they enjoy, not having honour nor obligation, they make Spanish men crazy causing them to commit innumerable sins, and the daughters that these mestizas bear bring about many more sins.' Cited in A. Queija, 'Mancebas de españoles, madres de mestizos: Imágenes de la mujer indígena en el Perú colonial temprano', p. 30 no. 40. The original source is Bernardino de Cárdenas, *Memorial y relación de las cosas muy graves y muy importantes el remedio y aumento de el reino del Perú y al consuelo de la conciencia del rey* (c. 1632), fl. 64v, Biblioteca Nacional de Madrid, Manuscritos, n.° 3198.

[44] A. Queija, 'Mancebas de españoles, madres de mestizos. Imágenes de la mujer indígena en el Perú colonial temprano', p. 30.

[45] Schwartz, 'Colonial Identities and the *Sociedad de Castas*', op. cit., p. 192. A case in point is Inca Garcilaso de la Vega, who may arguably be considered what P Bakewell labels an 'euromestizo', p. 172.

[46] Kuznesof, op. cit., pp.162-164.

[47] A. Queija, ''Un borracho de chicha y vino' La construcción social del mestizo (Perú, siglo XVI)', pp. 134-135.

[48] C. Rahn Phillips has argued that 'whatever their ethnic origin,' individuals in colonial Spanish America learned to function effectively within the colonial social world, at times by accommodating to colonial demands or by simply relying on or manipulating the colonial system; 'Twenty Million People United by an Ocean: Spain and the Atlantic World beyond the Renaissance', *Renaissance Quarterly*, Vol. 62, No. 1, Spring 2009, p. 38. People of mixed birth, and *mestizos* in particular, formed a new category that represented a challenge to categorization itself see Schwartz & Solomon, op. cit., p. 444. Negotiations surrounding these new categories would remain in flux during the colonial period.

[49] Schwartz, 'Colonial Identities and the *Sociedad de Castas*', op. cit., p. 193.

[50] A. Queija, ''Un borracho de chicha y vino': La construcción social del mestizo (Perú, siglo XVI)', op. cit., pp. 137-138.

[51] Schwartz, 'Colonial Identities and the *Sociedad de Castas*', op. cit., p. 193.

[52] 'In all this kingdom there are many who are negroes, mulatos, mestizos and other mixed people, and every day they grow in numbers.' (Carta del padre José de Teruel, rector del colegio de jesuitas del Cuzco, al rey; Cuzco, 1 de febrero de 1585, [AGI, Lima 316, fl. 1.])

[53] 'These people are raised with great vices and freedom, without work or trade; they eat and drink without measure and are reared with male and female Indians, and partake in their drunkenness and witchcraft, rarely attend mass during the whole year, and as a result do not know God's Law, our Creator, nor is there a

trace of His law in them.' (Carta del padre José de Teruel, rector del colegio de jesuitas del Cuzco, al rey; Cuzco, 1 de febrero de 1585, [AGI, Lima 316, fl. 1.])
[54] '[They] are reared with male and female Indians.'
[55] Kuznesof, op. cit., p. 169.
[56] Schwartz, 'Colonial Identities and the *Sociedad de Castas*', op. cit., p. 193. J. Lockhart (chap. X) offers details on Africans in colonial Peru. M.E. Martínez writes that by the early seventeenth century 'Iberians were regularly deploying the myth of the Course of Ham against dark-skinned Africans, thereby linking them to a stained biblical genealogy that was condemned to perpetual servitude'. See 'The Black Blood of New Spain: Limpieza de Sangre, Racial Violence, and Gendered Power in Early Colonial Mexico', *William and Mary Quarterly*, Vol. 61, July 2004, par.10).
[57] D.R. Cope, *The Limits of Racial Domination: Plebian Society in Colonial Mexico City, 1660-1720*, University of Wisconsin Press, Madison, 1994, p. 10. Schwartz and Lockhart note that Spanish American cities 'were built on the grid plan with a great central square, Spanish at the centre and Indian at the edges'; op. cit., p. 125.
[58] 'I have had no reports of any [monsters].' 'Except at the island called 'Quaris', [...] which is inhabited by a people who are regarded in these islands as extremely fierce and who eat human flesh; Cohen, op. cit., p. 121; Varela, op. cit., pp. 144-45.
[59] Palencia-Roth, op. cit., pp. 24-25 & 37-40.
[60] A. Pagden, (ed and trans), *Hernán Cortés: Letters from Mexico*, Yale University Press, New Haven, 1986, p. 147.
[61] W.F. Keegan, 'Columbus was a Cannibal. Myth and the First Encounters', *The Lesser Antilles in the Age of European Expansion*, RL. Paquette & S.L. Engerman (eds), University Press of Florida, Gainsville, 1996, p. 29.
[62] Loomba, op. cit., p. 93.

* Archival research in Seville, Spain for this project was funded by a 2007 grant from the Humanities Research Institute, Brock University.

Bibliography

Adorno, R., *The Polemics of Possession in Spanish American Narrative*. Yale University Press, New Haven and London, 2007.

Andrien, K.J., 'The Spanish Atlantic System'. *Atlantic History. A Critical Appraisal*. Greene, J.P. & Morgan, P.D. (eds), Oxford University Press, Oxford, 2009, pp. 55-79.

Ares Queija, B., 'Un borracho de chicha y vino: La construcción social del mestizo (Perú, siglo XVI)'. *Mezclado y sospechoso. Movilidad e identidades, España y América (siglos XVI-XVIII). Coloquio internacional (29-31 de mayo de 2000). Actas reunidas y presentadas por Gregorio Salinero.* Casa de Velázquez, Madrid, 2005, pp. 121-44.

——, 'Mancebas de españoles, madres de mestizos: Imágenes de la mujer indígena en el Perú colonial temprano'. Aizpuru, P.G. & Ares Queija, B. (coordinadores), *Las mujeres en la construcción de las sociedades iberoamericanas*, CSIC/Colegio de México, Sevilla/México, 2004, pp. 15-39.

Asúa, M. de & French, R., *A New World of Animals: Early Modern Europeans on the Creatures of Iberian America*. Ashgate, Aldershot, 2005.

Bakewell, P., *A History of Latin America*. Blackwell, Oxford, 2004.

Bildhauer, B., 'Blood, Jews and Monsters in Medieval Culture'. *The Monstrous Middle Ages*. Bildhauer, B. & Mills, R. (eds), University of Wales Press, Cardiff, 2003.

Braude, B., 'The Sons of Noah and the Construction of Ethnic and Geographical Identities in Medieval and Early Modern Periods'. *William and Mary Quarterly*, Vol. 34, 1997, pp. 103-42.

Cañizares Esguerra, J., 'New World, New Stars: Patriotic Astrology and the Invention of Indian and Creole Bodies in Colonial Spanish America'. *American Historical Review*. Vol. 104, No. 1, 1999, pp. 33-57.

Casas, B. de las, *Historia de las Indias, 1527-1559*. Millares-Carlo, A. (ed), 3 Vols., Fondo de Cultura Económica, Mexico City, 1951.

Cohen, J.M. (ed and trans), *The Four Voyages of Christopher Columbus*. Penguin Books, Harmondsworth, 1969.

Cope, R.D., *The Limits of Racial Domination: Plebian Society in Colonial Mexico City, 1660-1720*. University of Wisconsin Press, Madison, 1994.

Friedman, J.B., *The Monstrous Races in Medieval Art and Thought*. Harvard University Press, Cambridge, 1981.

Greenblatt, S., *Marvelous Possessions: The Wonder of the New World*. University of Chicago Press, Chicago, 1991.

Keegan, W.F., 'Columbus was a Cannibal: Myth and the First Encounters'. *The Lesser Antilles in the Age of European Expansion*. Paquette, R.L. & Engerman, S.L. (eds), University Press of Florida, Gainsville, 1964.

Kuznesof, E.A., 'Ethnic and Gender Influences on 'Spanish' Creole Society In Colonial Spanish America'. *Colonial Latin American Review*. Vol. 4, No. 1, 1995, pp. 153-76.

Jaffary, N. (ed), *Gender, Race and Religion in the Colonization of the Americas*. Ashgate, Aldershot, 2007.

Lizarraga, R. de., *Descripción breve de toda la tierra del Perú, Tucumán. Río de la Plata y Chile, Biblioteca de Autores Españoles*. Vol. 216, Atlas Ediciones, Madrid, 1968.

Lockhart, J., *Spanish Peru, 1532-1560: A Social History*. 2nd ed, University of Wisconsin Press, Madison, 1994.

Loomba, A., *Colonialism / Postcolonialism.* 2nd ed, Routledge, London, 2005.

Martínez, M.E., 'The Black Blood of New Spain: Limpieza de Sangre, Racial Violence, and Gendered Power in Early Colonial Mexico'. *William and Mary Quarterly*. Vol. 61, No. 3, 2004, 55 Pars, Viewed on 10 April 2009, <http://www.historycooperative.org.proxy.library.brocku.ca//wmindex.html>.

Mignolo, W., 'The Movable Center: Geographical Discourses and Territoriality During the Expansion of the Spanish Empire'. *The Latin American Cultural Studies Reader*. A. del Sarto, A. Ríos & A. Trigo (eds), Duke University Press, Durham, 2004.

Miles, R., *Racism*.Routledge, London, 1989.

Mörner, M., *Race Mixture in the History of Latin America*. Little, Brown, and Company, Boston, 1967.

Pagden, A., 'Dispossessing the Barbarian: The Language of Spanish Thomism and the Debate over the Property Rights of the American Indians'. *Theories of Empire. 1450-1800*. Armitage, D. (ed), Ashgate, Aldershot, 1998, pp. 159-178.

—, *Lords of all The World: Ideologies of Empire in Spain, Britain and France c.1500-c.1800*. Yale University Press, New Haven/London, 1995.

____, (ed and trans), *Hernán Cortés: Letters from Mexico*. Yale University Press, New Haven, 1986.

____, *The Fall of Natural Man: The American Indian and the Origins of Comparative Ethnology*. Cambridge University Press, Cambridge, 1986.

Palencia-Roth, M., 'Enemies of God: Monsters and the Theology of Conquest'. *Monsters, Tricksters, and Sacred Cows: Animal Tales and American Identities*, A.J. Arnold (ed), University Press of Virginia, Charlottesville, 1996.

Rahn-Phillips, C., 'Twenty Million People United by an Ocean: Spain and the Atlantic World beyond the Renaissance'. *Renaissance Quarterly*. Vol. 62, No. 1, 2009, pp. 27-40.

Schwartz, S.B., 'Colonial Identities and the *Sociedad de Castas*'. *Colonial Latin American Review*. Vol. 4, No. 1, 1995, pp. 185-201.

Schwartz, S.B. & Lockhart, J., *Early Latin America: A History of Colonial Spanish America and Brazil*. Cambridge University Press, Cambridge, 1988.

Schwartz, S.B. & Solomon, F., 'New Peoples and New Kinds of People: Adaptation, Readjustment, and Ethnogenesis in South American Indigenous Societies (Colonial Era)'. *The Cambridge History of the Native Peoples of the Americas*. Schwartz, S.B. & Solomon, F. (eds), Vol. 3, Pt. 2, Cambridge University Press, Cambridge, 1996-2000, pp. 443-501.

Seed, P., 'Are These Not Also Men?: The Indians' Humanity and Capacity for Spanish Civilisation'. *Journal of Latin American Studies*. Vol. 25, No. 3, 1993, pp. 629-52.

Sober, E., 'Evolution, Population Thinking, and Essentialism'. *Philosophy of Science: An Anthology*. Lange, M. (ed), Wiley-Blackwell, London, 2006, pp. 388-405.

Tzanaki, R., *Mandeville's Medieval Audiences: A Study on the Reception of the Book of Sir John Mandeville (1371-1550)*. Ashgate, Aldershot, 2003.

Varela, C. (ed), *Cristóbal Colón: Textos y documentos completos, relaciones de viajes, cartas y memoriales.* 2nd ed., Alianza Editorial, Madrid, 1984.

Wright, J.M., 'True Peoples and Their Monsters: Speculations on the Other in the Age of Exploration'. *Terrae Incognitae.* Vol. 37, 2005, pp. 1-15.

Zamora, M., *Reading Columbus.* University of California Press, Berkeley, 1993.

Protest and Pretence: Depicting the Monstrous Immigrant Body in *How the Other Half Lives* and *The Jungle*

Shelley Galliah

Abstract
This chapter explores one of the most dangerous, and accordingly, most stigmatised bodies in early twentieth century American literature - that of the immigrant, which marks and is marked by various ethnographic, economic, and social concerns. During the antebellum years, when America was confronting the contentious problems of secession, war, and reconstruction, and when there was 'a pervasive faith in social mobility, economic opportunity, and political equality,' immigration was not an issue.[1] In fact, immigrant workers were seen as crucial to building America. However, the belief that America's limitless body could easily embrace all the poor, needy, and downtrodden was repudiated when, at the turn of the century, the number of immigrants entering the country increased dramatically. When immigrants could not be consolidated with America's body - either because of their sheer numbers, their conflicting political beliefs, or, most obviously, their physical appearance - they were often re-imagined as hazardous to that body. In particular, this essay addresses how *The Jungle* and *How the Other Half Lives,* two influential texts by Upton Sinclair and Jacob Riis respectively, associated with social reform, register and react to this changing attitude. Ideologically confused, both of these texts make progressive statements while depicting the immigrant body as dangerous and monstrous.

Key Words: Abjection, body, charity writing, immigrant, immigration, meatpacking, muckraking, monster, poverty, slum.

*****

1. Introduction

In letter three of his *Letters from an American Farmer*, Crevecoeur is grateful that the colony contains no aristocrats and no boundary separating people, especially the rich and the poor. He celebrates how America's new ethnically diverse population is united by the noble occupation of farming. After further discussing the colony's almost utopian society, he speaks of its geographical vastness: 'Who can tell the millions of men whom it will feed and contain for no European foot has yet travelled half the extent of this mighty continent.'[2] He envisions the colony as a great asylum for Europe's impoverished, who were formerly 'not numbered in any civil lists of their country, except in those of the poor,' but now 'rank as citizens'.[3] Crevecoeur's optimism was no doubt influenced by America's desperate need for bodies; in the late eighteenth-century, to fulfil a quota of skilled trades people and common labourers, who were 'not forthcoming from the native population',[4] the country was launching campaigns to attract settlers of all ethnicities.

Years later, in 'Crossing Brooklyn Ferry,' Walt Whitman's voice resembles that of a compassionate, nostalgic Tiresias who has quietly, but blissfully, experienced all and moved with the multitudes.

> I too lived, Brooklyn of ample hills was mine,
> I too walk'd the streets of Manhattan Island, and bathed in the waters around it.
> I too felt the curious abrupt questionings astir within me,
> In the day among crowds of people sometimes they came upon me,
> In my walks home late at night or as I lay in my bed they came upon me.
> I too had been struck from the float forever held in solution,
> I too had receiv'd identity by my body,
> That I knew was of my body, and what I should be I knew I should be of my body.[5]

In this poem, and especially in the above passage, Whitman values the crowds stirring around Manhattan because he acquires identity from them. By mingling with other people and experiencing the outlines of their bodies, he is made both conscious and appreciative of his own physical nature. The crowds give him both solidity and *humanity*. The bodies he encounters, whether they belong to foreigners or his fellow native Americans, increase his sense of self and soul, and remind him that America is composed of wondrous multitudes.

However, in the years separating these two texts (1769 and 1865), the response to immigration shifted from a feeling of wholehearted welcome to one of guarded optimism. Various public figures saw immigration as a mounting threat. For instance, Samuel Morse, who helped invent the telegraph, was one of the leaders in the anti-Catholic and anti-immigration movement. His 1835 pamphlet on immigration blamed infiltrating Jesuit foreigners - 'hundreds of thousands of priest-controlled machines'[6] - for endangering the spirit of democratic Republicanism.

> He doubts that by the act of coming to this country, and being naturalized, their darkened intellects can suddenly be illuminated to discern the nice boundary where their ecclesiastical obedience to their priest ends, and their civil disobedience of them begins.[7]

Catholic immigrants are labelled as automatons who are plotting to overthrow the American government and install a papacy. Indeed, Morse's fearful pamphlet belongs to the transitional period from 1810-1860, which saw a number of practises to monitor and control immigration and categorize incoming groups. On March 2, 1818, the first restriction act was passed and the first official statistics of immigration were collected. And from the middle of the nineteenth-century onward,

> the influx of Italians, Poles, Jews, Russians, Armenians, Greeks, Syrians, Czechs, and Slovaks rapidly overshadowed the dwindling numbers of immigrants from the traditional sources in Great Britain, Germany, Scandinavia and the Low Countries.[8]

As the tide of immigration shifted to these more exotic groups, Americans, such as the leader of the Knights of Labour, distinguished between the better quality of immigrants arriving before the Civil War and 'the population that is coming today [which] is semi-barbarous. They are willing and used to living in filthy crowded conditions'.[9] Higham explains that

> more exclusively than most older immigrant groups, the new ones swarmed into the slums, the factories, and the mines .... In the crowded places where they made their homes, they lived as a class apart.[10]

The newer immigrant groups, then, seemed incapable of integration.

In the 1880s, when the seeds of xenophobia were firmly sown, the country experienced other crises: mounting unemployment, declining wages, increasing crime, a declining native population, and a disappearing faith in the ability to move both upward and westward.[11] And these changes, accompanied, in 1882, by a massive influx of 788,992 immigrants (a number not surpassed until 1903), necessitated the invention of a more complicated body of federal laws identifying those to be monitored by or excluded from the immigration process. These laws began in the act of August 3, 1882, which charged a head tax of $0.50 for each immigrant entering the country (which multiplied to $4.00 by 1907) and banned convicts, lunatics, and idiots. In 1894, after twelve years of laws, the Immigration Restriction League was formed which aimed to regulate the types and the numbers of people entering America.[12]

Although both Crevecoeur and Whitman envisioned America as a limitless body capable of absorbing all, towards the end of the nineteenth century, those writing about immigrant bodies, such as Robert Tomes, often saw them as frightening, diseased, and monstrous. The following passage enumerates the blatant stigmata of immigrants, who, in addition to being unnaturally ugly, have

> ... low heads and crumpled faces which look as if they had been squashed in the making; the nasal appendages fleshy and pendent, like abortive elephants' trunks; the ears tumid and misshapen as gigantic oysters; the thick lips, eviscerated mouths, and projecting underjaws, are generally of foreign importation.[13]

Tomes' catalogue of repulsive features reveals how the immigrant devolved from the papist/undemocratic/uncivilized other to a monstrous *it*. Foreigners became beastly aberrations defying nature's laws: their body parts are 'misshapen,' 'gigantic,' 'thick,' and in general 'disproportion.' Something has also gone wrong in both their creation and development: instead of normal, they are 'crumpled,' 'squashed,' and 'abortive.' Their association with elephants, oysters, and carnivores (the 'projecting underjaw') shows their violation of the margins separating the human and animal worlds. The excesses of this description are matched by the excesses (and regresses) of the immigrant body: the immigrant is a (de)formed human/thing which portends God's indifference (or wrath?) and prefigures the illness and eventual destruction of America's body. Therefore, the borders of America must be closed to exclude these monsters and to ensure the nation's health.

To consider the immigrant as monstrous, the origin of the word *monster* must be recalled. *Monster* derives from both *monstrum*, which means a divine omen, potent, and warning, and the Latin *mor-ere*, which means to show and to warn; both roots reveal how monsters were originally read as omens portending different events. Georges Canguilem documents how the definition of *monster* changed to include the concept of violating order. Whereas in the Middle Ages and the Renaissance, monsters were living, somewhat harmoniously, with the sane and the *normal*, in the eighteenth century, monsters were rejected and converted into objects of scientific study. Eventually, philosophical and teratological advances were incorporated into the term *monster*. Nineteenth-century scientists further distinguished the physically and mentally abnormal:

> ...the madman was in an asylum, where he was used as a foil for reason, and the monster was in the embryologist's jar, where it was used as a foil for the norm.[14]

The monster, then, (d)evolved from a divine portent to a harmless anomaly to, finally, a threatening beast/creature/freak that must be eliminated to preserve order. In the middle of the nineteenth century, then, immigrants who had been previously welcomed are often presented, either subtly or obviously, as monstrous (often leaking) bodies threatening the body of America and her homogenous, clean institutions.

The depiction of the immigrant as a monstrous, leaking body is connected to society's need, if not obsession, to maintain borders. Mary Douglas argues that cultures confront and categorize anomalous events by codifying the body and the pollution needing elimination from it. She argues that, for many cultures, the reaction to dirt, which is based on 'care for hygiene and respect for conventions,'[15] forms the basis of this model:

> [I]deas about separating, purifying, demarcating, and punishing transgression ... impose system on an inherently tidy experience ... [B]y exaggerating the difference between within and without, above and below, male and female, with and against, a semblance of order is created.[16]

Although bodily margins can symbolize any of society's precarious borders, each culture has its own perils and problems, depending 'on what situation the body is mirroring.'[17] If pulled this way or that, margins threaten to alter the shape of fundamental experience and the stability of the body politic. According to Douglas, bodily fluids most easily transgress these boundaries and verify the body's permeability, collapsibility, and the threat of the inside seeping to the outside. And Kristeva, in her revision of Douglas's work, likewise asserts that: 'bodily emissions affirm the priority of the body over subjectivity and remind humans of their materiality: they assert the leakiness of the self and the fragility of identity' and they 'represent a system that is leaking, and always at the risk of contaminating or being contaminated: they signify a society that is in crisis.'[18]

The order and the health of the body politic discussed by Douglas and Kristeva are two of the oldest concerns of political philosophy. If the *polis* is an organism, then menaces to civil order can be considered diseases or, in this case, infected bodies. Treatment is feasible only if the afflicted bodies are located, labelled, and separated (quarantined) from the body politic.

2. Investigating the Other Half with Jacob Riis

It is no coincidence, then, that pervasive images of immigrant bodies as both monstrous and diseased infiltrate three genres of writing emerging at the height of the immigrant problem: slum fiction, charity writing, and muckraking fiction.

Slum fiction, which will only be introduced here, was a minor branch of realism popular in the 1890s and beyond. It includes such titles as Alvan Sanborn's *Meg McIntyre's Raffle and other Stories* (1896), I. K. Friedman's *Poor People* (1900), Edward Townsend's *A Daughter of the Tenements* (1896), and his *Chimmie Fadden* tales (1895), Abraham Cahan's ghetto wedding stories, and his *The Rise of David Levinsky* (1917). Though these melodramatic works depicting the impoverished were of questionable literary merit, they were wholeheartedly enjoyed by the masses. According to Gandal, the majority of these depicted the slum as 'not so much a territory of strange habits and appearances as a den of vice and moral decay.'[19] This depiction enticed middle and upper-class Americans to take up slumming, a popular pastime in the 1880s and 1890s. In *The Rise of David Levinsky*, the main character refers to New York's East Side as 'the great field of activity for the American University Settlement worker and fashionable slummer.'[20] In the slums, social workers, journalists, and college students could find 'esoteric types and 'local color,'' as well as opportunites for 'philanthropy and 'uplift' work. To spend an evening in some East Side café was regarded as something like spending a few hours at the Louvre.'[21]

Charity writing, alternatively, which documented real, rather than fictional, excursions into the slums, examined the locale and its inhabitants while focussing on:

> crime, the Protestant virtues and vices (especially intemperance, disorder, uncleanliness, idleness, beggary, vagabondage), disease, the miserable conditions of dwellings (especially filth, heat and cold, lack of air and sunlight, overcrowding), the loss of modesty (especially among girls), the dissolution of families, the forms of unemployment and their moral and physical ills and dangers, the institutions devoted to their uplift, and the reform that still needed to be done.[22]

A strange mix of moral edification, sensationalism, and voyeurism, charity writing both educated people and satisfied the desire, of both the authors and the readers, to slum temporarily. From the safety of their middle-class homes, Americans could read about the other half, sympathizing before taking up a cause. And on the heels of charity writing came the muckraking movement, a branch of investigative journalism that began in 1902 dedicated to exposing 'injustices such as corruption in business, finance, government, the venality of the trusts, the horrors of working conditions and legions of other social abuses' and placing 'the causes of that corruption on the doorsteps of big business.'[23]

One such leading documentary journalist was Jacob Riis. By 1886, he was a seasoned reporter who had honed his investigative skills while working the New York precincts. Though Riis 'did not originally enter the slums for the purposes of reform,'[24] he was nonetheless one of the first American writers to consider the poor as victims. He was closely associated with a number of social welfare and reform organizations in New York, such as the Charity Organization and the Children's Aid Societies. Though he made many contributions to newspapers while advocating for various causes, Riis never bettered his immensely popular investigative work *How the Other Half Lives*. This landmark text, which depicting the crowded tenement district of New York's Lower East Side (the population density reached the startling 522 per acre), forced the public to re-imagine poverty's desolation, and to advocate philanthropy towards them.

The intensity and spirited reform of Riis's writing are apparent in the following passage describing a crowded tenement from 'No. Cherry Street.' The writer warns the reader to be careful, because,

> ...the hall is dark and you might stumble over the children pitching pennies back there. Not that it would hurt them; kicks and cuffs are their daily diet. They have little else.[25]

Then, continuing his journey, the world-weary narrator says,

> Here is a door. Listen! That short hacking cough, that tiny helpless wail - what do they mean? ... Oh! a sadly familiar story - before the day is at an end. The child is dying with measles. With half a chance it might have lived; but it had none.[26]

In this passage containing interjections, short sentences, fragments, questions, and exclamations, the narrator conveys both the urgency of the situation and his desire to amend it. Here, and throughout the rest of the text, the emphasis is on pathos: slanted language, graphic examples, and images invoking the sights, sounds, and sensations of the tenement are used to awaken the jaded reader. In this tour of the tenement's gothic environs, the reader is gradually enlightened to the rituals of tenement life, such as its physical abuse: the passage begins with minor injuries children receive from the darkness - kicks and cuffs - and ends with the death of a child from measles. This excerpt is one of many devoted to the plight of neglected and abandoned children. In fact, the book's most moving and carefully written chapters are those devoted to youngsters, such as 'Waifs of the City's Slums' and 'The Street Arab.'

However, what is also obvious in this passage is Riis's fear of the slums and the poor. Though the children themselves are victims, they are also denizens of a mysterious, dark world. This mixed attitude surfaces most clearly in 'The Problem with the Children' in which Riis predicts the effects of this environment. He argues that these children, though now victims, will soon become harmful as their numbers are tallied to the slum's growing masses. He speaks of 'the standing army of fifteen thousand dependent children in New York's asylums and institutions'[27] and of the poor as an unwieldy crop of weeds strangling the city's lifeblood. Though he argues for rescuing the children, he also relays middle-class fears about the contamination of the urban poor and the concomitant degeneration of society. Likewise, in a chapter examining the growth of New York gangs, 'The Harvest of the Tares,' Riis uses similar fatalistic biological language, describing the gang as the 'ripe fruit of tenement house growth,' which is fed by 'a generation that sacrificed home to freedom, or left its country for its country's good. The tenement received and nursed the seed.'[28] Drawing again on Darwinist terminology, Riis calls gang members atavistic beings terrorizing the weak, invading the body of America, and secretly establishing anti-democratic and anti-American institutions.

In a later segment, Riis blends the rhetoric of reform literature with familiar images of disease and infection. The slums are 'hotbeds of the epidemics that carry death to rich and poor alike; the nurseries of pauperism and crime that fill our jails and police courts.'[29] These tenements are productive of both disease and disorder, throwing off 'a scum of forty thousand-human wrecks to the island asylums and workhouses year by year'; turning out 'in the last eight years a round half million beggars to prey upon our charities'; and maintaining 'a standing army of ten thousand tramps.'[30] Here, Riis mixes stale metaphors ('hotbeds') with exaggerated language ('nurseries of pauperism and vice'), and again relies on the language of disease ('epidemics,' 'scum,' and 'contagion') and Darwinism (the description of the slum as a predatory creature). The ghetto, likewise, is a source of not only physical and moral contagion but also of ideological and political infection; pauperism is both physical and an economic disease. Here, immigrants and the urban poor - again, often there is little distinction between these groups - are presented as undemocratic, diseased, and threatening.

Likewise, in Chapter 10 of *The Other Half*, Riis pays homage to the popular belief that disease, rather than born in the slum's unsanitary conditions, is being created, transported, and nourished by foreign bodies. Typhus fever and smallpox are two

> filth diseases that sprout naturally among the hordes that bring the germs with them from across the sea, and whose first instinct is to hide their sick lest the authorities carry them off to the hospital to be slaughtered.[31]

According to Riis, the most diseased are the Italians, who, because they are inherently dirty and lazy, are content to live in the slum's worst pigsties. He is particularly preoccupied with Italian children, who spend much of their life in junkyards and who are worse than animals: 'even the pig I had encountered at one of the East River dumps was much the more respectable, as to appearance'[32] than the Italian youths there. The Italian who lives, works, and eats in garbage epitomizes the animalised, the diseased, and the abject.

Although Riis blames various ethnic groups for disseminating disease, he says that it is mostly in 'Jewtown,' a place uniting pestilence and capitalism, where there are atrocities, such as infested sweatshops. In his description, Riis reiterates the popular, but statistically false, association of Jewish people and tuberculosis. Kraut notes that although tuberculosis 'was neither peculiar to the Jews nor to those who worked in the garment industry,'[33] it came to be known as a Jewish illness and the tailor's disease. Exploiting this fear, Riis purveys loaded images, such as smallpox-infected children playing among the clothes, corpses rotting in busy work areas, and a typhus fever patient who, slowly expiring, is 'discovered in a room whence perhaps a hundred coats had been sent home that week, each one with the wearer's death warrant, unseen and unsuspected, basted in the lining.'[34] Townsend's *A Daughter of the Tenements* contains a strikingly similar example. When tenement worker Eleanor visits the Jewish quarter, she finds a typhoid stricken girl resting on some newly finished garments, each to 'be offered for sale over some counter the next day; a bargain, verily, for a death-warrant would be included free with every garment!'[35] The racial typing is obvious here: the Jewish tailor cares more about money than the health of those who will be handling, and eventually buying, the contaminated clothing.

Of course, there is other racial typing in this text: the Irish are hard-working and hard-drinking; the Bohemians are honest, stupid, but financially inept; the Chinese are secretive and cat-like; and the Arabs are a 'dirty stain spreading rapidly on a splash of ink on a sheet of blotting paper.'[36] But it is Jews whom Riis most dislikes and wants excluded from his ideal America, for he sees them as monstrous, leaking bodies, both physically contaminated and morally suspect. Their disease, like their capitalist practises, is too alien to be amalgamated.

This conflation of anti-democratic, subversive immigrants and dirty bodies was quite common in both reform literature and the popular press. Foreigners were increasingly blamed for spreading disease, undermining the American economy, and parasitically feeding off the nation's wealth. Such was the opinion of eminent turn-of-the-century social reformer Brace, who described immigrants as 'the refuse of Europe [who] congregate in our great cities and send forth ... wretched progeny, degraded in the deep degradation of their parents ... to be scavengers.'[37] Similarly, the Earl of Dunraven scorned the immigrant's ability to 'feed off the offal of the streets, and live in conditions, in respect of indecency, dirt and overcrowding, incompatible with any existence of an Englishman.'[38] Again, the immigrant's impoverishment is connected to violating social norms, such as willingly living in and eating garbage.

Although Riis thoroughly analyses the tenements with his fervent and enraged prose, his muckraking text is an uncomfortable compromise between protest and agreement. He enumerates the vices of different races in order to categorize the old *right* Americans (the Germans and Irish) from the newer *wrong* types (the Italian, Chinese, Jewish, and Arab peoples). Likewise, his text empathizes with the poor while depicting them as grotesque and deviant.

3. Slumming in *The Jungle*

Another leading muckraker was Upton Sinclair. Though he was primarily a journalist, he successfully combined investigative reporting and fictional writing in his realist novels. His *Oil!* (1917) and *King Coal* (1927) respectively investigated the inner workings of the oil business and coal mining, whereas his entire *Dead Hand Series* uncovered the capitalism's corruption. But it was *The Jungle* (1906), a novel based on the corruption of the Chicago meatpacking industry, which headlined the muckraking movement.

To create his text, Sinclair even attempted to erase the barrier between himself and his subject matter, transforming himself into an impoverished stock-yard worker and living, like a modern Thoreau, 'in a board cabin, eight feet by ten, set on a hillside north of Princeton, New Jersey.'[39] Notwithstanding Sinclair's desire to mingle his flesh with his subject matter, his outrage at the conditions of the Chicago stockyards, and his pride at 'dirtying his hands,' he could not, like Riis, totally forsake his prejudices or his reliance on certain racist typologies.

Although at the heart of *The Jungle* is the melodrama of immigrants Jurgis and his family as they attempt to survive in America, the text's main goals are exposing the meat packing industry and criticizing the principles of Taylorism, which create both an unsafe and dehumanising work environment. Though publicly lauded as progress, increased mechanization hardly benefited factory workers and actually halted their economic advancement; unskilled labourers, instead of climbing up the corporate ladder, usually remained as underpaid, undervalued machine-feeders. Though Packingtown's immigrant labourers can migrate from machine to machine, they cannot rise from the factory floor to management. In fact, they usually descend to lower and less-paying jobs as they become injured and/or literally consumed by the factory system. Likewise, Sinclair criticizes Packingtown's ruthless methods of ensuring a steady supply of labour, such as hiring too many men and creating a floating and impoverished labour force in Chicago that willingly accepts low wages. Thumbing his nose at America and his idolization of Fordism, Sinclair reveals how the so-called *efficient* factory system thoroughly promotes increased social stratification and consistently devalues human bodies.

In spite of this progressive view, the text is surprisingly conservative in its depiction of immigrants. For instance, before even beginning the story of Jurgis and his family, the narrator describes the immigrant's body as overly simplified, clearly legible, and hence, easily appropriated. Like the majority of the public, Sinclair portrays immigrants as backward, ignorant people who desperately need rescuing. He remarks that:

> with the exception of a very small minority, they had no idea that they had a right to a better way of life. It was moral, spiritual, and physical degradation, a jungle in which humans lived barely above the levels of animals.[40]

These comments easily recall charity writing, with its depictions of the poor and the immigrants as depraved and animalised.

On the one hand Sinclair thoroughly explains how the factory system dehumanises and destroys. In the meat packing plant, the workers are transformed from people to parts; they become hands that chop, pickle, and package. They are no longer valued as individuals but as useful or, eventually, useless parts of disposable machines. Those most wedded to the factory are the fertilizer men, who, even off duty, reek of the excrement they refine. Also recounted are the ways that the beef-luggers, the wool-pluckers, the picklers, the hoisters, etc., are marked and malformed by their dangerous jobs. Sinclair explains that:

> [o]f the butchers and floorsmen, the beef-boners and trimmers, and all those who used knives, you could scarcely find a person who had the use of his thumb; time and time again the base of it had been slashed, till it was a mere lump of flesh against which the man pressed his knife to hold it.[41]

Indeed, the text pays tribute to all the hands sacrificed to meatpacking's specialized but dangerous work. The factory equipment, designed for efficiency and not for comfort or safety, further disarticulates and remodels bodies: 'Durham's architects had not built the killing room for the convenience of the hoisters' for,

> at every few feet they would have to stoop under a beam, say four feet above the one they ran on; which got them into the habit of stooping, so that in a few years they would be walking like chimpanzees.[42]

In secondary ways, the factory system converts people into machines. It underpays and overcharges employees so that they are too exhausted to protest their mistreatment or to imagine a better life. Their bodies and minds drained, the workers are removed of their humanity.

In these descriptions of weary and beaten labourers, Sinclair voices his strongest criticism of the meat packing industry and aims his outrage at the public's heart. However, in his explanation of how this industry infiltrates the labourer's body and vice-versa, Sinclair definitely targets the public's stomach. That is, the author reserves many of his sensationalist tactics (the bathos, hyperbole, nasty coincidences) for Packingtown's various grotesque experiments, especially those involving the consumption of workers and the connection of the pure and the impure. Antanais, for instance, is one worker whose dissolution by and incorporation into the factory is depicted. After long months of standing all day in saltpetre, he begins eroding, from the feet up.

Antanais' transformation exemplifies how immigrants' bodies, usually thumbs and hands, are repeatedly blended into Packingtown's *pure* products. It is in these descriptions of the labourer's participation in an economy of filth and abjection that Sinclair's moral program is confused, if not undermined. When the public should be outraged at how immigrants are abused, it is instead worrying about how their bodies are leaking into and contaminating the public food supply.

Sinclair most thoroughly horrifies the public by showing the filth at all levels of meat production, one perpetuated by immigrant workers. Instead of *fresh*, most of the meat actually begins as *polluted*. Downers, or sick cattle that are supposed to be discarded, are slaughtered and disguised with fresh beef. The storage places are also exceedingly filthy: meat would be placed 'in great piles in rooms; and the water from leaky roofs would drip over it, and thousands of rats would race about on it.'[43] Later are depicted the repulsive process for making ham and sausage, in which bad meat and entrails of unknown origin (animal or human) are ground up, recycled, and disguised with flavouring.[44] For instance, into one such mixture for breakfast *meat* are:

> tripe, and the fat of pork, and beef suet, and hearts of beef, and finally the waste ends of veal, when they had any. They put these up in several grades and sold them at several prices; but the contents of the cans all came out of the same hopper ... there was 'potted game' and 'potted grouse,' 'potted ham,' and 'deviled' ham-de-vyled, as the men called it. 'De-vyled' ham was made out of the waste ends of smoked beef that were too small to be sliced by the machines; and also tripe, dyed with chemicals so that it would not show white; and trimmings of hams and corned beef; and potatoes, skins and all; and finally the hard cartilaginous gullets of beef, after the tongues had been cut out. All this ingenious mixture was ground up and flavoured with spices to make it taste like something.[45]

Almost jubilantly, the narrator reveals that although all of Packingtown's sausage,

> came out of the same bowl ... when they came to wrap it they would stamp some of it 'special,' and for this they would charge two cents more a pound.[46]

In a further grotesque parody of hygiene, cleaning products meant for disinfecting the factory are instead used to sanitize the meat, which is then 'dumped into the hoppers, in the dirt and sawdust, where the workers had tramped and spit uncounted billions of consumption germs.'[47] The Durham plant, then, is not only a nightmare of the abject but also a marvel of efficiency: it has factories to produce its operational necessities and to make fresh goods from its reprocessed and re-flavoured daily waste.

And the text depicts the immigrants as not only causing but also adding to the contamination; Jurgis and his fellow employees willingly make breakfast meat out of the contents of the waste barrels, along with dead rats and the bread used to poison them, and they regularly wash their grimy hands in the water pumped into the sausage. Still, Sinclair reserves his most startling sensationalism for Bubbly Creek, the most gratuitous example of the plant's wedding of nutriment and excrement. On the surface of these giant vats curdle various kinds of refuse - grease, chemicals, acids, animal and human hair, and other unidentifiable filth - which the packers 'gather and clean'[48] in order to process all into 100% pure lard. Here, waste and excrement from outside the bodies of both animals and immigrants are collected, refined, and repackaged into foodstuffs that will be taken inside the body again. This popular Durham product even recycles entire human bodies, such as those of the tank room men, whose:

> peculiar trouble was that they fell into the vats; and when they were fished out, there was never enough of them left to be worth exhibiting - sometimes they would be overlooked for days; till all but the bones of them had gone out to the world as Durham's Pure Leaf Lard.[49]

In these passages, the dangerous workplace conditions are secondary to the abhorrent process of lard-making. Of less notice to the readers is the fact that this economy of abjection also infects the immigrants. As Jurgis and his family fall further down the labour chain, they are poisoned by the affordable, yet tainted food they have helped produce. Kristoforas is sickened by bad sausage; little Antanais becomes a weak child susceptible to many diseases.

Throughout the text, then, overriding the potent message of social reform and the criticism of Taylorism are appalling, disturbing images more typical of a horror tale and more consistent with the conception of the immigrant body as animalised and polluted. The reader does not remember the injustices of the workers as much as their crimes as food producers. Sinclair also reinforces the image of the depraved immigrant body; that is, only the immigrant could adapt to such abominable conditions and continue supporting them. The immigrant also becomes a willing participant in an economy of abjection, establishing a sinister anti-order that threatens to corrupt both America's economy and food supply. Just as Riis could not disengage the terms *depraved* and *delinquent* from the terms *impoverished* and *immigrant*, neither could Sinclair. Branding the immigrant's body as dirty and degenerate was a way of classifying, excluding it, and ensuring that it and its strange, reviling customs would never be incorporated into the body of America.

As well, *The Jungle*, like other texts depicting immigrants, is, itself, a monstrous body composed of disparate parts. Firstly, Sinclair's text is confused on the issue of reform; it contains no clear program for amending the meat packing industry and seems, at times, divided in its opinion of the efficient factory system. That is, though horrified by Packingtown's procedures, the narrator is amazed by the plant's size and ingenuity. He will express wide-eyed admiration (supposedly expressed by Jurgis) of this factory, and then comment that the United States is the best nation on earth because it has 'been able to goad our wage-earners to this pitch of frenzy.'[50] An appreciation of production also clashes with a disapproval of how factories often abuse their power and degrade employees. Likewise, the text is part initiation story, part vicious plot of decline; it is also realist fiction, muckraking expose, and a model of proletarian writing.

Perhaps because of its confusion, *The Jungle*, then, both appeased and repulsed its middle-class readers. It assuaged them by carefully criticizing capitalism without denigrating democracy or promulgating socialism. The text also confirmed that immigrant labourers, though obviously abused, were extremely *different* from most native Americans, who would certainly not stomach Packingtown's dehumanising conditions. But the text's focus on the abject and the contagious immigrant body made readers less concerned with workplace safety and unfair labour practises than with the unhygienic conditions of the meat packing industry, which became known as one of the most heinous examples of fraudulent big business.

The inconsistencies of Sinclair's text, according to Riese,[51] are typical of proletarian literature, which, unfortunately came of age alongside mass culture and which developed as a response to and as part of certain changes coming to dominate the twentieth century, such as industrialization, incorporation, and consumerism. That is, as socialist and muckraker, Sinclair was supposed to stand behind his politics without openly antagonizing public opinion; as a result, he appeals to the bourgeoisie by mentioning socialism without expounding it, and by appropriating certain mass-cultural tactics, such as human interest stories, an exaggerated plot of decline, and sensationalism.

Riis, likewise, also appeased his readers. He called for the slum to be *improved* but not *abolished*, because he never saw it:

> as part of a metropolitan and national economy; he never absorbed the growing contemporary criticism of capitalism into his understanding of what he saw on the Lower East Side. For Riis, the slum was the product of individual greed, immigrant ignorance, political corruption, and the slipshod habits of previous generations.[52]

Although Riis abhorred the sweatshops, he did not suggest any feasible methods of eliminating them, such as refusing to buy from certain distributors. Instead, he proposed clean, cheap tenements and more hygienic working conditions, which would help protect public health. Unlike other muckrakers, such as Herrick and London, who preached the virtues of socialism and industry's corruption, Riis adopted a palatable political position that neither embraced socialism nor decried capitalism.

Despite their mixed programs and their depictions of the monstrous, leaking immigrant body, both writers effected change. Riis's simple strategy for amending poverty - renovate its breeding ground, the tenements - motivated studies, roused public concern, and provoked the 1901 tenement house law. As well, Sinclair's account of the way meat was handled (as well as recycled and reformulated) prompted Congress to pass the *Pure Food and Drug Act* of 1905, and, by extension, investigate the conditions on the factory floor. But sanitation came before socialism. It would take some time before working conditions were seriously improved; it would take even more time to view the immigrant as anything but monstrous, threatening, and *other* to the body of America.

Notes

[1] D. Ward, *Poverty, Ethnicity, and the American City, 1840-1925: Changing Conceptions of the Slum and the Ghetto*, Cambridge University Press, Cambridge, 1989, p. 15.

[2] Crevecoeur, *Letters from an American Farmer*, N. Baym, et. al. (eds), *The Norton Anthology of American Literature,* Norton, New York, 1989, p. 559.

[3] Ibid., p. 560.

[4] H.P. Fairchild, *Immigration: A World Movement and its American Significance*, MacMillan, New York, 1913, p. 60.

[5] W. Whitman, 'Crossing Brooklyn Ferry', N. Baym, et. al. (eds), *Norton Anthology of American Literature*, Vol. 1, 3rd ed, Norton, New York, 1989, p. 2032.

[6] S.F.B. Morse, *Imminent Dangers to the Free Institutions of the United States through Foreign Immigration, and the Present State of the Naturalization Laws*, E. B. Clayton, New York, 1835, p. 13.

[7] Ibid.

[8] S. Anderson, *Race and Rapprochement: Anglo-Saxonism and Anglo-American Relations*, 1895-1904, Associated University Press, Toronto, 1981, p. 54.

[9] Ward, op. cit., p. 51.

[10] Ibid.

[11] J. Higham, *Strangers in the Land: Patterns of American Nativism, 1860-1925*, Atherneum, New York, 1971, p. 87.

[12] Fairchild, op. cit., p. 112.

[13] M. Banta, *Imaging American Women: Idea and Ideals in Cultural History*, Columbia University Press, New York, 1987, p. 114.
[14] G. Canguilem, 'Monstrosity and the Monstrous', *Diogenes,* Vol. 40, 1962, p. 35.
[15] M. Douglas, *Purity and Danger: An Analysis of Concepts of Pollution and Taboo*, Routledge and Kegan Paul, London, 1966, p. 7.
[16] Ibid., p. 4.
[17] Ibid., p. 121.
[18] J. Kristeva, *Powers of Horror: An Essay on Abjection*, trans L.S. Roudiez, Columbia University Press, New York, 1982, p. 108.
[19] K. Gandal, *The Virtues of the Vicious: Jacob Riis, Stephen Crane, and the Spectacle of the Slum*, Oxford University Press, New York, 1997, pp. 27-28.
[20] A. Cahan, *The Rise of David Levinsky*, Harper & Brothers, 1917, p. 284.
[21] Ibid.
[22] K. Gandal, loc. cit.
[23] J.K. Smith, 'Scarred Hopes Outworn: Upton Sinclair and the Decline of the Muckraking Movement', *Upton Sinclair: Literature and Social Reform*, D. Herms (ed), Peter Lang, New York, 1990, pp. 58-59.
[24] K. Gandal, op. cit., p. 11.
[25] J. Riis, *How the Other Half Lives: Studies Among the Tenements of New York*, S. B. Warner (ed), The Belknap Press of Harvard, Cambridge, 1970, p. 4.
[26] Ibid.
[27] Ibid., p. 143.
[28] Ibid., p. 143.
[29] Ibid., p. 5.
[30] Ibid., p. 5.
[31] Ibid., p. 73.
[32] Ibid., p. 143.
[33] Ibid., p. 73.
[34] A.M. Kraut, 'Plagues of Prejudice', *Hives of Sickness: Public Health and Epidemics in New York City*, D. Rosner (ed), Brunswick University Press, Brunswick, 1995, p. 75.
[35] E.R. Townsend, *A Daughter of the Tenements*, Literature House, Upper Saddle River, 1970, p. 70.
[36] J. Riis, op. cit., p. 22.
[37] Cited in D. Ward, *Poverty, Ethnicity, and the American City, 1840-1925: Changing Conceptions of the Slum and the Ghetto*, Cambridge University Press, Cambridge, 1989, p. 51.
[38] Ibid.
[39] U. Sinclair, *The Jungle*, Harper & Brothers, New York, 1946, p. viii.
[40] Ibid., p. vii.
[41] Ibid., p. 98.

⁴² Ibid.
⁴³ Ibid., p. 135.
⁴⁴ Ibid., p. 97.
⁴⁵ Ibid.
⁴⁶ Ibid., p. 106.
⁴⁷ Ibid., p. 135.
⁴⁸ Ibid., p. 94.
⁴⁹ Ibid., p. 99.
⁵⁰ Ibid., p. 29.
⁵¹ U. Riese, 'Upton Sinclair's Contribution to a Proletarian Aesthetic', *Upton Sinclair: Literature and Social Reform*, D. Herms (ed), Peter Lang, New York, 1990, p. 14.
⁵² D. Warner, 'Introduction', *How the Other Half Lives: Studies among the Tenements of New York*, S.B. Warner (ed), The Belknap Press of Harvard, Cambridge, 1970, p. xi.

Bibliography

Anderson, S., *Race and Rapprochement: Anglo-Saxonism and Anglo-American Relations, 1895-1904*. Associated University Press, Toronto, 1981.

Banta, M., *Imaging American Women: Idea and Ideals in Cultural History*. Columbia University Press, New York, 1987.

Cahan, A., *The Rise of David Levinsky*. Harper & Brothers, 1917.

Canguilem, G., 'Monstrosity and the Monstrous'. *Diogenes*. Vol. 40, 1962, p. 35.

Crevecoeur, St. Jean de, *Letters from an American Farmer: The Norton Anthology of American Literature*. Bayam, N. et. al. (eds), Vol. I, Norton, New York, 1989, pp. 557-82.

Douglas, M., *Purity and Danger: An Analysis of Concepts of Pollution and Taboo*. Routledge and Kegan Paul, London, 1966.

Fairchild, H.P., *Immigration: A World Movement and Its American Significance*. MacMillan, New York, 1913.

Gandal, K., *The Virtues of the Vicious: Jacob Riis, Stephen Crane and the Spectacle of the Slum*. Oxford University Press, New York, 1997.

Higham, J., *Strangers in the Land: Patterns of American Nativism, 1860-1925*. Atherneum, New York, 1971.

Hunter, R., 'Immigration: The Annihilator of our Native Stock'. *The Commons*. April 1904, pp. 12-18.

Kraut, A.M., 'Plagues of Prejudice'. *Hives of Sickness: Public Health and Epidemics in New York City*. Rosner, D. (ed), Brunswick University Press, New Jersey, 1995.

Kristeva, J., *Powers of Horror: An Essay on Abjection*. trans. Roudiez, L.S., Columbia University Press, New York, 1982.

Morse, S.F.B., *Imminent Dangers to the Free Institutions of the United States through Foreign Immigration, and the Present State of the Naturalization Laws*. E. B. Clayton, New York, 1835.

Riese, U., 'Upton Sinclair's Contribution to a Proletarian Aesthetic'. *Upton Sinclair: Literature and Social Reform*. Herms, D. (ed), Peter Lang, New York, 1990.

Riis, J., *How the Other Half Lives: Studies Among the Tenements of New York*. Warner, S.B. (ed), The Belknap Press of Harvard, Cambridge, 1970.

Sinclair, U., *The Jungle*. Harper & Brothers, New York, 1946.

Smith, J.K., 'Scarred Hopes Outworn: Upton Sinclair and the Decline of the Muckraking Movement'. *Upton Sinclair: Literature and Social Reform*. Herms, D. (ed), Peter Lang, New York, 1990.

Townsend, E.R., *A Daughter of the Tenements*. Literature House, Upper Saddle River, 1970.

Ward, D., *Poverty, Ethnicity, and the American City, 1840-1925: Changing Conceptions of the Slum and the Ghetto*. Cambridge University Press, Cambridge, 1989.

Warner, D., 'Intro'. *How the Other Half Lives: Studies Among the Tenements of New York*. The Belknap Press of Harvard, Cambridge, 1970.

Whitman, W., 'Crossing Brooklyn Ferry'. *The Norton Anthology of American Literature*. Baym, N. et. al. (eds), 3rd ed, Norton, New York, 1989, p. 2032.

PART 2

Monstrous Transgressions in the Socio-Cultural and Political Imaginaries

Social Deviants and Freakish Misfits in the Short Stories of Annie Vivanti

Anne Urbancic

Abstract
A best selling author in Italy, England and America (with numerous translated editions in various European countries), Annie Vivanti (1866-1942) had a well-established reputation for writing women's novels, short stories and articles. Surface readings of her works provide fascinating and witty descriptions that may be categorized as comedy of manners. But there hides in these pieces a darker stratum. Closer reading of her writings reveals how much she also explored social deviance: drugs, promiscuity, murder, deliberate ostracism. All are elements that her social environment repelled. All entail physical or emotional violence. She develops her stories of deviants adeptly, subtly, unobtrusively, and then lets her readers form their own conclusions. This study examines how her English language short stories, published in the last years of the nineteenth century, evolve differently from the Italian short stories of the 1920s. It describes the nature of the changes and suggests social events in those thirty years that might explain them. It also looks at the events of Vivanti's own writing career that may have encouraged her changing perspectives of social deviants and freakish misfits.

Key Words: Vivanti, Italian short stories, deviants, *Perfect, A Fad, Landru, Tony Grant.*

*****

1. Introduction

Surreptitiously and cunningly, the freaks and deviants of Annie Vivanti's writings insinuate themselves into her pages. They look and act rather 'normally' until they inevitably confront the reader, at times unexpectedly, at times not, and leave us in perplexed loss of our cultural and social superiority as objective observers. Vivanti astutely pulls the rug out from under our readerly feet and forces us to fall right into the text, implicating and interrogating our own social mores as we continue reading.

Surface readings of her works offer fascinating and witty descriptions and dialogues, easily categorized as 'comedy of manners'. Most contemporary critics appraised her work from this perspective. Closer reading, however, reveals the dark deviance of the *topoi* she explores: drug abuse, promiscuity, murder, deliberate ostracism. All are elements overtly repelled by her own social environment of the late nineteenth and early twentieth century. All entail emotional or physical violence. Previous analyses of her stories have shown, however, that her English language short stories, published in the last years of the nineteenth century, evolve differently from the Italian short stories of the 1920s. What is the nature of the changes? What social events in those thirty years might explain them? What events of Vivanti's own writing career might have encouraged such a perspective?

Annie Vivanti was born in London in 1866. She began a career as a cabaret singer, which served as her own introduction to the world of social misfits. In this environment she was no passive observer, a fact readily confirmed by the steady newspaper gossip in which her name appeared and which she describes in a thinly disguised autobiographical first novel *Marion artista di caffè concerto* (1891). Her predilection for the bizarre underbelly of society's unwanted is clear even in this early writing venture. Vivanti had arrived into the Italian world of letters a year earlier with a small anthology of poems entitled *Lirica* (1890). Treves, the publisher, had accepted it because she had carefully convinced the most well known Italian poet of the day, Giosuè Carducci, to provide a preface endorsing the volume. When Carducci wrote the preface to Vivanti's first publication he did so because the works represented for him a breath of fresh air.[1] His observation sets her apart from contemporary Italian authors, women or men, of whom in fact, Vivanti did not know, except cursorily, since she had been educated outside of Italy. Connections have yet to found between her and writers of her day, including Marchesa Colombi, Neera, or others. Even Carolina Invernizio whose gothic 'romanzi d'appendice' were much in vogue in the late nineteenth century seems not to have been an influence. Vivanti was more likely formed by readings in English and German; in fact, there is at least a modicum of truth in her assertion that of Italian writers she knew little. Of Dante, she claims, she knew only the illustrations by Gustave Doré.[2]

Carducci's preface, in essence, marked Vivanti as being 'different' from other Italian poets. In *Lirica* we find ample evidence of her emphasis on nonconformity, on difference. In a perceptive study entitled 'Maculate Conceptions: Annie Vivanti's Textual Reproductions', Graziella Parati refers to this phenomenon of differentiation as, 'Vivanti's excesses of literary representations of hybridity [wherein] Vivanti depicts her own cultural, linguistic, ethnic hybridity that will become fragmented in various narratives and characters, and plots.'[3] Parati accurately points out that from the outset of her career, in the very first poem of the anthology, appropriately entitled *Ego*, Vivanti establishes the dichotomy of outsider/insider, of exclusivity/inclusivity that will consistently inform her works. Vivanti writes: 'Do you ask of my native land? I answer you/ I have no native land,' placing herself outside the regularized human experience of a geopolitical identity.'[4] But before we might voice sympathetic protest that she must certainly have a country to call home, that she cannot be excluded from belonging to a nationality, she produces the unexpected reason for not belonging to any one nation: 'All the earth is mine' ('è mia tutta la terra!').[5] She thus includes herself far beyond what we might have done for ourselves. Her answer deviates from an anticipated response of someone who feels excluded; instead, she unsettles the archetypal understanding of 'native land', producing the excess or hyperbole to which Parati has referred. Vivanti has neither represented nor really misrepresented herself; instead she has captured our attention by staging herself as different from us. How could we not have known that she considered herself to act beyond mere nationalistic hegemony? After all, 'impetuosa e strana/per nuove vie fugge la vita mia/Fugge nel buio e crede nella luce.'[6] Why did we assume a homogeneous self-identity? Furthermore, she had already previously warned the World, her poetic interlocutor in the same poem, that all along she had planned to stymie her listeners, her readers: 'Sono in contravvenzione, o Mondo astuto./Volea truffarti con la merce mia:/Non è tabacco, sigari o liquori,/Nulla di spiritoso: è poesia.'[7]

So while no physical deformity marks Annie Vivanti as a freak or monster, she points to herself nonetheless as a social misfit. She does not play by socially sanctioned rules, preferring instead to create her own subversion and implosion of societal forms. Such an attitude can be intimated even in Benedetto Croce's comparison of Vivanti to the gypsy Carmen: ever changing, facile, and very sophisticatedly smooth.[8] And sharply intelligent.

Her short stories, both English and Italian, provide a rich exemplar of how the avowed authorial misfit creates literary misfits. She develops her stories of deviants adeptly, subtly, unobtrusively, allowing her readers to come to their own conclusions, textually interrogating all the while our preconceptions of difference and deviance, of freak and misfit.

This study will explore Vivanti's fascination with social deviants and freakish misfits by examining a selection of her short stories. While the distinctions of the typologies of freaks, as described by Leslie Fiedler in *Freaks Myths and Images of the Secret Self* (1978), are valuable, in this chapter the terms freak, misfit, deviant and at times monster will be used as if synonymous to indicate a patent separation from established social norms. Stories both in English and then in Italian will be described and the narrative changes between the two collections explored.

2. The Social Deviants of Vivanti's English Stories

Vivanti's early short stories, written in English, have only recently been collected and translated into Italian.[9] Originally they were published under various names used by Vivanti in several popular magazines intended for women.[10] This chapter will examine how Vivanti develops the idea of social deviants and misfits in two of the stories, 'Perfect' and 'A Fad'.

In 'Perfect', Francesca Verdon a young wife and mother, has travelled alone to Europe. In Florence she catches the attention of a handsome German singer, Karl Helmuth, who admires her for her 'dark hair and a clear, strong face. She looked like one of Murillo's gipsy-eyed Madonnas, powerful and serene'.[11] She becomes his lover; their relationship cuts him to the quick because of the cruel games she plays with his sincere feelings toward her. After some weeks with Karl, she decides suddenly that it is time to return to her husband and child in New York. She seems quite unaffected by her departure from Karl, while he mourns his loss of perfection.

> She was perfection, perfection! If she had been less than perfect, if her life had been less complete, he would have loved her less ... It was the glory of her complete goodness, of her full happiness, that brought his placid German heart in worship to her feet.[12]

Eventually, he follows her to New York where he becomes the laughingstock of her household, compared to the mangy dog who lived in their garden and to whom the family threw leftover scraps. Francesca's husband tolerated Karl 'with broad and genial benevolence'.[13] Karl comes to understand his mistake in thinking that the affair might be anything more than a casual encounter; he realizes that it has no future. With a loss of some dignity and also of a substantial amount of money invested into the trip to New York, he returns to Europe.

The description of Francesca's eyes, twice characterized disparagingly as gypsy eyes, alert us to the darker side of the affair. As we discover later, her perfection resembles a surface veneer; it belies the corrupt material lying beneath. Beyond her beauty, 'her clever face',[14] her 'happy-family, 'bon-ménage air'[15] could be found someone who today would be categorized a sociopath. She was callous, yet charming, without remorse, unfaithful, contemptuous, pleased to have a person in her thrall but unwilling to offer any empathy. After she told her husband of the affair, he

> growled in his fat comfortable way and told her she ought to be ashamed of herself ... Really, he was sorry for the poor fellow. But Francesca laughed and laughed ... perfectly happy, utterly at peace.[16]

She proves herself capable of profound cruelty, with no sense of social or moral responsibility. Her conflation of the mangy dog, Ribs, and her lover Karl, is particularly poignant as she embraces the animal, whom she normally ostracizes, a few days previous to Karl's arrival

> I have been very unkind to you, Ribs. ... I have made fun of you and called you names. And you are so good and sad and faithful. And I cannot help being glad you are coming three thousand miles to see me.[17]

The encounter between Ribs and Karl only emphasizes the lack of any remorse on her part for having led the young man to believe that theirs was a true love.

> 'You have a friend' she said, lifting mild, almost wistful eyes to [Karl's] glowing young face, 'who knows all about you, and whom you have never asked to see...We have spoken together by the hour about you...'[18]

Karl is repulsed by Ribs, who 'maudlin with age and affliction went up to him affectionately',[19] and asks to see this special friend of Francesca's. Her response is laughter: 'Oh! That was - that was not true,' she said. 'I was only joking'.[20] But Karl has understood that Ribs was the friend, and that he, Karl, holds the same status in Francesca's life as the unwanted dog. It is at this point that he decides to return to Europe. As his ship departs the harbour, Francesca's last thoughts of him are actually thoughts of herself.

> She saw herself, as he saw her, moving away with her fat, contented husband and her healthy little child - a tender wife; a patient mother, a good housekeeper. He had thought he loved her for all this; he had said he loved her because she was a perfect woman. It was not true. Men do not love perfect women. ... except perhaps, it be men [like her husband] who do not understand the blue things of the soul.[21]

Even her husband, he of the 'commonplace, Wall Street eyes - the eyes that could not see the pale things of the spirit',[22] and who simply accepts her misfit character, admits that 'we would make fools of ourselves to please you. We would do a great deal more'.[23]

For all her beauty and charm, Francesca Verdon remains a social deviant, operating solely according to her own rules, incapable of rising above her own self. And enjoying the havoc she wreaks as a result.

Similarly in 'A Fad', Vivanti describes another situation filled with thinly veiled deviance from contemporary social norms. The story opens with a scene that presages in physical terms the psychological cruelty that will follow. Cicillo, a young Neapolitan, accompanies English ladies on their tour of Mt. Vesuvius on a rather sickly looking pony. When the latter balks at moving, Cicillo stabs him with a penknife to incite him to proceed. If the rider should protest, Cicillo insists that Garibaldi, the pony, actually likes being abused in that way. Similar abuse is repeated later with another pony. But it is not until Cicillo repeats that he too likes being treated in a psychologically abusive way that the story becomes one of deviance.[24]

Lucy Van Cleef and her mother, two wealthy New York ladies, have hired Cicillo as their guide. Taken in by his charming ways, they decide to employ him for the rest of their trip. They learn that during the winter season, when few tourists require his services as guide, Cicillo models for various artists. He is so unusually beautiful with his long blonde curls (inherited from an English grandmother) that they decide they must have him; along with various false Michelangelo drawings, a fake relic supposedly the bone of Saint Theresa, they buy his services from his parents, and they bring him to their Madison Avenue home to add to their collection of souvenirs. 'He would be the fad of the day. People would come to ... see him, just as they go to Paderewski's concerts. He is worth his weight in dollar-bills'.[25] In the tradition of late nineteenth century souvenir collection, Cicillo is symbolically added to the Van Cleef '*wunderkammern*' or display cabinet.

For the next two years they dress him up, undress him, and show him off to their friends in various artistic poses. Unlike the artists, they do not draw or paint him. Nor is he a servant. He has no other role than pose for their guests during their dinner parties. He is no longer a person, simply a 'medieval picture' as Dick Norden, Lucy's suitor, tells them.[26] Relegated to the role of spectacle for their gaze, Cicillo is truly a *tableau vivant*, a form of entertainment still very much in fashion in the late nineteenth century.

> Cicillo was the rage. All New York flocked to the stately old house in Madison Avenue, where the Van Cleefs' Italian 'find' was to be seen perched on a bronze velvet pedestal, with bare legs crossed and flower-crowned head like a young Faun ... He was passed round from one guest to the other. After a dinner-party he was brought in with the liqueurs, beribboned, perfumed, and shining with jewels, to sing Neapolitan street-songs and Sicilian love-lays against a background of turquoise velvet curtains ... It was aesthetic, it was romantic, it was charming.[27]

As he becomes further depersonified and fetishised, he also grows in beautiful appearance. Any attempts to remove him from his objectified state do not last long (lessons to teach him to write, for example, are soon abandoned). Dick Norden, attempts to warn Lucy of the perversion she has compelled upon Cicillo: 'This is an insane, unwholesome business'.[28] The warning remains unheeded. Nonetheless his words asking what Lucy will do with her 'souvenir' in the years to come, when they are both much older, hit their mark.

When Lucy asks Cicillo what the future might hold, he repeats that he can live only as the object of her gaze and admiration. Just as she has trapped him into becoming so objectified and fetishised, he has trapped her in a cage of her own making: she can only and always be the voyeur. She tells him she loves him and desires him, but he does not accept her declaration. He repeats that he only wants her gaze and her admiration. She turns away but he forces her to watch him in his final *tableau vivant* as he kills himself in front of her.

That evening Lucy enters the room where he is laid out in preparation for his funeral. She comes to gaze upon him once more. But this time she sees only the hard lines of the face of an uneducated peasant. She is shocked that she could ever have had feelings of desire for this face. Averting her eyes away, she leaves.

This story of sadistic scopophilia is one that Baudrillard might have called obscene, a tale of hyperreal, pornographic voyeurism, 'a voyeurism of representation and its perdition, a dizziness born of the loss of the scene and the irruption of the obscene'.[29] The scenes described in 'A Fad' point, again in Baudrillard's words, to

> a culture of the desublimation of appearances: everything is materialized in accord with the most objective categories. A pornographic culture par excellence; one that pursues the workings of the real at all times and in all places'.[30]

In essence Lucy has practiced what Rosemarie Garland-Thomson refers to as 'enfreakment': 'enfreakment emerges from cultural rituals that stylize, silence, differentiate and distance' those whom 'freak-hunters' either colonize or commodify'.[31] Both Lucy and her mother could engage in the commoditization or objectification of Cicillo because their actions were socially sanctioned in the reaffirmation on the part of their friends and acquaintances that the boy was an easily recognizable Other, clearly freakish even in his own Neapolitan environment where his long blonde curls set him apart from his peers. Their own deviance, on the other hand, remained overtly undetectable to everyone except Lucy's ex-suitor.

3. Vivanti's Misfits After the English Short Stories

In the early years of the twentieth century, soon after the publication of these stories, Vivanti turned to the theater, producing two comedy hits.[32] She also wrote several romance novels. Additionally, she concentrated her energies on daughter Vivien's career as child violinist. She may or may not have divorced her husband, John Chartres; certainly this was the period when their lives began to take separate paths although they continued to overlap sporadically, including in her publicly declared pro-Irish, pro-Sinn Fein, anti-English political stance. In 1910, her new novel, *The Devourers*,[33] thrust her into the spotlight again. And once again the theme, how daughters metaphorically devour their mothers, dealt with social misfits, economic and ethnic certainly, but also psychological. Vivanti had clearly learned some lessons from the new studies in psychosocial disturbances that were being proposed at the time by Sigmund Freud and others. We know from her books on the adulteress Marie Tarnowska,[34] which followed the *Devourers*, that Vivanti was interested in such phenomena and their effects on the human psyche; she had gone to great lengths to have her Tarnowska books supported by the professional opinion of alienist L. M. Bossi, who wrote the preface for the her American edition. At her 1910 trial in Venice, the Countess Tarrnowska, had titillated both Europe and North America with descriptions of her nymphomaniac tendencies and the crimes ascribed to her sexual deviancy.

Vivanti continued to probe the darker aspects of the human soul in most of her works of the post World War I period, with attitudes that included ever greater degrees of degrading violence exacted by social deviants: rape and abortion (*L'Invasore,* 1914), white slavery, drug and sexual abuse (in both *Naja Tripudians* (1920) and its sequel *Salvate le nostre anime*, 1932), and later miscegenation (*Mea culpa,* 1927). Ever ingenious and entrepreneurial, Vivanti took advantage of the *zeitgeist* as she wrote her works. She held a mirror to her middle- and upper-class social milieu, and reflected back at her readers their own fears and phobias. In *Naja tripudians*, for example, she points to just how deeply rooted the fear of white slavery was at the time she was writing, and how extensively the topic was treated particularly in the British and American press, in literature and in the nascent field of cinematography.[35]

Thomas Fahy has commented on the ontology of freaks by noting that 'the freakish body revealed surprisingly insecure power structures and suggested underlying anxieties about the ways individuals defined and related to each other'.[36] While Vivanti may not have consciously subscribed to such a perspective, she knew her reading market well, and she intuited how, in the rapidly changing world that followed the first World War, the unprecedented transformations in so many aspects of life had become the locus for widespread and profound social angst.

In this period, the one exception to her portrayals of deviants and misfits was her first anthology of Italian short stories, *Zingaresca* (1918). The collection is interesting for a new literary trope that she began to employ; namely the consistent inclusion of a persona named Annie Vivanti, who narrated the events, and who was, and also simultaneously was not, autobiographical. An earlier study called her approach pseudo-autobiographical.[37] She had previously written in the first person, as herself, in 'The Story of a Wunderkind as told by her mother, Annie Vivanti' (1905) where she was more intent on producing a promotional piece to complement her daughter's burgeoning career. *Zingaresca*, however is different. The hyperbolic narration, the quasi unreal qualities of some of her descriptions, point to the possible influence of Massimo Bontempelli who was himself experimenting with the technique of magical realism at the time and whom she had come to know at least since 1915 when he reviewed her play *L'Invasore* in the *Nuova Antologia*. Their limited correspondence found to date, reveals a personal friendship, but given the lack of reliable biographical confirmation, the effect of Bontempelli's ideas must be further investigated. Certainly Vivanti's publication of her 'magic' children's story, *Sua Altezza! Favola candida* (1923) would indicate some influence. One other characteristic describes the stories of *Zingaresca*: they are humorous, a laugh-aloud type of humour, with wry commentary by the authorial persona who participates in the joke.

4. The Monsters of Vivanti's Italian Stories

Two more anthologies of short stories in Italian comprise Vivanti's career. *Gioia. Novelle* (1921) and *Perdonate Eglantina* (1926) contain seventeen tales, many published in various periodicals before being anthologized. The humour begun in *Zingaresca* continues, becoming, however, much darker. And, in these two collections the freaks and misfits who had previously hidden their deviance in their souls, now embody themselves openly. They are truly, etymologically speaking, 'monsters': they show themselves (from the Latin *monstrare*) and simultaneously, we can understand them as a warning (from the Latin *moneo*) An examination of one story from each collection will exemplify just how Vivanti's writing of the 1920s repositioned the misfits of her early short stories. Jacques Derrida's observation on monsters is of paramount relevance here. He reminds us that a monster

> is always alive, let us not forget. Monsters are living beings. The monster is also that which appears for the first time and, consequently, is not yet recognized. A monster is a species for which we do not yet have a name, which does not mean that the species is abnormal, namely the composition or hybridization of already known species. Simply ... it shows itself in something that is not yet shown and that therefore looks like a hallucination, it strikes the eye, it frightens precisely because no anticipation had prepared one to identify this figure.[38]

Quella che Landru non uccise (*The Woman Landru Did Not Murder*), from *Gioia*, could pass without difficulty into the genre of horror story (with which Vivanti had experimented in sections of *Naja tripudians,* published in the previous year). The story assumes the reader's background knowledge of the real life case surrounding notorious French serial killer Henri Désiré Landru who, in the years of World War I, had lured ten women and one young man to his villa near Paris where he killed them and disposed of their bodies by burning them in his kitchen oven. Sentenced to death by guillotine, he was executed in late February 1922, that is, after Vivanti published her tale.[39]

The story challenges us to recognize in it two levels of abnormal scopophilia. First there is the voyeuristic narrator, the Vivanti-persona[40]; she is an author going about her business in Paris when a young woman, the second voyeur, is pointed out to her as the one woman who had not become Landru's victim. The author/narrator reviews briefly for herself (and her readers) the notorious facts known about the case, and decides to approach the woman because she wanted to see if her face might reveal visible traces of the horror she had experienced.[41] To put this differently, the narrator seeks the one who was Other, marked as monster by her face. She stops the woman and invites her to tea, and encouraged by the nervous facial tic that the narrator feels is indicative of the other's status as monster, she hopes to hear the whole sordid story. She does not ask for the woman's name. What the latter reveals is beyond anything the narrator might have expected; to call on Baudrillard once more, it is simply obscene. Landru had not lured her at all to his gruesome lair; instead the nameless woman had enticed him quite deliberately to invite her there. She wanted to know, she confides to the narrator, what happened to her best friend, Céline, who had gone there previously and had never returned. She had already guessed what had transpired, and had surmised that the same fate would befall her as well. She wanted to know how one dies at the hands of a serial killer. She wanted to die because in death she could find the brilliant finale to her lacklustre life.[42] Her friend had written several hasty missives describing Landru's horrible preparations for what would become her own murder. The letters describe him as a maniac,[43] and crazy.[44] Having gained entrance to the villa, the nameless interlocutor becomes the voyeur: 'Ed io lo guardavo. ... lo guardavo. Guardavo le sue mani scure e nervose. ... e me le figuravo intorno al sottile collo di Céline'.[45] Then suddenly she confronts him by asking how he will kill her, revealing her desire 'di morire sgozzata da lui che sapevo assassino'.[46] She begs him: 'Uccidetemi! Uccidetemi! ... ho bisogno di morire così! Mettetemi le mani alla gola. ... e stringete! Stringete! Cacciatemi le unghie nelle carni.'[47] The deviant aspect comes from the sudden realization that the parameters of the story have changed; the situation has become explicitly sado-erotic. The young woman continues to say

> Parlava piano, chino in avanti, accarezzandosi la barba colle mani scure e sottili.
>
> -Tu mi hai capito, tu sola! - sussurrava. -Tu sai che gli altri uomini quando vedono una donna si domandano: 'Come sarà quella donna nell'amore?'. Ebbene, io no! Io, quando vedo una donna, mi domando: 'Come sarà quella donna ... nella morte?' Si dibatterà come una furia, con urli orrendi che bisognerà soffocare? O si torcerà con piccoli gemiti e strilli come un cagnolino che si tortura ? ... Il bisogno di veder morire le donne che mi piacciono è in me come una frenesia, come un parossismo di desiderio...[48]

In his seminal study of freaks, Leslie Fiedler has noted that

> all freaks are perceived to one degree or another as erotic. Indeed, abnormality arouses in some 'normal' beholders a temptation to go beyond looking to *knowing* in the full carnal sense the ultimate other.[49]

And so in this story we are left wondering how many freaks there actually are: Landru certainly for he does know the carnal Other, but also the nameless woman who desires to be the carnal Other. The narrator finally protests that the story must stop, but is taunted by the anonymous woman for not having nerves strong enough to hear the entire story.[50] The narrator too is a freak, cognizant of her own desire for voyeurism, for wanting to watch the carnal Other, for wanting to experience vicariously the transgressive social order of the carnal Other. She wonders if she has looked for an instant into the deepest abyss of human monstrosity.[51] But the nameless woman has walked away, and the narrator will never know if deviance goes deeper. The ontological instability about the nature of the freak or monster in this story destabilizes and cancels any sense of closure.

A similar technique that also raises the question of what or who may be defined a monster or freak is *Il Natale di Tony Grant* (*The Tony Grant Christmas*) found in Vivanti's later anthology *Perdonate Eglantina (Pardon Eglantina)*. Here as before, the addition of the implicated narrator compels a consideration of a multi-layered deviance. The story is a deceptively simple one of a young girl who is assigned a new room-mate, recently arrived from Uganda, at her Swiss boarding school. She is most displeased by this event and plays a cruel trick on her new companion with the result that the latter begs to be removed from the school and returns home to Africa.

The most obvious reading of this story juxtaposes skin colours and brings to the fore open racist attitudes. But Vivanti writes far more cleverly; in this story of black and white, nothing, it appears, is really black and white. As she has done in previous works, here too she problematises what is meant by deviant, by social misfit. As we look at the story from that perspective, we might bear in mind Allen S. Weiss' axiom that a 'true monster [or deviant] will be remembered for the shock it produces, breaking all chains of associations'.[52] As readers we must decide who or what brings about the greater shock.

The story unfolds as a memorialistic tale of *autonoesis*, that is, Annie Vivanti clearly identifies herself as the protagonist who remembers experiencing the event. Whether or not this story is actually autobiographical is not as relevant as is the fact that the author wishes her readers to believe it is. She reveals that despite her fourteen years, she is known at the Swiss school for her immature behaviour: 'Tu hai l'età della ragione, Annie Vivanti,' the principal admonishes, ' e non dovresti fare le sciocchezze che fai'[53] And one of her teachers is more specific: 'Non capisco, Annie, come tu possa sempre escogitare delle cose fantastiche, delle bizzarrie che a nessuna delle tue compagne verrebbero in mente. Ma cerca dunque di mettere giudizio!'[54] These reprimands alert us to the fact that Annie Vivanti, the schoolgirl, is different from the other students, and not in a positive way. She is a misfit. This is confirmed by her shrewd and almost malicious acceptance of the teacher's challenge that by the new year she must turn over a new leaf: 'Ma questo era ancora l'anno vecchio. Feci un rapido calcolo mentale: oggi era il nove dicembre. Avevo dunque ventidue giorni prima did dover mettere giudizio. Molto me ne rallegrai.'[55] Her deliberate nonconformance, therefore, would remain as such, at least for the foreseeable future.

When the new student is announced some evenings later, she too is introduced as 'different': she is of another race, she is black, the principal informs the schoolgirls.[56] However, this is not in itself the reason for any discrimination against the girl; Annie in fact is quite eager to meet this Sudanese princess (from Uganda!) named Tony Grant. She imagines a beautiful young woman resembling the model in painting entitled *Daughter of the Desert*, which hangs in one of their classrooms. But Tony Grant is a disappointment: she appears ugly to Annie who calls her 'un grande animale strano', 'quella temibile e formidabile creatura [che] doveva dormire con me, nella mia stanza bianca, al posto della snella, mite e lattea Cécile Klaus'[57] someone with orangutan arms[58] who, animal-like, sheds hair everywhere.[59] Having immediately dehumanized her, Annie then begins to focus deliberately on all Tony Grant's negative characteristics. Slowly but surely, Tony Grant unwittingly becomes a monster in Annie's eyes, and furthermore, a monster who has developed a schoolgirl crush on Annie. While the issue of xenophobia is relevant, the intent here departs from the immediate racial dichotomy of us/Other. Graziella Parati notes correctly that in this story, as in all her works, Vivanti explores the deviant that is within us, the monster that we are.[60] Annie, the protagonist, decides to embody herself as 'monster' in order to rid herself of Tony Grant. She borrows a fur boa from a schoolmate and leads Tony Grant to believe that due to a congenital deformity, she, like her family members, was born with a tail which they all tie around their waists during the day but loosen in the evenings, and which hangs out from under their nightgowns at night. Unaware that she herself is considered a monster, Tony Grant thus encounters a monster of her own. Terrified, she runs for comfort to her teachers. The teachers and principal all gather to reprimand Annie for her cruel joke, but Annie is quick to notice that even as they scold her, they are laughing.[61] Their complicit laughter serves to 'unfreak' the cruelty Annie has unleashed, normalizing it, so that, despite the repeated assurances that the tail constituted a joke, Tony Grant withdraws from the school. The laughter of the teachers embodies their anxieties about the Other, whether the Other be different in skin colour as was Tony Grant, or whether the Other be a misfit, like Annie, who could easily have made them the objects of her cruel prank. In the same way children often befriend the bully so as to escape being bullied.

The Tony Grant Christmas portrays a most cogent example of how deviance and monstrosity are first, socially sanctioned constructions, and secondly, unstable. In a different time and in a different context, the monstrosity could have been a joke, even as the teachers had remarked. Unlike the previous story of Landru, we understand some sense of closure in Tony Grant's terrified departure from the monster that has a tail. There remains, however, the problematicity of what that closure means. There is no moral, no final edifying lesson. Not only does the story sanction the deviant social deportment of the protagonist but it does so in the guise of an autobiographical account. In other words, Vivanti the narrator would like us to believe that the anecdote really happened, and that it really was a harmless prank after all. She confirms that the memory of this particular Christmas still brings her much exhilaration whenever she recalls it.[62]

5. Conclusion

In interweaving into her later stories a narrator who is implicated in their plot, Vivanti adds a layer of literary sophistication missing from her third person narrations of the English language stories. In a sense, the participation of her literary persona adds a sinister quality to the deviances she describes. She plays with narratorial authority, challenging us to find our own way to understand deviants as deviant, monsters as monstrous. Her narrator will not help us because she is involved in the story. In these latter examples, unlike in the former, when Vivanti-as-narrator 'defictionalises' her tale we as readers must understand, as Rosemarie Garland-Thomson suggests, that Vivanti's deviants and misfits 'cannot be relegated to metaphorical figures of otherness, but rather they are enfleshed as they are enfreaked, always particular people in particular lives at particular moments at particular places.'[63] By involving her persona she is taking a risk, removing herself from cultural and social superiority as objective observer. Without an omniscient, neutral buffer, we too have no choice but to implicate and interrogate our own social mores in reading these stories.

Vivanti knew her reading market extremely well. Her stories of the darker, the monstrous, side of human nature, couched as they may have been in upper and middle class social niceties, sold. Greatly. Consistently. Being a misfit herself, she knew how to create other misfits and how to insert them into acceptable social milieus. Her monsters, unmarked by physiological aberrations, both show and warn of the darker underbelly of those milieus. Undoubtedly her readers found in her stories the tension between monster and normal that spoke to their own anxious instability in a rapidly changing world, whether in the Anglo-American environment of the late nineteenth/twentieth century, or in the Italian environment of the 1920s, both rife with political and social upheavals, tensions and crises, both times when the world prepared for major military conflicts, with increasingly powerful arsenals. Contemporary critics often relegated Vivanti to a lesser category of 'women's writer'. This she is not. As subtle and surreptitious as they may be, her misfits, deviants and monsters point to an author who is deliberately transgressive, and most keenly aware of how to draw us into a place where misfits and monsters are given a voice: their voice, her (pseudo-) autobiographical narrative voice, and what frightens most, our own readerly voice.

Notes

[1] Giosuè Carducci in his preface to *Lirica* wrote: A Lei, la fisonomia dell'immagine, la tempera del colorito, la qualità della frase e l'andamento del verso vengono e spirano col movimento del fantasma e della passione che Le dan la poesia. Tutto ciò è sempre bene? Io so e dico che molte volte mi rapisce ('For you, the shape of an image, the tempera of the colors, the quality of the phrase and the cadence of the verse, come and breathe with the movements of spirits and passion which give you poetry. Is all this always for the good? I know so and say that it often enraptures me'). A. Vivanti, *Lirica*, Prefazione di Giosuè Carducci, Fratelli Treves Editori, Milano, 1890, np.
[2] A. Vivanti, 'Giosuè Carducci', *Zingaresca*, Quintieri, Milano, 1918, p. 281.
[3] G. Parati, 'Maculate Conceptions: Annie Vivanti's Textual Reproductions', *RLA: Romance Languages Annual*, Vol.7, 1995, p. 327.
[4] Vivanti, 'Ego', *Lirica*, Prefazione di Giosuè Carducci. Fratelli Treves Editori, Milano, 1890, p. 14.
[5] Ibid., p. 16.
[6] Ibid., pp. 27-29: 'Impetuous and strange/my life flees down new paths/It flees through the dark and believes in the light'. All translations mine.
[7] Ibid., pp. 5-8: 'But I contravene against you/oh clever World./I wished to trick you with my wares:/Not tobacco, cigars or liquor/No spirits, but poetry'.
[8] B. Croce, *La letteratura della nuova Italia*, Vol.6, Laterza Bari, 1974, p. 284.
[9] Vivanti, *Racconti americani*, a cura di Carlo Caporossi, Sellerio, Palermo, 2005.
[10] A. Vivanti-Chartres, 'Perfect,' *Cosmopolitan*, Vol. 22, December 1896, pp. 185-200; Vivanti-Chartres, 'En passant', *The Idler*, Vol.11, February-July 1897, pp. 234-41; Vivanti-Chartres, 'Houp-là!', *Musnseys Magazine*, Vol. 18, October 1897, pp. 25-32; Vivanti-Chartres, 'A Fad', *Leslie's Weekly*, February 9 1899, pp. 105-6; February16 1899, pp. 25-126; February 23 1899, pp. 145-46; 'The Story of a Wunderkind as Told by Her Mother, Annie Vivanti', *The Saturday Evening Post*, June 3 1905, pp. 13-14 and also 'The True Story of a Wunderkind Told by Its Mother, Annie Vivanti,' *Pall Mall Magazine*, Vol 35, January/June1905, pp. 55-59.
[11] Vivanti-Chartres, 'Perfect', *Cosmopolitan*, Vol .22, December 1896, p. 186.
[12] Ibid., p. 188.
[13] Ibid., p. 196.
[14] Ibid., p. 199.
[15] Ibid., p. 198.

[16] Ibid., p. 192.
[17] Ibid.
[18] Ibid., p. 198.
[19] Ibid., p. 199.
[20] Ibid.
[21] Ibid., p. 200.
[22] Ibid.
[23] Ibid., p. 193.
[24] Vivanti-Chartres, 'A Fad', *Leslie's Weekly*, February 16, 1899, p. 125.
[25] Ibid.
[26] Ibid., p. 126.
[27] Ibid., February 23. 1899, p. 145.
[28] Ibid.
[29] J. Baudrillard, *Seduction*, trans B. Singer, New World Perspectives, Toronto, 1990, p. 29.
[30] Ibid., p. 34.
[31] R. Garland-Thomson (ed), *Freakery: Cultural Spectacles of the Extraordinary Body*, New York University Press, New York, 1996, p. 10.
[32] *That Man*, 1898, shown also on Broadway and *The Ruby Ring*, 1900.
[33] Published first in English (in London by Heinemann and in New York by Putnamand Sons) and later translated by Vivanti as *I divoratori*, Treves, Milano, 1911.
[34] A. Vivanti, *Circe,* Quintieri Milano, 1912 and later in her own English translations *Marie Tarnowska*, Heinemann, London, 1915; and *Marie Tarnowska*, with an introductory letter by L.M. Bossi of the University of Genoa, The Century Company, New York, 1915.
[35] A. Urbancic, 'Plagiarism or Fantasy: Examining *Naja Tripudians* by Annie Vivanti', *Quaderni d'italianistica*, Vol. 24, No. 2 , 2003, pp. 23-36.
[36] T. Fahy, *Freak Shows and the Modern American Imagination: Constructing the Damaged Body from Willa Cather to Truman Capote*, Palgrave Macmillan, New York, 2006, p. 2.
[37] A. Urbancic, 'L'io narrante autobiografico di Annie Vivanti: madre scrittrice', *Campi immaginabili*, Vol 1/2, 1991, pp. 145-152.
[38] J. Derrida, *Points...Interviews, 1974-1994*, P. Kamuf (ed), Stanford University Press, Stanford, 1995, pp. 385-386.
[39] Vivanti generally carefully avoided mentioning dates in her stories, especially those in which the pseudo-autobiographical narrator might be obliged to an accountability of times and events. This is especially notable in her supposed travelogue *Terra di Cleopatra*, Mondadori, Milano, 1925. A full discussion of this avoidance is found in A. Urbancic, 'Picturing Annie's Egypt: Terra di Cleopatra by Annie Vivanti', *Quaderni d'italianistica*, Vol. 27, No. 2, 2006, pp. 93-106. 'Quella

che Landru non uccise', however is dated November 26, at the same time as the press was reporting on his trial (Nov. 7 to Nov. 30).

[40] The narrator's status as voyeur is several times reinforced by seemingly casual commentary on how she was advised to use her pointed gaze in order to discover the depths of another's soul. In this, the narrator also displays her anxiety about her own normality. Catherine Heard has commented that 'monsters have been mankind's shadow companions', 'The Persistence of Monsters', *Beauty and the Abject*, L. Boldt-Irons, C. Federici & E. Virgulti (eds), Peter Lang, New York, 2007, p. 29). She explains: We are never fully assured of our own normality, and seek that reassurance through comparison with models of the normal and abnormal. We have an innate need to closely examine the other and to make minute comparisons of difference, but there is an inherent guilt associated with this examination'; Ibid., p. 35.

[41] A. Vivanti, 'Quella che Landru non uccise', *Gioia! Novelle*, Bemporad, Firenze, 1921, p. 109.

[42] Ibid., p. 113.

[43] Ibid., p. 114.

[44] Ibid.

[45] Ibid., p. 116: 'I watched him … I watched him. I watched his dark nervous hands … I imagined them around Céline's slender neck…'

[46] Ibid., p. 117: 'to die with my throat slit by him, whom I knew to be a killer.'

[47] Ibid.: 'Kill me, kill me! … I need to die like this! Put your hands around my throat … squeeze! Squeeze! Dig your nails into my flesh…'

[48] Ibid., p. 118: 'He spoke softly, inclined towards me, and stroked his beard with his slender dark hands. 'You, you alone, have understood me!' He whispered. 'You know that other men, on meeting a woman wonder: How will she be in love? Not I, however. I, when I see a woman, wonder: How will she be in death? Will she fight like a Fury, with horrific screams that will need to be suffocated? Or will she twist away with little whimpers and cries, like the puppy you torture? …The need to see the women I find attractive die is like a frenzy within me, like a paroxysm of desire…'

[49] L. Fiedler, *Freaks: Myths and Images of the Secret Self*, Simon and Schuster, New York, c1978, p. 137.

[50] A. Vivanti, 'Quella che Landru non uccise', *Gioia! Novelle* , Bemporad, Firenze, 1921, p. 118.

[51] Ibid., p. 119.

[52] A.S. Weiss & S. Allen, 'Ten Theses on Monsters and Monstrosity', *The Drama Review*, Vol. 48, No. 1, Spring 2004, p. 124.

[53] A. Vivanti, 'Il Natale di Tony Grant', *Perdonate Eglantina*, Mondadori, Milano, 1926, p. 75: 'You have reached the age of reason, Annie Vivanti, and you should not do the stupid things you do.'

[54] Ibid., p. 76: 'I don't understand, Annie, how you come up with such exaggerated and bizarre things that would never cross the minds of any of your companions. Do try to be a bit more judicious.'
[55] Ibid. 'But this was still the old year. I calculated rapidly: today was the ninth of December. So I had 22 days before I had to become more judicious. I was really happy when I realized this.'
[56] Ibid., p. 77.
[57] Ibid., p. 84: 'a large and strange animal', 'that frightful and formidable creature [who] was to sleep in my little white room instead of the slender, sweet and milky-white Cécile Klaus'.
[58] Ibid.
[59] Ibid.
[60] G. Parati, op. cit., p. 330.
[61] A. Vivanti, 'Il Natale di Tony Grant', *Perdonate Eglantina*, Mondadori, Milano, 1926, p. 93.
[62] Ibid., p. 75.
[63] R. Garland-Thomson, 'Foreword', *Victorian Freaks: The Social Context of Freakery in Britain*, M. Trump (ed), Ohio State University Press, Columbus, Ohio State UP, 2008, p. xi.

Bibliography

Baudrillard, J., *Seduction*. trans. Singer, B., New World Perspectives, Montreal, 1990.

Croce, B., *La letteratura della nuova Italia*. Vol.6. Laterza, Bari, 1974.

Derrida, J., *Points...Interviews, 1974-1994*. Weber, E. (ed), Kamuf, P. (trans), Stanford University Press, Stanford, 1995.

Fahy, T., *Freak Shows and the Modern American Imagination: Constructing the Damaged Body from Willa Cather to Truman Capote*. Palgrave Macmillan, New York, 2006.

Fiedler, L., *Freaks: Myths and Images of the Secret Self*. Simon and Schuster, New York, 1978.

Garland-Thomson, R., (ed), *Freakery: Cultural Spectacles of the Extraordinary Body*. New York University Press, New York, 1996.

——, 'Foreword'. *Victorian Freaks. The Social Context of Freakery in Britain.* Trump, M. (ed), Ohio State University Press, Columbus, 2008.

Heard, C., 'The Persistence of Monsters'. *Beauty and the Abject.* Boldt-Irons, L., Federici, C. & Virgulti, E. (eds), Peter Lang, New York, 2007.

Parati, G., 'Maculate Conceptions: Annie Vivanti's Textual Reproductions'. *RLA: Romance Languages Annual.* Vol. 7, 1995, pp. 327-332.

Urbancic, A., 'L'io narrante autobiografico di Annie Vivanti: madre scrittrice'. *Campi immaginabili.* Vol. 1/2, 1991, pp. 145-152.

——, 'Picturing Annie's Egypt: Terra di Cleopatra by Annie Vivanti'. *Quaderni d'italianistica.* Vol. 27, No. 2 (2006), pp. 93-106.

——, 'Plagiarism or Fantasy: Examining Naja Tripudians'. *Quaderni d'italianistica.* Vol. 24, No. 2 (2003), pp. 23-36.

Vivanti, A., *Gioia! Novelle.* Bemporad, Firenze, 1921.

——, 'Giosuè Carducci'. *Zingaresca.* Quintieri, Milano, 1918.

——, *Lirica.* Prefazione di Giosuè Carducci. Fratelli Treves Editori, Milano, 1890.

——, *Perdonate Eglantina.* Mondadori, Milano, 1926.

Vivanti-Chartres, A., 'A Fad'. *Leslie's Weekly.* February 9, 1899.

——, 'Perfect'. *Cosmopolitan.* Vol. 22, December 1896, pp. 185-200.

Weiss, A.S., 'Ten Theses on Monsters and Monstrosity', *The Drama Review.* Vol. 48, No. 1, Spring 2004, pp. 124-25.

The Zombie's Great Escape in René Depestre's *Hadriana dans tous mes rêves*

Tamara El-Hoss

Abstract
In *Hadriana dans tous mes rêves* (1988), the Haitian author René Depestre examines the myth, the representation, as well as the role of the zombie in Haiti, and analyzes its symbolic implications. The premise of the story is simple: Hadriana Siloé, a beautiful young woman, who although white skinned is one hundred percent Haitian (in the sense that she was born in Haiti and is well aware of Haitian history, beliefs, myths and folklore), is the object of desire of all those who know her and/or meet her, including the narrator (Patrick), a childhood friend. Hadriana is what Depestre calls a *femme-jardin*, a beautiful earthly sensual woman who is closely linked to Haiti. On her wedding day, January 29, 1938, in Jacmel (a Haitian coastal town), Hadriana collapses in Church and is deemed to be dead. But is she? As the novel progresses, it is announced that she has disappeared from her grave, thus setting in motion the myth of the zombie and zombification which will serve as the anchor of the novel. Hadriana's zombification in the novel is parallel to Haiti's, since both names begin with an H, both are feminine nouns in French, and because Haitian authors, including Depestre, tend to personify their native land. The purpose of this article is to investigate the manner in which Depestre rewrites the myth of the zombie in this novel by creating a 'monstrous' woman, Hadriana, who at the end will be able to escape her monstrosity. But what will be the price of her 'great escape'?

Key Words: Zombie, Haiti, René Depestre, Hadriana.

*****

In *Hadriana dans tous mes rêves* (1988), the Haitian author René Depestre (1926-) investigates the myth of the zombie and zombification in his native land. Through the story of his female protagonist, Hadriana, the author reexamines the representation as well as the role of the zombie in Haiti, and reinterprets its symbolic meaning. The purpose of this article is to investigate the manner in which Depestre rewrites the myth of the zombie by creating a 'monstrous' woman, Hadriana, who at the end will be able to escape her monstrosity. But what will be the price of her 'great escape'?

The premise of the story is simple: Hadriana Siloé, a beautiful young woman from one of the most important French families in Jacmel (a Haitian coastal town), who, although white skinned is one hundred percent Haitian (in the sense that she was born in Haiti and is well aware of Haitian history, beliefs, myths and folklore). She is also one hundred percent *Créole* (according to Jean Barnabé, Patrick

Chamoiseau and Raphaël Confiant's definition of the term as proposed in *Éloge de la créolité* [*In Praise of Creoleness*]) and is the object of desire of all those who know her and/or meet her, including the narrator, Patrick, a childhood friend. Hadriana, whom Depestre calls a *femme-jardin*, in other words a beautiful earthly sensual woman closely linked to Haiti[1] in general and to Jacmel in particular is, according to Joan Dayan in her article 'France Reads Haïti: René Depestre's *Hadriana dans tous mes rêves*,' 'implicitly identified with Erzulie-Fréda, the nearly white loa [goddess] of love, the embodiment of gorgeous femininity in Haiti.'[2] On her wedding day in Jacmel, on Saturday January 29, 1938, Hadriana collapses in Church and is pronounced dead. But is she? As the novel progresses, it is announced that she has disappeared from her grave, thus setting in motion the myth of the zombie and zombification which will serve as the anchor of the novel. Joan Dayan maintains the following:

> Depestre seems to join with other black writers of the diaspora who return to the gods, to the call of a past designated by the 'standard' histories. But Depestre's recollection is more deeply shaped by a very French surrealism than by vodou practices, with its fragmented rituals, and recollected or reexperienced gods that make belief a reliving of history.[3]

I partly agree with Dayan, Depestre's novel *is* heavily influenced by French surrealism, but it is also heavily influenced by Vodou[4] and local myths, as I will demonstrate in this study. Therefore, before analysing Depestre's reinterpretation of the myth of zombification and its symbolic meaning in the novel, it would be useful to have a brief history of the zombie in Haiti and explain what the author precisely means by that term. In order to do so, a quick overview of Haiti's history would be extremely pertinent.

In 1670, Haiti officially becomes a French colony. In order to maintain the production of sugar canes on its plantations, France will import African slaves who, once in the colony, will be converted to Catholicism by force. This conversion, however, will not succeed in abolishing their various African religious beliefs; the combination of Catholicism and African religions will produce a new religion in Haiti: Vodou. When the country gains its independence from France in 1804 and becomes the first free black Republic in the world, Haitians are free to leave for 'greener pastures,' if they wish, and some will decide to move to Louisiana, thus exporting Vodou. Ninety five percent of Haitians today are descendants of African slaves, which explains the speed at which Vodou developed and why it is still practiced by Haitians in Haiti, and even outside of Haiti. Vodou in Haiti is a religion practiced alongside Catholicism, and there is no contradiction in a Haitian's mind who may go to Catholic mass on Sunday and practice Vodou during the week. A substantial number of Haitians living in Haiti are *vodouisants*, in other words, they actively practice Vodou.

For the *Vodouisants*,[5] the risk of zombification is real and therefore zombies are real. But what, or who, are zombies exactly? And what is zombification? A zombie is a 'creature' neither living nor dead, sometimes referred to as the 'living-dead' in Western cultures. However, as John Mbiti explains in *African Religions and Philosophy*, the concept of the leaving-dead is quite different for Africans, and by extension, their descendants in Haiti have

> Human relationships with the spirits vary from society to society. It is, however, a real, active and powerful relationship, especially with the spirits of those who have recently died - whom we have called the living-dead. Various rites are performed to keep this contact, involving the placing of food and other articles, or the pouring of libation of beer, milk, water and even tea or coffee (for the spirits who have been 'modernized').[6]

In Western imagination, and mainly thanks to Hollywood motion pictures, a zombie is a monster who crawls out of a grave and terrorizes the living, attempting to zombify (make a zombie of) all those who cross its path, all the while terrorizing the audience watching the movie. Zombies for *Vodouisants* are not the Hollywood version.[7] *Vodouisants* believe that a human being's soul is composed of two parts: the *gwo-bon-ange* (*gros bon ange* in French and in Depestre's novel, literally translated as 'big good angel') and the *ti-bon-anj* (*petit bon ange* in French and in Depestre's novel, literally translated as 'little good angel'). According to Leslie Desmangles in *The Faces of the Gods: Vodou and Roman Catholicism in Haiti*, the *gwo-bon-ange* 'is a life-force, an internal dynamism planted within the body that serves as its shell,'[8] which can be very loosely interpreted to be the body, while the *ti-bon-anj* 'is personality, conscience, the moral side of one's character,'[9] and which can be interpreted to be a person's consciousness. There are two necessary stages to zombification: in the first stage, a *houngan* (sorcerer) injects a person with a poison that will paralyse him/her and slow his/her pulse dramatically, making him/her appear to be dead. The victim will then (usually) be buried in a Christian cemetery, only to be quickly unburied by the *houngan* who will set the second stage of zombification in motion: he will administer the antidote to 'wake up' the *gwo-bon-ange* (the body) of the victim and will proceed to capture his/her *ti-bon-anj* (consciousness) by putting it in a bottle, like a Coke bottle, for example. The victim, who at this point has been fully zombified, will then regain some of his/her physical faculties but will remain lethargic and, more importantly, will be unable to think, dream, or have any desires or emotions, thus becoming a 'zombie' who will obey all orders without ever questioning them.

A person who has been zombified has usually committed an act of aggression or a crime and zombification becomes his/her social punishment. This is not the case of Depestre's Hadriana, however, who seems to be an innocent victim: 'J'étais punie par le destin pour un péché que je n'avais pas commis,'[10] she declares. *Vodouisants* believe that zombies are condemned to housework, field labour (*zombie-champs*), factory labour (*zombie-z'outil*) or other physically demanding tasks. The parallel between a zombie's life and that of a slave is quite clear. It is important to note, however, that a zombie, unlike a slave, does not have a state of consciousness and that the only thing that can 'wake it up' according to popular beliefs, in the sense that it regains its consciousness, is salt (perhaps because of the belief that salt has purifying properties and can ward off evil). Zombification is so deeply rooted in the Haitian psyche that it has been included in the Haitian Penal Code. In his book, Leslie Desmangles states the following:

> It is interesting that the Haitian Penal Code takes cognizance of zombies. Article 249 reads: 'Also shall be qualified as attempted murder the use against any person of substances that, without causing actual death, produce a more or less prolonged lethargic coma. If after administering of such substances, the person has been buried, the act shall be considered murder no matter what result follows.'[11]

Returning now to René Depestre's novel. The zombification of Hadriana takes place in 1938, after the American Military Occupation of Haiti (1915-1934). Furthermore, Depestre's novel was published in 1988, after the Duvalier dictatorships.[12] The almost thirty year period under the Duvaliers is deemed to be one of the darkest in Haitian history. The country was ruled by terror and an iron fist; a large number of intellectuals left the country while those who stayed behind were often tortured and/or killed by the *tonton-macoutes* (bogeymen) who were the Duvaliers' secret military police. Depestre was one of the intellectuals who succeeded in leaving, he will write in exile and will always be aware of the risks of becoming what he calls a 'zombie-writer' if he conforms to Western styles of writing and forgets his Caribbean roots.

In Haiti, myth is often mixed with reality; according to Jean-Marie Salien, in his article 'Croyances populaires haïtiennes dans *Hadriana dans tous mes rêves*,' Haitian discourse mixes beliefs and facts, the natural and the supernatural, reality and dreams,[13] which forms *le merveilleux haïtien*[14] in Haitian literature. Depestre's *Hadriana dans tous mes rêves* is an excellent example of the 'merveilleux haïtien' and what makes the novel stand out from other Haitian novels, however, is the fact that the author also has a high regard for vodou mythology, which strengthens the novel's 'haïtienneté', or in other words, what makes it Haitian. By anchoring his novel in the Haitian myths of the zombie and zombification, Depestre condemns the Western myth of voodoo, which confuses sorcery and the sacred, and desecrates the *Vodouisant*'s religious traditions.[15] As Desmangles explains,

> in popular literature and film the term voodoo has been misconstrued as sorcery, witchcraft, and in some cases cannibalistic practices, all of which are false and have kindled many foreigner's prejudices not only about Vodou, but about Haitian culture in general.[16]

Hadriana dans tous mes rêves is divided into three movements. The first and longest movement, which serves as the backdrop to the story and immerses the reader into the *merveilleux haïtien*, starts with the erotic adventures of the butterfly-sorcerer Balthazar Granchiré with Hadriana's godmother, Madame Villaret-Joyeuse. Balthazar Granchiré is a phallic butterfly who deflowers virgins (an excellent example of the *merveilleux haïtien*). According to Joan Dayan 'in Creole chiré means 'gash' or 'tear'; and used idiomatically for 'fuck' or 'fucked', [Granchiré's] last name could be translated both as 'Bigfuck' or 'Biggash'.'[17] In this movement, we learn that Hadriana 'est le don princier que la France de Debussy et de Renoir a fait à [Haïti]. Plus qu'une jeune fille de dix-neuf ans, la fée tutélaire de Jacmel est une rose piquée au chapeau du Bon Dieu.'[18] Jacmel's beautiful guardian angel is the anchor of this movement as she is the object of desire of every Haitian man in Jacmel. After her death at the Church on her wedding day, local rumours link her tragedy to Granchiré. The latter apparently found Hadriana so beautiful that 'il en a eu les antennes coupées'[19]

> Madame Brévica Losange, une voisine des Siloé qui avait une réputation de mambo, ... affirma ensuite tout haut que le décès d'Hadriana n'était pas dû à une cause naturelle. On n'avait pas besoin du talent de Sherlock Holmes pour découvrir la piste qui conduisait à l'auteur du forfait. Celui-ci était signé Balthazar Granchiré ![20]

Regardless of these rumours, and because Hadriana came from a white French Roman Catholic family (her parents were not *vodouisants*), she was buried according to their beliefs and traditions. Towards the end of the movement, we learn that she has disappeared from her grave, which in Haiti implies that she has probably been zombified. The inhabitants of Jacmel are 'petrified' and subsequently lock their doors to protect themselves from the *virgin-zombie* - the marriage was never consummated. Hadriana is doubly threatening because, as a virgin, she has never been touched by man while as a zombie, no man *wants* to touch her. No further facts are given about her 'disappearance' and the movement ends with oncle Féfé (Patrick's guardian) explaining the scientific details of zombification to the young narrator, in an obvious attempt by Depestre to demystify the process and educate the Western reader.

The second movement, the shortest of the novel, is for the most part written in the form of a socio-ethnographic essay in which the narrator tries to explain the roots of the 'art' of zombification in Haiti, along with its history and socio-political implications. It is 1977, Jean-Claude Duvalier (Baby Doc) is Haiti's dictator and Patrick is a writer in exile, or rather a 'zombie-writer,' still obsessed with Hadriana's disappearance and possible zombification. We learn of Jacmel's decline after the vanishing of its guardian angel, its 'descent into hell' under the Duvalier dictatorships. The second movement ends with a 'coup de théâtre': Patrick is a professor at the University of West Indies (Jamaica) when Hadriana walks into his classroom: thirty-nine years have passed since her wedding day.

In the third movement, all is revealed: the reader learns what *really* happened to Hadriana through her own narrative. She is obviously alive and well, and describes how she was able to escape zombification. We learn, in Hadriana's version of events, that she drank, unbeknown to her at the time, poisoned lemonade before leaving for the Church on her wedding day. On her way to her destination, she started feeling ill but was unable to express her discomfort to those around her because she had lost her voice due to the effects of the poison on her vocal chords. At the altar, she gathered all her strength to pronounce (or rather scream) the ritual 'yes', after which she collapsed and was pronounced dead at the scene by a Doctor attending the wedding. Even though she appeared to be physically dead, she was in fact still alive but paralysed, with an imperceptible pulse, slipping in and out of consciousness, able to recount what she was seeing and hearing around her, unable to move or speak.

She describes, for example, how her casket was set up in the middle of a public space, 'l'allée des Amoureux' [the Alley of Lovers], and how she had observed various historical figures (French, Haitian, and other) as well as numerous Vodou gods and goddesses walk in front of her. One may think that Hadriana was hallucinating because of the poison; the explanation, however, is as follows: the night of her death, the Carnival had been celebrated and all those who did not attend the wedding, and who consequently were not 'officially' attending the wake, were celebrating the former. Among the participants were some of the world's greatest 'zombifiers' like Alexander the Great, Napoleon Bonaparte's generals, even Stalin, to name only a few, as well as other historical figures like Queen Elizabeth I, Toussaint Louverture (the Haitian hero of independence), and the Tsars of Russia. The Carnival episode is another excellent example of the 'merveilleux haïtien' through which Depestre illustrates how life and death are often intertwined in Haiti.

Hadriana slips in and out of consciousness throughout her ordeal – an effect of the poison - and is 'buried alive'. She recounts that gruesome experience.

> À mon réveil sous la terre, j'étais toujours dans le même état de pseudo-mort ou de pseudo-vie. ... Il n'y avait rien à voir. Je ne pouvais qu'écouter. ... Je m'écoutais mourir. Ce qui me restait d'existence était coincé dans la cécité absolue de mon foyer souterrain. Pour un forfait que je n'avais pas commis, on a laissé tomber ma vie dans un lieu sans lien temporel ou spatial avec l'extérieur. J'étais perdue dans le vide stupéfiant baptisé zombie en Haïti.[21]

While underground, her sense of hearing becomes extremely sharp. She can hear the sea, which gives her hope.

> La mer de Jacmel me rabattait secrètement vers l'espace lumineux de tout ce que j'étais à un doigt de perdre à tout jamais. La victoire était encore possible sur les forces démoniaques qui me zombifiaient.[22]

Hadriana is quickly unburied and given the antidote by Rosanfer, a Haitian of African descent who wished to capture her and keep her as a sex slave (let us remember that Hadriana was the object of desire of all the men in the novel, including the narrator). Rosanfer had subsequently hired the butterfly-sorcerer Balthazar Granchiré who had prepared the poison to be administered. Once unburied, her 'master' decides to give her a new name.

> Hadriana Siloé, ça ne va pas à une zombie, il y a trop de sel blanc dans ce nom. Je te baptise à mon tour: Eolis Anahir-dah ! Voici ton nom de négresse-femme-jardin à papa Rosanfer.[23]

Before her captor was able to put her *ti-bon-anj* in a bottle (the second stage of zombification), and mainly thanks to her youth (she was 19 years old at the time), Hadriana is able to outrun him in the graveyard and escape the last stage of her zombification.[24] She will never become Rosanfer's *négresse-femme-jardin* (an obvious play on words on René Depestre's concept of the Haitian *femme-jardin* mentioned at the beginning of this article). Rosanfer's use of the word *négresse* in Hadriana's case, who is white, does not necessarily refer to the colour of her skin but rather to the state of zombification, which is deemed to be parallel to slavery. Depestre maintains that by choosing a female protagonist who is white, he shows the universality of zombification in the sense that anyone can be a victim of the latter. In other words, anyone can lose his/her consciousness. There is, however, another possibility that cannot be ignored. By choosing a white victim from a prominent French family in Jacmel (in other words, a descendent of French colonizers), a victim who was 'a gift from France', Depestre instigates a role reversal. The colonizer, who has zombified the region for decades, is now himself zombified. In this context, zombification can certainly be perceived as an act of vengeance against the oppressor. If we accept the hypothesis that Hadriana symbolizes the colonizer/oppressor, her zombification consequently exposes the 'monster within', hidden under the mask of a fairy-like *femme-jardin*. In this case, Hadriana is not an innocent victim as she claims to be in the novel, and her possible transformation into a *négresse-femme-jardin* by a Haitian of African descent *could* be 'justifiable.' Nevertheless, the fact that she ultimately escapes her zombification seems to imply that the colonizer/oppressor still has the upper hand in old colonies.

After her escape from the graveyard, Hadriana, who was still wearing the wedding dress she was buried in, runs into town and tries to get help by knocking on various doors in her path, but nobody answers her knock. 'C'était à ne pas y croire', she declares, 'en moins de vingt-quatre heures, ma vie a cessé d'être un sésame à Jacmel. Mon nom n'ouvrait plus aucune porte.'[25] Hadriana is no longer the object of desire; the sensual Haitian *femme-jardin* has rather become a zombie, an object of fear. Haitians are not afraid of zombies because they are 'monsters' who will attack and eat them, as Hollywood would have us believe, what frightens them about the zombie is the reminder that anyone can be zombified, that anyone can lose his/her consciousness and become a slave. According to Maximilien Laroche in his article 'Mythe africain et mythe antillais: le personnage du zombi'

> Le personnage du zombi est une adaptation au contexte haïtien de la croyance africaine de la mort. Il est le symbole de l'esclave, de l'être aliéné, dépossédé de sa volonté, réduit à l'esclavage, obligé de travailler pour un maître.[26]

Slavery is deeply rooted in Haiti's collective memory and is often referred to in *Hadriana dans tous mes rêves*. Saint-Domingue (Haiti's colonial name) was a French colony (1670-1804) where slaves were governed by the *Code Noir* (literally translated as 'Black Code'), a decree passed by Louis XIV in 1685 in which, for example, slaves were considered to be a 'good' owned by a master. As mentioned earlier, slaves were forced to convert to Catholicism upon their arrival in the colony and were also given Christian names. They were forbidden from gathering, except for the purpose of a funeral, which explains why funerals are still sometimes 'celebrated' (in the sense that there is music playing and some dancing) in some old French colonies of the Americas. As Desmangles states: 'The impacts of the Code Noir ... still persist in Haiti.'[27] Depestre's novel reinforces Desmangles' assertion when Patrick states that ' le destin du zombie serait comparable à celui de l'esclave des plantations coloniales de la Saint-Domingue d'autrefois.'[28] Hadriana's escape could be compared to the escape of the slaves from plantations; these runaway slaves were called the *Marrons*. She takes a similar path through a dense tropical forest, but ends up by the coast as opposed to the mountains where the *Marrons* had historically hid.

Depestre's female protagonist is well aware of her new status within the Haitian society of Jacmel; in order to completely and successfully escape her zombification, Hadriana must leave Jacmel, where she is well known and is now a perceived to be a 'monster', and eventually Haiti. Her destiny is parallel to that of the Haitian writer who must leave his native land if he is to survive; the price of Hadriana's escape will ultimately be her exile. After her flight from the cemetery, Jacmel's guardian angel walks all night by the sea - the salt water completely awakens her senses - and reaches Bainet, a Haitian coastal village where nobody knows her, at dawn

> J'ai essayé de mettre un peu d'ordre à ma tenue de zombie, avant ma première rencontre, en plein jour, avec les vivants. En ajustant tant bien que mal ma toilette, j'ai eu une surprise qui cadrait parfaitement avec le surréalisme échevelé de mon aventure. Dans ... ma ceinture, j'ai trouvé l'enveloppe de ma dot.[29]

The fact that she attempts 'to put some order in her clothes' demonstrates that she is fully aware of her monstrous appearance and is quite 'conscious' of the fact that she no longer belongs with the 'living' in her native country. She is, on the other hand, pleasantly surprised when a group of local inhabitants, getting ready to set sail and leave Haiti for Jamaica, think that she is the Haitian *loa Simbi-la-source* (literally translated as *Simbi-the-Spring*)[30] who has come out of the sea to bless their trip, and they greet her accordingly. Hadriana has metamorphosed once again, this time into an object of worship, accompanies them on their journey and leaves Haiti, never to return. When she arrives in Jamaica, her white skin serves as her passport and she is allowed to enter the country without any official documents (let us remember that it is 1938): 'En ce temps-là, la peau blonde, mieux qu'un passeport diplomatique, avait la valeur d'un visa de droit divin.'[31] Hadriana Siloé the Haitian *femme-jardin* who was an object of desire, became an object of fear (zombie), then an object of worship (*Simbi-la-source*), before becoming *politically* white once she leaves Haiti (in Haiti her white skin was not an issue, since she was considered *Créole*).

Hadriana's zombification in the novel is parallel to Haiti's: both words begin with the letter H and are feminine nouns in French. Furthermore, Haitian authors, including Depestre, tend to personify their native land in their writings. Haiti, according to Depestre and other Haitian intellectuals, has been zombified by various powers (colonial as well as local) since its birth in 1804. In the twentieth century, we can trace this zombification back to the American Military Occupation of the country from 1915-1934 and to the Duvalier dictatorships spanning from

1957 through 1986. According to Stanley Péan: 'Haïti a bel est vécu, sous le régime duvaliériste, presque trente ans de 'zombification', de perte du corps, de la tête et surtout de l'âme.'[32] If Hadriana symbolizes Haiti, then the loss of her *femme-jardin* status implies that Haiti has lost its *pays-jardin* status (*pays* means country in French). The *zombie-country* has lost its body, its mind and its soul. Haitians live in a country that has been turned inside out, the monster within (the zombie) has petrified and paralysed them. In an interview with Joan Dayan, Depestre upholds the following:

> The notion of zombification replaces the theory of alienation. It is the concrete form of the alienation of a people. ... Haiti is a zombified country, a country that has lost its soul. Political and colonial history has plunged Haiti into an unrelenting state of total alienation.[33]

Patrick reinforces Depestre's beliefs when he declares in the novel: ' Mon pays natal ne serait-il pas un zombie collectif?'[34]

History demonstrates that Haiti has been unable to escape its zombification as the country is, to this day, a 'zombie collectif' trapped in a state of pseudo-life, pseudo-death. As Dayan declares, 'Depestre evokes the zombie as the most powerful emblem of anonymity, loss, and neo-colonialism.'[35] Hadriana Siloé, on the other hand, escaped her fate alone, without the help of anyone, possibly because of her youth, perhaps even because she was an innocent victim, and/or maybe because she was white skinned and a descendant of French colonizers. More importantly, however, her escape was possible as well as successful, because she refused to accept her monstrosity in Haiti and had the *will* to break away from her misfortune. The price of her freedom, or rather the price of her 'rebirth', which she was willing to pay without any hesitation, was her exile. Only by leaving Haiti was she able to bury the monster in order to live her life as a woman. In Jamaica, thirty-nine years after that fateful day at the altar, she finds Patrick and, according to a note at the end of the novel, 'they live happily ever after', a true 'fairy tale' ending. Now that Haiti has been zombified, how can it 'wake-up' from its state? What will be its 'salt'? Depestre's novel, perhaps suggesting a sense of fatalism and/or impotence, does not answer this question.

Notes

[1] It would be interesting to point out that the concept of the *femme-jardin* first appeared in *Le Mât de cocagne* (1979) and later in a collection of short stories by Depestre entitled *Alléluia pour une femme-jardin* (1981). The latter is heavily influenced by André Breton and French surrealism, as is *Hadriana dans tous mes rêves*.

[2] J. Dayan, 'France Reads Haiti: René Depestre's *Hadriana dans tous mes rêves*', *Yale French Studies*, Vol. 2, 1993, p. 171.
[3] Ibid., p. 166.
[4] Even though there are numerous spellings of 'vodou' (*vodoun, vodun*), I have chosen to use the former because it is the closest spelling to the Haitian pronunciation of the word.
[5] When referring to *Vodouisants*, I'll be specifically referring to Haitian *vodouisants*.
[6] J. Mbiti, *African Religions and Philosophy*, 2nd edition, Heinemann, London, 1990, p. 81.
[7] Haitian beliefs in zombies differ from those in Guadeloupe, Martinique, and the rest of the Caribbean. This article will focus on the meaning of the zombie in Haiti in general and in Depestre's novel in particular. For more information regarding zombies (in Haiti and elsewhere), please refer to Ackermann and Gauthier's article 'The Ways and Nature of the Zombi.'
[8] L. Desmangles, *The Faces of the Gods: Vodou and Roman Catholicism in Haiti*, The University of North Carolina Press, Chapel Hill, 1992, p. 66.
[9] Ibid., p. 67.
[10] R. Depestre, *Hadriana dans tous mes rêves*, Gallimard, Paris, 1988, p. 168. The English translation of *Hadriana dans tous mes rêves* has been out of print for years. All translations of the novel are my own. 'I was punished by destiny for a crime I had not committed.'
[11] L. Desmangles, op. cit., p. 195, note 7.
[12] François Duvalier, Papa Doc, from 1957 to 1971, and his son Jean-Claude Duvalier, Baby Doc, from 1971 to 1986.
[13] J.M. Salien, 'Croyances polpulaires haïtiennes dans *Hadriana dans tous mes rêves* de René Depestre', *The French Review*, Vol.74, No.1, October 2000, p. 91.
[14] Scholars use this French term, even when writing in another language. A literal English translation would be the 'Haitian marvellous'.
[15] Salien, op. cit.
[16] Desmangles, op. cit., p. xi.
[17] Dayan, op. cit., p. 169.
[18] Depestre, op. cit., p. 38. Hadriana 'is the princely gift that Debussy and Renoir's France gave Haiti. More than a nineteen year old young woman, the guardian fairy of Jacmel is a rose picked from God's hat.'
[19] 'his antennas were cut.'
[20] Ibid., p. 49. 'Madame Brévica Losange, a Siloé neighbour who had the reputation of being a mambo, … asserted out loud that Hadriana's death wasn't due to natural causes. One didn't need Sherlock Holmes' talent to discover the path that lead to the author of the deed. The latter was signed Balthazar Granchiré!'

[21] Ibid., pp. 187-88. 'When I awoke underground, I was still in a state of pseudo-death or pseudo-life. ... There was nothing to see. I could only listen to myself. ... I was listening to myself die. What remained of my existence was stuck in the absolute blindness of my underground home. For a deed I had not committed, my life was left in a place without a temporal or spatial link with the outside. I was lost in the stupefying emptiness baptized zombie in Haiti.'

[22] Ibid., pp. 188-89. 'The sea of Jacmel secretly pulled me towards the luminous space containing the things I was about to lose forever. Victory over the demonic forces that were zombifying me was still possible.'

[23] Ibid., p. 197. 'Hadriana Siloé does not suit a zombie, there's too much white salt in that name. I baptize you Eolis Anahir-dah ! Here's the new name *négresse-femme-jardin* that papa Rosanfer gives you.'

[24] Traditionally it is the *houngan* who captures the victim's *ti-bon-anj* and puts it in a bottle. In Depestre's novel, however, it is a character who is not a sorcerer, which perhaps further explains Hadriana's escape (Rosanfer is inexperienced in the art of zombification).

[25] Depestre, op.cit., p. 202. 'It was hard to believe, in less than twenty-four hours, my life ceased to be a sesame in Jacmel. My name didn't open a single door.'

[26] M. Laroche, 'Mythe africain et mythe antillais: le personnage du zombi'. *Revue canadienne des études africaines/Canadian Journal of African Studies*, vol. IX, no. 3, 1975, p. 487. 'The character of the zombie is an adaption of the African belief in death to the Haitian context. He is the symbol of the slave, the alienated being deprived of his will, reduced to slavery, forced to work for a master.'

[27] Desmangles, op. cit., p. 52.

[28] Depestre, op. cit., p. 137. 'the destiny of the zombie would be comparable to the destiny of the colonial plantation slaves in the former Saint-Domingue.'

[29] Ibid., p. 205. 'I tried to put some order in my zombie outfit before my first meeting, in daylight, with the living. While trying to adjust my attire, I had a surprise that captured my surreal adventure perfectly. In my belt, I found the envelope containing my dowry.'

[30] There are numerous white *loas* in Vodou.

[31] Depestre, op. cit., pp. 207-8. 'At that time, blond skin, better than a diplomatic passport, had the value of a divine right.'

[32] S. Péan, 'Vodou et Macumba chez René Depestre et Mário de Andrade', *Études littéraires*, Vol.25, No.3, 1993, p. 53. 'Haiti has altogether lived, under the Duvalier regimes, almost thirty years of zombification, loss of the body, the mind, and above all, the soul.'

[33] J. Dayan, 'France Reads Haiti : An Interview with René Depestre', *Yale French Studies*, Vol. 2, 1993, pp. 146-147.

[34] Depestre, op. cit., p. 134. 'Isn't my native land a collective zombie?'

[35] J. Dayan, 'France Reads Haiti: René Depestre's *Hadriana dans tous mes rêves*', p. 174.

Bibliography

Ackermann, H.W. & Gauthier, J., 'The Ways and Nature of the Zombi'. *The Journal of American Folklore*. Vol.104, No.414, Autumn 1991, pp. 466-94.

Barnabé J., Chamoiseau, P. & Confiant, R., *Éloge de la créolité*. Gallimard, Paris, 1989.

Depestre, R., *Hadriana dans tous mes rêves*. Gallimard, Paris, 1988.

Desmangles, L., *The Faces of the Gods: Vodou and Roman Catholicism in Haiti*. The University of North Carolina Press, Chapel Hill, NC, 1992.

Dayan, J., 'France Reads Haiti: An Interview with René Depestre'. *Yale French Studies*. Vol.2, 1993, pp. 136-53.

___, 'France Reads Haiti: René Depestre's *Hadriana dans tous mes rêves*'. *Yale French Studies*. Vol.2, 1993, pp. 154-75.

Laroche, M., 'Mythe africain et mythe antillais: le personnage du zombi'. *Revue canadienne des études africaines/Canadian Journal of African Studies*. Vol. IX, No.3, 1975, pp. 479-91.

Mbiti, J., *African Religions and Philosophy*. 2nd ed, Heinemann, London, 1990.

Péan, S., 'Vodou et Macumba chez René Depestre et Mário de Andrade'. *Études littéraires*. Vol. 25, No. 3, 1993, pp. 49-59.

Salien, J.M., 'Croyances polpulaires haïtiennes dans *Hadriana dans tous mes rêves* de René Depestre'. *The French Review*. Vol. 74, No. 1, October 2000, pp. 82-93.

The Labyrinth, Lustrate and Liminal in *Requiem for a Beast*: The Monster Resurrected as Multi-Modality

Phil Fitzsimmons

Abstract
In 2008 Matt Ottley's *Requiem for a Beast* won the Australian Book Council, Picture Book of the Year award, receiving both critical acclaim and public outrage. While billed as a graphic novel, it has been created in a multi-modal form with elements of whole text, large sections of picture plates, parallel narratives and an accompanying CD. While the plot deals with a young man working on an outback cattle station, the subtext highlights the current Australian narrative that is 'struggling to free itself from residual colonial ideologies.'[1] However, while focusing unanswered contemporary issues such as the 'stolen generation,' masculinity, indigenous genocide and adolescent self-concept, *Requiem for a Beast* negotiates the tension between past and present through one of the oldest monstrous sign-signifier connections, the use of the Minotaur as an 'apophasis metaphor of socio-cultural transgression.'[2] As such, this text becomes more than simply a liminal format of 'pastiche, hybridization and interdeterminancy'[3] but a 'metaphysical liminality' in two ways. Firstly, in its multi-modal structure it allows the monster to be multi-voiced or intersemiotic, as has always been the case with the appearance of archetypal monsters,[4] providing a visual metaphor of a 'harbinger of category crisis that dwells at the gates of difference.'[5] However, perhaps more importantly the portrayal of this monster reveals its primary and primeval function of not only 'to show forth or teach, as determined by is etymological roots of 'monstrare'[6] but to act as a symbolic bridge between physical and spiritual dimensions.

Key Words: Australian narrative, labyrinth, mindscapes, monster theory, *Requiem for a Beast*.

*****

1. Are We Seeing Eye to I? An Auto-Ethnographic Introduction to Incongruity

In 2008 Matt Ottley's *Requiem for a Beast* won the Australian Book Council Picture Book of the Year award. While it received critical acclaim in several magazine articles, internet forums and book distributor websites, the voice of public disquiet and condemnation in the print news media was by far the loudest and longest. It seems the use of the 'f-word', several other elements of swearing and sexual references had raised the ire of many journalists, commentators, parents of children and the public at large. Questions were asked in regard to its suitability as a children's book, why the Book Council had conferred this award and the need to use profanity in a supposed children's text, or in any text? The sexual references, unambiguous detailing of post-colonial injustices to the indigenous population and the explicit use of the Minotaur as metaphor were by and large overlooked in the ongoing debate. However, perhaps the most important aspect overlooked in this debate was the question of why did these facets arise? If both the human and physical topography in literature reflects the cultural mindscapes of how a nation views itself, then why does *Requiem for a Beast* return to illustrated scenes of a past 'desert pastoriphilia'[7] with its national mythic underpinnings of death, hardship and the laconic outback stockmen, when children's literature in Australian has in more recent times 'looked to the coast and found it good.'[8]

The forms and focus of Ottley's book suggests that the national gaze has been blinkered, as does the overall initial reaction and questioning of Ottley's language use. Public outbursts such as these have always been markers of a populist reaction to any liminal space, or 'set of models or templates that periodically reclassify reality or man's relationships to culture, society and nature.'[9] As in this case, typically the outcry is that this literature 'transgresses the boundaries and norms of childhood innocence,'[10] but in fact this is a verbal smokescreen representing denial that there is tension between 'mixed cultural codes'[11] or two competing paradigms. Below the surface level of language use these texts bend and transgress boundaries by breaking the typical 'home-away-home' flow of what are deemed as suitable children's books, 'showing us the deceptive feeling of being at home in the world.'[12]

However, not only did Ottley's book have all of the previous characteristics but his use of the Minotaur as an ongoing metaphoric thread gave voice to the monster which 'haunts the edges of civilizations uneasy sleep.'[13] The unashamed narrative footprint of this monster had never before been unleashed in the Australian canon. In *Requiem for a Beast*, the typical 'Australian narrative mindscapes'[14] of open space for the taking, the emotionless white male living in a pastoral home, the strip of English garden in a binary connection with the absence of water and femininity had become symbolically inhabited by the 'scapegoat emissary of the unconscious, ... the critical touchstone for communal renewal and for individual redemption.'[15] As Conty asserts, this beast and its labyrinthine lair represents 'the life death-crossing or chiasmus, accompanied by a similar crossing of truth with fiction, reality with illusion and speech with sign.'[16]

As one of the oldest monstrous sign-signifier 'life affirming' as well as 'life destroying' connections, this 'bull hybrid motif' is often used as allegory to represents the most poignant 'apophatic metaphor of socio-cultural transgressions.'[17] In itself this symbol tends to unsettle any reader as its appearance tends to appear in deeply 'troubling stories, ...ones that that touch the core of what it means to be human.'[18]

Hence, it could be argued that *Requiem for a Beast* was pilloried, not because of its language use but because it brought a monstrous transgressive voice to the developing 'easy going beach-city narrative' of Australian culture and associated developments in children's literature. While the narrative was based in and on the 'Dead Heart' of the Australian continent and the related cultural myth of the powerful unassuming laconic white stockman, *Requiem for a Beast* directly challenged this notion as well the post millennial view that the largest island nation has genuinely shifted away from its racist Anglophile past. The common theme in Australian art and literature of the 'veranda around the homestead' is shown to represent distance from the traditional owners of the land and not the view from 'a justifiable place of leisure of a wealthy democracy.'[19]

Also, the Australian educational context was in the throes of being refocused by right wing political forces and had begun reverting to a more conservative viewpoint of what constituted quality children's literature. As a graphic novel, *Requiem for a Beast* also challenged this viewpoint. However, it is one of the new breeds of graphic novella hybrids in that it incorporates not only the typical graphic novel form of stand-alone visual facets, and text-visual relationships but also various combinations of textual elements. Ottley had created an even more evolved multi-modal form as all of the narrative elements are fractured in someway with parenthetical 'gutters' (or gaps between the text), visual sequences that not only run parallel but provide alternate narratives within these frames and an accompanying CD. With a continual explicit focus on monstrosity and as a graphic novella containing other overlapping narratives and points of interstitial cultural contestation, *Requiem for a Beast* automatically acted as a textual breeding ground for reflection on other monstrous forms, the darker elements of the 'social self' whereby readers 'contemplate monsters of its own creation.'[20] These monsters tend to be those shadowy forces that the human condition knows exist within but are pushed deep down into the cultural psyche, but never for long. There always come a time when societies and groups have to come face-to-face with repressed ideologies or 'the monster of grim prospects, ... the beginner's monster. It attacks when we are untried, or when we are tried in a situation unlike any that has confronted us before.'[21]

Requiem for a Beast was also published at a time of political and social confrontation and is a socio-psycho reservoir that gives both form and voice to the re-surfacing of this aspect of the monster. In this case its pointed focus honed in on a national identity that is still in a state of flux, grounded in the tension between genuine ownership of the land and the mythic concepts held by white Australia concerning 'mateship' and taming of the outback. While there is usually a subtle dystopian underpinning to young people's literature arising out of the Australian context here was a reversal of that 'writing into thought' process with a clear message that the socio-cultural dystopian slide can only be halted through encountering, 'eucharising' and embracing the monster. To do this produces 'category crisis, ... the beginning of the hermeneutic spiral into a new interconnected method of perceiving the world.'[22]

Requiem for a Beast is constructed through just such a spiral of narratives that become increasingly microscopic in regard to a monster that does not exist and yet must still be captured, and telescopic with respect to the universality of this beast's lair that exists at the labyrinthine centre of 'us'. The following paragraphs follow the circular path of 'us as the beast', touching on the key points of microscopic narrative and its related vision and resurrection of where 'the dream of reason produces monsters.'[23]

2. Connections between the Covers: Ancient Forms as New Associations

Just as the entire book is encased with an overall set of visual paratext, these 'thresholds of interpretation' related to concepts of the 'monstrous,' departure, loss, sacrifice and death are continued as 'architext,'[24] or different genres or narratives within the text. In this instance the 'architectural' form is developed not only through the graphic novel format but also through the use of four subsections within the book with the subtitle of each section being a verse of the Catholic 'Requiem.' Ottley's narrative is also a 'transtextual'[25] interlocking of narratives in that it forces the reader to become increasingly introspective, as with each turn of the page there is an increasing synoptic intermingling wherein the oldest forms of mythic narrative are recast 'monstrously' anew. In *Requiem for a Beast,* white Australia becomes connected to the Aboriginal landowners, who in turn are bonded together through the use of the Knossian motif. Each section uses this monster as a metaphor to reveal the darker elements of what is commonly called, the 'Australian Dream', and an echo of the mythic call to change.

Following on from the subtitle *Dies Irate,* Latin for 'The Day of Wrath', the first pages of this opening subsection introduces the sense of loss and departure from the supporting structures that give meaning to the Australian indigenous people, and the ultimate day of reckoning to come that results from this loss. In a series of panels an Aboriginal female elder laments the loss of her cultural memory and sense of self. In a reference to the 'dream time' stories, the narratives that underpin the Aboriginal culture to an interconnected sense of person, people, place and past, she inscribes a tone of bereavement not only for these four facets, but for the entire text. However, in a liquid like movement to the next section, which is characteristic of the whole text, there is a change of tense from the past to the present continuous carrying forward the sense of demise, aloneness and disconnectedness into the here and now. But more importantly, this section of written text re-introduces the polyvalent paratextual 'bull' connection named as '[T]hat Bull.'[26]

As Barber and Barber note, a reference to the 'one bull' while having direct labyrinthine connotations automatically sets up another layer of interstitial framework where by this metaphor articulates meaning that is associated with a sense of 'quality of place and quality of action.'[27] While having the same metaphoric implications through its constant return to the monster's death,

Requiem for a Beast questions the quality of the current Australian sense of place. Any reference to follow the bull in narrative always infers the need to return to the place of cultural birth and the societal womb to gain this understanding. However, while always a place representing the possibility of rebirth, it is also a place of death.

In this first section, although cast in an Australian outback context, the bull is described as having the same purpose as the Knossian beast with reference to its 'calling to him in the night, ... that it is leading somewhere,'[28] and when it disappears the landscape has become altered and barren. In this initial section while there is a call for a boy to follow he is not mentioned by name and just as he is figuratively lost in the text, he also loses sight of the bull as 'he stops at the edge of the world.'[29] His body and sense of situation metaphorically enacts the lost sense of place and rejection experienced by his people. More importantly this sense of loss is also framed in the narrative through the rejection of the boy by his family, and more pointedly rejection by his father. While carrying on the narrative tradition that the father represents absence, often both physical and emotional, and allows the introduction of evil, in this text all the adults in this narrative appear as being absent in the sense they have no understanding of place or genuine purpose. As cattle workers and wives in the Outback, both male and female appear to have lost their own sense of story as reflected in the natural wasteland that surrounds them; a land these white men struggle to tame, subdue and eke out a living but which in turns drains them of the ability to form relationships as they hide in their work and loneliness. More importantly, the indigenous cattle workers are kept at the same sense of distance as the white wives and children.

As Cohen and Eliade contend, when a people or space are profaned, a competing narrative of the monstrous arises to fulfil one of its key roles of leading the human condition back to a once known reality and once experienced grounded sense of story. This monster's enduring narrative is that it speaks of and to a people going into sleep and sleep walking, 'denoting a plunge and dissolution of consciousness in the darkness of non-being', as a 'child enters the womb for birth.'[30] Thus from the outset this narrative speaks of a need to change by somehow connecting with the Minotaur, and though it is seen as a creature that can kill, the beast is also seen to be a creature that can recreate. The reference to the lack of water and the shift into panelled illustrations in this opening section is also an archetypal-monstrous reference to both the loss of the essence of life and the promise that it will return. There is pain signalled in these metaphors but also promise. A return is never easy and just as Theseus found it more difficult to find his way out of the labyrinth than to find his way in, so too the characters in *Requiem for a Beast*, both black and white and the peoples they represent, suffer the same sense of stumbling in the dark to find a sense of story, purpose and direction.

These facets are further revisited in the graphic novel panels as the stand-alone text of the initial dream sequence. This then shifts into an Aboriginal child's vision of a church school in a parched landscape. The narrative is now in graphic novel form reflecting to some degree the oral-storytelling elements of the aboriginal culture, however only the child's brown skinned hand can be seen opening the school door. Alone he sits at a school desk and through the window a rider is seen approaching wearing a horned bull-like helmet. Described by the dreamer as a 'man-beast', as it approaches it begins chanting 'the boy, the boy' and this mantra becomes the 'growling of a beast'. As the beast-man crashes through the wall of the building, the Dreamer grabs the boy and pushes the young child out of the window to safety. As he falls with outstretched hand another dreamer's hands are seen. Cast as a white female the vector draws the reader's vision to her left hand on which she is wearing watch. The lost matriarch's narrative in the first pages is drawn into another metaphor of an absent mother, with its ensuing nexus of death, loss, abandonment and a different sense of time. The hand that opened the door to get in, the hand held up in horror and the hand that pushed the boy out are only conjoined as opposite forces. The monster will not give up searching for the boy and will not let the faceless white woman escape as well.

In doing so this entire section reveals not only the fractures within the apparently egalitarian Australian society but also begins to show how the Aboriginal people are given only limited tenancy in their own broad and seemingly limitless expanse of land. The school rectangularity is held in stark contrast to the expansive horizons as illustrated through the classroom's window. However, in this conjoined dream sequence the monster simultaneously has impinged on the nightmare of a white child. While this section of narrative hints at the white resistance to accepting the narratives of the traditional landowners, as the aboriginal child falls out of the white space, he looks back for help. While this version of the Minotaur creates the typical highly signified ongoing chaos created by narrative monsters, the connecting gazes between the two cultures also reveals the other parallel role of the monster in also 'creating a bridge between two rational categories.'[31]

This binary of connectivity and relentless chaos of this narrative monster representing 'human nature's sense of cosmic disorder, chaos and loss'[32] is further revealed as the beast then crashes into the school room. The shape shifting nature of the Minoan Beast, and all its associated relatives, is further revealed as it morphs into a representation of the Minotaur seen in the fractured frames akin to a broken pain of glass. On the subsequent page the beast again changes, as also indicated by the written text, into a more demonic or alien form. Its eyes are looking at the reader, and also turned to the right, both visually denoting a sense of place and immediacy combined with positive movement to the completion of a goal and a final place of rest. This 'dazzling allegory of the monster's double presence,'[33] once again reveals the chaos and uncertainty that humans create is simply an agent for possible change.

In this six-page set of graphic transitions there are no page numbers, and this also occurs wherever the monster appears in later visual vignettes. While continuing on the flow of the plot the removal of the pagination highlights a space and time of white invasion when the Aboriginal sense of space and time ceased to exist. Their 'Dream Stories' of living with the land were replaced by ownership and pastoral demarcation by the first settlers who also brought in a new set of religious and cultural stories that were forced onto the indigenous peoples. With an ongoing visual and textual linkage to places of wildness and desert, these pages become the key markers which in a more global sense, call into question the ongoing narrative discourse of the Western Culture that has perpetuated the view of itself as the 'perfect and ultimate state of humanity,'[34] and in particular the Australian narrative focus of being the 'lucky country'. The latter is a colloquialism for 'the safety and security in a place of isolation, wealth, natural beauty and mineral resources'. However, on the whole it is 'lucky' for whites only. These unpaginated sections of *Requiem for a Beast* act as labyrinthine centres allowing the monster to return, providing an opportunity for it to demonstrate how much Australia has become 'the other within'.

> Monsters are personifications of the *unheimlich*. They stand for what endangers one's sense of at-homeness, that is, one's sense of security, stability, integrity, well being, health and meaning. They make one feel *not at home at home*. They are figures of chaos and disorientation within *order* and orientation, revealing deep insecurities in one's faith in oneself, one's society and one's world.[35]

As the monster in narrative also 'defines human identity'[36] the beast in *Requiem for a Beast* inhabits the psyche of the Aboriginal child in this first section by defining this young person as a victim of white culture. However, at this point the narrative converges and explores the story of a white boy who is also a victim of the same imagination of a forced will that has the appearance of power and self control but is itself deeply wounded. Ottley reveals that the beast in his text is a reflection of the new beast to be overcome on the driest continent, the 'beast of colonial complacency within'. The *Requiem for a Beast* narrative has arisen to reveal the necessity to expunge this twin beast of imposed post-colonial order, ownership and its deception that all is well without and all is well within.

As the reader moves on, this 'beast within' focus now morphs into a series of smaller text and graphic vignettes transforming the text into an intersection of all of the previous narratives. The first tells of the white boy beginning life as a station hand. His thoughts, and love of reading are held in stark relief to those of the other 'hard living' older workmen. A smaller 'graphic novel like' twin panel reveals there have been problems in his home and if fact when the muster is over he is staying on at the station. The first parallel panel tells of his ongoing remoteness as well as that of Ellie, a disillusioned station hands wife. Through the panels he is seen as a young child falling back on a swing, and while his mother can just be made out behind Ellie's narrative, only her hand pushing him can be seen clearly.

While a hand is once again depicted as a primary point of care and trust it represents the only sense of emotional and protective cathexis in the entire narrative. All other places or psychological domains of protection have fallen to the wayside for both the indigenous and white children. In what Uebel would term a 'flickering point of contact,' it symbolizes the creation of a problematic space or grey area of exchange between 'translation and mutation.'[37] Although only a momentary point of contact, it also a point of loss opening the door for the re-entrance of the monster.

Through the shift in each of these smaller stories the tension in this unnamed white boy's life is further revealed. Commencing with the loss of culture revealed in the opening pages, and then unpacked metaphorically through the desert scenes, the first attack of the beast and the slow death of the parched landscape, there is also a parallel set of narratives revealing the death of relationships amongst the main characters, the drying up of the elements constituting a genuine life and a sense of desertion, loneliness and rejection of each as people. This notion of abandonment and destruction of relationships is also a primary polyvalent layer in the Knossian myth, and subsequently another ensuing key archetypal underpinning for all narratives. Ariadne's betrayal of her half brother is also recognized as being a cause and effect signage in which the Minotaur is an integral component of the cosmic cycle of destruction that creates a new beginning. This cycle is recognized in the continuation of this mythic story in that being an accomplice to his death in the underground 'death womb,'[38] Ariadne commenced her own death-abandonment path with her foreign lover which in turn led to the eventual irrevocable loss of her homeland and culture. After having fled with Theseus and left on the deserted island of Naxos, a parallel desertification occurred on Crete and in particular within the labyrinth. Thus death of the beast and the desertion of Ariadne was a mircrosm, signalling the constant cycle of death to be experience by all mankind and an inability to find and maintain relationships, unless the monster could once again be found.

In *Requiem for a Beast* the dead landscape and falling backwards of the children can also be equated as being lowered into the same mythic grave. This motif is continued through the ensuing vignette which returns the reader's focus to the wife of one of the drovers as told through the eyes of the young cattle worker. As is often the case in Australian narrative, she too is a lost soul in the typical isolation trope of the Australian males who are yearning for pastoral control, leaving their wives to figuratively die alone in the stifling anti-cultural aspects of rural life and the oppressive micro-culture of the outback existence. This sets up a smaller set of narrative cycles where the boy unpacks his family's ongoing fall; the emotional distance between father and son, how he wanted to be like his father and have the same stories. However, this notion of why the boy's father is so distant is then unpacked through parallel columns of narrative on the next page. While there are only fragments of detail in the text based narrative and the pastiche of overlapping visual elements they reveal glimpses of the father's unfulfilled dreams, the hint that he killed a young aboriginal boy in a night time accident, an attempted suicide by the young story teller, the story of an aboriginal woman in town, a song of the first meeting of the aboriginal people with the white settlers and the meshing of these facets with his own story. However, these snippets of larger and integrated narrative web are summarized in the perceived disappointment his father felt for him as he wanted to become a jackeroo, and 'the silence'[39] that followed. A turn of the page focuses this 'silence' of the 'absent father' into the boy's confession that the Minotaur has always haunted his dreams. As the 'gutters' framing this section of graphic novel construction fade, the text slides into an almost full-page spread where the boy transforms into this beast give illustrative voice to his pain of abandonment. The narrative then returns to the day's muster and a brief paragraph linkage to the other stockmen who are also emotionally and socially 'absent', as they ride off in silence of a dark morning in the Outback.

As the 'narrative as text' returns, so too the reader is returned to 'the bull' and the Minotaurian narrative, as it leads the boy alone into a clearing in the bush. He hears the echo of his father's voice, and something 'deep within his fear calls to him. ... Go with the bull. You must take the bull.'[40] And in silence bull and boy face each other. However, in the next set of stand-alone visuals and text, it is the man and beast that are facing each other. As the illustrations of the bull again fracture into more focused elements the aboriginal child is seen reflected in the eye of the bull. While signifying the taming of the child and its people, this last scene also represents the child needing to stare into the eyes of the beast and see its potential. As Scutter believes, the notion of tameness has within it 'a potential shadow self, of wildness.'[41] In this text the two facets have become conflated within the gaze of the monster revealing the potential of Aboriginal people to draw on both sides of this binary and reach a full potential.

The second section is entitled *Mors Stupebit et Natura,* translated as death and nature. This begins with the same graphic novel format and a return to the white boys arrival in his new outback home and then expands on the binary of tameness and the sense of the wild. His memory is also returned through a graphic novel framework to the recollections of the Aboriginal woman and her memories of the stolen generation. As the boy is pictured sitting up the back of a community hall with only a handful of white audience members there is greater focus, amplification and increasing introspection regarding 'how they no longer knew their place in the world'.[42] This narrative chunk is small in comparison with the other sections but is the most important as it is a summary of the intersection of points and places of cultural contestation over ownership of the land, and a place of stark opposites. The Knossian cycle of death and resurrection of the monster is further clarified as it is in this section that the child in the first school room narrative is revealed as being representative of the children who were taken from their parents along with the brutality of the new schools for the 'stolen generation' is told with their cycle of beatings, loneliness and silence. It is in this section that the restoration of the loss of the indigenous children and Aboriginal culture as a whole is cast as a return to an understanding of the concept of land. In direct contrast to the 'silences' of the previous narratives restoration of the land, ownership of story and language in this section it seen as a place of healing and interaction, which also includes the white culture.

As another layer of connection, the coming of the bull is mentioned again but framed as a coming darkness of storm clouds. 'All have to stand in the rain.'[43] While it is made clear that the first iteration of the bull at the school was representative of white society, here another form is conceived. It would appear that while the injustices of some elements of the white society were cruel in the extreme, Ottley adds a different focus in that the indigenous culture needs to focus on a process of 'healing ourselves,'[44] as well as the white members of Australia. *Requiem for a Beast* appears to be offering an alternate view to the reconciliation process that has only just begun in the 'land down under'. The answer to overcoming the racism still inherent in Australian culture and in exorcising the remnant cruelty of the recent past, the indigenous residents should not accept help from the white geo-politic but seek to understand and enact the true nature of their much richer cultural past and identity. In finding and re-establishing for themselves their sense of connectedness to the land and their own stories they will become more empowered and able to reveal to the broader Australian context what it really means to re-vision the colonial view point of this continent as 'Terra Nullis'. At this point *Requiem for a Beast*'s emergent theme is that there were inhabitants here for thousands of years before white settlement, who lived with the land and not off it. Thus in later visual frames the aboriginal child, without comment from the written text is depicted riding off into the wild untamed desert on the back of the Brahmin bull. In a parallel narrative the white jackeroo has to also face this beast, emblematic of the need to remove the cultural injustices that he represents, as well learn to follow the path that beast is leading him on.

> The monstrous metaphor as object becomes the critical touchstone for communal renewal and for individual redemption, the sacrificial victim, the scapegoat emissary from the unconscious.[45]

The third section of *Requiem for a Beast,* 'Lacrymosa,' takes up the visual narrative ending of part one and the final warning of the previous section regarding the 'coming darkness,'[46] again shifting through a series of graphic narratives. In the first the young white boy is seen following the bull into a circular gully, and then after an initial monstrous charge he again follows the beast into a landscape that is 'strangely familiar, ... deeper into the day and into himself.'[47] In stark contrast to the illustrated glare of the desert, the illustrations shift into the darkness of night as the boy realizes he has entered a dream he had the previous night which focused on one of his fellow Aboriginal workmen, Rudy. The indigenous stockmen is pictured as trying to tame a wild horse that was trying to not only throw him off but take him away. Both horse and rider then morph into a bellowing Minotaur as the dreaming adolescent runs into the desert. On the next page through a series of widening panels an indigenous mother comes to the dreaming boy and asks where is her son? Over the next sixteen pages the graphic narrative shifts in and out of the boys current confrontation with the bull and flashback sequences to his fractured familial past, emotional dislocation with his father and the constant dream he had of the Minotaur. In the final pages the textual narrative of the disappearance of the Aboriginal child does not fit precisely with the visual narrative. Instead the dreaming boy is pictured holding onto the wild Brahmin bull as the panels fold into smaller parallel frames of the lost Aboriginal child as part of the stolen generation and the young white boys dislodgement from his father. These continually diminishing panels then morph into a final double page spread where on one side both the boy and bull are locked in death struggle finally collapsing over a precipice. On the parallel page the Minotaurian rider of the first narrative is seen coming in from the desert holding a bloodstained axe having killed indigenous woman and children. This section ends with an illustrative return of the roaring Minotaur and the indigenous child holding onto a rope.

With the ever-increasing focus on the desert space and confrontation with the monster in a confined space in the desert, the underpinning representation is the sense of an ever-increasing 'assimilation into chaos.'[48] While this section of *Requiem for a Beast* is typical of the to and fro narrative movement of any labyrinthine narrative leading to an eventual slide into narrative dystopia, Ottley has used this pattern of the Minotaur-labyrinth configuration of plot and subtext to comment on the lack of the overall Australian political and social will to acknowledge the present indigenous claims and rights to land ownership and discrimination. The only space they have been granted occupancy are at the remote special and social margins. Thus *Requiem for a Beast* typifies Cohen's contention that in monster narratives such exiles are framed as '…monstrous children. Hidden away in the remote recesses of our minds.'[49] However, just as the Minotaur in Ottley's text always returns, so do the monsters we exile. It is these monsters that fully reveal the social condition that forced them into being the marginalized. However, as Deardorf and Cohen believe they posses a sacred or spiritual knowledge about the human condition, 'asking us to re-evaluate our cultural assumptions about race, gender, sexuality, our perceptions of gender, our perceptions of difference, our tolerance towards its expression. They ask why we created them.'[50] Unless this question is answered the fragility and desertification of the desert environment painted in Ottley's text will be reflected in the urban social plane of Australiana.

The switching frames of section three ending in the raging Minotaur are continued on in the final section, 'Pie Jesu,' however, in this final narrative the young jackeroo awakes to find himself wounded and bleeding having been unconscious for some time. As he turns he realizes that bull is immobilized because of a broken pelvis, but the boy also senses the Brahmin has been watching over him. Through his pain and blood he realizes that he must kill the bull to protect it from a slow agonizing death and attack from predators. Asking for its forgiveness he pulls the beast's head back, and as it roars he slits its throat. He then waits for it to turn cold, and knowing he is lost in the dark and the incessant rain he walks away in peace.

The final pages of the narrative end in a mythic return with both the young stockman's rescue by another lost 'bushie' in parallel with the emblems of a coming monsoonal rain. While there is a remembering of the white boy's story and the need to tell the truth about how his father killed an Aboriginal child, the indigenous narrative remains hidden in the motif of the need for cleansing rain 'that will allow the land and people to grow again.'[51]

Thus *Requiem for a Beast* ends on a somewhat ambivalent note. *Requiem for a Beast* appears to be stating that unless reconciliation occurs in Australia a monster will arise and fill the existing voids, emptying the large open spaces of political entrapment and eradicating the constant fear of post-colonial domination of the land and all its peoples. The dystopian labyrinth of old could return.

> It is remarkable that in our age, when the idea of the Fates unwinding the thread of our destiny seems old fashioned and makes us smile, the labyrinth is still the linked to the problem of the meaning of our existence and even haunts our consciousness with renewed vigour as the symbol of a quest that has become even more obscure.[52]

Notes

[1] G. Huggan, *Australian Literature: Postcolonialism, Racism and Transnationalism*, Oxford University Press, Oxford, 2007, p. ix.

[2] P. Fitzsimmons, 'A Rebirth of Myth and Monster', *Myth and Symbol*, Vol. 2, 2008, p. 52.

[3] S. Broadhurst, *Liminal Acts: A Critical Overview of Contemporary Performance and Theory*, Cassell, New York, 2009, p. 1.
[4] D. Williams, *Deformed Discourse: The Function of the Monster in Medieval thought and Literature*, McGill-Queen's University Press, Montreal, 1996, p. 235.
[5] J. Cohen, 'Monster Theory: Seven Theses', *Monster Theory: Reading Culture*, J. Cohen (ed), University of Minnesota Press, Minneapolis, 1996, p. 6.
[6] Williams, op. cit., p. 4.
[7] J. Hoorn, *Australian Pastoral: The Making of a White Landscape*, Fremantle Press, Fremantle, 2007, p. 195.
[8] H. Scutter, *Displaced Fictions*, Melbourne University Press, Melbourne, 1999, p. 46.
[9] D. Deardorrf, *The Other Within: The Genius of Deformity in Myth, Culture and Psyche*, Whitecloud, Ashland, 2004, p. 12.
[10] J. Rose, *The Case of Peter Pan or the Impossibility of Children's Fiction*, University of Philadelphia Press, Philadelphia, 1993. p. 118.
[11] Broadhurst, op. cit., p. 23.
[12] G. Steiner, *Heidegger*, Harvest Press, Sussex, 1978, p. 195.
[13] Deardorrf, op. cit., p. 8.
[14] Scutter, op. cit., p. 46.
[15] D. Gilmore, *Monsters: Evil Beings, Mythical Beasts and All Manner of Imaginary Terrors*, University of Philadelphia Press, Philadelphia, 2003, p. 172.
[16] P. Conty, *The Genesis and Geometry of the Labyrinth*, Inner Traditions, Rochester, 2002, p. 54.
[17] P. Fitzsimmons, op. cit., p. 52.
[18] L. Nieme & E. Ellis, *Inviting the Wolf In: Thinking about Difficult Stories*, August House, Little Rock, 2001, p. 10.
[19] W. Stanner, *White Man Got No Dreaming, Essays 1938-78*, ANU Press, Canberra, 1979, p. 332.
[20] M. Warner, *Phantasmagoria*, Oxford University Press, Oxford, 2006, p. 258.
[21] R. Johnson, 'The Monster of Grim Prospects', *The Inner Journey: Myth, Psyche and Spirit*, M. Heynemann (ed), Morning Light, Sandpoint, 2008, pp. 247-254.
[22] Cohen, op. cit., p. 11.
[23] M. Warner, *Managing Monsters: Six Myths of Our Time - The Reith Lectures*, Vintage, London, 1996, p. 18.
[24] G. Genette, *Introduction to the Architext*, University of California, Berkeley, Berkeley, 1992, p. 53.
[25] Genette, op cit., p. 42.
[26] M. Ottley, *Requiem for a Beast*, Lothian, Melbourne, 2008, p. 29.
[27] E. Barber & P. Barber, *When They Severed Earth From Sky: How the Human Mind Shapes Myth*, Princeton University Press, Princeton, 2004, p. 114.
[28] Ottley, op. cit., p. 29.

[29] Ottley, op. cit., p. 9.
[30] J. Campbell, *Primitive Mythology*, Condor, New York, 2000, p. 65.
[31] Williams, op. cit., p. 227.
[32] T. Beale, *Religion and its Monsters*, Routledge, New York, 2002. p. 90.
[33] Warner, op. cit., p. 21.
[34] M. Shelton, 'Primitive Self: Colonial Impulses in Michel Leiris's L'Afrique fantome', *Prehistories of the Future: The Primitivist Project and the Culture of the Modern*, E. Barkan & R. Bush (eds), Stanford University Press, Stanford. 1995, p. 327.
[35] T. Beal, 'Our Monsters, Ourselves', *The Chronicle of Higher Education*, Vol. 48, no. 9, 2001, pp. 18-31.
[36] Warner, op. cit., p. 20.
[37] M. Ubel, 'Unthinking the Monster: Twentieth-Century Response to Saracen Alterity', *Monster Theory: Reading Culture*, J. Cohen (ed), University of Minnesota Press, Minneapolis, 1996, p. 265.
[38] Conty, op. cit., p. 55.
[39] Ottley, op. cit., p. 21.
[40] Ibid., p. 32.
[41] Scutter, op. cit., p. 243.
[42] Ottley, op. cit., p. 43.
[43] Ibid., p. 45.
[44] Ibid., p. 45.
[45] D. Gilmore, op. cit., 172.
[46] Ottley, op. cit., p. 49.
[47] Ibid., p. 47.
[48] M. Eliade, *The Myth of the Eternal Return*, 2nd ed, Princeton University Press, Princeton, NJ., 2005, p. 9.
[49] Cohen, op. cit., p. 20.
[50] Ibid., p. 20.
[51] Ottley, op. cit., p. 81
[52] Conty, op. cit., p. 8.

Bibliography

Angerer, M., 'Space Does not Matter: On Cyber and Other Bodies'. *European Journal of Cultural Studies*. Vol. 21, 1999, pp. 209-229.

Anstey, M. & Bull, G., *Reading the Visual*. Harcourt, Sydney, 2000.

Anzieu, D., *Das Haut Ich-The Skin Ego*. Surhkamp, Frankfurt, 1992.

Barber, E. & Barber, P., *When They Severed Earth From Sky: How the Human Mind Shapes Myth*. Princeton University Press, Princeton, NJ, 2004.

Beal, T., 'Our Monsters, Ourselves'. *The Chronicle of Higher Education*. Vol. 48, no. 9, 2001, pp. 18-31.

——, *Religion and its Monsters*. Routledge, New York, 2002.

Broadhurst, S., *Liminal Acts: A Critical Overview of Contemporary Performance and Theory*. Cassell, New York, 2009.

Campbell, J., *Primitive Mythology*. Condor, New York, 2000.

Cohen, J., 'Monster Theory: Seven Theses'. *Monster Theory: Reading Culture*. Cohen, J. (ed), University of Minnesota Press, Minneapolis, 1996, pp. 3-25.

Conty, P., *The Genesis and Geometry of the Labyrinth*. Inner Traditions, Rochester, 2002.

Deardorrf, D., *The Other Within: The Genius of Deformity in Myth, Culture and Psyche*. Whitecloud, Ashland, 2004.

Eliade, M., *The Myth of the Eternal Return*. 2nd ed, Princeton University Press, Princeton, 2005.

Fitzsimmons, P., 'A Rebirth of Myth and Monster'. *Myth and Symbol*. Vol. 2, 2008, pp. 49-56.

Genette, G., *Introduction to the Architext*. University of California Press, Berkeley, 1992.

Gilmore, D., *Monsters: Evil Beings, Mythical Beasts and All Manner of Imaginary Terrors*. University of Philadelphia Press, Philadelphia, 2003.

Grosz, E., *Space, Time and Perversion*. Power Publications, New York, 1995.

Johnson, R., 'The Monster of Grim Prospects'. *The Inner Journey: Myth, Psyche and Spirit*. Heynemann, M. (ed), Sandpoint, ID, Morning Light, 2008.

Hoorn, J., *Australian Pastoral: The Making of a White Landscape*. Fremantle Press, Fremantle, 2007.

Huggan, G., *Australian Literature: Postcolonialism, Racism and Transnationalism*. Oxford University Press, Oxford, 2007.

Nieme, L. & Ellis, E., *Inviting the Wolf In: Thinking about Difficult Stories*. August House, Little Rock, 2001.

Ottley, M., *Requiem for a Beast*. Lothian, Melbourne, 2008.

Rose, J., *The Case of Peter Pan or the Impossibility of Children's Fiction*. University of Philadelphia Press, Philadelphia, 1993.

Scutter, H., *Displaced Fictions*. Melbourne University Press, Melbourne, 1999.

Shelton, M., 'Primitive Self: Colonial Impulses in Michel Leiris's L'Afrique fantome'. *Prehistories of the Future: The Primitivist Project and the Culture of the Modern*. Barkan, E. & Bush, R. (eds), Stanford University Press, Stanford, 1995.

Stanner, W., *White Man Got No Dreaming, Essays 1938-78*. ANU Press, Canberra, 1979.

Steiner, G., *Heidegger*. Harvest Press, Sussex, 1978.

Ubel, M,. 'Unthinking the Monster: Twentieth Century Response to Saracen Alterity'. *Monster Theory: Reading Culture*. Cohen, J. (ed), University of Minnesota Press, Minneapolis, 1996.

Vanderbeck, R. & Deinkley, C., *Children's Geographies*. Routledge, London, 2007.

Warner, M., *Managing Monsters: Six Myths of Our Time - The Reith Lectures*. Vintage, London, 1996.

——, *Phantasmagoria*. Oxford University Press, Oxford, 2006.

Williams, D., *Deformed Discourse: The Function of the Monster in Medieval Thought and Literature*. McGill-Queen's University Press, Montreal, 1996.

Barbarians at the Gate in Tom Clancy's *Ghost Recon: Advanced Warfighter* Series

Tracy Crowe Morey

Abstract
Game theorists have proposed that a computer game is not simply a text to be read but an experience to be had. In locating popular computer games as important cultural texts, the following chapter proposes to consider the relationship between gameplay and representation in Tom Clancy's *Ghost Recon: Advanced Warfighter* Series (*GRAW* and *GRAW2*) with respect to ideological notions of deviance and conformity manifested within a specific political and socio-cultural context of the U.S./Mexico border. Banned in some states in Mexico for its nefarious depiction of the Mexican rebel, *GRAW* is a military computer game that boasts an impressive ludic play from the standpoint of multiplayer agency. The modern infantry combat computer game places the player in the role of U.S. army Captain and his Special Forces Group south of the border in Mexico whose mission is to quell the potential threat of civil war about to spill over onto U.S. soil. Sharing with the American western genre of the first half of the twentieth century, the players must ride out to achieve glory (and accumulate wins) in the midst of violent contending forces on the border. The enemy in the game, stereotypically depicted as the vicious *bandido* represents the incontrovertible example of America's foreign bugaboos. For the purposes of the following chapter, I am interested in the tests faced by the players of the game, which manifest particular xenophobic fear of the depraved other and align the game with challenges of legitimacy and conformity. The military combat computer game revisits questions of civilization and barbarism worked out in the liminal spaces/frontiers in game play. The game's textual and performative reliance on notions of race and ideology will be argued as relevant to current political and social realities between the United States and Latin America.

Key Words: Tom Clancy, *Ghost Recon*, U.S./Mexico border, stereotypes in the media, and the Mexican *bandido*.

*****

Intel says the enemy may be in possession of some nasty technology. Your orders are to punch a hole through the enemy lines to Juarez and neutralize all possible dirty bombs.[1]

Of this unrest I myself saw nothing. In private I observed that once in every generation, without fail, there is an episode of hysteria about the barbarians.[2]

For at least the past decade, game theorists have been interested in the narrative or representational dynamics of computer games as well as the performance or gameplay context. It is agreed that video games are not simply texts to be observed but incorporate a ludic mode of experience and participation unlike that of previous media engagements between, for example, reader and novel or viewer and film. The player's involvement in the compositional aspects of narrative in which he/she may be given the choice to plot out character and/or setting indicates that computer games go beyond traditional modes of storytelling. Narrative elements concerning race, gender, or class, to name a few, and how these are represented at the level of game play also prove to be valuable insights into the ideologies and suppositions of software companies, developers, and/or gaming audiences. In the most recent years, game theorists have begun to consider videogames as important cultural texts that take into account both the formal elements of narrative as well as the structural and rule-based aspects of gameplay. Frans Mäyrä's theoretical introduction to games in culture defines the methodological contours of game studies distinguishing between *structural gameplay analysis* as 'paying special attention to how game rules and interactions with game objects and other players are structured'[3] and *thematic analysis* which 'highlights the experience of players sensitive to the symbols and messages conveyed by the game's operation as a cultural medium.'[4] Working within these theoretical parameters, the following chapter explores the relationship between gameplay and representation in Tom Clancy's *Ghost Recon: Advanced Warfighter* series (*GRAW* and *GRAW2*) with respect to ideological notions of deviance manifested within a specific socio-cultural context of the U.S./Mexico border. I argue that the *GRAW* series dehumanizes America's newest foreign bugaboo based on earlier stereotypes perpetuated at the border, especially that of the clichéd Mexican *bandido*. In addition, I demonstrate the techniques by which the game naturalizes hegemonic ideologies of civilization and barbarism at the level of gameplay. Ultimately, I contend that the game's textual representation and game strategy manifest spectres of terror lurking south of the border and as a result align the game with socio-cultural fears regarding America's newest threat to national borders and security.

The border shared by Mexico and the United States has forever been a site of exchange, crossings, and conflict. Since the re-bordering of territories in 1848 between Mexico and the United States through to the events of the Mexican Revolution spilling out over its boundaries, American media has depicted the region as a frontier divide between order and democracy and chaos and barbarism. In early Hollywood films, during the events of the drawn out Mexican Revolution, the crossing of the Rio Grande became 'a place of exile for all sorts of North American ruffians fleeing from the law of their own country.'[5] Mexico had always conjured images of 'bandits, arbitrary crimes and perpetrators who go unpunished.'[6] Border towns such as Tijuana and Ciudad Juárez were portrayed by the American media as sites of moral corruption as well as political and social lawlessness, especially during Prohibition and thereafter. Édgar Cota-Torres points out that

> illicit activities in the United States took place on the other side of the border on a grand scale, and the border, Tijuana especially, became the escape valve for American Puritanism.[7]

Nowadays, Tijuana has become the postcard picture of the popular and cheap tourist outpost for gambling, drugs, and illicit sex visible on its main street, Avenida Revolución. The Mexican border town in the American imaginary is replete with poverty, disease, moral inferiority, endemic corruption, and most prominently threatens the American side of the border with illegal immigration and drug trafficking into the United States. An increase in violence occurring near the U.S. border due to Mexico's drug wars has been the most current preoccupation for both government and media channels and has resulted in the continued support of a militarization of the border and the release of a tourist alert for travellers crossing over into Mexico by the United States Department of State.[8] Other media channels include U.S. border town newspapers where daily claims of drug warfare and violence are common. One such editorial captured the increase in violence with a recent title, 'Mexico Drug War is Drenched in Blood' and when the journalist details that 'headless bodies in Tijuana, kidnapped children in Phoenix, and shootouts on the streets of Vancouver' are the 'unwanted by-products of progress in the Mexican drug war,'[9] it is not hard to miss the sarcasm and perhaps frustration of Mexico's stereotypical latency in cleaning up its internal corruption and violence.

The frenzy of borderland security and defence also took on a dramatic and urgent priority with U.S. policy makers since the 9/11 attack on America. As Peter Andreas signals,

> security is back with a vengeance. Yet, this time, the primary security threat is not the traditional concern of intense military conflict, but rather terrorism, a distinct form of organized violence orchestrated primarily by non-state actors.[10]

Mass media and popular fiction and entertainment have capitalized on the panic-stricken American distrustful of his own neighbour.[11] In *GRAW* and especially *GRAW2* there is a corresponding emergence of U.S. border fears post-9/11. Most prominently, the border town of Ciudad Juárez fits into the background of *GRAW2*'s simulation of chaos and violence at the borderlands. The geographic locales throughout the game are marked by border fences and bridges that appear to lack adequate defences with the violence finally spilling out onto U.S soil in El Paso, Texas. Friendly tourist-welcoming signs such as 'Feliz viaje' ('Nice Trip') and 'Gracias por su visita' ('Thank You for Your Visit') are bypassed very quickly and transform into urban locales of deserted cantina and curio shops alongside abandoned vehicles and crushed garbage of shanty towns. While game designers and marketers are advised that 'players want reality and authenticity'[12] for the backdrop of a game story that mimics real-world settings, the objects depicted in the cityscapes of Tom Clancy's *GRAW* series reflect the negative fears and alarm of widespread violence and subsequent descent of the border region.

The premise of *GRAW* and *GRAW2* involves an élite team of futuristic soldiers who must quell a civil war raging in Mexico before its violence spills out onto U.S. soil. The videogame publisher and developer Ubisoft Entertainment based the *GRAW* series on Tom Clancy's legacy of military novels, *Red October*, *Red Storm Rising*, *The Cardinal of the Kremlin*, and *Patriot Games*. *Patriot Games* was endorsed by U.S. Defence and State Department and together with his other works

> stand out as strategic simulations. Jammed with technical detail and seductive ordinance, devoid of recognizably human characters, and obliquely linked to historical events, they have become the perfect free-floating intertext for saving the reality principle of the national security state: namely that the sovereign state's boundaries, like those between fiction and fact, simulation and reality, can once again be made impermeable to the Soviet threat, the terrorist attack, and even the launch of ICBMs.[13]

As an adaptation of the novelistic military genre, *GRAW* and *GRAW2* are futuristic counter-terrorist videogames set in the years 2013 and 2014 when the newly constructed border wall between the United States and Mexico comes under threat from rebel forces. The video gamer takes on the role of a futuristic and elite soldier of a covert Ghost squad - whose acronym stands for Global Humanitarian Operation and Special Tactics - but whose name also suggests stealth and cunning the gamer must adapt to in the netherworld south of the border. The clandestine operation of Captain Scott Mitchell and his Ghost squad begins in Mexico City where a summit involving the President of the United States (Ballantine), the Canadian Prime Minister (unnamed), and the President of Mexico (Ruiz-Peña) are to sign the North American Joint Security Agreement (NAJSA), a historic new policy designed to share the policing responsibilities along the borders of these three countries. The game begins just after the ghost soldiers are informed of the coup d'état that has taken place on the eve of the new treaty by Mexican Nationalists against the Security Agreement. The Ghosts also learn that the Prime Minister has been assassinated and that the Vice-President of Mexico has requested American military support in the capital city. In *GRAW2* the soldiers having just left Mexico City are ordered to the border town of Ciudad Juárez to work with the Mexican loyalist army in cleaning up the remaining rebels after they learn that missing weapons of mass destruction are heading toward the U.S. border. As the official game guide details, the country has fallen into a 'full-scale civil war that threatens to spread its violence north into the U.S.'[14] The mission entails the ghosts secure the U.S. borders by hunting down and killing the rebel insurgents along with destroying the nuke and missile launchers thereby 'prevent[ing] the mercenaries from launching a nuclear weapon at the United States, and sav[ing] millions of citizens.'[15]

According to Juárez newspaper, *El diario*, the Governor of the State of Chihuahua, José Reyes Baeza Terrazas ordered the confiscation of all copies on sale of Ubisoft's *GRAW2*. As stated in the report, government officials consider the game an insult to the entire country for portraying poor values and violence on the border towns.[16] The filmmaking industry in Hollywood received similar protests in the 1920s regarding its nefarious depiction of America's so-called good neighbour. However, as Edward Buscombe argues, 'Hollywood films, especially Westerns, remained unable to conceive of any Mexican character other than malevolent bandits or their peasant victims.'[17] Such critiques against American media and entertainment are warranted given the perpetuation of viewing Latin America in uncivilized and unsophisticated terms especially when compared to developed first world nations. The purely fantastical image of the 'savage' or 'barbarian' dating back to antiquity's 'monstrous races' and travelling to the New World often became expressions of 'otherness' through the widespread use of animal categories such as the dog-headed cannibal or the wild man, culturally inferior due to his gibberish language and animal-like tail.[18] Common stereotypes of the Mexican today include expressions such as 'dog,' 'half-breed,' 'locust,' and 'cockroach,'[19] all of which underline the association of the Mexican - especially the Mexican American or the illegal Mexican immigrant - with bestial and pestilent properties; such stereotypes also underscore the idea that the U.S. views their southern neighbours as pesky invaders. During the nineteenth and twentieth centuries, 'the image of the Mexican as a barbarian, unable to solve his own problems'[20] becomes foremost in the figure of the social bandit or outlaw and most recently in the figure of the narcotrafficker. At the beginning of the twentieth century during Mexico's revolutionary period, its most infamous *bandido*, Pancho Villa quickly became known for his incursions across the U.S./Mexico border.[21] Villa is the epitome of the revolutionary macho; Alfredo Mirande, citing Mexican psychologist Anciento Aramoni[22] writes of Mexican machismo as an exhibition of 'narcissism, petulance, aggressiveness, intense destructiveness, considerable hatred of superiors (not just in the hierarchical sense), profound disdain and fear of the woman.'[23] The Mexican's penchant for violence and rebellion against the state was often viewed from U.S. interventionists as non-compliance and a threat to the neo-liberal policies of both the Mexican and U.S. governments. Just a century earlier, the Mexican outlaw rendered the country 'a dangerous and disorderly place.'[24] In nineteenth-century Mexico it is the savage and often extraordinary violent nature of the bandits that terrify and trouble the English travellers.[25] In some nineteenth-century travelogues, Anglo-Saxon foreign officials and diplomats who came to Mexico after 1821 to evaluate the new republic refer to the bandit as monstrously dangerous since he portrayed 'a latter-day Hannibal whose depredation would endanger the entire country.'[26] By the twentieth century, the typical portrayal of the Mexican rebel was

> irresponsible, treacherous, vengeful and prey to an uncontrolled sexuality. He is also represented physically in a specific way: his poncho and wide sombrero become a kind of uniform added to his dark skin and wide moustache.[27]

In his analysis of the classic Hollywood Western, *The Magnificent Seven*, Buscombe reiterates that 'In early cinema a Mexican was almost invariably a villain, cowardly, treacherous and lascivious, explicitly vilified as a greaser.'[28] Mark Cronlund Anderson traces the racial discrimination of the Mexican in the American media as a result of Mexico's Hispanic and Indian *mestizaje:*

> Since Mexico achieved independence from Spain in the early 1820s, Mexicans have been portrayed in the United States as the products of blended Spanish and Indian heritage - as *mestizo*, in short. This Hispanic-Indian admixture has been twisted in the United States into a creature that adds up to less than the sum of its half-breed parts. While the Hispanic was held to be racially and culturally superior to the lowly Indian, Mexicans were viewed as 'mongrels' who represented the worst and most depraved extremes of both races and cultures.[29]

Regarding Mexico's revolutionary leaders, Anderson points out that the common themes that proliferated in the American press were images of moral decrepitude, innate violence, and infantile backwardness.[30]

A similar discourse appears in nineteenth-century Latin America among the newly formed governments of the independence movements. Latin American élites envisioned a modernized and progressive nation-state with no place for a criminalized *mestizo* vagrant or peasant rebel with ties to the barbaric rural backlands. This barbarian was conceived to be unsophisticated and destructive of the modernizing endeavours of the élite creole leaders. For these state élites, 'The enemy of 'la patria' was not perceived as the nation next door, but as those in the population who threatened the social and economic status quo.'[31] Juan Pablo Dabove demonstrates that the bandit along with the Indian and the runaway slave were considered the demonic and adversarial forces in the liberal discourses of the early nineteenth century.[32] Since these 'undesirables' were the forces that threatened the governability of the newly formed republics, Latin American élites defined the *bandido* in nonhuman terms to justify the eradication of such barbaric forces from the nation-state. Latin America's monsters - ranging anywhere from bloodthirsty bandits to disease-ridden immigrants and harpy-like black females - 'are not the children of a bizarre 'Latin' imagination but urgent political responses to real conflicts.'[33]

The nineteenth-century civilization/barbarism dichotomy was employed at the service of liberal initiatives under the newly formed Latin American governments. This same discourse on barbarism and civilization seems to have made a startling return since the events of 9/11. The now famous presidential speech to congress on 8 November 2001 when the President declared that 'We wage a war to save civilization itself'[34] was made in reference to Al Qaeda and their attacks on America on 11 September, 2001. However, as Anna M. Agathangelou and L.H.M. Ling point out, the political discourse on terror is 'a return to old-fashioned colonialism: that is, (Western, Christian) civilisational discipline against all 'terror' ... the semantic shift from 'terrorism' to 'terror' offers one small indication of this change from a political to cultural agenda.'[35] In terms of barbarism re-imagined in the twenty-first century we are not too far from the Latin American nineteenth-century rhetoric of civilization and barbarism first phrased by Argentine President, Domingo Faustino Sarmiento. In his documentation of Sarmiento's mediations on civilization and barbarism, Dabove comments that Sarmiento saw bandits as 'enemies of humankind and to kill them on the spot, without due process.'[36] Now the conflict concerns global terrorists, a nasty creature that fits too perfectly into the nineteenth-century mould of the demonic force of banditry, out to destroy humanity as a race. The Americas post-9/11 are returning to the epic battle between the forces of good and evil where the rebel of Latin America is in need of the civilizing processes of the Americans - the dark rogue must either submit to neo-liberalist rule or face extermination.

In the Clancy video games American soldiers must deal with the consequences of Mexican insurrections and defeat a horrific and colossal threat against the American people and civilization in general. Such victimization requiring foreign intervention in the name of freedom is not a new concept depicted on the American screen. Noël Carroll's discussion of the central ideological function of the classic Hollywood film as a justification for American foreign policy easily translates over to the rhetoric posited in the Clancy video game entailing U.S. intervention south of the border in the name of freedom and security.

> Quite clearly, from a political point of view these films are about an opposition to oppression and the support of social liberation. Underlying these films is the presupposition of a principle that the justification of professional prowess rests in its service for freedom and against tyranny. At the same time, there is a pretty

clear-cut association of the professionals in these films with the military. They either have military backgrounds (Ben Trane, Rico Fardan, Bill Dolworth), or they wear military regalia (Rico Fardan, the Wild Bunch), or they exhibit military behaviour (the *Magnificent Seven* training the peasants). Putting this together with the previous principle, we see that these films rest on the view that the justification of the military is its promotion of freedom.[37]

In the original *GRAW* the ghost soldiers must save the Presidents of the United States and Mexico from the rebel insurgents - inconsequentially the Canadian Prime Minister is already assassinated before the game even begins. These well-trained ghost soldiers are representative of discipline, daring and virility and, similar to the earlier Hollywood Western films, it is the American who is the only one 'capable of bringing peace, order, justice and progress to a country like Mexico.'[38] Given that the primary obstacle in the videogame faced by the main characters concerns the defeat of Mexican villains and the subsequent rescue of the American President, the theme of the computer game pertains to the fate of Western civilization over the barbaric forces of unbridled evil. In earlier Hollywood Western films it was often the damsel in distress - the Mexican *señorita* - who must be rescued.

In *The Mexican's Faith* a labourer attempts to rape the rancher's wife, in *Mexico* a Mexican federal soldier assaults Villa's wife, while in *Lieutenant Danny USA* it is only the intervention of an American lieutenant that saves the Mexican girl from violation by a group of Mexican bandits.[39]

Director and producer Deedee Halleck demonstrates the American stereotype of Latin America in her documentary *Gringo en mañanaland*, a montage of several hundred clips showcasing U.S. film portrayals of Latin America from 1910-1960. The essential plot recapitulates a romance version of paradise found, lost, and recovered in which American heroes quell Latin American problems with civil war and banditry and leave once these southern neighbours have been taught courtesy, civility, and U.S. free enterprise. In the *GRAW* series the American soldiers are no longer saving the beautiful Mexican damsel but the heads of democratic states.

Mexico, on the other hand, is in the denigrated position of the Other representing everything the United States does not: barbarism versus civilization, lawlessness versus order, degeneration versus progress, murder versus innocence. In *GRAW2* the Mexican *bandido* has returned as both rebel and loyalist to the American political agenda. However, what makes this game different from earlier stereotypes of the Mexican south of the border, is that the Mexican is no longer outfitted in the typical poncho and sombrero nor is he carrying primitive weapons; he is no longer racially marked by the colour of his skin; in fact, he looks similar to the Mexican soldier loyal to the Mexican army and with whom the Ghosts must join forces. This inability to detect the enemy is even more terrifying to those societies who fear they are under attack for 'the enemy who looks just like us, talks like us, and is just like us' as Philip Cole argues, 'is one of the traditional guises of the Devil.'[40] The gaming experience produced from such enemies across the border is what generates an imaginary evil created within a particular socio-cultural context. The Mexican *bandido* now manifests a spectral image of global terror and speaks to the fear and panic of Americans regarding security at their borders. The first *GRAW* was about murderous envy of innocent victims and irrational barbarity - the Mexican bandit killed even his own for no apparent reason. The enemy rebel also becomes the feared monster who has power to assassinate the Canadian Prime Minster taking on superpowers of extraordinary capability, strength and power in plots of ultimate destruction. The kidnapping and assassination of the Prime Minister serves as an example of the power of a global evil and what could happen if unchecked and ignored. In *GRAW2* the American citizen now becomes the enemy's prey; the barbarian is now knocking down the gates of civilization with no other goal in mind but annihilation. What becomes even more disturbing is the rebel's ability to pass the border undetected, appearing to be a part of humanity but secretly scheming its destruction.

Due to such constructions of the degeneracy of the Mexican rebel, the need for surveillance and discipline naturally follow in the game. *GRAW2* is about directing the player to protect one's own borders watching and surveying enemies post-9/11. With respect to the gaming industry and the military post-9/11, Clive Thompson comments that 'Not only did the military seek out game designers, but after 9/11 there were instances of game designers reaching out to the military to offer their services.'[41] As a first-person shooter game, *GRAW* and *GRAW2* form part of a larger gaming industry where certain real-time, military strategy and simulation computer games have been utilized by the U.S. military. The 'military-entertainment complex' coined by mainstream commentator J.C. Herz acknowledged the close relationship between the gaming industry and military research back in the 1990s and has since been stepped up post-9/11. A number of different first-person shooter and real-time strategy military games have crossed over from commercial to military appropriation and adaptation: *Full Spectrum Warrior* (Pandemic, 2004) and *America's Army: Operations* (U.S. Army/Department of Defence, 2002) have provided the U.S. military with certain training and recruitment tools. *Full Spectrum Warrior*, for example,

> was created by the Institute for Creative Technologies, with the help from the Army, to teach soldiers realistic strategies for

surviving what the armed forces call 'military operations in urban terrain.'[42]

The realism of urban-warfare scenarios played out on a global level and in real time potentially allows for soldiers around the world, whether they are new recruits or long-time officers, to train with one another.[43] Not to mention that many of the younger soldiers spend their downtime playing, for example, Xbox military strategy games such as *Call of Duty* (Activision, 2003) or *Gears of War* (Epic, 2006).[44] The connection between military initiatives and entertainment is also demonstrated in the use of combat videogames for socio-cultural propaganda. For example, the computer game image posted on the Minuteman Project website of the United States Department of State tourist advisory represented a biased version of the state advisory regarding the violence that tourists may expect if they cross the border into Mexico. The computer game scenario portrayed the danger of the borderland, as the Minutemen Project would have their readers believe, as a literal war zone sensationalized by the images from computer games such as *Gears of War* and *GRAW* and *GRAW2*.

I would argue that military-entertainment crossover games such as the *GRAW* series placate to the fear-mongering of potential attacks and conflict at the border. From a ludic mode of experience, the player is entirely restricted and bound to the rules of game play regarding choices of mission assignments and objectives. The player can at times execute in any order the targets and mission goals, however these objectives remain unchanged. In realistic, military video games

> the player is presented with an objective, and then guided and instructed by the game in how best to achieve this objective using the tools at his or her disposal. To complete the game, the player must learn and internalize these rules of warfare and therefore learn how to win wars according to the logic of the game. The rules of the game instruct the player in how the game should be played; it is from this instruction that the player derives an understanding of the logic of games, but also the logic of war.[45]

In *GRAW* and *GRAW2* the player is trained at the outset to achieve the game objectives through the use of surveillance technology; the advantage of this technology is at its best when played in collaboration with others as multi-player; for the player interested in micromanagement and reaction time challenges,[46] the squad system in the *GRAW* series allows the player to manage the resources and characters through simulated, real-time satellite images on the cross-com. The key to mission success is to know how to use the technology, how to move, and how to work best together. The satellite communications system or the cross-com is the most talked about and attractive aspect of the *GRAW* series, as the player must reach his/her objectives through the use of the near god-like view for detection of the position of enemy soldiers. In multi-player scenarios, one gamer uses the crosscom to ascertain the position of rebel insurgents. His teammate then places himself/herself strategically for quick kills without harming any other of the squad members. As long as the satellite system has the targets in sight the god-like view also detects for the player the position of the loyal soldiers as well as the enemies demonstrated by either a blue or red diamond-shaped reticule. This allows the gamer precision and the ability to shoot at the right target. In perfecting this technological means to detect and target the enemy, game play becomes much more controlled and organized.

The surveillance techniques in *GRAW* and *GRAW2* support the type of xenophobic fear-mongering that has been carried out recently at the border due to the threat of terror and drug-related violence. As Edward Williams and Anne Johnson point out, in 2007 under projects financed by the Secure Fence Act of 2006, Sasabe, Arizona saw the construction of a 'virtual barrier decorated with nine nearly 100-foot-tall towers and a bewildering array of other sky-wars wizardry calculated to look through the darkness and around corners.'[47] The star war devices used to detect the presence of illegal border crossers from Mexico have the feel of the military technology at the command of the video gamer. The capabilities of policing and surveillance available to both the border patrols post-9/11 and the video player reflect a wider discourse of power and discipline as explored by Michel Foucault in *Discipline and Punish: The Birth of the Prison*. In his chapter on the 'Panopticon,' Foucault describes the measures taken in one seventeenth-century plague-stricken town as the answer to the perfectly governed city. Surveillance and hierarchy maintain this ideal state through what Foucault refers to as a 'double mode; that of binary division and branding (mad/sane; dangerous/harmless; normal/abnormal).'[48] The hierarchy of a society can only be maintained through surveillance by the type of architectural construction found in Bentham's Panopticon: 'The panoptic mechanism arranges spatial unities that make it possible to see constantly and to recognize immediately.'[49] It is the outcome of such visibility that becomes the mechanism of control and discipline for as Foucault explains, 'the major effect of the Panopticon: to induce in the inmate a state of conscious and permanent visibility that assured the automatic functioning of power.'[50] That is to say, the consequence of surveillance from the tower is the very means of disciplinary power: 'So to arrange things that the surveillance is permanent in its effects, even if it is discontinuous in its action; that the perfection of power should tend to render its actual action unnecessary.'[51]

While Foucault speaks about the constant visibility of the Panopticon and the effects this visibility has on the observed and therefore docile body, I am interested in the effects of such mechanisms on the observer. Surveillance of the terrorist body is the very essence of knowledge and power in the United States post-9/11.

The *GRAW* videogames perform such mechanisms of control at the level of game play. The player's viewpoint is always on the opponent in the face of imminent terrorist attack and dismantling of the U.S. security systems. Through the process of a user-friendly interface, the player is led to see the cross-com/gaze as the most attractive application of *GRAW* and *GRAW2*. The real-time satellite serves the logistics of game play such that when forced to be without such targeting gear the player feels most vulnerable. Gamers have commented that this is the most intense part of the game in *GRAW2* in addition to Mexican enemies incorporating more gripping fighting as they play a kind of hide-and-seek line of attack which adds a further element of suspense and duress for the gamer.[52] In the rules of the game and the terms of victory - such as the rescue of the kidnapped Presidents in *GRAW* and the capture of the weapons of mass destruction in *GRAW2* - cooperative game play as interactive with the story itself 'is really what allows the story to unfold.'[53] That is, the stories of *GRAW* and *GRAW2* are only revealed when the player navigates through mission controlled directives and stereotypical landscapes. In this digitalized version of America post-9/11, game play is all about the player's totalising gaze on the enemy through organized teamwork and planning while in conjunction with superior, military satellite technology and weaponry. The game's objective at the point of dénouement essentially entails navigation through a virtual environment in which the players of *GRAW* and *GRAW2* are victorious in safeguarding the borders against a demonic threat lurking at the edges of civilization.

In the Tom Clancy *GRAW* video game series the adrenaline rush of game play can be attributed to an imaginary evil lying in wait at the border whose scare tactics include ghostly movements that can go undetected by the players and whose 'barbaric' cruelty entails atrocious acts of assassination and destruction. The earlier stereotype of the *bandido* included an innate evil and violence often demonstrated in stories of rape and murder. However, in this new version of the border town 'badlands', the American fear of its permeable borders are personified in the Mexican insurgent and his wraith-like qualities to move across boundaries with ease. Therefore, the strategies and rules of game play focus on collaborative ability and skill to search and destroy. The hunted now becomes the hunter and, with superior U.S. weaponry and technology at the hands of the video gamer, the panoptical gaze on the savage ruffian south of the border candidly becomes part of the entertainment package of military simulation and strategy. In the end, the destruction of the Mexican bugaboo satisfies the game's programming design and the player's gameplay experience. Ultimately, however, the videogame dramatizes our own fears of imaginary monsters and one wonders if in doing so we do not become monsters or 'Ghosts' ourselves as Sarmiento succinctly intimated regarding the paradox of Latin America's civilizing mission (now dressed as Global Humanitarians) and its own barbarism.[54]

Notes

[1] M. Knight, *Prima Official Game Guide for Ghost Recon: Advanced Warfighter2*, Random House, Roseville, CA, 2007, p. 44.
[2] J.M. Coetzee, *Waiting for the Barbarians*, Penguin, New York, 1980, p. 8.
[3] F. Mäyrä, *An Introduction to Games Studies: Games in Culture*, Sage Publications, Los Angeles, 2008, p. 165.
[4] Ibid., p. 163.
[5] M. de Orellana, 'The Circular Look. In the Incursion of North American Fictional Cinema 1911-1917 into the Mexican Revolution', *Mediating Two Worlds: Cinematic Encounters in the Americas*, J. King, A.M. López & M. Alvarado (eds), British Film Institute, London, 1993, p. 9.
[6] Ibid., p. 9.
[7] E. Cota-Torres, 'Dispelling the Border Myth: Zonkey Writers and the Black Legend', *Border Transits: Literature and Culture across the Line*, A.M. Matazanas (ed), Rodopi, New York, 2007, p. 59.
[8] The United States Department of State's tourist alert for Mexico was released on their website on 20 February, 2009 stating that this alert will expire on 20 August, 2009. The United States Department of State, The Office of Electronic Information, Bureau of Public Affairs, Viewed on 15 April 2009, <http://www.state.gov/>.
[9] T. Carl, 'Mexico Drug War is Drenched in Blood', *Valley Morning Star*, March 2009, Viewed on 13 March 2009, <http://www.valleymorningstar.com/sections/local-news/>.
[10] P. Andreas, 'A Tale of Two Borders: The U.S.-Canada and U.S.-Mexico Lines after 9-11', *The Rebordering of North America. Integration and Exclusion in a New Security Context*, P. Andreas & T.J. Biersteker (eds), Routledge, New York, 2003, p. 19.
[11] Such panic is manifested in the recent establishment of the Minuteman Organization, a National Citizens Neighbourhood Watch based out of Arizona. This group has gained widespread political attention and rapid expansion through its use of web-media resources which monitor news channels and government plans regarding immigration policies and border control.
[12] J. Novak, *Game Development Essentials: An Introduction*, Thomson Delmar Learning, New York, 2005, pp. 124-125.
[13] J. DerDerian, 'The Simulation Syndrome: From War Games to Game Wars', *Social Text*, Vol. 24, 1990, p. 191.
[14] Knight, op. cit., p. 4.
[15] Ibid., p. 118.
[16] T. Surette, 'Mexican Mayor Slams *GRAW2*', *Game Spot*, March 2007, Viewed on 15 April, 2009, <http://www.gamespot.com/ps3/action/graw2/news.html?sid=6167149>.

[17] E. Buscombe, '*The Magnificent Seven*', *Mediating Two Worlds: Cinematic Encounters in the Americas*, J. King, A.M. López & M. Alvarado (eds), British Film Institute, London, 1993, p. 16.

[18] P. Burke, 'Frontiers of the Monstrous: Perceiving National Characters in Early Modern Europe', *Monstrous Bodies/Political Monstrosities in Early Modern Europe*, L. Lunger-Knoppers & J.B. Landes (eds), Cornell University Press, Ithaca, 2004, p. 25.

[19] S.W. Bender, *Greasers and Gringos: Latinos, Law, and the American Imagination*, New York University Press, New York, 2003, pp. 114-153.

[20] Cota-Torres, op. cit., p. 58.

[21] Ibid., p. 58.

[22] A. Aramoni, *Pscioanálisis de la dinámica de un pueblo*, B. Costa-Amic, Mexico, 1965, p. 151.

[23] A. Mirande, *Hombres y machos: Masculinity and Latino Culture*, Westview, Boulder, 1997, p. 41.

[24] C Frazer, *Bandit Nation. A History of Outlaws and Cultural Struggle in Mexico, 1810-1920*, University of Nebraska Press, Lincoln, 2006, p. 69.

[25] Travel narratives from classical antiquity down to the medieval and the early modern periods are fraught with images of the Other as a representation of the unknown and the exotic. Nineteenth-century travelogues of Mexico are no different.

[26] Frazer, op. cit., p. 69.

[27] de Orellana, op. cit., p. 10.

[28] Buscombe, op. cit. p. 16.

[29] M.C. Anderson, *Pancho Villa's Revolution by Headlines*, University of Oklahoma Press, Norman, 2000 p. 120.

[30] Ibid., p. 123.

[31] M.A. Centeno, *Blood and Debt. War and the Nation-State in Latin America*, Pennsylvania State University Press, University Park, 2002, p. 90.

[32] P. Dabove, *Nightmares of the Lettered City: Banditry and Literature in Latin America, 1816-1929*, University of Pittsburgh Press, Pittsburgh, 2007, p. 1.

[33] Ibid, p. 2.

[34] G.W. Bush, 'President Discusses War on Terrorism', *Address to the Nation*, World Congress Centre, Atlanta, GA, 8 November 2001, Viewed on 15 April, 2009, <http://www.whitehouse.gov/news/releases/2001/11/20011108-13.html>.

[35] A. Agathangelou & L.H.M. Ling, 'Power, Borders, Security, Wealth: Lessons of Violence and Desire from September 11', *International Studies Quarterly*, Vol. 48, 2004, p. 520.

[36] Dabove, op. cit., p. 32.

[37] N. Carroll, 'The Professional Western: South of the Border', *Back in the Saddle Again: New Essays on the Western*, E. Buscombe & R.E. Pearson (eds), British Film Institute, London, 1998, p. 60.
[38] de Orellana, op. cit., p. 6.
[39] Ibid., p. 3.
[40] P. Cole, *The Myth of Evil: Demonizing the Enemy*, Edinburgh University Press, Edinburgh, 2006, p. 2.
[41] C. Thompson, 'The Making of an X Box Warrior', *New York Times*, August 2004, Viewed on 15 April, 2006, <http://www.nytimes.com/2004/08/22/magazine/22GAMES.html>.
[42] Ibid., p. 35.
[43] Ibid., p. 36.
[44] Ibid., p. 36.
[45] M. Thomson, 'From Underdog to Overmatch: Computer Games and Military Transformation', *Popular Communication*, Vol. 7, Issue 2, 2009, p. 93.
[46] Novack, op. cit. p. 189-90.
[47] E. Williams & A. Johnson, 'Walls and Fences: Perspectives from Universities and Museums'. *Journal of the Southwest*, Vol. 50, Issue 3, 2008, p. 2.
[48] M. Foucault, *Discipline and Punish: The Birth of the Prison*, trans. A. Sheridan 2nd edn., Vintage Books, New York, 1995, p. 199.
[49] Ibid., p. 200.
[50] Ibid., p. 201.
[51] Ibid., p. 201.
[52] B. Dalupan & J.D. *Morey, Personal Interview*, 22 November, 2008.
[53] Novack, op. cit., p. 177.
[54] A. Dorfman, *Other Septembers, Many Americas: Selected Provocations 1980-2004*, Seven Stories Press, Toronto, 2004, p. 113.

Bibliography

Agathangelou, A. & Ling, L.H.M., 'Power, Borders, Security, Wealth: Lessons of Violence and Desire from September 11'. *International Studies Quarterly*. Vol. 48, 2004, pp. 517-538.

Anderson, M.C., *Pancho Villa's Revolution by Headlines*. University of Oklahoma Press, Norman, 2000.

Andreas, P., 'A Tale of Two Borders: The U.S.-Canada and U.S.-Mexico Lines after 9-11'. *The Rebordering of North America: Integration and Exclusion in a New Security Context*. Andreas, P. & Biersteker, T.J. (eds), Routledge, New York, 2003.

Aramoni, A., *Pscioanálisis de la dinámica de un pueblo*, B. Costa-Amic, Mexico, 1965.

Bender, S.W., *Greasers and Gringos: Latinos, Law, and the American Imagination*. New York University Press, New York, 2003.

Burke, P., 'Frontiers of the Monstrous: Perceiving National Characters in Early Modern Europe'. *Monstrous Bodies/Political Monstrosities in Early Modern Europe*. Lunger-Knoppers, L. & Landes, J.B. (eds), Cornell University Press, Ithaca, 2004.

Buscombe, E., '*The Magnificent Seven*'. *Mediating Two Worlds: Cinematic Encounters in the Americas*. King, J., López, A.M. & Alvarado, M. (eds), British Film Institute, London, 1993.

Bush, G.W., 'President Discusses War on Terrorism'. *Address to the Nation*. World Congress Center, Atlanta, GA, 8 November 2001, Viewed on 15 April 2009, <http://www.whitehouse.gov/news/releases/2001/11/20011108-13.html>.

Carl, T., 'Mexico Drug War is Drenched in Blood'. *Valley Morning Star*. 11 March 2009, Viewed on 13 March 2009, <http://www.valleymorningstar.com/sections/local-news/>.

Carroll, N., 'The Professional Western: South of the Border'. *Back in the Saddle Again: New Essays on the Western*. Buscombe, E. & Pearson, R.E. (eds), British Film Institute, London, 1998.

Centeno, M.A., *Blood and Debt: War and the Nation-State in Latin America*. Pennsylvania State University Press, University Park, 2002.

Coetzee, J.M., *Waiting for the Barbarians*. Penguin, New York, 1980.

Cole, P., *The Myth of Evil. Demonizing the Enemy*. Edinburgh University Press, Edinburgh, 2006.

Cota-Torres, E., 'Dispelling the Border Myth: Zonkey Writers and the Black Legend'. *Border Transits: Literature and Culture across the Line*. Manzanas, A.M. (ed), Rodopi, New York, 2007.

Dabove, P., *Nightmares of the Lettered City: Banditry and Literature in Latin America, 1816-1929*. University of Pittsburgh Press, Pittsburg, 2007.

de Orellana, M., 'The Circular Look: In the Incursion of North American Fictional Cinema 1911-1917 into the Mexican Revolution'. *Mediating Two Worlds: Cinematic Encounters in the Americas*, King, J., López, A.M. & Alvarado, M. (eds), British Film Institute, London, 1993.

DerDerian, J., 'The Simulation Syndrome: From War Games to Game Wars'. *Social Text*. Vol. 24, 1990, pp. 187-192.

Dorfman, A., *Other Septembers, Many Americas: Selected Provocations 1980-2004*. Seven Stories Press, Toronto, 2004.

Foucault, M., *Discipline and Punish: The Birth of the Prison*. trans. Sheridan, A., 2nd ed, Vintage Books, New York, 1995.

Frazer, C., *Bandit Nation: A History of Outlaws and Cultural Struggle in Mexico, 1810-1920*. University of Nebraska Press, Lincoln, 2006.

Halleck, D., *Gringo en Mañanaland*. D. Halleck Productions, 1995.

Herz, J.C., *Joystick Nation: How Video Games Ate Our Quarters, Won Our Hearts, and Rewired Our Minds*. Little Brown, Boston, 1997.

Jim Gilchrist's Minuteman Project. Gilchrist, J. (ed), Viewed on 24 February 2009, <http://minutemanproject.com/>.

Knight, M., *Prima Official Game Guide for Ghost Recon: Advanced Warfighter2*. Random House Inc., Roseville, 2007.

Mirande, A., *Hombres y machos: Masculinity and Latino Culture*. Westview, Boulder, 1997.

Mäyrä, F., *An Introduction to Games Studies: Games in Culture*. Sage Publications, Los Angeles, 2008.

Novak, J., *Game Development Essentials: An Introduction*. Thomson Delmar Learning, New York, 2005.

Surette, T., 'Mexican Mayor Slams *GRAW2*'. *Game Spot*. 9 March 2007, Viewed on 15 April 2009, <http://www.gamespot.com/ps3/action/graw2/news.html?sid=6167149>.

Thompson, C., 'The Making of an X Box Warrior'. *New York Times*. 22 August 2004, pp. 32-37, Viewed on 15 April 2009, <http://www.nytimes.com/2004/08/22/magazine/22GAMES.html>.

Thomson, M., 'From Underdog to Overmatch: Computer Games and Military Transformation'. *Popular Communication*. Vol. 7, Issue 2, 2009, pp. 92-106.

Tom Clancy's Ghost Recon: Advanced Warfighter. Ubisoft, 2006.

Tom Clancy's Ghost Recon: Advanced Warfighter 2. Ubisoft, 2007.

The United States Department of State, The Office of Electronic Information, Bureau of Public Affairs, Viewed on 15 April 2009, <http://www.state.gov/>.

Williams, E. & Johnson, A., 'Walls and Fences: Perspectives from Universities and Museums'. *Journal of the Southwest*. Vol. 50, Issue 3, 2008, pp. 1-10.

PART 3

Mad Women (And Not Necessarily Just in the Attic)

Monstrous Minds, Boundless Bodies: Madness, the Monstrous Feminine and the Victorian Imagination

Elizabeth Hollis Berry

Abstract
Historically, the conflation of both madness and the feminine with monstrosity reaches back to traditional connections with chaotic forms, women's boundless bodies, and specifically it has been long associated with excess and hysteria. After During the eighteenth century theories and treatment of madness underwent a shift in which the monstrous representations of insanity in the form of the frightful madman were replaced by the figure of the psychologically intriguing madwoman, a character of compelling interest to Victorian novelists. During the mid-century, Charlotte Brontë's *Jane Eyre*, George Eliot's *Adam Bede* and Charles Dickens's *Great Expectations* construct deranged female characters who fall outside the parameters of normative identity. These representations of aberrant women almost invariably conjoin derangement with female sexuality to produce the character of the monstrous madwoman. Cultural anxieties about social chaos and contagious disease thus embodied in the disorderly female figure render her increasingly represented as requiring forceful confinement - whether in an attic, asylum, prison cell, or grave. Yet, despite discursive containment within the space of meta-human Otherness according to hierarchical binaries of normative identity, in these mid-Victorian novels the deranged woman's monstrous potencies persistently challenge and disturb categorical fixity, opening up boundless bodies of resistance.

Key Words: Hysteria, madness, mania, monstrosity, moral insanity, post-modern analysis, psychology, puerperal insanity, repression, the uncanny.

*****

> … the body, unreason, sensuality, sexuality; the varied but static figure of Woman becomes the container for all that is excised and women are in turn contained in a private world. She is an object, occulted in order to be revealed, continually open to reinvention.[1]

> What the classical period had confined was not only an abstract unreason … but also an enormous reservoir of the fantastic, a dormant world of monsters supposedly engulfed in the darkness of Hieronymus Bosch, which had once spewed them forth.[2]

Monsters tease out and tangle with the imagination's enfolded recesses, embodying great fears about disfigurement, disease or death. As productions of the mind, culturally and discursively constructed, the madhouse monsters described by Foucault - prodigious creatures emerging from their 'dormant world' of pre-Enlightenment confinement - also deliberately characterise madness and suggest threats of corruption, contagion and chaos informing the modes whereby the insane (especially mad women) were imagined and confined. Historically, the conflation of both madness and the feminine with monstrosity reaches back to traditional connections with chaotic forms, women's flowing, swelling, boundless bodies, in particular, long associated with excess and hysteria. Views linking monstrosity and madness were maintained even after eighteenth-century reforms replaced the medieval madhouse such as Bedlam with the more enlightened asylum such as the York Retreat. Although practitioners actively pursued reform, nineteenth-century fears about social disorder and contagious disease found shape in these iconic monsters of unreason dredged up from the imagination's deeps. Thus discursively correlated with different categories of body and mind, monstrosity itself has taken many forms. Monsters since antiquity have been known by the excess of their physicality or bodily parts, some by the evil in their minds, others by a hidden monstrosity so unspeakably great it defies description.[3]

Since the very idea of monstrosity implies prodigious ills or disorder, Foucault's dormant monsters perform an instructive function, linking unreason with disease and showing how the insane were assigned a cultural position 'in the geography of evil' wherein lepers had formerly been contained.[4] The term *monster* also connotes various other meanings: a prodigy or a marvel (qua Chaucer), deviations from natural form, hybrid beings, part brute, part human, and creatures of mythic ferocity or excessive size.[5] Categories of monstrosity thus interconnect along a trajectory - from the marvellous and prodigious, to the unnatural, the deviant, the excessive and the unwieldy - marking out historical variants in constructions of hysteria or madness. Issuing from evolving philosophies of the self and sensationalist psychology, theories of madness (along with its treatment) underwent a shift during the eighteenth century, as more or less enlightened practitioners ditched the demonological for the disease model.[6] Pope's quip in the *Dunciad* about two nude male statues of 'Lunaticks over the gates of Bedlam-hospital' (the monumental madness in 'Great Cibber's brazen, brainless brothers')[7] gave a satirical twist to monstrous representations of insanity in the form of the frightful madman, archetype of the possessed lunatic, as Elaine Showalter points out, replaced over the next century by the cultural icon of the psychologically intriguing female hysteric or madwoman.[8]

These female figures can be read as representations of the monstrous feminine: wild, disruptive, transgressive, contaminating, through their excessive emotionality and sexuality. Images of madness in the early nineteenth-century Romantic imagination demonstrated a fascination with the spectacle of sexuality and emotionality combined in such figures as Ophelia and Crazy Jane, cultural constructions that crossed over into psychiatric ideologies and entered the period's psychiatric discourse.[9] As definitions of the lunatic, monstrous feminine, these terms are never absolute or stable, since they vary according to the discourse (itself potentially monstrous or chaotic) in which they are used.[10] Although in mythic, fantasy, medical or novelistic discourse, the ubiquity of misogynistic language is undeniable, one would be hard pressed to argue that either Charlotte Brontë or George Eliot was writing from a misogynistic position; but they, with other writers of the period, were representing female figures through an always-already misogynistic discourse. Repeatedly, in these mid-Victorian novels - whether Brontë's, Eliot's or Dickens's - the monstrous feminine is constituted, I will argue, to occupy a space somewhere in between categories, an unnamed or even unspeakable place, outside both the essentialist patriarchal (Freudian) definition of the passive or natural victim[11] and the later Victorian concept of liberated New Woman. During the mid-century, Charlotte Brontë's *Jane Eyre*, George Eliot's *Adam Bede* and Charles Dickens's *Great Expectations* construct disturbing female characters who fall outside the parameters of normative identity. Imagined through such fictional creations as Bertha Mason, Hetty Sorrel and Miss Havisham, these representations of women who deviate from some theoretical norm almost invariably conjoin derangement with female sexuality to produce the character of the monstrous madwoman, a figure that discursively resists societal containment with prodigious power.

In a way suggested by ancient and post-modern theorists (Aristotle, Derrida, Irigaray, Kristeva, amongst others) concerned with identity and power relations, the question of monstrosity weaves itself around the very definition of the normative self - for these fictional characters no less than for characters or beings elsewhere. Even before Christian patriarchy rendered Eve and woman exegetically condemned to the domain of demonic monstrosity, Aristotle would have it that to be born a woman was already to occupy the category of the monstrous: since the female body deviated from the morphology of the ideal male body, he termed the birth of girls a type of monstrosity or deformity.[12] Post-modern analysis opens up the idea of defining the self as an exclusionary process, in Derrida's hierarchical binary, for example, or in Kristeva's theory of abjection; the monstrous and the feminine together ambiguously signify a presence both within and without normative (humanist) identity. Mad (emotional, wilful, eccentric, hysterical, disruptive) women are thus doubly relegated to monstrous extremes in exclusionary discursive practices, for they spill outside containing boundaries of cultural propriety and are by definition always already in a state of becoming other (than man) and other than centrally, properly human. Erring chaotically out of bounds, the madwoman suggests the kind of monster that threatens destruction through embodying prodigious excess, un-nameable power or alien values,[13] a figure so disruptive to the patriarchal economy that it opens up the question of containment.

Perhaps this cultural anxiety about containing chaos and contagion explains why the nineteenth-century imagination produced diverse narratives featuring monsters and also why novels about iconic monsters frame the century: both *Frankenstein* (1818) and *Dracula* (1897) emerged from threatening currents of revolutionary force and sexual anarchy. Early nineteenth-century Romanticism fostered the novelistic creation of Mary Shelley (whose infamously excessive parent Mary Wollstonecraft drew fire as the mother of feminism before she became the grandmother of *Frankenstein*),[14] exploring monstrosity and constructions of the self. When his Romantic friend is killed by Frankenstein's monstrous scientific creation, this not only signals the death of Romanticism, but also prefigures movements in science. The fin-de-siècle saw brute science in the form of Darwinian psychiatry putting a throttlehold on transgressive expressions of the self embodied in the New Woman, rendered pathological as the 'neurotic' woman (any woman) who dared attempt self-fulfilment or self-cultivation. Over the years of the mid-century, when political and social reforms announced a dedication to straightening out Victorian life's messy corners (factory hours, public health and divorce), novels depicted troublesome, wayward women as deviating from accepted behavioural modes in diverse ironic and provocative ways. The novels of Brontë, Eliot, and Dickens draw on a shared psychological and social discourse to explore the identity of the disorderly woman who undergoes a grotesque metamorphosis in such characters as Bertha Mason, Hetty Sorrel and Miss Havisham, paradigmatic figures representing female sexuality variously as a complex of insane violence against men, monstrous self-indulgence and wilful resistance to patriarchal structures.

Considering how the term 'monster' functions as a common slur circulated in the discourse of prejudice or hatred, one can trace the range of those resistant subjects targeted for abuse and, in so doing, comprehend the shifting or permeable boundaries that mark monstrosity as both without and within. On the question of these permeable borders, Margrit Shildrick's analysis of the 'un-containable' monstrous as a 'deeply disruptive force' offers useful insights.[15]

> That which is different must be located outside the boundaries of the proper, in black people, in foreigners, in animals, in the congenitally disabled, and in women; in short, in all those who might be seen as monstrous. At the least contentious level, monsters ... evoke opposition to the paradigms of a humanity that is marked by self-possession. At the very moment of definition, the subject is marked by its excluded other, the absent presence which primary identification must deny, and on which it relies. The monster is irreducible to the selfsame, but is also within.[16]

While such post-modern analysis of difference theorises a moment of defining the self through marking the subject by its excluded or abjected (monstrous) other, for bourgeois nineteenth-century women who dared to get out (away from patriarchal or family control) or speak out (against the status quo), the threat of embodying the shunned, monstrous other loomed large. Women writers such as Florence Nightingale (1820-1910), Charlotte Brontë (1816-1855) and George Eliot (1819-1889) approached their craft as embattled outsiders, marked by difference. Nightingale saw herself in childhood as a 'monster,'[17] as did Eliot in adulthood,[18] whereas Brontë battled against criticism that the author of *Jane Eyre* must be a woman monstrously 'unsexed,' the creator of 'odious' work. In her response, Brontë refused reductive binaries of gendered identity by claiming a space outside the corporeal self: 'To you I am neither Man nor Woman - I come before you as an Author only.'[19]

For many such women (and the fictional characters they created) the spectral presence of a monstrous, forbidden identity hovered over their attempts to break out from confining borders and for some, as Nightingale argues, insanity was the only way out, the sole form of agency available. Beyond Foucault's limiting comments (outlined in *The History of Sexuality*) about the 'hystericization of women's bodies' as an effect of power saturation, Elizabeth Grosz theorises women's inhabiting hysteria as a 'strategic' move that functions as a 'form of resistance to the demands and requirements of heterosexual monogamy and the social and sexual role culturally assigned to women.'[20] While not fully a liberation from oppression, here in the realm of the female third term, outside the binaries of normative identity lies the eccentric or deranged woman's agency, her power. Echoing Nightingale's timely analysis of women's need to resist restrictive social pressures, her concerns about links between women's insanity and their confinement in the 'prison which is called a family,'[21] and her sense of monstrous difference from others, suggestive interconnections between madness and the idea of the monster within, together with the shadow self and the double, recurrently surface in Victorian writers' constructions of female characters. Some of the monsters engendered in the Victorian imagination originated in hybrid monsters of antiquity such as the Medusa and the Hydra - part woman part serpent - monsters of excess and chaos; others, excessive in a contrary direction, come from the realm of dwarfish imps and demons, monsters of diminution whose evil propensities are hidden.

Arguably a quintessential Victorian monster of mad excess (the prototypical madwoman in the attic)[22] Charlotte Brontë's Bertha Mason in *Jane Eyre* embodies the unruly, passionate contradictions to be found in the spirited childhood self of the novel's eponymous heroine. For all her outward difference, lunatic Bertha, the Creole woman transplanted from the tropics, functions as Jane's unsettling double, a doubling suggested by the title's poly-vocal quality: plain Jane's down-to-earth fixity juxtaposed against airy, wandering Eyre, the mutable, aberrant feminine.

Announcing and resisting categorical models,[23] the novel exposes uncanny ironies underpinning normative feminine identity. When Jane is imprisoned in the psychologically unhinging red-room, she is shown a mirrored reflection of monstrous defiance and waywardness, only to grow later into a good English wife whose proper virtue is defined all the more starkly against the savagery of her hidden, diabolical wifely counterpart - the immured yet un-containable Bertha. Critics have noted that the madwoman functions as a fiery, destructive double for Jane, acting out the untamed, disruptive feminine already apparent in Jane's childhood self. Bertha represents the sexually excessive, savage self that Jane must learn to abject in order to function as a proper wife in Victorian society. Rochester's mad wife also acts both as Jane's deranged agent (unwittingly setting her free) and as the complex of passionate, exotic, subversive qualities ultimately repudiated by both Victorian society and Jane Eyre. Presenting a negative mirror image of Jane and other properly Victorian female figures, Bertha Mason suggests, Showalter argues, 'the dark double who stands for the heroine's anger and desire, as well as for all the repressed creative anxiety of the nineteenth-century woman writer.'[24]

To this end, Charlotte Brontë's narrative about Jane Eyre's journey into selfhood deploys tropes of lunar influence, incendiary emotion and monstrous excess, suggestively marking the girl Jane's place outside accepted modes of behaviour, just as Bertha Mason's character is later stigmatised according to the politics of identity and difference as that of the monstrous (foreign, depraved, mad) outsider. Brontë's interest in the psychological effects of social hierarchy, confinement, and abuse connects these female figures through detailed references to depression and breakdown, mapped out in spatial metaphors that connote the asylum. In the Gothic 'spare chamber' of the symbolic red-room, with its 'half-shrouded' windows, Jane suffers 'a species of fit.'[25] A palimpsestic Antigone, locked in a space chilled by death, 'so lonely' and 'solemn' in its isolation, the young Jane experiences what many incarcerated in prisons and asylums knew: the harrowing effects of solitary confinement.[26] Her sole escape, as for others Victorian society isolated for punishment or penitential mind control, is the way of madness, a yet 'more terrifying' alternative.[27] Emblematised through images of death, burial and wildfire, Jane's terrified resistance to the correctional chamber connects her with other wayward female characters whose only viable passage led into a place of insanity. The question of societal control over those deemed marginal (female) or outsiders (alien, eccentric, deranged) and Brontë's reliance on a vocabulary of images drawn from contemporary texts about insanity bring Bertha Mason's doubling presence into the frame early. These images also prefigure Brontë's own later impressions of people subjected to solitary confinement when she visited Bethlem Hospital and Pentonville prison in 1853, where she observed the ill-effects of solitary confinement detailed in *Villette* as leading to madness or mania.

Bertha, to whom Brontë referred in a letter as the Maniac, a 'shocking ... but too natural' character degraded by sin,[28] embodies the monstrous-feminine identity, an unruly spirit of rebellion with potent occult energies, a parallel identity also earlier reflected in the red-room's looking-glass where Jane sees her younger self. What the girl discerns mirrored in its 'visionary hollow' hints at the free, demonic double, the other side of the feminine binary self, limned outwardly in the glass.[29] At this liminal moment, Jane envisions her spirited, monstrous potential and fears its power: a 'strange little figure,' white-faced, 'like one of the tiny phantoms, half fairy, half imp.' Brontë's habitual reliance on descriptors of diminution and pallor for her heroines works against an immediate linkage between this view of Jane's defiant other self and the apparition of Bertha, the Creole Other, the monstrous wife who comes as a warning in the dark at Thornfield Hall, yet Bertha's identity slips through the binary's exclusionary process of definition. Despite Brontë's deliberate differentiation between the two female figures, Jane's view of her motherless self in the mirror scene as diminutively subhuman, thus ironically foreshadows her vision of Bertha who resembles 'the foul German spectre - the Vampyre' or 'some strange wild animal,'[30] suggesting ancient, mythic links with the monstrous, lunar-influenced, cannibalistic forms of the werewolf and the archaic mother.[31]

Disturbing the definitive categories of good and bad wife, pure little woman and evil, monstrous woman, these connections between Jane and Bertha also work as contradistinctions. At Thornfield, Bertha appears 'tall and large,' her face 'discoloured' and 'savage' with 'the fearful, blackened inflation of the lineaments' that mark her as both raving and alien.[32] As for the earlier red-room episode, Brontë's language suggests contemporary Victorian sources for the description, interweaving mania with monstrosity. James Cowles Prichard's 1835 *Treatise on Insanity* describes the maniac's features: 'the eye-brows drawn up; the hair bristled' as 'the eyes become fiery,' combined with 'impetuous, audacious, shameless habits,' also 'shrieking, roaring, raging,' tearing 'clothes to tatters,' then 'Whoever touches . . . is abused or struck.'[33] Even Bertha's dark hair and physical build fit the classification of the 'furious' maniac presented by J.E.D. Esquirol in his 1845 *Mental Maladies* which offers the startling generalization that 'those who have black hair, who are strong, robust, and of a sanguine temperament, are maniacs, and furious.'[34] In a similar vein, Bertha's appearance reminds Jane of a vampiric monster, with her 'fiery eye,' purple coloration, lips 'swelled and dark,' 'black eye-brows widely raised over the bloodshot eyes.'[35] Neither beast nor human being, the bellowing, purple-faced 'maniac' or 'lunatic' is shaped by feral features, including 'a quantity of dark grizzled hair, wild as a mane,' and objectified as a creature: 'it grovelled, seemingly, on all fours; it snatched and growled like some strange wild animal.'[36] Also exceeding the normative in size (another meaning of monster), Bertha, a 'big woman, in stature almost equalling her husband, and corpulent besides,' shows 'virile force' enough to wrestle Rochester (but not quite enough to throttle him).[37]

While Brontë constructs Bertha's insanity through language comparable to the discourse of Victorian psychiatric texts,[38] conjoining the roots of her madness in both 'inherited taint' and 'personal responsibility,'[39] she also suggests the fleshly (feminised) excesses of a distant country and race as causative. Rochester locates the 'germ of insanity' within her mother 'the Creole' who was 'both a madwoman and a drunkard' but insists on Bertha's depraved sexuality, her 'pigmy intellect' and 'giant propensities' as the 'excesses' that hasten her madness.[40] After one of her episodes of mania, typically associated with female sexuality in general and menstruation in particular, when the moon's reflection is 'broad and red' in the waves, Rochester claims he made the decision to transport his lunatic wife to England, despite the threat of 'such a monster in the vessel.'[41] Bespeaking domination, this 'fearful voyage'[42] with a cargo marked as monstrous or subhuman offers a telling inversion of the triangle trade in slaves going the other way from Africa to the West Indies, shipping stricken African women and men to work the plantations which enriched generations of Englishmen. This discourse of enslaved otherness pervades the narrative and opens up questions about whether the monstrosity encoded in racist or sexist slurs meant to diminish others is in actuality located elsewhere.

Cathected in iterative signs of subjection, this cultural anxiety about slavery (in both distant colonial and immediate familial contexts) disturbs the narrative's traditional romance. When Rochester determines to fix the 'aerial' Jane within a lexical power-play that denominates his ownership of 'Fairfax Rochester's girl-bride,' her reaction registers an intuitive (intelligent) panic about imminent subjection: feeling 'smote and stunned,' she recognises the effect on her of something that causes 'almost fear.'[43] Brontë conveys the threat through emphasis on verbs and substantives that signify enslavement, as Rochester vows to encircle, enchain, and load his bride with jewels: 'I will myself put the diamond chain round your neck ... and I will clasp the bracelet on these fine wrists, and load these fairy-like fingers with rings.'[44] Hovering over the symbolic rhetoric that conflates romance with ruin, monstrosity rears its fearful head at each shift in meaning. When Mrs. Fairfax voices a cryptic warning about Rochester's proposal (cultural concerns about age, class and other disparities), Jane wonders, 'Why - am I a monster?'[45]

This question about monstrosity locates Jane's uncertainties in the troublesome area of feminine identity where the slippage in defining the self (from angel to thing or monster) seems as insistently agitating against the narrative surface as the monstrous potential in that mysterious unknown, the spectral threat of murderous secrets drawn from the symbolic realm of monitory fairy tales. Brontë keeps the threat of monstrous excess in play as Bertha's identity takes shape through a series of discursive uncertainties that draw the reader in to wonder (along with Jane) who or what haunts the ancestral manor at Thornfield, with its suggestively thorny questions in a field of Bosch-like horrors. An uncanny, unspeakable monstrosity lurks on all sides in unanswered questions about the source of Rochester's treasure hoard, an inexplicable connection with the West Indies, a crime 'incarnate,' the mysterious female creature, a snarling 'tigress' who bites and stabs when the moon is full, the 'Fury,' 'wild beast' or 'fiend in yonder side-den' of Thornfield's sequestered third-floor, his curious 'capital error' associated with 'heartless, sensual pleasure' in a foreign land.[46] The colonial source of Rochester's wealth and the captive state of his Creole wife in the secret attic chamber offer an ironic corollary to any fairy-tale bracelet symbolically clasped on Jane's fine wrists to signal her belonging - whether to Rochester as bride, to the ranks of the privileged, elevated in marriage beyond spinsterhood (Victorian society's odd woman out)[47] or to the servant class as governess.

Through Bertha's looming presence implied conjunctions linking marital fetters to slave-chains press in discursively. In her genesis from enchained West-Indian slave populations whence her misbegotten wealth has come, she embodies the threat of contagion and miscegenation. Added to the antithetical metaphorical spaces implied in Bertha's earthy, infernal connections set against 'aerial' Jane's ascent, other spatial ambiguities unsettle the binaries differentiating the two. Again, Brontë's rhetorical emphasis on hellish excess charts both Bertha's monstrosity and her insanity. A mix of feminine chaos and psychological disorder, she originates in those infernal regions of the tropics and the psyche, beyond reach of civilization or reason: Rochester's voice places his mad wife's shrieks in the 'fiery West-Indian night,' the air 'like sulphur steams,' and life itself a 'bottomless pit' of 'hell.'[48] Bertha's alien, sexual heat provides a powerful threat even after her containment in Thornfield's cold darkness. There, her oddly chthonic presence up above (the lady of the house in servants' quarters), whence she descends to undo Rochester's marriage plans, has the unsettling effect of revealing her as both monstrous destroyer and lunatic sibyl. Although Brontë distances Jane from Bertha, the madwoman slips through the hierarchy of identity and difference in her elevation to the ambiguous position of liberator, serving the narrative's need for an agent of both destruction and change whose incendiary actions enable the governess's mobility (from servitude and entrapment) upward, to her ultimate place as lady of the manor, a space ironically devoid of passion once its mad, monstrous-feminine being is dispatched.

If Brontë's Bertha Mason represents madness and monstrosity through the passionate excesses of an exotic alien figure, both morally and racially Other, for George Eliot's Hetty Sorrel, the monstrous is paradoxically shaped by diminution and hybridity, in the form of a home-grown, farm-fresh English country-girl, 'that distracting kitten-like maiden,'[49] whose crazed actions are domesticated in the form of puerperal insanity. Eliot's portrayal of Hetty, who loses her virginity, her societal status and her mind in quick succession, offers a deconstruction of a cultural ideal (village life) and the idealised feminine (tiny, perfect) by revealing ugly contradictions inherent in the politics of both Victorian society and identity. Repeatedly categorised by an acerbic narrator in ambivalent terms both undermining and connoting innocence and sweetness, Hetty represents a monstrous crux of matter over mind. Violating Victorian society's belief in motherhood, this outwardly ideal pastoral figure of the milkmaid belies her diminutive femininity through the unspeakable act of child murder. Although by the time her story ends Hetty would not have been construed as raving mad, her crime of infanticide would often have been mitigated by a legal defence of insanity and her psychological state understood then as puerperal insanity, recognised as a weakening of the already (naturally) weak female mind after childbirth.[50]

Opening up contemporaneous questions about nature and monstrosity,[51] the natural world features largely in Eliot's characterization of Hetty. Throughout the earlier part of the narrative, before her unfortunate fall into the disgrace of unsanctioned pregnancy (enshrined in phallocentric terms also as a state of 'nature' for women), Hetty is repeatedly characterised as a diminutive creature, a 'little rose' with a 'little butterfly soul.'[52] Eliot heaps the image clusters of small, round, dimpling, fleshly features, calves and kittenish young animals, constructing her ironically as both culpably shallow in her excessive, seductive beauty and infantile (thus vulnerable) in her rash desires. If it were not for the evidence of her vanity, superficiality and wilfulness adduced along the way, Hetty's failing could be read as the natural outcome of immature desires fired by ambition, but she is condemned for aspiring beyond her station and misusing her beauty to subvert the natural order of village life. Even though the girl - who replicates nature's bounty 'as if she had been made of roses' - cannot help her God-given features, the narrator's voice implicates Hetty for knowing her beauty is of an exceptional, even excessive order which 'seems made to turn the heads not only of men, but of all intelligent mammals, even of women' and elicits 'unmistakable avowals of luscious strawberries and hyperbolical peas.'[53] Its effects go prodigiously beyond the usual 'causing men to make fools of themselves,' and, while hardly monstrous in itself, her beauty 'like that of kittens, or very small downy ducks' encompasses metamorphosis and hybridity, linking her to the Medusa and other serpent-women who fascinated Victorian artists and poets.[54] While Eliot later chooses the epithet of 'that wondrous Medusa face' to show how Hetty has metamorphosed into the Medusa's hybrid monstrosity after her fall, already in her pre-lapsarian state she embodies excessive animal propensities.[55]

Seemingly personifying Hetty's human value through iterations of *beauty,* the narrator's identification of her as such is swiftly destabilised as 'a beauty ... you feel ready to crush for inability to comprehend the state of mind into which it throws you.'[56] The girl emerges from these tropes cataloguing emotional affect as a curious prodigy of diminution and excess. A hybrid being whose adorable physicality prompts overwhelming (even destructive) emotionality, she represents the diminutive beauty with monstrous potential. Here, while Eliot's unflinchingly rigorous narrator appears on the surface to offer a condemnatory analysis of the beautiful girl's superficiality and knowing beguilement of her suitors in unambiguous, patriarchal language (causing men to make fools of themselves, engaging in conscious mischief), the overloading of kitten, duckling, infant imagery also suggestively offers slight room for mitigation of baby-faced Hetty's later criminal actions. Since these traditional, infantilising images diminish the impression of Hetty's conscious self into that of the animal or natural primitive (conveying her child-like inability to understand much beyond instant gratification), they insistently problematise her terrible fate.

Categories identifying Hetty shift continually as the narrative is focalised in her mind and physical awareness, others' impressions, society's views and external judgments, all interchanging with almost dizzying complexity. Characterizing the dairymaid through the environment of her pastoral workplace, the dairy is defined by its provocative tactility, fragrant freshness, liquid plenty, its 'soft' coloration of creamy milk and rosy or ruddy flesh redolent of an entrancing allure:

> such coolness, such purity, such fresh fragrance of new-pressed cheese, of firm butter, of wooden vessels perpetually bathed in pure water, such soft colouring of red earthenware and creamy surfaces.[57]

A kind of performative rhetoric takes over: the narrator's artful reliance on anaphora - through the onomatopoeic intensifier *such* - produces a metonymic excess of arousal. The bountiful dairy space with its 'calves ... not all weaned,' where Hetty responds to Captain Donnithorne's entry and words by blushing 'a deep rose colour,' conveys both her prodigious corporeality and childish limitations. Eliot's carefully pointed tactile imagery of earthy abundance, hard surfaces undone by creamy softness, constructs the maiden through contradictory impulses as delectable temptation and incipient crime. While the body language of Hetty's blush (juxtaposed against Arthur's speech) sexualises the dairymaid from one viewpoint, from another, the scene plays up the local disparity in power between landowning squirearchy and comely peasantry, thus allowing Eliot some leeway in placing the blame for Hetty's monstrous crime as it sets out the underlying facts of the case: Arthur Donnithorne's careless seduction of a seventeen year-old girl who is not only his social inferior, but also chronologically and psychologically his junior.

Eliot's construction of this 'distractingly pretty girl' whose cheek is 'like a rose petal' shifts ambivalently from focalisation sometimes in the adoring male gaze, sometimes in the harsh eye of social surveillance.[58] The direction of seductive motion seems undone by narratorial insinuations that the object of the gaze is actually seeing herself being seen, thus defining her sexual identity (and its monstrous implications) simultaneously from without and within. Hetty blushes in apparent confusion; 'but,' chides the narrator, 'it was not at all a distressed blush, for it was enwreathed with smiles and dimples,' the girl 'slyly conscious' of her body's potency.[59] Defined against a conventional ground of traditional patriarchal culture, the embodied feminine emerges through the sinuous schemata of paralipsis: 'It is of little use for me to tell you ... dimples played about her pouting lips.'[60] The narrator's voice repeatedly insists the girl's beauty and power beggar description, while all the while cataloguing their impact and inserting damning modifiers to reveal guile.

> I could never let you know what I meant by a bright spring day. Hetty's was a springtide beauty: it was the beauty of young frisking things, round-limbed, gambolling, circumventing you by a false air of innocence.[61]

Eliot undercuts any conventional alignment of youth with innocence or beauty with truth by positing a mechanics of seductive technique, the 'prettiest attitudes and movements,' the coquetry set out in Hetty's butter-making prowess, as she makes

> little patting and rolling movements with the palm of the hand ... which cannot at all be effected without a great play of the pouting mouth and the dark eyes.'[62]

Whereas the narrator censures this sexual excess or 'great play' of the eroticised female body as evidence of transgressive and dangerous ways, the violent superlatives suggestively analyse a patriarchal culture's dehumanising response to Hetty's superabundant physical presence and then later to her deranged (adjudged criminal) actions, thus refusing to let anyone off easily.

Guilty of the unnatural, Hetty is ironically constructed through an analogous environment of lush, natural profusion and the natural beauty of her young body, a characterization conjoined with Eliot's narratorial focalisation in her shallow, immature thought-processes to present her as the kind of creature whose monstrosity lies hidden within. Metaphorically aligned with the transient flowering of the natural world and its primitive sexuality, Hetty's outward self, marked superficially with the 'blooming health' of youth, can betray her inner horrors about unwanted pregnancy only 'by the desperation of terror,' for 'it would take a great deal of such mental suffering as hers to leave any deep impress.'[63] This focalisation in Hetty's callow mind reveals her experience of anguish moving randomly between disappointment and dread. Terrorised 'that the eyes of her aunt and uncle would be upon her,' she finds 'the self-command which often accompanies a great dread' and is thus situated in the context of moral surveillance, a subject to be controlled.[64]

Through the narrator's piercing eye, focused by perceptions of the family and society, Hetty is judged and the societal punishment for excessive female behaviour (or sexuality) in the form of imprisonment is assured. Already doomed, despite futile attempts to hide her 'secret misery' from family and society, she looks out 'as the sick and weary prisoner might think of the possible pillory. They would think her conduct shameful; and shame was torture. That was poor little Hetty's conscience.'[65] Yet, while the narrator would have it that her conscience, like her kittenish form, might be slight, and her crime judged unnatural or monstrous, Eliot's insistent positioning of Hetty as an Eve in 'that leafy, flowery, bushy time,' blazoned by Edenic fruition, with her ripe body 'bending over the red bunches, the level rays piercing the screen of apple boughs, the length of the busy garden beyond,' also tends to humanise her as woman in an originary state of nature.[66] Since her pregnancy can also be read as a natural biological state (together with the accompanying frequency of puerperal insanity), these shifting meanings around the Hetty-as-Nature construction destabilise traditional patriarchal taxonomies of criminality, femininity and monstrosity.

When Eliot maps the privatives of Hetty's later wanderings in an alien landscape, she also particularises the plight of countless women cast out into rootless destitution under Victorian social ideologies and public policy. Focalised in the interior space of her thoughts and mirrored in the exterior world of unknown territory, Hetty's narrative emblematises the acute mental distress that caused women to deviate from the paths of normative behaviour. 'Poor wandering Hetty,' as she journeys along unfamiliar byways, takes on not only the face of Medusa 'with the passionate, passionless lips,'[67] but also the features of a wild Ophelia, a type favoured by Victorian asylum superintendents and psychiatrists, since her picturesque tractability implied the containment of both sexualised femininity and madness.[68] Through the narrator's commentary on Hetty's search for a watery grave, the reader is offered a window into the process of derangement. For one so thoroughly embodied in nature to seek disembodiment through drowning and natural decay, she becomes a walking paradox, her deranged mind revealed by grotesque contradictions. Figuratively beside herself as she roams wearily up and down, this child of untrammelled nature finds not life but the beguilement of death in the natural world where a woodland pool in a wild brake promises oblivion. She feels 'as if she were dead already,' viewing the future erasure of both self and sin; by summer, here a paradoxical season of both her defining fecundity and the quickened decomposition she wants, she would be a bloated corpse, unrecognised.[69] Although Hetty takes refuge in a sheep hovel rather than drowning, she becomes a savage Ophelia, marked as 'a wild woman,' by the old man who discovers her awakening from troubled sleep, her body framed by the hovel's straw and gorse. Now seen 'trapesin' about the fields like a mad woman,' she is lost to the ways of social or moral propriety.[70]

Eliot's treatment of the girl's mental affliction with mitigating pathos also introduces a figurative connection that enters into Hetty's ultimate recuperation through her closeness with the evangelical Dinah. When she seeks the sheep hovel's protective warmth, Hetty gains the 'energy of a new hope' by following the exemplars of both Hayslope's shepherd and lost lambs, familiar tropes of salvation, whether pastoral or biblical in origin.[71] Similarly, when she is a prisoner looking 'as if a demon had cast a blighting glance upon her, withered up the woman's soul in her and left only a hard despairing obstinacy,' a 'corpse' of her former self, it is another good shepherd in the form of Dinah who gives her warmth and life.[72] From earlier scenes, Hetty has been presented as Dinah's dark, monstrous double, 'the little minx' who dresses herself in black for coquettish sport as a parody of the Methodist woman's plain, decent self.[73] Offered as a species of unspeakable monstrosity, Hetty's crime is dramatised as such for the court when she stands statue-like in her aphasic, deranged state, while the account is delivered entirely through eye-witness testimony about one whose full identity is unknown, although her unnatural, incriminating actions are observed.

Re-inscribing the fallen woman's identity in a transfigured form after Hetty Sorrel's name at the beginning of the small red-leather book found in her pocket when she is arrested, Dinah's name appears 'near the end' and registers her revivifying force after Hetty's figurative death.[74] That the old Hetty has effectively died by retreating into an un-nameable place outside nature is confirmed by the narrator's closing comments, a view focalised in the jury's unsympathetic eyes before the judge puts on his black cap to announce her punishment by hanging: 'the unnaturalness of her crime stood out all the more by the side of her hard immovability and obstinate silence.'[75] While Hetty faints away and Adam tries but fails to save her, Dinah enters into the picture as the salvatory sign of empowerment and change. Eliot blends the figures psychologically through a clinging so tight that the two seem conjoined. Hetty's cold 'marble' front is melted into tears, and with her cheek 'against Dinah's,' she finds the power to give and receive forgiveness.

> It seemed as if her last faint strength and hope lay in that contact;
> and the pitying love that shone out from Dinah's face looked like
> a visible pledge of the Invisible Mercy.[76]

Her positioning of the figure that personifies spiritual rather than bodily love allows Eliot to reformulate the question of identity.[77] As the form that lends humanizing agency to the monstrous fallen woman, this female power shifts correlative meanings away from simple, exclusionary binaries informing hierarchical values and offers a discursive space beyond the usual categories of containment.

Whereas Eliot's representation of feminine monstrosity opens up a powerful space through the discursive nuances of the compassionate feminine, Dickens's characterization of Miss Havisham in *Great Expectations* allows less room for recuperation. By means of Pip's wounded voice, the voice of privation and longing, Dickens constructs a monster of repression in Miss Havisham, the anti-mother, another savage Ophelia who stops life, but here by wilfully poisoning her charges. While Brontë's Bertha Mason embodies excessive life through her madness, Miss Havisham embodies the disordered repression of a living death. Through her mad inhabitation of death's domain, enacted in a morbid obsession with lost love and revenge, she can only live on through repressing life, stopping life's clocks both literally and figuratively.

Drawing on the spatial trope of the tomb, Dickens characterises Miss Havisham indirectly through the 'dismal' features of Satis House, a strangely half-living mortuary space, it

> was of old brick, and dismal, and had a great many iron bars to it. Some of the windows had been walled up; of those that remained, all the lower were rustily barred,' a Gothic prison of the mind, shut up in gloomy fastness.[78]

Within this metaphorical womb of a mausoleum, Dickens assembles terrifying effects that anticipate Freud's definition of the uncanny as 'something familiar and old-established in the mind ... alienated from it if only in the process of repression.'[79] Surrounded by familiar but unreadable signs (the faded bridal flowers in white hair and 'once white dress'), this perverse reversal of the maternal, who curses her young charges into emotional sterility, also embodies the castrating monstrous-feminine in the traditional figure of a witch.[80] Dickens shows the alarming mental processes of Miss Havisham's repression contaminating all - even the very space she inhabits as the living symbol of her disorder, a broken heart: 'She held the head of her stick against her heart ... the once white cloth all yellow and withered; everything around, in a state to crumble under a touch.'[81] Imagined as the witch's lethal power[82] to curse, destruction (her definitive, vengeful broken-heartedness) has become her identity. As she stands looking at the table, projecting her corpse's placement post mortem 'in my bride's dress' on the 'bride's table,' she enacts repressive processes, turning her pain into a curse on the world of the living and her betrayer inward upon herself. When Miss Havisham claims her prospective place in death on the table set for a wedding feast (the funereal feasting 'upon me'), this polyvalent discourse of marriage rites and death rituals dramatises both derangement and feminine monstrosity.[83] Her macabre symbolic sacrifice constructs a monstrous, cannibalistic inversion of the wedding feast.

Thus constructed, the ghastly figure also presents a case study, which harkens back to Prichard's definition of moral insanity as 'a morbid perversion of the natural feelings, affections, inclinations, temper, habits, moral dispositions, and natural impulses.'[84] Miss Havisham's distortion of the feast into one of cannibalistic assault allows Dickens to implicate Victorian society in the relatives' money-grubbing rapacity and her ultimate destruction. The aged crone in faded white tatters is constructed along the mythic lines of a nightmarish fairy tale's awful warning to the young. Neither Pip nor the reader can miss the threat of mental corruption, as the poison of her obsessive and deranged mind turns inward to reveal her in a ruthless repression of the marriage myth, the darker side of romance. Thus discursively produced, Miss Havisham's body instantiates the uncanny, chaotic effects of monstrous femininity, perhaps replicating Dickens's earlier memory of a jilted woman (seen 'always' walking in 'ghastly' white bridal clothes on Berners Street in London), another 'conceited old creature, cold and formal in manner,' who had gone 'simpering mad on personal grounds alone.'[85] Echoing Dickens's reflections on the familiar but odd woman in white, Pip's emphasis on the strange sign of Miss Havisham, 'the strangest lady I have ever seen or shall ever see,' shows her body as a site of contested meaning.[86] Several shades of contradiction, Miss Havisham's weird form disturbs the process of reading the body: she incorporates the indecipherable mystery with its uncanny power and the definitive sign predictably embodied, personifying a demented performance of excessive femininity, acted out contrariwise through forms of repression.

This figure also occupies the Freudian category of hysterics, who 'suffer ... from reminiscences' and offers a symbolic allusion to cultural constructions of femininity.[87] While her diseased psyche exemplifies the hysterical woman whose life is held back by the past, her moral insanity also warns against the monstrous-feminine's disruptive power. This old 'lady,' who reminds Pip of a 'ghastly' fairground exhibit, 'wax-work and skeleton' combined in a cryptic signature of withered maidenhood, emits corruption and embodies aporia.[88] The uncanny impact of her in the bridal dress, 'withered like the dress and like the flowers,' corrupts the outward sign of the young bride, just as her body's inward shrinking away to 'skin and bone' betokens skeletal dissolution and undoes the 'rounded figure of a young woman' for whom the dress was fitted.[89] Miss Havisham's overwhelming physical and psychological decay engulfs Pip, threatening his youthful self with her corrupting influence, a perversion already insidiously underway in her pathological hardening of Estella into the breaker of hearts and her manipulation of Pip into a victim of that destruction.

> In the heavy air of the room and the heavy darkness that brooded in its remoter corners, I even had an alarming fancy that Estella and I might presently begin to decay.[90]

With its uncanny, brooding presence, this space of repressive fears becomes an anti-womb, a synecdoche for Miss Havisham. Obsessed with the socially constructed identity of wife as the only role for normative women in the patriarchal economy of Victorian society, she is warped into a non-mother, a familiar but unknown (or Freud's *unheimlich*)[91] destroyer of young hearts, cutting off conventional attempts at love in the novel, for neither Pip nor Estella can effectively withstand her monstrous reach or ruinous effects.

The sepulchral dimensions of Satis House (which operates spatially as a conflation of asylum and grave) hold fast its demented mistress while simultaneously holding her back from life, suspended monstrously in some archaic stratum of feminine identity where she embodies the core (also *coeur*) identity of brokenness without a husband, arrested in the premarital moment when the clocks were stopped at a quarter to nine. Along the semiotic lines of Satis House's ironic name, its chatelaine who insatiably lusts after revenge has had enough of life. From the socially imposed straitjacket that was feminine identity she has turned the whole performance upside down to take refuge in a crazed reflection of the normative world. Like the Ophelia figures preferred by Victorian asylum keepers and psychiatrists in their categorization of insane types (presumably because the broken-hearted madwoman was imagined more affectively diminished), Miss Havisham, the spurned bride with her 'sick fancies,' fits the prototype of the woman crazed by unrequited love.[92] Yet, while Dickens's characterization takes the figure into account, he gives her a perverse agency that places her outside the realm of those wistful or pathetic constructions of forlorn maidenly madness. As mistress of her own house and fortune, she maintains an independent (albeit wayward or monstrous) power to control the lives of herself and others. This control reaches beyond life, as she - 'the faded spectre' in her 'grave-clothes' - welcomes the contrary prospect of being laid out in death on her birthday.[93] Yet even as she sees her past life in the 'heap of decay' on the wedding table 'gnawed at' by mice while 'sharper teeth than teeth of mice have gnawed at me,' her power is embodied in the form of a castrating monster as she promises to gnaw away at Pip's future life and hopes.[94] The broken heart she points to in an emphatic gesture of self-definition announces her identity as a type of feminised madness proverbially encoded as the insane 'fury' of a woman scorned. Miss Havisham's case demonstrates the repression of any such passion into an outwardly pathetic but inwardly seething form, an aged Ophelia, bent on revenge.

Just as another Shakespearean almost-bride, Hero in *Much Ado About Nothing* becomes 'but the sign and semblance of her honour,'[95] the readable embodiment of her faulty sexualised self, Dickens's characterization of his deranged Bride manqué suggests a reading of the embodied mind through the space it occupies. Seething with symbolically verminous, primitive creatures, 'these crawling things,'[96] the space of Miss Havisham's self-imposed entombment since before Pip was born (significantly both in and out of historical time) also replicates other tomb-like areas of containment[97] in Victorian fictions about women whose lives have been pathologically stopped. Like them, she is held captive outside time and society, contained within a deadly purdah. Dickens's characterization of Miss Havisham - the relic of some former life suspended in iconic alienation - echoes these familiar Victorian characterizations of accursed, corpse-like women. Evincing a preoccupation with earthly and unearthly potencies combined in the female form, such figures appear insistently all over the Victorian cultural map from waxwork exhibitions of Sleeping Beauty[98] to Pre-Raphaelite paintings and Tennyson's poems. His 'Lady of Shalott' and 'Mariana' feature women doomed to a death-in-life suspension, either lost to the marginal space of embowered isolation in the Lady's island tower or relegated to the moated, Gothic grange where Mariana wastes away in a self-immolation of waiting while singing her death-dirge. For Miss Havisham and Mariana, the deranged woman's space is marked by harbingers of bodily corruption and decay: the 'black fungus' of Miss Havisham's mouldy wedding cake interconnects with the mice 'rattling behind the panels'[99] to convey a world of morbidly repressed energies.[100] Unlike either Bertha Mason or Hetty Sorrel, however, Miss Havisham ends her fictional life without escaping the containing boundaries imposed by her male creator through the adult voice of Pip. Characterised in a posture of subjection to the end, either on her knees begging forgiveness, 'What have I done!' or shrieking 'with a whirl of fire blazing all about her,' then cast down to the floor in her death throes when Pip grapples with her 'like desperate enemies,' she is dealt the witch's punitive burning for undermining the symbolic order of patriarchal society.[101] Unable to find words to answer or comfort her, Pip's voice knowingly categorises her madness and feminine monstrosity:

> And could I look upon her without compassion, seeing her punishment in the ruin she was, in her profound unfitness for this earth on which she was placed, in the vanity of sorrow which had become a master mania, like the vanity of penitence, the vanity of remorse, the vanity of unworthiness, and other monstrous vanities that have been curses in this world?[102]

Seemingly open to humanitarian possibilities, the rhetorical question quickly withholds the space it offers and forces the problems of mental illness and feminine identity back into a prejudicial realm of socially-sanctioned categories, fixing Miss Havisham in fiery ruin - the punishment of her unfitness for this earth (un-humanity), a text-book case of monomania or an ancient Ophelia, meant not for this world but for the pages of patriarchal discourse.[103]

These representations of insanity in such figures as savage Ophelia or the Maniac madwoman reductively situate the complexities of women's lived experience - mental, spiritual or otherwise - within the putatively weaker vessel of an oversimplified, sexualised body. Thus embodied in a sexualised form, female madness and monstrosity are discursively imbricated, whether in the discourses of Victorian psychology or art: emblematising these cultural preoccupations, Millais' drowned Ophelia looks eerily more orgasmic than tragic, supine on her watery bed, glowing in a vivid, enflowered embrace. As Luce Irigaray suggests in her challenge to Jacques Lacan about his and Bernini's (mis)reading of Saint Teresa's mental and spiritual capacity for ecstasy (minutely detailed in her writings but evidently ignored by some male interpreters), women who experience intense encounters with the world (beyond the notional norm) have been represented within a discursive taxonomy that rendered them corporealised, excessive, always already beyond logos or reason. During the nineteenth century, amongst the many stories created in both psychiatric and literary texts about disorders embodied in the madwoman, Charlotte Brontë's Bertha Mason, George Eliot's Hetty Sorrel and Charles Dickens's Miss Havisham, imagined in various shades of monstrosity (whether monsters of the unspeakable, of excess, or of repression), enact behavioural deviations or sexual extravagance stigmatised by Victorian culture as disruptive, dangerous, and contaminating to the social organism. Cultural anxieties about social disorder and contagious disease embodied in such a figure who spills out monstrously beyond the boundaries of social propriety in a patriarchal economy render her increasingly represented as requiring forceful confinement - in an attic, an asylum, a prison cell, a grave, for example. Yet, despite discursive containment within the space of meta-human Otherness according to hierarchical binaries of normative identity, in these mid-Victorian novels the deranged woman's monstrous potencies persistently challenge and disturb categorical fixity, opening up boundless bodies of resistance.

Notes

[1] T. Heffernan, *Post-Apocalyptic Culture: Modernism, Postmodernism, and the Twentieth-Century Novel*, University of Toronto Press, Toronto, 2008, p. 141.
[2] M. Foucault, *Madness and Civilization*, Random House, New York, 1988, p. 209.
[3] For Kant the unspeakable held a paradoxical relationship to the sublime and chaos; for Derrida an apocalyptic shift would cause the 'unnameable' in the 'form of monstrosity.' See S. Neiman, *Evil in Modern Thought*, Princeton University Press, Princeton, 2002 on Kant, p. 83 and T. Heffernan's op. cit., on Derrida, p. 22.
[4] Foucault, op. cit., p. 205.
[5] These can be found among the OED's many (seven) definitions of monster.

⁶ See R. Porter's valuable analysis of medical history in *Enlightenment: Britain & the Creation of the Modern World*, Penguin, London, 2000, p. 216. He later explains 'moral management,' the new strategy which 'radically altered the treatment of the insane, and thereby changed the shape of discourse about madness' as, close observation of the everyday behaviour of the insane became the great priority and the course of the disorder under treatment was charted. For the first time, the criterion for proper knowledge about madness became the close encounter with patients under confinement. *Body and Flesh in the Age of Reason*, Norton, New York, 2004, p. 316.

⁷ A. Pope, *The Dunciad, Poetry and Prose of Alexander Pope*, A. Williams (ed), Houghton Mifflin, Boston, 1969, p. 308.

⁸ E. Showalter, *The Female Malady*, Penguin, New York, 1987, p. 8. Her compelling study of women and madness provides detail about the cultural, scientific, and literary context discussed here: pp. 7-10 and pp. 11-13.

⁹ This 'traffic between cultural images and psychiatric ideologies,' Showalter mentions in her comments on Crazy Jane and Ophelia, citing Esquirol's influence on attempts to represent the physiognomy of madness through drawings of female inmates such as an 'erotomaniac' in the character of Crazy Jane: Ibid., pp. 13-14.

¹⁰ Wilson identifies Menippean discourse as one of chaotic variety. 'On Disgust: A Menippean Interview with Robert Wilson,' *Canadian Review of Comparative Literature/Revue Canadienne de Littérature Comparée*, Vol 34, No, 2, 2007, p. 208.

¹¹ B. Creed, *The Monstrous-Feminine: Film, Feminism, Psychoanalysis*, Routledge, London, 1993, p. 7.

¹² Shildrick discusses ambivalent responses to the monstrous body such as Aristotle's use of the term 'monstrosity' to describe forms of corporeal excess, deficiency or displacement, not just in those bodies which were malformed by disease, accident or birth, but more widely … all beings that are a deviation from the *common* course of nature' and his 'famously' characterizing 'the birth of girls as the most common form of deformity. She cites from *Generatione Animalium*, 728a18, 737a27: 'Monstrosities belong to the class of things contrary to nature, not any and every kind of nature, but Nature in her usual operations.' *Embodying the Monster: Encounters with the Vulnerable Self*, Sage, London, 2002, pp. 11-12.

¹³ Such monsters embody 'an alien set of values' and pose 'the problem of containment.' See R.R. Wilson, *The Hydra's Tale: Imagining Disgust*, University of Alberta Press, Edmonton, 2002, p. 198.

¹⁴ Wollstonecraft was dismissed as monstrous by Walpole.

¹⁵ Shildrick, op. cit., p. 1.

¹⁶ Ibid., p. 5.

¹⁷ This 'private autobiographical note' is cited from C. Woodham-Smith by Showalter, op. cit., p. 62.

[18] Eliot's biographer F. Karl notes she saw herself as 'an old hag' and 'increasingly as Medusa.' *George Eliot: Voice of a Century*, Norton, New York, 1996, p. 148.

[19] Brontë's letter of 16th August 1849 to W.S. Williams emphatically resists the judgment-by-gender slight. She claims authorship as 'the sole standard by which you have a right to judge me - the sole ground on which I accept your judgment.' See *The Letters of Charlotte Brontë*, M. Smith, (ed.), Vol. II 1848-1851, p. 235. In the preface to the second edition of *Jane Eyre* she answers 'carping' critics 'in whose eyes whatever is unusual is wrong.'

[20] E. Grosz, *Volatile Bodies: Toward a Corporeal Feminism*, Indiana University Press, Bloomington, pp. 157-158.

[21] Nightingale, *Suggestions for Thought to Searchers After Religious Truth*, cited in Showalter, op. cit., p. 262.

[22] S. Gilbert & S. Gubar, *The Madwoman in the Attic: The Woman Writer and the Nineteenth-Century Imagination*, Yale University Press, New Haven, 2000, pp. 336-71.

[23] *Jane Eyre* is 'a distinctively female *Bildungsroman*,' says Gilbert and Gubar, op. cit., p. 339. Shuttleworth argues the novel offers a reiteration of conflicts, the 'very reverse of a progressive, linear history:' *Charlotte Brontë and Victorian Psychology*, Cambridge University Press, Cambridge, 1996, p. 159.

[24] Showalter, op. cit., p. 68.

[25] C. Brontë, *Jane Eyre*, Sally Shuttleworth (ed), Oxford University Press, Oxford, 2000, p. 13 and p. 18.

[26] Ibid., p.14.

[27] Gilbert, op. cit., p. 341.

[28] To W.S. Williams, on 4th January 1848, she wrote of a phase of insanity, which may be called moral madness in which all that is good or even human seems to disappear from the mind and a fiend-nature replaces it. The sole aim and desire of the being thus possessed is to exasperate, to molest, to destroy, and preternatural ingenuity and energy are often exercised to that dreadful end. The aspect, in such cases, assimilates with the disposition; all seems demonised. See *Letters*, op. cit., p. 3.

[29] Brontë, op. cit., p. 14.

[30] Ibid., p. 284 and p. 293.

[31] Creed defines *sarcomens* (Greek for vampire) as 'flesh made by the moon,' while the Medusa and Gorgon are thus linked to the female vampire who '*is* the archaic mother.' Creed, op. cit., pp. 64, 66 & 72.

[32] Brontë, op. cit, p. 283.

[33] J. Cowles Prichard, *A Treatise on Insanity and Other Disorders Affecting the Mind*, Sherwood, Gilbert and Piper, London, 1835, p. 76.

[34] J.E.D. Esquirol, *Mental Maladies: A Treatise on Insanity*, trans. E.K. Hunt, Lea & Blanchard, Philadelphia, 1845. Repr. Gryphon, Bethesda, MD, 1987, p. 38.

[35] Brontë, op. cit., p. 284.
[36] Ibid., p. 293.
[37] Ibid., p. 293.
[38] Both Shuttleworth and Showalter make similar points.
[39] Shuttleworth, op. cit., p. 166.
[40] Brontë, op. cit., p. 292.
[41] Ibid., p. 309.
[42] Ibid., p. 309.
[43] Ibid., pp. 259, 258.
[44] Ibid., p. 259.
[45] Ibid., p. 265.
[46] Ibid., pp. 210, 212 & 310.
[47] G. Gissing's references to 'sexual anarchy' and unmarried women in his novel *The Odd Women* are cited in E Showalter, *Sexual Anarchy: Gender and Culture at the Fin de Siècle*, Viking, New York, 1990, pp. 3, 19 & 31.
[48] Brontë, op. cit., pp. 307-308.
[49] G. Eliot, *Adam Bede*, Stephen Gill (ed), Penguin, London, 1985, p. 85.
[50] J. Connolly the humane reformer (& Dickens's friend) observed 'in no form of insanity is the suicidal tendency so well-marked.' Judges were reluctant to sentence these women to death. Showalter, op. cit., pp. 58-59.
[51] Apropos evolution (Lyell's *Geology*), Tennyson links Nature with prehistoric monsters. A. Tennyson, *In Memoriam, LV, Poems of Tennyson*, Oxford University Press, Oxford, 1921, p. 349.
[52] Eliot, op. cit., pp. 134-136.
[53] Ibid., pp. 186, 84 & 97.
[54] N. Auerbach connects these 'mermaids, serpent women' of the Victorian imagination with 'a triumph larger than themselves,' the triumphant power of the Medusa's laugh, as argued by Hélène Cixous. Auerbach, *Woman and the Demon: The Life of a Victorian Myth*, Harvard University Press, Cambridge, 1982, pp. 8-9.
[55] Eliot, op. cit., p. 386.
[56] Ibid., p. 84.
[57] Ibid., p. 84.
[58] Ibid., p. 85.
[59] Ibid., p. 84.
[60] Ibid., p. 85.
[61] Ibid., p. 85.
[62] Ibid., p. 86.
[63] Ibid., p. 336.
[64] Ibid., p. 337.
[65] Ibid., pp. 336, 337.
[66] Ibid., pp. 218, 221.

[67] Ibid., pp. 391, 386.
[68] J.C. Bucknill refers to 'Ophelia's plasticity and yieldingness of character.' Bucknill, *The Psychology of Shakespeare*, Longman, London, 1859, p. 121.
[69] Eliot, op. cit., p. 388.
[70] Ibid., p. 390.
[71] Ibid., p. 388.
[72] Ibid., pp. 433, 432.
[73] Ibid., p. 228.
[74] Ibid., p. 410.
[75] Ibid., p. 438.
[76] Ibid., p. 460.
[77] In medieval iconography and morality plays (such as *The Castle of Perseverance*), Mercy appears as one of the Four Daughters of God.
[78] Dickens, *Great Expectations*, R. Douglas-Fairhurst (ed.), Oxford University Press, Oxford, 2008, p. 50.
[79] Ibid., p. 241.
[80] Ibid., p. 81.
[81] Ibid., p. 81.
[82] Creed refers to the tradition of a deadly 'mother's curse,' even more lethal in witches; she also quotes from the *Malleus Maleficarum* apropos witches stealing 'male organs' and fears of castration. Creed, op. cit., pp. 74-75.
[83] Dickens, op. cit., p. 80
[84] Prichard, op. cit., p. 6.
[85] See *Great Expectations*, op. cit., n. 15, p. 463.
[86] Ibid., p. 52.
[87] See S. Freud, *Studies in Hysteria*, trans. N. Luckhurst, Penguin, New York, 2004, p. 11.
[88] Dickens, op. cit., pp. 52, 53.
[89] Ibid., p. 52.
[90] Ibid., p. 81.
[91] While '*unheimlich*' can mean 'everything that was intended to remain secret, hidden away, and has come into the open,' the uncanny '(*das Unheimliche*, the unhomely) is in some way a species of the familiar (*das Heimliche*, the homely.' See S. Freud, *The Uncanny*, trans. D. McLintock, Penguin, London, 2003, pp. 132, 134.
[92] Dickens, op. cit., p. 53.
[93] Ibid., pp. 113, 85.
[94] Ibid., p. 81.
[95] W. Shakespeare, *Much Ado About Nothing*, 4.1. 32. See *The Complete Works of Shakespeare*, D. Bevington (ed), Longman, New York, 1997, p. 239.
[96] Ibid., p. 77.

[97] Kathleen Komar notes how, 'enclosed spaces that echo the biological space of the female become arenas of punishment or at least confinement in which women can themselves be contained and separated from male social space' and 'Woman is forced back in upon herself to keep her from contaminating patriarchal society.' K. Komar, 'Feminist Curves in Contemporary Literary Space,' *Reconfigured Spheres: Feminist Explorations of Literary Space*, M.R. Higonnet & J. Templeton (eds), University of Massachusetts Press, Amherst, 1994, pp. 91-92.

[98] Auerbach discusses Victorian myths, Sleeping Beauty and the 'mystic powers of control' lurking behind the silence of these figures in Pre-Raphaelite paintings and elsewhere: op. cit., pp. 41-42, 35-62.

[99] Dickens, op. cit., p. 77.

[100] See 'Mariana,' line 1, the 'blackest moss,' and lines 63-64: 'the mouse / Behind the mouldering wainscot shriek'd.' Tennyson, op. cit., pp. 7-9.

[101] Dickens, op. cit., pp. 367, 364.

[102] Ibid., pp. 364-65.

[103] Even the Victorian discourse of humanitarianism situated reformed asylums, workhouses and penitentiaries within practices of control and 'domination.' Showalter, op. cit., p. 50.

Bibliography

Auerbach, N., *Woman and the Demon: The Life of a Victorian Myth*. Harvard University Press, Cambridge, 1982.

Brontë, C., *Jane Eyre*. Shuttleworth, S. (ed), Oxford University Press, Oxford, 2000.

Bucknill, J.C., *The Psychology of Shakespeare*. Longman, Brown, Green, Longmans & Roberts, London, 1859. Repr. AMS, New York, 1970.

Creed, B., *The Monstrous-Feminine: Film, Feminism, Psychoanalysis*. Routledge, London, 1993.

Cixous, H., 'The Laugh of the Medusa'. *New French Feminisms*. Shocken, New York, 1981.

Dickens, C., *Great Expectations*, Douglas-Fairhurst, R. (ed), Oxford University Press, Oxford, 2008.

Eliot, G., *Adam Bede*. Gill, S. (ed), Penguin, London, 1985.

Derrida, J., *Writing and Difference*. trans. Bass, A., Routledge & Kegan Paul, London, 1978.

Esquirol, J.E.D., *Mental Maladies: A Treatise on Insanity*. trans. Hunt, E.K., Lea & Blanchard, Philadelphia, 1845.

Foucault, M., *Madness and Civilization*. Random House, New York, 1988.

Freud, S., *The Uncanny*. trans. McLintock, D., Penguin, New York, 2003.

—, *Studies in Hysteria*. Penguin, New York, 2004.

Gilbert, S. & Gubar, S., *The Madwoman in the Attic: The Woman Writer and the Nineteenth-Century Imagination*. Yale University Press, New Haven, 2000.

Grosz, E., *Volatile Bodies: Toward a Corporeal Feminism*. Indiana University Press, Bloomington, 1994.

Heffernan, T., *Post-Apocalyptic Culture: Modernism, Postmodernism, and the Twentieth-Century Novel*. University of Toronto Press, Toronto, 2008.

Irigaray, L., *This Sex Which Is Not One*. Cornell University Press, New York, 1985.

Karl, F.R., *George Eliot: Voice of a Century*, Norton, New York, 1996.

Komar, K., 'Feminist Curves in Contemporary Literary Space'. *Reconfigured Spheres: Feminist Explorations of Literary Space*. Higonnet, M.R. & Templeton, J. (eds), University of Massachusetts Press, Amherst.

Neiman, S., *Evil in Modern Thought: An Alternative History of Philosophy*. Princeton University Press, Princeton, 2002.

Pope, A., *The Dunciad: Poetry and Prose of Alexander Pope*. Williams, A. (ed), Houghton Mifflin, Boston, 1969.

Porter, R., *Body and Flesh in the Age of Reason*. Norton, New York, 2004.

—, *Enlightenment: Britain & the Creation of the Modern World*. Penguin, London, 2000.

Prichard, J.C., *A Treatise on Insanity and Other Disorders Affecting the Mind*. Sherwood, Gilbert and Piper, London, 1835.

Shakespeare, W., *The Complete Works of Shakespeare*. Bevington, D. (ed), Longman, New York, 1997.

Shildrick, M., *Embodying the Monster: Encounters with the Vulnerable Self.* Sage, London, 2002.

Showalter, E., *The Female Malady: Women, Madness and English Culture, 1830-1980*. Penguin, New York, 1987.

—, *Sexual Anarchy: Gender and Culture at the Fin de Siècle*. Viking, New York, 1990.

Smith, M. (ed), *The Letters of Charlotte Brontë*. Vol. II 1848-1851. Clarendon Press, Oxford, 2004.

Shuttleworth, S., *Charlotte Brontë and Victorian Psychology*. Cambridge University Press, Cambridge, 1996.

Sywenky, I. & Juliana T., 'On Disgust: A Menippean Interview with Robert Wilson'. *Canadian Review of Comparative Literature/Revue Canadienne de la Littérature Comparée*. Vol. 2, No. 34, 2007, pp. 203-213.

Tennyson, A., *Poems of Tennyson*. Oxford University Press, Oxford, 1921.

Wilson, R.R., *The Hydra's Tale: Imagining Disgust*. University of Alberta Press, Edmonton, 2002.

Offended Readers and Monstrous Texts: Theorising Monstrosity and Narrative

Jonathan A. Allan

Abstract
This chapter discusses the concept of monstrosity in literary and cultural studies. Initially, I favour a theoretical consideration of monstrosity and then move to close readings of texts: Valentine Penrose's *La comtesse sanglante* and Alejandra Pizarnik's *La condesa sangrienta*. It is held that no detailed close reading can occur without the necessary theoretical framework that is established in the opening sections of this study. I argue that authors must allow for a process of distanciation so as to write about monstrosity; and that this allows for: (1) the author to distance themselves from the textual subject; and (2) that it allow the reader to actualise the text because the reader will not see themselves in the textual subject. This chapter draws on texts ranging from fiction through to historical texts through to official histories. Finally, this study is written predominantly from the standpoint of phenomenological hermeneutics, especially the writings of: Paul Ricoeur, Mario J. Valdés, and Daniel Frank Chamberlain.

Key Words: Erzsébet Báthory, Bloody Countess, Valentine Penrose, Alejandra Pizarnik, vampire, phenomenological hermeneutics.

*****

1. Introduction

Valentine Penrose opens *La comtesse sanglante*: 'De la comtesse qui se baignait dans le sang de jeunes fille, voici l'histoire'[1] meanwhile Alejandra Pizarnik opens her novella *La condesa sangrienta* paying homage to Penrose who 'ha recopilado documentos y relaciones acerca de un personaje real e insólito: la condesa Báthory, asesina de 650 muchachas.'[2] Both narratives open in a similar fashion in that they summarise the tales, which the reader is about to read; namely, the account for a woman who kills young girls and bathes in their blood. Yet, the questions that seem necessary to ask are: how and why does one read this type of (monstrous) narrative?

Before moving into the textual analysis, though this has been foreshadowed already, it becomes necessary to account for the idea of monstrosity and literary texts. Frederick Whiting argues that 'monsters have traditionally provoked causal explanations that attempt to reinscribe them in the order of things.'[3] It would seem that this idea is commonplace, that is, there is a desire to categorise which seems implicit in most theories of literature, whether it is at the level of form (for instance, genre theory) or at the level of content (for instance, theories of identity). Thus, it has become common practice in the academy to tautologically categorise monsters in one fashion or another so that they 'fit' within some rubric which will assist the critic in studying the given text; the 'histoire' of Erzsébet Báthory, or the Bloody Countess as she has become known in Penrose's and Pizarnik's works.[4] This chapter, instead, seeks not to answer to genealogies, tautologies, or categories, but rather, it is interested in answering to the initial questions regarding reading about monsters and monstrous acts.

It seems that critics are often content to speak simply of monstrosity as a term which is distinct from 'other' insofar as the 'other' seeks a discourse based on power dynamics while monstrosity works to create the 'other' in a de-humanizing light. Or perhaps, the monster becomes the extreme other.[5] Monstrosity requires offence while 'othering' is often more about ignorance. In the texts by Penrose and Pizarnik, the reader does not see an 'other' but rather a monstrous human. The challenge thus becomes how does the reader overcome the offensive (monstrous) narrative content so that the reader is still able to engage with and fully read the text? The solution is found, I would suggest, in a shift from a textual 'other' to a monster that is no longer human (like the reader or like an 'other'). Instead it is monstrous (not like the reader). The solution that is proposed here is one which allows - if not requires - the reader to distance themselves far enough away from the protagonist of the narrative so that the reader is no longer able to identify - recognise themselves - with the monster.[6] In developing this understanding of monstrosity, this study will, at least initially, draw on phenomenological hermeneutics in an attempt to establish a series of observations on monstrosity as trope and on the reader's experience of the text. Thus, this study provides first a theoretical overview and then a departure from this theory to engage with and read the texts by Penrose and Pizarnik.

2. Theorising Monstrosity and Readers

The challenge that is to be overcome is that of readers who engage with a textual subject which is offensive to their ethos, morality, values, etc. The author is certainly aware of this challenge which is imposed upon him/her when they - as authors - want to engage with a subject who/which is morally questionable or reprehensible. This initial challenge relates directly to the prefiguration of the reader and author. Paul Ricoeur sees 'prefiguration' as the first mimetic level and he argues that to 'imitate or represent action is first to preunderstand what human acting is, in its semantic, its symbolic system, its temporality.'[7] Simply put, it 'constitutes a 'repertory' common to the writer and his or her reader' and further that '[i]f human action can be recounted and poeticised, in other words, it is due to the fact that it is always articulated by signs, rules, and norms.'[8] There is a necessary challenge with the prefiguration of the author/reader that must be accounted for in the second mimetic level, or the configuration, of the text. The configuration of the text is the actual process of reading/writing the text. The reader must enter into the world of the text. At this level, we enter into emplotment of the text, that is, the 'organization of the events.'[9] This second mimetic level finds itself 'between the antecedence and the descendance of the text';[10] it is the mediating function. Hence, for the reader, it is necessary that his or her prefiguration be addressed in the configuration of the text. It therefore stands that if the reader's prefiguration is offended, it must be accounted for in the prefiguration of the text before any possible refiguration, the ultimate mimetic level, can occur. The matter of prefiguration is further complicated as it is never absolute or complete. Ricoeur's argument is thus that 'self-knowledge is an interpretation'[11] and that, as Ricoeur notes, 'reading creates a new ego.'[12] The presupposed reality permits one to be offended by a text or to embrace a text. While the reader's identity is in a constant process of configuration, the reader is persistently aware of his or her own prefiguration. Thus, the reader can never shatter the past and live intrinsically in the present and presence of the text.

Reading, in most instances, requires that the reader accept a 'textual assertion to be true.'[13] However, this is fundamentally polemic precisely because of its inherent supposition of truth which itself may be problematic. Indeed, it is only through phenomenological hermeneutics that we can begin to account for the reading (actualisation) of the text. It may appear self-contradicting for this chapter not to privilege reception theory, which intrinsically represents the reader in critical theory, or makes the reader's consciousness the focus of the ontological-appropriative event. However, reception theory fails to consider the textual experience beyond the relation of text and reader. Cristina Santos in her chapter develops a hermeneutical reading of the Countess and this chapter continues along her Valdesian hermeneutical approach and returns to earlier works of Mario J. Valdés on phenomenological hermeneutics. Thus, it is necessary to attempt an understanding of the Countess's 'psychopathic behaviour' and her 'inherited madness, capriciousness, and sexual pleasure'[14] by returning to the hermeneutics of textual experience.

It is necessary that the 'function of interpretation [be] to produce understanding'[15] and moreover, it is necessary to consider this action as a 'dialogical engagement with another's text across time and space.'[16] Perhaps, the reader of the text ought to consider a colloquium of influences in which a multitude of literary and critical voices can be heard. I hold that a 'dialogical engagement' is necessarily also a hermeneutical engagement with the text and the 'literary universe,' which as Northrop Frye would have it, is to say that

> the centre of literary universe is whatever poem we happen to be reading. One step further and the poem appears as a microcosm of all literature, an individual manifestation of the total order of words.[17]

We cannot therefore study a text in a literary vacuum unto itself. In keeping with this, it is essential that the reader also recognise that 'we must not fall into the common error of postulating [that] everything has meaning.'[18] Reading should therefore be a 'constant interweaving of the anticipated words and thoughts with a retrospection to what has come before and is now the context for what is emerging.'[19] Moreover, as Northrop Frye writes,

> Whenever we read anything, we find our attention moving in two directions at once. One direction is outward or centrifugal, in which we keep going outside our reading, from the individual words to the things they mean, or, in practice, to our memory of the conventional association between them. The other direction is inward or centripetal, in which we try to develop from the words a sense of the larger verbal patter they make. In both cases we deal with symbols, but when we attach an external meaning to a word we have, in additional to the verbal symbol, the thing represented or symbolised by it.[20]

Frye has seemingly anticipated the phenomenological hermeneutics of Valdés. Thus, as readers, we must reconcile our own literary histories with literary history as a whole in order to understand the specific text we are reading at a specific moment in time.

Phenomenological hermeneutics holds 'the idea that the hermeneutic encounter is one of overcoming the initial alienating strangeness of the text for the reader.'[21] This principle that becomes most evident when reading *La Comtesse sanglante* and *La condesa sangrienta* because of its persistent violence, which becomes an overall strangeness. Phenomenological hermeneutics is a theoretical starting point which demands much of the reader; for instance, Daniel Frank Chamberlain argues that 'every reader is ultimately an 'experience I' that enters into a relationship with a narrative voice of 'you' and a narrated world.'[22] Unfortunately, it does appear that both Chamberlain and Valdés have not accounted for the text which and/or a protagonist who offends the reader. Thus, the central polemic of this study becomes: how does one respond to a text which is offensive to the subjectivity of the reader, and what strategies can be used to 'grasp the meaning of a literary text'?[23]

In accounting for the self, it becomes necessary to consider the ideas of distanciation and the truth-claim, which will, I argue, come to dominate much of the theoretical discussion necessary to allow for theoretical observations on monstrosity. The tale of the Countess Báthory will – as perhaps it should – offend most readers and thus serves as our textual example. Santos summarises that the Penrose text presents 'fictional elements of vampire and witch folklore with true historical facts to create the quasi-mythical figure of the Bloody countess.'[24]

Valentine Penrose opens her text with, '[d]e la comtesse qui se baignait dans le sang des jeunes filles, voici l'histoire.'[25] Alejandra Pizarnik writes of '[l]a perversión sexual y la demencia de la condesa Báthory.'[26] In these instances, both critical and literary, there is a consensus that the Countess is perverse and mad. Indeed, in most studies of the Countess, she has been reduced to one or a combination of the following: psychopath;[27] demon;[28] sociopath; and/or lesbian/queer.[29] The motivation for these categories is one which attempts to reconcile the 'truth' of the textual world, 'a textual assertion [which] is considered true by the reader',[30] with the 'experiencing I'[31] and the necessary process of distanciation (the distancing of the experiencing I from the textual world).

The creation of tautologies like psychopath, demon, sociopath, and lesbian/queer are necessary for the reader, as these tautologies function as a means of distanciation. A label is put on the protagonist, who thus moves far enough away from the label that the reader may carry or may hold to be part of their own subjectivity. Chamberlain argues that '[d]istanciation is the basis of cultural solitude and historical alienation' in contrast to '[a]ssimilation [which] forms the basis of cultural belonging.'[32] In doing this, readers recognise a difference (distance) between themselves and the text and by so doing, readers are better able to actualise the text. Paul Ricoeur suggests that '[d]istanciation is not a quantitative phenomenon; it is the dynamic counterpart of our need, our interests, and our effort to overcome cultural estrangement.'[33] Moreover, Chamberlain summarises that '[d]istanciation is assimilation's very reason for being because assimilation exists only to overcome distanciation.'[34] Accordingly, it is necessary that distanciation become a part of a theory of monstrosity because the construction of the monstrous becomes a process of distanciation. In many regards, it is important to recall that the 'text plays upon the reader's acceptance of the narrative world.'[35] It becomes essential to account for the 'initial truth-claim' in which 'the reader accept[s] the extraordinary events'[36] of the given text. For instance, it is the reader who accepts the 'extraordinary events'[37] of the Countess Báthory as 'true to life' for a psychopath, demon, deviant, monster, or whatever tautological signifier is deemed appropriate and acceptable to the reader.

3. Distance Reading

In considering the textual world, the first thing that the reader must account for, aside from the author's name, is the title of the book, poem, etc. Indeed the title of both works is essentially the same *La comtesse sanglante* or *La condesa sangrienta*; the English translation is: *The Bloody Countess: Atrocities of Erzsébet Báthory*. Here, I will speak about the three titles, which all seemingly agree that the focal point ought to the Bloody Countess, which now supersedes her proper name, Erzsébet Báthory. This titular naming functions as the first instance of distanciation. In naming her the Bloody Countess, the author has taken away the identity of Erzsébet Báthory and replaced this identity with a misnomer, which creates an *imaginary* title. Indeed, this becomes a process of metaphorisation. In this process, it is necessary to recall that 'interpretation has specific subjective implications, such as the involvement of the reader in the process of understanding the reciprocity between the *text*-interpretation and *self*-interpretation.'[38] Hence, the subjective nature of the reader will impact the interpretation of the title. Accordingly, the author intends - and I recognise all the polemics involved with this claim - for the title 'The Bloody Countess' to provoke a reaction that has now allowed the Countess to become *less real* by the addition of the adjectival 'bloody.' That is, 'the Countess' can stand alone and 'make sense'; however, when 'bloody' is added, it imposes itself upon the noun, thus adding a condition, which takes away from the stand-alone structural sign. The inclusion of 'bloody' is not intended as a colloquial outburst, but rather, as metonymous with her actions. The term as a whole, 'The Bloody Countess' becomes a metaphor for the Countess Erzsébet Báthory. Further to this, the use of 'bloody' requires a response that goes directly to the human, in that blood carries a variety of symbolic, religious, mythical, and historical meanings. Indeed, it might be suggested that blood becomes entirely archetypal in that in most cultural imaginaries blood carries symbolic value. Thus, the metaphor, 'the Bloody Countess,' becomes an all-encompassing misnomer for the Countess Báthory and her identity is lost in favour of this misnomer.[39]

The opening line of Penrose's text, the line which opened this study, reads, 'De la comtesse qui se baignait dans le sang de jeunes fille, voici l'histoire.'[40] This line very clearly and quickly directs the reader and allow for the immediate process of distanciation and monsterisation of the Countess (who the reader already knows as 'the Bloody Countess'). The reader, we can assume, most likely will be baffled - if not horrified - by the idea of 'bathing in the blood of girls.' Further, the second sentence begins with a truth claim: 'Une histoire authentique, et inédite en France'.[41] Indeed, this is a 'textual assertion [which] is to be considered true by the reader.'[42] The hermeneutics of the phrase require that one accept the text as being *true*. In considering the two sentences in conjunction with one another, the central idea is that the reader is dealing with 'Une histoire authentique'.

The process of monsterisation is furthered in the second paragraph which reads: 'La Bête de Csejthe, la Comtesse sanglante, hurle encore la nuit dans les chambres dont les fenêtres et la porte furent, et restèrent, murées'[43]. There is an immediate monsterisation of the Countess. The reader will recognise the metaphorization of the Countess into 'the Beast' and 'the Bloody Countess' (an uncanny repetition of the title). The inclusion of 'Beast' is entirely related to the monstrous in the Countess as her being has now been dehumanised in favour of the animalesque. The Countess has taken on a bestial character, wherein her humanness has been distanced. This allows for readers to recognise the difference between themselves and the Countess.

Paradoxically the text does engage with a negotiation between the process of distanciation and one of assimilation wherein the reader takes steps backward and forward. Thus, while there is a process of monsterisation, there is also a process of humanization. This negotiation occurs, for instance, when the reader is told: 'En vérité Erzsébet Báthory, à sa venue sur terre, n'était pas un être humain achevé'.[44] Again, this idea of not being fully human establishes the process of distanciation because readers are likely to understand themselves as complete humans being. Furthermore, a monsterisation is occurring by means of the dehumanising narrative strategy. In addition to these two processes coinciding with one another, one must recall the principle of the 'truth-claim' that Valdés has established, which is once again at play here. However, when this idea is considered in contrast to the following, the reader can begin to understand the negotiation: 'Elle n'écouta, sans doute, que d'une oreille fort distraite la nouvelle musique de Valentin Balassa et les poésies sur les roses, les pivoines et l'alouette de la plaine'.[45] Just previous to this example, the readers learn 'Erzsébet pensait certainement avec sérieux à l'établissement de ses trois filles'.[46] In these instances, we have a process of humanisation, or perhaps re-humanization. One might, perhaps, go so far as to speak about the maternalisation of the Countess here. Thus, while Penrose has established a distance between reader and subject, here the author is attempting to draw the reader into the subject. However, this is only momentary as very quickly we are reminded: 'Les Báthory, dès leur plus lointaine origine, s'étaient toujours distingués dans le bien comme dans le mal'.[47] Thus, this negotiation is indeed on which privileges the 'evil' in favour of the 'good.' In most cases, perhaps all, the reader is not quite certain what 'good' may exist in the Countess. Indeed, this negotiation is akin to Charles Taylor's suggestion that 'we become good when reason comes to rule, and we are no longer run by our desires.'[48] Hence, the negotiation is one that is dominated by 'reason' over 'desire.' However, as we shall see with respect to the Countess, it is 'desire' that dominates 'reason' and this directly relates the process of monsterisation.

Since there is very little development of the psyche of the Countess, it becomes necessary, therefore, to constitute this process of distanciation in terms of the narrative-ontological construction of the Countess. The text provides an onto-historical understanding of the Countess by outlining her familial bonds and traditions; indeed, the text goes so far as to recall that: 'Mais cela allait-il jusqu'à la crise d'épilepsie? C'était une maladie héréditaire chez les Báthory'.[49] A process of distanciation occurs by means of the reader not having, likely, the same list of hereditary diseases (for instance, gout is also included). Moreover, this signifying characteristic is furthered by means of allusions to the lesbianism of the Countess: 'Cet univers exclusivement féminin'[50] – the exclusively feminine universe – or

> En matière d'horoscope féminin, tout mauvais aspect que
> Mercure reçoit de la lune, elle-même en relation avec Mars,

> cause la tendance à l'homosexualité. Voilà pourquoi la lesbienne, souvent, est aussi sadique.[51]

When one reads this, not only is the Countess, the Bloody Countess, she is now also, among other things: a lesbian, an epileptic, a victim of gout, a sadist, etc. All of these signifiers are inherent to the process of distanciation as they are terms that will likely not represent the vast majority of readership.[52]

Considering these processes of initial distanciation, the reader can clearly see that Penrose is attempting to distance the reader from the textual subject. In that this initial distance has been established, it becomes necessary now to consider how this distance is maintained throughout the textual world. In this regard, the distance is maintained by the highlighting of cruelty, a cruelty which some, including the text itself, have called sadism.[53] The text quickly turns to matters of brutality and the cruel nature of the Countess.

> Elle parlait et criait durant les tortures, arpentait la chambre, puis comme un animal de proie revenait à sa victime ... Elle riait d'un rire effrayant, et ses dernières paroles avant de sombrer dans la concluant pâmoison étaient toujours : 'Encore, encore plus, encore plus fort !'[54]

Again, this process of *distanciation* is benefited by the inclusion of the *monsterization* of the Countess by means of *animalesque* imagery. The animalesque is found in various examples throughout the text ranging in form of direct illusions 'un animal de proie'[55] or through to the *metaphorization* of the animal through language 'la chassait comme le cerf, avec des chiens'.[56] All of this being recognised, the process of *distanciation* is one which relies on *monsterization* through metaphors and animal imagery. However, I would contend that the most *distancing* narrative strategy is that of torture, which is intrinsically related to the 'monstrous' character of the Countess. Thus, at this point, I am interested in how torture and monstrosity come to participate in this dialectic of space, and, in particular, distance. Hence, I shall look at Penrose's text alongside Alejandra Pizarnik's text and examine how they explore the performance of torture.[57]

Each of the episodes of torture in the texts seem to mimic the sexual, but always in a violent and sadistic manner. The reader learns that the Countess

> Elle-même avait un vocabulaire que les femmes de bonne compagnie employaient rarement, et dont elle usait surtout pendant ses crises d'érotisme sadique, à l'égard des jeunes filles affolées de douleur par les épingles qu'on leur avait plantées

sous les ongles, ou lorsque dans sa passion forcenée elle brûlait elle-même leur sexe avec un cierge.[58]

Immediately, the reader will recognise that both practices involve phallic imagery: a candle and needles. Furthermore, the reader will note that the verbs being used are also masculinised in that they both seem to allude to penetration. Finally, it must also be seen that the 'girl' is humanised by the inclusion of pain, which does not seem to bother the Countess; she is immune to the pain being seen around her. Indeed, the Countess is a sadist and Penrose writes of her sadist eroticism. The torture continues

> Sa compagne inconnue devait avoir le même sentiment, et appliquées toutes deux, pour satisfaire leur passion cruelle, à déchiqueter avec des pinces le buste d'une jeune fille dans un chambre reculée du château.[59]

The text maintains that this practice of torture was an erotic performance insomuch as the language mimics the theatrical, in a room out of the way. In many regards this recalls the idea that Shakespeare's Ophelia does not die 'on-stage' but rather in 'another space.' The audience is only aware of her death when the Grave-digger asks: 'Is she to be buried in Christian burial, when she wilfully seeks her own salvation?'[60]

The performance of torture is demonstrated throughout the text, and indeed the text does provide explanation at times for a given torture:

> Il [Nadasdy] vit, un jour, en entrant dans un petit jardin privé du château, une de ses jeunes parentes pleurante et nue attachée à un arbre, toute enduite de miel et couverte de fourmis et de mouches.[61]

As mentioned above, this performance of torture is also one relegated by sexuality in that the reader will be aware of the erotic-symbolic value of honey and ants. The reader will learn that the girl had stolen fruit and thus was punished for her actions. The performative value of the torture is not shown, that is, the reader is not given a 'step-by-step' reading, but rather is given an image of the girl 'smothered in honey.'

Returning to a more performative example of torture in the text by Penrose, the reader learns that '[p]our se venger elle piquait ses femmes avec des épingles'[62] which again returns to the erotics of torture by means of phallic imagery. While the reader is already likely offended by the performances of torture and/or by the erotic nature of these performances, the reader will almost certainly begin to further distance themselves from the Countess when they read: 'Comme on s'inquiète soudain, come le feu prend, comme on arrache ses habits, subitement la soif de sang s'emparait d'Erszébet',[63] and moreover, the reader comes to understand that 'en racontant des histoires de sang coulant dans la rue, le cris de filles assassinées de d'imprécations de moines s'élevant d'un proche monastère.'[64] The reader at this point is most likely distancing themselves once again from the protagonist because of the hyperbolisation of cruelty and torture being considered.

In addition to this process of distanciation, one must consider where this hyperbolization becomes almost fantastical in that it seems near impossible to believe; but the reader must recall the 'initial truth-claim.'[65] The text reads,

> Une légende prétendait qu'à la fin d'un long banquet réunissant plus de soixante filles d'honneur, toutes belles, la diabolique Comtesse avait tout simplement fait fermer les portes et égorger les beautés qui, à genoux, la suppliaient. Puis, arrachant ses fourrures et ses velours, Erszébet Báthory s'était plongée dan une cuve remplie de leur sang pour y baigner son éblouissante blancheur.[66]

For one reason or another, the reader accepts this account of torture, likely due to that initial truth-claim (in both Penrose and Pizarnik); it is thus 'authentic' as the text would have the reader believe. There is no question of 'reliability'[67] of the narrator and/or character within the textual world. Indeed, very few readers will be able to *assimilate* themselves toward the idea, let alone the act of bathing in the blood of sixty 'maids-of-honour' with every one of them being 'beautiful'. Furthermore, it would seem that most readers would also not be able to *assimilate* themselves with the idea, again not of the act, of murdering each of these women, and then bathing in their blood. Penrose has thus allowed the Countess to be defined by means of an explanation of her actions but only through a carefully constructed process of distanciation.

Pizarnik (who openly admits to being influenced by Penrose) proposes another vision which is equally polemic for the reader. Pizarnik, like Penrose, focuses on the role of cruelty and the performance of torture in sustaining her narrative. She also allows the reader to read the text by means of this necessary process of distanciation. Pizarnik requires her reader to recall the 'initial truth-claim' which Penrose establishes when she writes: 'Valentine Pernose ha recopilado documentos y relaciones acerca de un personaje real e insólito: la condesa Báthory, asesina de 650 muchachas.'[68] As such, the reader must recall that Penrose establishes the truth-claim and now Pizarnik, like many readers, accepts it. Indeed, Pizarnik, like Penrose, pathologises the Countess: '[l]a perversión sexual y la demencia de la condesa Báthory son tan evidentes.'[69] Pizarnik herself recognises that the Countess is *different* from the norm by means of the necessary inclusion of perversion and dementia as indicators of distance and hence, distanciation.

As this essay comes to a close, I want to briefly consider a scene from Pizarnik's text called 'Baños de sangre' which accounts for the scene described above in Penrose: the bathing in blood scene. Pizarnik attempts to provide a reason for these bloody baths, 'para preservar su lozanía, tomaba baños de sangre humana.'[70] The reader here will note that the rationale is to maintain her beauty, lushness, and/or abundance. However, the reader also ought to note the process of distanciation and metaphorization that occurs by means of bathing in human blood. It is not enough that it is 'blood'; instead, it is 'human blood.' The inclusion of 'human' makes the blood less real, in that it is no longer 'blood' but rather 'human blood'; however, paradoxically and purposefully the blood becomes *more* real for the reader.

Pizarnik, like Penrose, elaborates on these blood baths when she explains the process of how this idea becomes an action

> De este modo, en la sala de torturas, Dorkó se aplicaba a cortar venas y arterias; la sangre era recogida en vasijas y, cuando las dadoras ya estaban exangües, Dorkó vertía el rojo y tibio líquido sobre el cuerpo de la condesa que esperaba tan tranquila, tan blanca, tan erguida, tan silenciosa.[71]

In this instance, the *distance* is maintained; the reader has come to understand the purpose and method used in collecting and dispersing the blood. It was to maintain her youthful beauty - 'tan tranquila, tan Blanca, tan eguida, tan silenciosa' - which Penrose has also attested to The Countess's bathing in blood is made available by 'la sangre de muchachas - en lo posible vírgenes.' Again, the preference for virgins seems to further allow for distanciation in that virgin blood is being used during an erotic performance of torture, the non-sexualised being suddenly becoming sexualised - that is, they are being violated and then ultimately murdered. The Countess later realises this does not maintain her beauty and decides to use the virgin blood of noble girls. Hence, the blood of virgins is no longer adequate; it must now be virgin and noble blood.

There is a constant negotiation of distance between the textual world and the real world of the reader. Within this analysis of two texts, admittedly an analysis primarily of Penrose's *La comtesse sanglante*, it becomes obvious that the reader will accept the initial truth claim and consequently will respond by means of distanciation and the monsterisation of the textual subject. Additionally, both Penrose and Pizarnik attempt to maintain the reader's attention by means of a necessary process of distanciation which begins at the earliest moment possible: the title. This process is carried throughout both texts, however, intentionally or not, both authors maintain the 'initial truth-claim'[72], which requires that the reader accept the texts as authentic. Thus, from the standpoint of Ricoeur-inspired phenomenological hermeneutics, the reader must contend with this initial truth-claim alongside the process of distanciation. There is, I argue, an essential consideration of a perspective, which must incorporate, or perhaps assimilates and appropriates, phenomenological hermeneutics to explain texts such as these. In considering these texts it is necessary that the reader consider how they are able to read such a text. Indeed, it is my position that the reader, like the author intends, must distance themselves from the text. That is, there is no attempt by the reader or the author to recognise themselves in the Countess. Hence, by means of a process of monsterisation the reader is able to recognise that the Countess is nothing like themselves and thus they are comfortably far enough away from the Countess that they are thus able to read the text.

Notes

[1] V. Penrose, *Erzsébet Báthory, La Comtesse sanglante*, Mercure de France, Paris, 1969, p. 7. Trans. 'This is the story of the Countess who bathed in the blood of girls.' V. Penrose, *The Bloody Countess*, trans. A. Trocchi, Solar Books, Creation Books, London, 2006, p. 5. Unless specified all translated citations are from Alexander Trocchi's translation (2006) of Penrose's text and appear directly following the citation information for Penrose. The 2006 translation is a revision of the earlier translation published in 2000. There are many issues with this 'translation' insofar as it is often more of an 'adaptation' in that the structure of the narrative has been changed, chapters shuffled, etc.

[2] A. Pizarnik, *La condesa sangrienta*, Aquarius, Buenos Aires, 1971, p. 9. 'Valentine Penrose has summarised documents and reports about a real and usual personage: the Countess Báthory who killed 650 girls.' A. Pizarnik, 'The Bloody Countess,' trans. A. Manguel, *The Oxford Book of Gothic Tales*, Oxford University Press, Oxford, 1992. p. 466. Unless specified all translated citations are from Alberto Manguel's translation in *The Oxford Book of Gothic Tales* and appear directly after the citation information for Pizarnik.

[3] F. Whiting, 'Bodies of Evidence: Post-War Detective Fiction and the Monstrous Origins of the Sexual Psychopath', *The Yale Journal of Criticism*, Vol. 18, No.1, 2005, p. 166.

[4] As I have already addressed the idea of genre theory, I am hesitant to ascribe a 'genre' category to these texts given that Penrose's text does not follow the traditional definition of novel insofar as it is not principally fictitious. In some regards, the 'non-fiction novel' might be a better term, though this also is unsatisfactory. For the purpose of this essay, I will, as much as possible, avoid naming the genre and rather oscillate between terms like text or work which are more ambiguous terms (perhaps more monstrous, recalling here Derrida's use of 'monstrosity' in his 'La Loi du genre' [J. Derrida, *Parages*, Gallilée, Paris, 1986, pp. 251-287.]). Another option available to the reader concerned with issues of genre would be Linda Hutcheon's notion of 'historiographic metafiction' which

'are both intensely self-reflexive and yet paradoxically lay claim to historical events and personages' (L. Hutcheon, *Poetics of Postmodernism: History, Theory, Fiction*, Routledge, New York, 1988, p. 5).

[5] For instance, Colin Nazhone Milburn observes that: 'Monsters, denizens of the borderland, have always represented the extremities of transgression and the limits of the order of things' ('Monsters in Eden: Darwin and Derrida.' *MLN*, Vol. 118, No. 3, 2003, p. 603); moreover, Milburn writes: '[t]he monster represents 'the species of the nonspecies,' the nascent germ of a species about-to-become' (Ibid., p. 604). In this instance, the monster is certainly not human which situates it outside of the realm of the 'other' insofar as it has yet to fully 'become' anything; it is 'unnameable' (Ibid.).

[6] Literary and filmic texts often challenge a reader's engagement with the text; for instance, we could think of Pedro Almodóvar's, *Hable con ella*, which forces the viewer to re-evaluate their judgments of the principal character when it is realised that he raped a comatose patient he was taking care of. The patient becomes pregnant and gives birth; but through this, the comatose patient 'returns to life' and is able to resume her previous life. Thus, a number of ethical and moral questions are asked of the viewers, ranging from their engagement with the nurse to how they were able to sympathise with this character and so forth.

[7] P. Ricoeur, *Time and Narrative*, 3 Vols., trans. K. McLaughlin & D. Pellauer, University of Chicago Press, Chicago, 1984-1988, Vol.1, p. 64.

[8] P. Ricoeur, 'Mimesis and Representation', *A Ricoeur Reader: Reflection and Imagination*, M.J. Valdés (ed), University of Toronto Press, Toronto, 1991, p. 140.

[9] Ricoeur, *Time and Narrative*, Vol. 1, p. 64.

[10] Ricoeur, 'Mimesis and Representation', p. 147.

[11] T.C. Wright, 'Phenomenology an the Moral Imagination', *Logos*, Vol. 6, p. 4, 2003, p. 106.

[12] Ibid.

[13] M.J. Valdés, *World-Making: The Literary Truth-Claim and the Interpretation of Texts*, University of Toronto Press, Toronto, 1991, p. 3.

[14] C. Santos, 'Vampires and Witches and Werewolves…Oh My!', *Defiant Deviance: The Irreality of Reality in the Cultural Imaginary*, C. Santos & A. Spahr (eds), Peter Lang, New York, 2006, p. 37.

[15] Valdés, *World-Making*, p. 4.

[16] Ibid., p. i.

[17] N. Frye, *Anatomy of Criticism: Four Essays*, R.D. Denham (ed), Vol. 22 of *Collected Works of Northrop Frye*, A.A. Lee (ed), University of Toronto Press, Toronto, 2006, p. 112.

[18] Valdés, *World-Making*, p. 4.

[19] M.J. Valdés, *Shadows in the Cave: A Phenomenological Approach to Literary Criticism Based on Hispanic Texts*, University of Toronto Press, Toronto, 1982, p. 46.
[20] Frye, *Anatomy of Criticism*, p. 67.
[21] Valdés, *Phenomenological Hermeneutics and the Study of Literature*, University of Toronto Press, Toronto, 1987, p. 61.
[22] D.F. Chamberlain, *Narrative Perspective in Fiction: A Phenomenological Mediation of Reader, Text, and World*, University of Toronto Press, Toronto, 1990, p. 131.
[23] Valdés, *Phenomenological Hermeneutics and the Study of Literature*, p. 60.
[24] Santos, op. cit., p. 36.
[25] Penrose, op. cit., p. 7.
[26] Pizarnik, op. cit., p. 9.
[27] Santos, op. cit., p. 36.
[28] K. Humphreys, 'The Poetics of Transgression in Valentine Penrose's *La Comtesse sanglante.*' *The French Review*, Vol. 76, No. 4, 2003, p. 741.
[29] Santos, op. cit., p. 37; as well, D.W. Foster, *Gay and Lesbian Themes in Latin American Writing*, University of Texas Press, Austin, 1991, p. 101; and S. Chávez Silverman, 'The Look that Kills: The 'Unacceptable Beauty' of Alejandra Pizarnik's 'La condesa sangrienta', *¿Entiendes? Queer Readings, Hispanic Writings*, E.L. Bergmann & P.J. Smith (eds), Duke University Press, Durham, 1995, p. 284.
[30] Valdés, *World-Making*, p. 3.
[31] Chamberlain, op. cit., p. 131.
[32] Ibid., p. 55.
[33] P. Ricoeur, *Interpretation Theory: Discourse and the Surplus of Meaning*, Texas Christian University Press, Fort Worth, 1976, p. 43.
[34] Chamberlain, op. cit., p. 54.
[35] Valdés, *World-Making*, p. 25.
[36] Ibid., p. 24.
[37] Ibid.
[38] P. Ricoeur, 'Metaphor and the Main Problem of Hermeneutics,' *A Ricoeur Reader: Reflection and Imagination*, M.J. Valdés (ed), University of Toronto Press, Toronto, 1991, p. 303.
[39] With respect to the English translation, if one looks semiotically at the text, 'The Bloody Countess' is privileged over 'Atrocities of Erzsébet Báthory' in that the title is clearly at the top, whereas the subtitle is at the bottom of the cover, below the author's name (indeed, even below the translator's name). Moreover, further analysis of the subtitle reveals that it is as influential as the first part of the title as there is yet another process of distanciation at work: the reader is required to assume that there exists a direct correlation between the two parts of the title.

Continuing, it is noticeable that her name is the very last construct to appear, prior to her name the reader will recognise that 'The Bloody Countess' is directly related to the 'Atrocities of Erzsébet Báthory.' As well, there is a notion of *relationality* between the 'Atrocities' and 'Erzsébet Báthory' who is 'The Bloody Countess.' The only aspect of the title that does not symbolically relate to another is 'Atrocities,' that is, there is no corollary term within the titular construct. However, the reader is certain that 'atrocities' is metonymously (not a synecdoche) associated with 'the Bloody Countess' and 'Erzsébet Báthory.' Thus, the atrocities are understood to be hers alone. In all of this, there is a negotiation between the author and the text. The author carefully ensures that her reader recognises these 'atrocities' not to be of Valentine Penrose, but of 'the Bloody Countess' and 'Erzsébet Báthory.' Hence, the double-naming (literal and metaphoric) is a process of distanciation.

[40] Penrose, p. 7; trans. 'This is the story of the Countess who bathed in the blood of girls,' p. 5.

[41] Penrose, p. 7; trans. 'An authentic story, hitherto unpublished in its horrific entirety anywhere,' p. 5. This is another example of the liberties taken by the translator. The original would suggest 'An authentic story, hitherto unpublished in France.'

[42] Valdés, *World-Making*, p. 3.

[43] Penrose, p. 7; trans. 'The Beast of Csejthe, the Bloody Countess, still shrieks in the night, in that very room whose door and windows were, and still remain, walled up.' p. 5.

[44] Penrose, p. 12; trans. 'To tell the truth, Erzsébet Báthory, when she came into the world, was far from being a complete human being.' p. 10.

[45] Penrose, p. 13; trans. 'Undoubtedly, she listened rather absentmindedly to the new music of Valentin Balassa and to rose romance poetry, to the bullfinches and skylarks.' p. 10.

[46] Penrose, p. 13; trans. 'Erzsébet was most seriously concerned with the proper upbringing of her three daughters.' p. 10.

[47] Penrose, p. 13; trans. 'The Báthory family, from its earliest origins was distinguished in good as well as evil.' p. 10.

[48] C. Taylor, *Sources of the Self: The Making of Modern Identity*, Harvard University Press, Cambridge, 1989, p. 115.

[49] Penrose, p. 25; trans. 'But does all this amount to epilepsy? The latter was an hereditary illness of the Báthorys.' p. 23.

[50] Penrose, p. 27.

[51] Penrose, p. 25; trans. 'In matters of the female horoscope, every evil aspect which Mercury receives from the Moon - itself in conjunction with Mars - exacerbates the tendency towards homosexuality. That is why the lesbian is often sadistic too.' p. 20.

[52] Consider, for instance, that the World Health Organization cites that fifty-million people worldwide suffer from epilepsy (*Atlas: Epilepsy Care in the World*, WHO Press, Geneva, 2005, p. 3). Or, that Alfred Kinsey, dated research to be sure but within the historical framework of Penrose's writing, suggested that between 2-6% of women are exclusively homosexual (*Sexual Behavior in the Human Female*, Saunders, Philadelphia, 1953).

[53] This sadistic question becomes apparent in Alejandra Pizarnik's *La condesa sangrienta* that will be discussed below.

[54] Penrose, p. 30; trans. 'She talked and shouted throughout the tortures, pacing up and down her room like a rapacious animal, returning to her victim ... She had a terrifying laugh, and her last words before sinking into the final swoon were always, 'More, more still, harder still!' p. 25.

[55] Ibid.

[56] Penrose, p. 36; trans. 'they [the victims] were hunted with dogs.' p. 27.

[57] Alejandra Pizarnik's *La condesa sangrienta* can, and perhaps should be, read as a testimonial text. It must be recognised that Pizarnik is writing in Argentina during a time where torture was quite common and the torture described in the text would be similar to that of Argentina. It must be recalled that Argentina is 'a very wealthy, highly sophisticated, highly literate, highly differentiated society with a large number of interest associations. Yet, for precisely those reasons, Argentina is the most prone to fragmentation and crisis' (H.J. Wiarda, *The Soul of Latin America: The Cultural and Political Tradition*, Yale University Press, New Haven, 2001, pp. 301-302). Furthermore, it is necessary to recognise that: '[c]ultural life was meticulously screened by censorship committee, and all universities and unions came under government control'; *The Argentina Reader: History, Culture, Politics*, G. Nouzeilles & G. Montaldo (eds), Duke University Press, Durham, 2002, p. 395. The role of torture in Argentina during the life of Pizarnik cannot be denied and as such, a cultural reading is very possible with respect to *La condesa sangrienta*, in which the text is read as a criticism of Pizarnik's society. D.W. Foster contends that it 'can be read as an allegory of patriarchal, with Báthory constituting one of Mary Daly's token torturers, an understanding of the text that both explains how the Countess was able to pursue her sadistic rituals with relative impunity and why Pizarnik's treatment has provoked so much interest in the context of analysing the neofascist ideology of Argentine dictatorships' (Foster, op. cit., p. 62).

[58] Penrose, pp. 29-30; trans. 'She herself employed a vocabulary seldom used by women in society, particularly during her fits of sadistic eroticism, when she confronted young girls maddened by the pain of having needles stuck under their nails, or when her frantic lust moved her to burn a girl's sex with a candle', p. 25.

[59] Penrose, p. 30; trans. 'Her unknown companion must have shared her sentiments. And so, with the object of satisfying their cruel passion, together they

applied themselves to the task of tearing the breasts of the girl to shreds. Such acts were done in an out-of-the-way room in the castle', p. 25.

[60] W. Shakespeare, *Hamlet*, R. Gill (ed), Oxford University Press, Oxford, 1999, V.i.1-2.

[61] Penrose, pp. 49-50; trans. 'One day, on entering a tiny private garden on the castle grounds during a stroll with his wife, Nádasdy caught sight of one of his kinswomen, naked and in tears, tied to a tree, her body smothered in honey, and now a heaving mass of flies and ants', p. 34.

[62] Penrose, p. 71; trans. 'she took her revenge upon women of her bedchamber, sticking pins into them', p. 44.

[63] Penrose pp. 72-73; trans. 'As one suddenly becomes anxious, as fire takes hold, as one tears off one's clothes, so very suddenly the thirst for blood would seize Erzsébet.' p. 45.

[64] Penrose, p. 81; trans. 'There were tales of blood flowing in the streets, of shrieks of murdered girls, and of the imprecations of monks coming from a nearby monastery', p. 51.

[65] Valdés, *World-Making*, p. 24.

[66] Penrose, pp. 86-87; trans. 'Legend has it that at the end of a long banquet at which more than sixty maids-of-honour were present, every one of them beautiful, the fiendish countess simply locked all the doors and massacred each and every one of them while on their knees begging for mercy. Then, tearing off her furs and her velvet gown, Erzsébet Báthory plunged herself into a tub overflowing with their blood to bathe her dazzling whiteness', p. 55.

[67] Chamberlain, op. cit., pp. 132-7.

[68] Pizarnik, p. 9; trans. 'Valentine Penrose has summarised documents and reports about a real and usual personage: the Countess Báthory who killed 650 girls.' (translation mine)

[69] Pizarnik, p. 9; trans. 'The Countess Bathory's sexual perversions and her madness are so obvious', p. 466.

[70] Pizarnik, p. 55; trans. 'in order to preserve her comeliness, took baths in human blood.' p. 474.

[71] Pizarnik, p. 55; trans. 'Therefore, in the torture chamber, Dorko applied herself to slicing veins and arteries; the blood was collected in pitchers and, when the victims were bled dry, Dorko would pour the red warm liquid over the body of the waiting countess – ever so quiet, ever so white, ever so erect, ever so silent', pp. 475-475.

[72] Valdés, *World-Making*, p. 24.

Bibliography

Chamberlain, D.F., *Narrative Perspective in Fiction: A Phenomenological Mediation of Reader, Text, and World*. University of Toronto Press, Toronto, 1990.

Chávez Silverman, S., 'The Look that Kills: The 'Unacceptable Beauty' of Alejandra Pizarnik's 'La condesa sangrienta'. *¿Entiendes? Queer Readings, Hispanic Writings*. Bergmann, E.L. & Smith, P.J. (eds), Duke University Press, Durham, 1995.

Derrida, J., 'La Loi du genre'. *Parages*. Gallilée, Paris, 1986.

Foster, D.W., *Gay and Lesbian Themes in Latin American Writing*. University of Texas Press, Austin, 1991.

Frye, N., *Anatomy of Criticism: Four Essays*. Denham, R.D. (ed), University of Toronto Press, Toronto, 2007, Vol. 22 of *Collected Works of Northrop Frye*. Lee, A.A. (ed), 1996.

Humphreys, K., 'The Poetics of Transgression in Valentine Penrose's *La Comtesse sanglante*'. *The French Review*. Vol. 76, No. 4, 2003, pp. 740-751.

Hutcheon, L., *A Poetics of Postmodernism: History, Theory, Fiction*. Routledge, New York, 1988.

Kinsey, A.C., *Sexual Behavior in the Human Female*. Saunders, Philadelphia, 1953.

Milburn, C.N., 'Monsters in Eden: Darwin and Derrida'. *MLN*. Vol. 118, No. 3, 2003, pp. 603-21.

Nouzeilles, G. & Montaldo, G. (eds), *The Argentina Reader: History, Culture, Politics*. Duke University Press, Durham, 2002.

Penrose, V., *Erzsébet Báthory, La Comtesse sanglante*. Mercure de France, Paris, 1969.

——, *The Bloody Countess: Atrocities of Erzsébet Báthory*. trans. Trocchi, A., Solar Books, Creation Books, London, 2006.

Pizarnik, A., 'The Bloody Countess'. *The Oxford Book of Gothic Tales*. trans. Manguel, A., Oxford University Press, Oxford, 1992, pp. 466-77.

——, *La condesa sangrienta*. Aquarius, Buenos Aires, 1971.

Ricoeur, P., *Interpretation Theory: Discourse and the Surplus or Meaning*. Texas Christian University Press, Fort Worth, 1976.

——, 'Metaphor and the Main Problem of Hermeneutics'. *A Ricoeur Reader: Reflection and Imagination*. Valdés, M.J. (ed), University of Toronto Press, Toronto, 1991.

——, 'Mimesis and Representation'. *A Ricoeur Reader: Reflection and Imagination*. Valdés, M.J. (ed), University of Toronto Press, Toronto, 1991.

——, *Time and Narrative*. 3 Vols., trans. McLaughlin, K. & Pellauer, D., University of Chicago Press, Chicago, 1984-1988.

Santos, C., 'Vampires and Witches and Werewolves…Oh My!'. *Defiant Deviance: The Irreality of Reality in the Cultural Imaginary*. Santos, C. & Spahr, A. (eds), Peter Lang, New York, 2006.

Shakespeare, W., *Hamlet*. Gill, R. (ed), Oxford University Press, Oxford, 1999.

Taylor, C., *Sources of the Self: The Making of the Modern Identity*. Harvard University Press, Cambridge, 1989.

Valdés, M.J., *Phenomenological Hermeneutics and the Study of Literature*. University of Toronto Press, Toronto, 1987.

——, *Shadows in the Cave: A Phenomenological Approach to Literary Criticism Based on Hispanic Texts*. University of Toronto Press, Toronto, 1982.

——, *World-Making: The Literary Truth-Claim and the Interpretation of Texts*. University of Toronto Press, Toronto, 1991.

Whiting, F., 'Bodies of Evidence: Post-War Detective Fiction and the Monstrous Origins of the Sexual Psychopath'. *The Yale Journal of Criticism*. Vol. 18, No. 1, 2005, pp. 149-78.

Wiarda, H.J., *The Soul of Latin America: The Cultural and Political Tradition.* Yale University Press, New Haven 2001.

World Health Organization, *Atlas: Epilepsy Care in the World.* WHO Press, Geneva, 2005.

Wright, T.C., 'Phenomenology and the Moral Imagination'. *Logos.* Vol. 6, No. 4, 2003, pp. 104-21.

Vampire, Witch, Serial Killer or All of the Above? The Bloody Countess Elizabeth Bathory

Cristina Santos

Abstract
The legend of the Countess Erzsébet Bathory presents a unique case in which the fictional elements of vampire and witch folklore combine with true historical facts to create the quasi-mythical figure of the Bloody Countess.[1] Alejandra Pizarnik wrote the short story 'La condesa sangrienta' (1968, 'The Bloody Countess') based on the historical figure of the Countess Erzsébet Bathory as compiled in the socio-historical text *The Bloody Countess: Atrocities of Erzsébet Bathory* by Valentine Penrose. In addition, Andrei Codrescu, using Hungarian archival documents, writes the novel *The Blood Countess* in 1995 and Gia Bathory publishes her 'Intimate Portrait' of the Countess in 2006. Even though Pizarnik is transparent about the fictionality of her text, Codrescu's truth claim of basing his 'novel' on historical documents does not make his text any more historically reliable than Pizarnik's. This study will focus primarily on a discussion of how the 'monstrous' character of the Bloody Countess is a product not only of her murdering over 650 virgins but also of her various sexual perversions and psychopathic madness. The weaving and inter-weaving of history, fiction and popular culture will be key to examining how the 'monstrous' characterization of Bathory is unfairly and predominantly linked to her sexual deviance: her suspected lesbianism, her marital infidelities and an overall deviation from the proscribed role for women in her society and culture.

Key Words: Erzsébet Bathory, Bloody Countess, female vampire, Alejandra Pizarnik, Valentine Penrose, serial killer, witch, torture, sexual deviance.

*****

> A pagan who hid beneath the skirts of reverent Protestantism, while at the same time, learned the ancient lores of the Sisterhood. Wytch, Vampyre, Murderer, so many titles have been given to her.... History has perverted her beyond imagination, as it has with nearly all other powerful creature in time that did not conform to the standards of social 'Normality'. To modern man, Erzsébet has become a lesbian vampire icon, a token Goddess of their own perverse desires.[2]

The legend of the Countess Erzsébet[3] Bathory presents a unique case in which the fictional elements of vampire and witch folklore combine with true historical facts to create the quasi-mythical figure of the Bloody Countess. Alejandra Pizarnik wrote the short story 'La condesa sangrienta' (1968, 'The Bloody Countess') based on the historical figure of the Hungarian Countess Erzsébet Bathory (1560-1614) as compiled in the socio-historical text *The Bloody Countess: Atrocities of Erzsébet Bathory* (2000) by Valentine Penrose. In addition, Andrei Codrescu, using Hungarian archival documents, writes the novel *The Blood Countess* in 1995 and Gia Bathory publishes her 'Intimate Portrait' of the Countess *The Trouble with Pears* in 2006. Even though Pizarnik is transparent about the fictionality of her text, Codrescu's truth claim of basing his 'novel' on historical documents does not make his text any more historically reliable than Pizarnik's. This study will focus primarily on a discussion of how the 'monstrous' character of the Bloody Countess is a product not only of her murdering over 650[4] virgins but also of her various sexual perversions and psychopathic madness. The weaving and inter-weaving of history, fiction and popular culture will be key to examining how the 'monstrous' characterization of Bathory is unfairly and predominantly linked to her sexual deviance: her suspected lesbianism, her marital infidelities and an overall deviation from the proscribed role for women in her society and culture which includes suspected vampirism, witchcraft and murder.

The Penrose text provides the reader with the historical context and events in the life of Elizabeth Bathory and is the very text that the Argentinean Pizarnik reveals as the foundation for her fictional short story 'The Bloody Countess'.[5] On the other hand, Codrescu and Gia Bathory present unique and problematic cases with respect to the truth claims as to their approach to the 'history' of Elizabeth Bathory. Codrescu, as previously mentioned, bases his work on Hungarian historical texts the Hungarian American Drake Bathory-Kereshtur (a direct descendant of Elizabeth Bathroy) and on his testimony (unsupported by witnesses) to the District Attorney of New York.[6] Similarly, Bathory esoterically reveals on her dedication page that she is dedicating her book to: 'All my Sisters, for everything.... / Most of all to Erzsébet: I kept my promise'.[7] Out of the four mentioned texts, Penrose's text is proven to be the 'most historical' text and without possible bias of familial ties as in Codrescu's and Gia Bathory's texts. In addition, Gia Bathory makes a valid point in her Preface that is helpful in our discussion of the truth claim system surrounding these approximations to Elizabeth's life - unlike Penrose and Codrescu, Gia Bathory does not purport to be writing an historical 'document' regarding Elizabeth, instead she instructs her reader to

> let the imagery flow through your head and allow the *flow of madness* to enter. The story makes much more sense when you look through the eyes of the mad... which is why it has little

time, date or reference to documentation. I could go on for chapters explaining the facts and 'facts' of her life (most of which have been corrupted by historians and the Church.[8]

Interestingly it is the two male writers that indicate that they have written historically sound texts regarding Elizabeth, whereas it is the two women authors that are more transparent in the fact that their novellas are simply 'approximations' to Elizabeth's life story. Nevertheless, Pizarnik[9] makes it clear that she based her novella on her reading experience of Penrose's account, thereby blurring the line between fact and fiction even further. By examining and comparing these texts one will note an interesting relationship between history and fiction in the appropriation of the figure of Elizabeth as the Bloody Countess[10] into popular culture.[11]

Let us begin by basing ourselves on Penrose's presuppositions provided in his historical document on Elizabeth, in which the origin of Elizabeth's vicious homicidal behaviour is attributed to the environment into which she was born. That is to say: she was a child of aristocratic inbreeding[12] during a time of warfare where torture and violence were an everyday occurrence and to some extent provided a more tolerant cultural backdrop to her own cruel inclinations. Comparable to Cavallaro's discussion of the Marquis de Sade's behaviour, Elizabeth's 'own society was violently abusive and ... the appalling scenarios [she] portrays are more of an incarnation than a vicious misrepresentation of [her] culture's prevailing trends.'[13] Penrose also draws on Elizabeth's environment in revealing that: '... Erzsébet was surrounded, particularly in Pistyán,[14] by a society which she took pleasure in choosing for its corruption, for its infinite variety and vice.'[15] Overall, Elizabeth was able to indulge in a life of privilege as well as sexual and intellectual freedom that her social ranking allowed her. During her lifetime she witnessed the struggle between the Reformation and Counter-Reformation as well as the Turkish wars for the conquest of Europe (the same wars that kept her husband away from her years at a time).[16] Elizabeth was, above all, an educated woman for her time, with a strong sense of megalomaniacy based primarily on her sense of entitlement that her noble birth and social standing provided her. It is this façade of aristocracy and noble power that intrinsically masks her degenerative murderous impulses, that is until she crosses the line and begins to take victims of noble lineage.

In the attempt to rationalize Elizabeth's sexual and murderous perversions as related to her psychopathic madness Penrose reveals that not only was Elizabeth born in 1560 'within the mould of sorcery'[17] but she wasalso the product of much inbreeding typical of the Hungarian upper class[18] to which her family belonged: a family genealogy that included an aunt that was known to be a witch and a lesbian and 'a notorious corrupter of young girls' as well as an uncle who was a sorcerer and worshipped the Devil.[19] Coupled with the fact that she had she received a traditional education by both a Protestant minister and Catholic monk in her childhood as well as instruction in the art of witchcraft, magic and Satan worship by her nurse Ilona Joo and later, Darvulia.[20] Let us recall that prior to the sixteenth century the term 'witch' tended to be a term used by the learned elite to define a traditional culture based on folk magic and sorcery. It is interesting to point out that it is entirely possible that Elizabeth was educated more so in the branch of sorcery in that she relied on the powers of ritual (such as the bathing in blood) and potions (virginal blood) than on diabolism that required the intervention of a supernatural being. One could say that genetics only account for part of Elizabeth's psychopathy since her use of manipulation and intimidation to satisfy her own selfish needs were traits better associated with the psychopathic killer component to her personality and were further accentuated by the lack of empathy for her victims or remorse for her actions.

Figure 1. Bathory's Castle by Rudy Ramos

But can the murder of over 650 young girls be blamed entirely on moments of epileptic madness?[21] On the contrary, I would argue that her attention to detail in the torturing and killing of young girls could not have been caused solely but episodes of uncontrolled madness and/or epilepsy but rather a sign of a more deeply rooted sadistic inclinations. Elizabeth's methods of torture evolved with time from simply biting and piercing servants who did not do their task properly to more intricate and elaborate methods of extracting personal pleasure from inflicting pain and ultimately death on her victims.[22] Some of the contraptions she used to arouse pain (and pleasure) included: the Iron Maiden, a iron cage in the shape of a woman embedded with precious stones that would close upon its victim piercing her with its daggers located in the interior of the cage;[23] in 'death by water' the victim would be taken outside in the middle of winter naked and water repeatedly poured over her, freezing her to death;[24] a cage lined with sharp blades that would be pulled up to the ceiling piercing the victim's flesh as it swayed;[25] also other modes such as branding, piercing, biting, the severing of body parts and even forced cannibalism.[26] Throughout the various episodes of torture and killing, Elizabeth would sometimes talk and shout 'employ[ing] a vocabulary seldom used by women in society, particularly during her fits of sadistic eroticism.'[27] During the torture sessions she would also at times 'pac[e] up and down her room like a rapacious animal[28] and at other times have breakthrough moments in her cold demeanour of genuine emotion.

One cannot ignore that Elizabeth's sexuality plays an important part in her monstrous characterization, but to say it is the only reason would be essentialising the psychological complexity of her murderous impulses and would also undermine the morbidity of her numerous killings. Let us recall that serial killers have been profiled as being motivated by psychological impulses and/or sexual compulsion. Of the texts examined here it is only Gia Bathory's 2006 novella that mentions the term 'serial killer' in relation to Elizabeth's behaviour. She states that Elizabeth was 'the most notorious female serial killer in world history'[29] - the same history corrupted by patriarchy and Church - but also emphasizes that her novella is not to show 'the world not what she did, but why she did it.'[30] Nevertheless, using Elizabeth in the first person narrative voice, Bathory reveals within this 'flow of madness' that

> these things I did, yes they were horrible...but they were in fact acts of humanitarian mercy. If I had not killed them they would have died of plague, been raped and murdered on the journey to and from the castle or even eaten by wild animals while picking flowers.[31]

Not only does Elizabeth view killing them as merciful but, most importantly, she has no regret for her actions. Although Penrose, Codrescu and Pizarnik also point to Elizabeth's madness as a contributing factor to her actions, Bathory does so more poignantly by having Elizabeth's own 'voice' come through the text. In so doing it highlights both her disconnectedness from those of lower social standing but also her megalomaniacy in rationalizing that she was only expediting what would have been an early death for her victims regardless of her involvement.

However, it is only Penrose, Pizarnik and Codrescu that bring forth the idea that Elizabeth experienced both the psychological and sexual gratification in her killings: not only would the torturing of her victims alleviate her epileptic seizures and attacks of melancholy (and anger), but they would also replenish the youthfulness of her skin. Some critics attribute the first time that Elizabeth noticed the power of virginal blood to an occurrence when she scratched a servant for having tugged her hair too hard while brushing it. It is then that she noticed that the spot on her hand where the young girl's blood had fallen seemed to plump up and become youthful. All the same, Foster also points out that Elizabeth's violent actions were used to 'allay the tedium of her melancholy,'[32] which, as part of Pizarnik's masked criticism of the Argentine dictatorship, Elizabeth's methods of torture 'had no more goal than the aesthetic display of the ingenuity of violence ... [similar to that of] some of the agents of military repression.'[33]

Figure 2. *Bathory- Power* by Rudy Ramos

Even though her noble class provided her with more freedom than women of lower social standing, Elizabeth was not beyond reproach.[34] Prior to the rumours of lesbianism[35] and other 'unnatural' sexual tendencies Elizabeth had already established a questionable reputation. At the age of eleven she had an affair with a peasant villager and gave birth to a daughter from this encounter. Elizabeth's family hid her pregnancy and at the birth of the child quickly gave it to the peasant man 'with a substantial amount of money to keep the affair and offspring a secret.'[36] At the age of fifteen she was married to Ferencz Nadasdy (1555-1604)[37] but this did not stop her from having had extramarital affairs during her husband's prolonged absences while away at war against the Turks. One such affair led to her eloping 'with a young man rumoured to be a vampire,[38] but was short-lived and she hastily returned to her position at the castle. That is to say, Elizabeth's moments of a purported genetically inherited epilepsy and insanity were tied to the established Bathory family trait of 'a marked taste for monstrous or unnatural acts of lust.'[39]

The figure of the female vampire has a well-established history in the Greek mythological figure of the *Lamia,* a woman who sought revenge for the murder of her children by Hera, by killing children. There is also the biblical reference to Lilith, Adam's first wife who 'rejected him on the grounds of his sexual ineptitude.'[40] Cavallaro goes on to extrapolate a quintessential metaphorical interpretation of the female vampire figure in that the female vampire embodies 'the threat posed by a supposedly predatory female sexuality upon masculine integrity.'[41] In both instances, the dangers of uncontrolled and unchecked female sexuality are accentuated along with its emasculating power, especially when combined with lesbian tendencies. Similar to Lilith, Elizabeth's sexual appetite is seen as 'unnatural' and 'abnormal' by reigning socio-cultural norms and, coupled with her intelligence and megalomaniacy, it is easy to see why she is able to carry out acts of abuse and exploitation for so many years. Nevertheless, it would be this 'deviant' sexual behaviour that would open her to censure and persecution at the end of her murdering spree.

But to say she was monstrous based solely on her lesbian tendencies and sexual perversions would be essentialist and would take away from our present discussion. Notwithstanding, it is interesting to note that Penrose compares Elizabeth, at various points in his text, to another serial killer: Gilles de Rais (1400-1440). In his own right Gilles de Rais was accused of murdering eight hundred young boys[42] from 1433-1440 as well as sodomy, necrophilia and making pacts with demons.[43] Similar to Elizabeth, De Rais also took sadistic pleasure in torturing and smearing the blood of his victims on himself, but unlike Elizabeth, in the end he did show remorse for his crimes and was never classified as having vampiric qualities.

I would argue that Elizabeth's vampiric and witch qualities revolve around her obsession with blood and its mysterious powers. As a woman living in a dominantly patriarchal society, Elizabeth recognized that the sign of menstrual blood brought on not only the loss of childhood innocence but also 'separated her forever from the world of men'[44] and opened her to the 'world of women and the suffering of the flesh.'[45] Codrescu also makes a point of 'explaining' Elizabeth's fascination with blood as part of her cultural imaginary:

> I [Elizabeth] grew up listening to stories about the miraculous restorative powers of blood. Hungarian folklore awash in blood. Blood and beauty are wedded in fairy tales, folk sayings, and conventional wisdom.... Given this red liquid medium in which I spent my life, it would have been surprising if I *didn't* bathe in blood. To bathe in blood was simply to acknowledge the literal reality.[46]

Elizabeth's infamous blood baths were supported not only by the recommendations of her witches but her obsession with maintaining her youthful beauty in order to avoid becoming an 'uncharitable void of nothingness.'[47] At first Elizabeth was instructed by her witches that bathing in the blood of a young virgin girl would help preserve her beauty and youth: 'Everywhere the blood touched seemed to glow with the radiance of youth and vitality.'[48] But as time began to show itself in her appearance, despite these baths in virginal blood, Elizabeth is advised by her witches[49] that she must bathe in blood similar to her own: the noble blood of young ladies. At this point, Elizabeth, with the aid of her witches, is able to secure young noble ladies to come to her castles under the premise that they would be receiving special training in good manners and languages.

It is important to mention that for years rumours were widespread of the mysterious disappearances of pretty young girls while in the service of the Countess of Bathory. Although very organized at the beginning of her murdering spree, towards the end Elizabeth (and her assistants) began to show signs of carelessness in disposing of the dead bodies and of answering to questioning parents looking for their daughters. At this point it seems that Elizabeth becomes all consumed with the torturing and killing in order to fulfill both her psychotic and sexual pleasure and her obsession with her youthful beauty and not so much in taking the necessary precautions so that her deviant behaviour not be exposed.

> The more I performed the blood rites, the more addicted I finally became to the substance itself.... I needed more. Within a few years I was killing one every other day to keep up my face and body against the ravages of time.[50]

In essence, she loses control of her murderous impulses leading ultimately to the discovery and disclosure of her crimes. Notwithstanding, it is only when the young ladies of noble lineage begin to vanish that the gossip of Elizabeth's strange behaviour and alleged murderous penchant is demanded to be formally investigated.

Some critics question the validity of said investigation due to the unique circumstances that Elizabeth's nobility and social status allowed her (yet again). In this particular instance it is important to note that the King Matthias himself owed much money to the Bathory-Nadasdy family and if Elizabeth were to have been formally charged by the King's court the family riches would have automatically passed on to the reigning monarch. In order to prevent the Bathory-Nadasdy fortune from being passed onto the reigning monarch Elizabeth's cousin, Count Thurzo, leads the raid of her home on New Year's Eve 1610 and formally charges and arrests her on January 2nd, 1611 of murdering 610 young women.[51] Thus, what occurs is the questioning, torturing and eventual execution of Elizabeth's witches and other servants for their participation in the ritualistic killings of the victims.[52] However, due to the financial implications and the tarnishing of the family names, Elizabeth herself is only 'investigated' under the aegis of the family court (and never formally charged in the king's court). She is found guilty of torture, murder, witchcraft and bathing in human blood and is condemned to live out the remainder of her life walled in one of her rooms in her castle at Cahtice until her death on August 14, 1613. Bathory indicates that the 'trial' itself only lasted two weeks and carried out in Elizabeth's absence from the courtroom.[53] In the end, Elizabeth falls victim herself to a higher power: she had struggled so vehemently to preserve her status within her patriarchal society by preserving her youthful beauty only to be judged and punished for her transgressions into the masculine world of power and violence.

The relationship between fact and fiction surrounding the macabre story of the Bloody Countess has not only attracted historians and writers but also filmmakers, musicians and artists in various forms. In *The Trouble with Pears* the author comments on the appropriation of Elizabeth's personality in the twenty-first century.

> I find it rather sad, all the lies and twists of fact that have come to be associated with my story. So many fantastic tales of magick and demons and feasts of Vampyrism ... if they only knew that truth was stranger than fiction ... I [Elizabeth] was ... turned into a lesbian at some point in time and then became an idol to hundreds of pathetic little girls who think they are 'Elizabeth Bathory' because they read Anne Rice books and wear black nail varnish, preposterous! I find it sickening what I have become to the modern world.[54]

As a brief example, in 2004 the film *Eternal* is released based loosely on the story of Elizabeth Bathory. This particular film takes place at the same time as its production and follows the murderous and sexual escapades of Elizabeth Kane (the reincarnated/immortal version of Elizabeth Bathory for the twenty-first century). Similar to her historical counterpart (and alluded to at various points in the film itself) Elizabeth thrives on the blood of young women to maintain her beauty and immortality and is able to lure her victims with the help of Irina, her loyal assistant. Each time she kills her victim, Elizabeth with a sense of superiority, says to her beautiful victim: 'I thank you for your beauty'. This same sense of regal class distinction even at a moment of such visceral murderous behaviour is also repeated in Bathory's novella: 'I thanked the girls sincerely for giving up their lives so that I could be beautiful again.'[55] In *Eternal*, it is Irina, who takes on the role of companion and aid fulfilled in history by Elizabeth's loyal witches. However she also provides the antithesis to Elizabeth for the viewer: she is more like a fledgling - a vampire in training - preying on young men and women alike, killing out of lust and without the calculated coolness of her mistress, waiting for the moment that Elizabeth grant her the gift of eternal life.

Unlike other films of the vampire genre, *Eternal* depicts a defiant and self-assured female protagonist (Elizabeth) in control of her environment and her actions, even at the end of the film when she finds herself imprisoned in a cell in an old church in Europe. Historically we know that Elizabeth was walled in one of the rooms in her castle in Csjethe, in *Eternal* the directors seem to appropriate a similar scene from *Silence of the Lambs*,[56] although in this case the serial killer is being held in the dungeon of a church and the genders of the psychotic serial killer and detective are reversed. In doing so, the directors of *Eternal* insinuate the involvement of the church in Elizbeth's final imprisonment whereas, as we have already discussed, the elements leading to the 'real' Elizabeth's punishment revolved around the financial implications of her actions on the Bathory-Nadasdy families rather than on religious tenets. *Eternal*, in my opinion, is one of the few films identifying itself as based on the historical account of the Bloody Countess Elizabeth Bathory that substantiates the truth claim insomuch as to include a scene in a Venetian bookstore in which the shopkeeper recounts to the detective the historical account of the Bloody Countess. Nevertheless, the film does tend to focus more so on Elizabeth's lesbianism and mythical vampiric qualities: in which Elizabeth not only bathes in the blood but also sucks it and ingests it from her young and beautiful victims as a typical vampire.

Similarly, *Blood Scarab* (2008) in its opening scene explicitly confesses that it is based on 'historical facts' surrounding the Countess Elizabeth Bathory but that 'the rest is speculation', thereby, intrinsically not negating that the film could be simply fiction. Nevertheless, the 'believability' of the truth claims made at the beginning is quickly suspended once the viewer is presented with a highly sexualized and semi-nude Elizabeth who reveals that she is unhappily married to Count Dracula. Interestingly enough, this film provides a plausible explanation to Elizabeth metamorphosis into a vampire: in one particular scene Elizabeth remembers her past that: 'they called me the Blood Countess because I bathed in the blood of young virgins so many centuries ago ... blood baths preserved my beauty - to remain young' but it is only when she meets her 'fellow Transylvanian' (Count Dracula) does he provide her with a new means of forever remaining young and beautiful - as a vampire. Unlike the depiction of Elizabeth in *Eternal*, the Countess Dracula (Elizabeth) in *Blood Scarab* is explicitly linked to the vampire lore related to Count Dracula as a method by which to explain how she has survived until the twenty-first century, a point that is left more to an open interpretation in *Eternal* as revealed by the film's co-director in his interview with *Offscreen*.

> *Offscreen*: ... Is Elizabeth the nearly 500 year old Countess, or does she just think she is?

The script is written so that you can read it both ways.

> *Federico Sánchez*: We tried to craft an unusual, sexual suspense thriller, with an original spin on vampirism. As to whether she is or not a vampire, we will leave [sic.] that decision to the public.[57]

In her 2009 production *The Countess* director/writer Julie Delpy also leaves it up to her viewers to decide if Bathory could have been a vampire. Unlike the other films prior to the release of *The Countess* Delpy produces one of the first historically acceptable film but focused more so on the romantic rather than the political reasons behind her obsession with blood baths.

Contrary to the previous discussions in this chapter regarding the possible causes for Bathory's behaviour, Delpy (who both wrote and directed) foregrounds the romantic relationship between Bathory with the younger Istvan Thurzo as her reason for wanting to maintain her youthful beauty. Even though the attention to historicity is commendable (and much awaited in films purportedly dealing with Bathory's story) the amount of time given to the *Romeo and Juliet* plot line between Elizabeth and Istvan diminishes the historical accounts of her political and personal accomplishments. In this film Elizabeth is depicted almost as a victim of Gyorgy Thurzo, her late husband's cousin and Istvan's father. Denied by Elizabeth after Ferencz's death, Gyorgy prohibits her relationship with his son (out of jealousy?) and subsequently leads not only the team that discovers Elizabeth's gruesome crimes but also the persecution at court. Despite the historical romance approach to Elizabeth's life one cannot discount the critical apportation this film has brought to developing scholarship on the historical person of Elizabeth and not adding to the superficiality of her purported (and much touted) lesbianism and vampirism.[58]

As we have already discussed, there is a wealth of historical documents and evidence substantiating the gruesome details of Elizabeth Bathory's serial murders and psychopathic behaviour, however, we have also seen that the line between fact and fiction often become blurred and at times even blend together. To date the Bloody Countess' story continues to draw the interest of historians, critics and artists. In the process, one could argue that this intrinsically victimizes her victims for a second time: many of them, especially those who did not belong to the noble class, are destined to remain faceless and nameless in the legend of the Bloody Countess. It is clear that Elizabeth Bathory had the traits of a psychotic megalomaniac serial killer. She was spurred in her killings by her belief in the occult and witchcraft to grant her most desired wish: to remain youthful and beautiful forever. I would say that maybe she has succeeded in this immortality - at least in the pages and images dedicated to the details of her life story.

Notes

[1] This article is an expanded version of a conference paper presented at the 6th Global Conference on *Monsters and the Monstrous* held at Mansfield College, Oxford University in September 2008.

[2] G. Bathroy Al Babel, *The Trouble with Pears: An Intimate Portrait of Erszebet Bathory*, Authorhouse, Bloomington, 2006, p. 6.

[3] Some texts on the Countess Erzsébet Bathory use, Elizabeth, the English version of her name.

[4] This number tends to vary from 50 to 600 to 650. In his novel Codrescu proposes that it was in truth 650 since at the inquisition of the witnesses to her crimes on January 7 and 11, 1611: 'Jacob Silvazy, the overseer at Castle Cahtice, produced in evidence a register in the Countess's own handwriting where she had recorded the names of 650 girls she had killed' (p. 333). Bathory cites that Elizabeth's murders totaled 'over seven hundred women and numerous men as well', p. 9.

[5] Originally published in Spanish as 'La condesa sangrienta', *Extracción de la piedra de locura. Otros poemas*, 1968.

[6] In Prefatory Note.

[7] On one of her personal blogs Gia Bathory reveals that she is: 'I am a Transsexual [sic.] ... a High Priestess as well as a published novelist. ... I am mad, not crazy, but then again...have you ever met a writer that was not?' ('Deeper'). The fact that she identifies herself as a High Priestess and esoterically refers to Elizabeth as one of her 'Sisters' would imply that they both practice witchcraft. However, this is further complicated by the fact that Gia also shares the last name of Bathory - thereby also insinuating a blood relation. This two factors paired with her having kept 'her promise' to Elizabeth establishes a rather complicated case better left for future study.

[8] Bathory, op. cit., p. 11; emphasis mine.

[9] Foster goes so far as to suggest that Pizarnik may of used Elizabeth's story 'as a symbol of the absolute power of the persecutions of the military tyranny in Argentina at the time in which *La condesa sangrienta* was written', p. 148.

[10] In some cases she is also referred to as the 'Blood Countess', as in Codrescu's novel.

[11] The history of Elizabeth Bathory has been adapted into music, theatre, film and even sculpture.

[12] Codrescu also stipulates that Elizabeth's witnessing the vicious murders of her two sisters at the age of nine may have also affected her murderous sensibility, p. 44. Nevertheless, there does not seem to be any mention of this fact in Penrose's historical text even though Codrescu purports that the details of Bathory's life that he uses in his novel are 'taken from historical documents in the Hungarian State Archive' ('Prefatory Note').

[13] D. Cavallaro, *The Gothic Vision: Three Centuries of Horror, Terror, and Fear*, Continuum, New York, 2002, p. 175.

[14] Located in present day Slovakia.

[15] V. Penrose, *The Bloody Countess: Atrocities of Erszébet Bathory*, Alexander Trocchi (trans), Creation Books, London, 2000, p. 29.

[16] The Reformation is said to have begun when Martin Luther released his Ninety-Five Theses in 1517 and ended in 1648 with the Treaty of Westphalia. The Counter-Reformation began in 1560 and ended with the same Treaty in 1648. The fact that Ferencz Nadasdy was born in 1555 it is more than likely that he served in the Crimean war of 1576-1581 and not the Russo-Turkish war of 1568-1570.

[17] Penrose, op. cit., p. 13.

[18] Inbreeding amongst the aristocracy of sixteenth-century Europe was not uncommon since it was viewed as a method of guaranteeing the purity of the noble family line.

[19] A. Howard & M. Smith, *Rivers of Blood: Serial Killers and their Victims*, Universal Publishers, Boca Raton, 2004, p. 33.

[20] Codrescu, op. cit., pp. 142-42.

[21] Penrose, op. cit., p. 24 and p. 26.

[22] Codrescu also points to the deliberateness in the torturing: Reluctantly, the commission concluded that, 'these carefully designed devices are proof that she was not simply the victim of uncontrollable anger'. In other words, she may have begun by cruelly lashing out in an accepted manner at her insubordinate servants, but in her maturity she had prepared refined, sophisticated means of gradually and skilfully arousing pain and, very likely, pleasure. (p. 339)

[23] See Pizarnik, pp. 466-467; Codrescu, pp. 45-46 and Bathory, p. 145.

[24] See Pizarnik, pp. 467-468 and Bathory, p. 145.

[25] See Pizarnik, p. 468 and Codrescu, p. 297.

[26] See Pizarnik, pp. 468-470; Penrose, p. 167 and Bathory, p. 145.

[27] Penrose, op. cit., p. 29.
[28] Ibid., p. 29.
[29] Bathory, op. cit., p. 11.
[30] Ibid.
[31] Ibid., p. 193.
[32] D.W. Foster, 'Of Power and Virgins: Alejandra Pizarnik's La condesa sangrienta', *Structures of Power: Essays on Twentieth-Century Spanish-American Fiction*, T.J. Peavler & P. Standish (eds), State University of New York Press, Albany, 1996, p. 157.
[33] Ibid.
[34] Penrose, op. cit., p. 29.
[35] Elizabeth's Aunt Klara was purported to have been a woman who 'liked to dress like a man and kept a large retinue of beautiful young girls whose only job was to pamper their mistress' (Codrescu p. 42).
[36] Howard & Smith, op. cit., p. 33.
[37] The Bathory family was more powerful and richer than the Nadazdy family, therefore, upon their marriage Elizabeth retained her maiden name while Franz added the name Bathory to his (Codrescu p. 193).
[38] Howard & Smith, op. cit., p. 33.
[39] Penrose, op. cit., p. 24, and p. 26.
[40] Cavallaro, op. cit., p. 180.
[41] Ibid., p. 181.
[42] These numbers also tend to vary greatly, at times as low as 100, primarily because of the lack of investigative documents kept at the time.
[43] Howard & Smith, op. cit., p. 33.
[44] Codrescu, op. cit., p. 141.
[45] Ibid., p. 140.
[46] Ibid., pp. 313-14.
[47] Penrose, op. cit., p. 71.
[48] Bathory, op. cit., p. 147.
[49] Specifically Majorova, as indicated by Penrose and Darvulia as described by Bathory.
[50] G. Bathory, op. cit., p. 147.
[51] Howard & Smith, op. cit., p. 35.
[52] The reliability of witness testimonies is questionable at best since the testimonies were acquired through the customary methods of torture or threat of torture of the time.
[53] Bathory, op. cit., p. 9.
[54] Ibid., p. 155.
[55] Ibid., p. 191.

[56] See Totaro's interview with Sánchez for further discussion of this point; D. Totaro, 'The 'Eternal' Interview with Federico Sánchez', *Offscreen*, Vol. 9, No. 10 (October 2005), pp. 1-13.
[57] Totaro, op. cit., p. 3.
[58] 2008 also saw the release of the Czech production of the film *Bathory,* which to date has not been released as of this date for English audiences.

Bibliography

Bathory Al Babel, G., 'Deeper'. <http://people.tribe.net/babylonpriestess>. Viewed on 27 June 2009.

——, *The Trouble with Pears: An Intimate Portrait of Erzsébet Bathory.* Authorhouse, Bloomington, 2006.

Cavallaro, D., *The Gothic Vision: Three Centuries of Horror, Terror, and Fear.* Continuum, New York, 2002.

Codrescu, A., *The Blood Countess*. Simon & Schuster, New York, 1995.

Foster, D.W., 'Of Power and Virgins: Alejandra Pizarnik's La condesa sangrienta'. *Structures of Power: Essays on Twentieth-Century Spanish-American Fiction.* Peavler, T.J. & Standish, P. (eds), State University of New York Press, Albany, 1996, pp. 145-58.

Howard, A., & Smith, M., *River of Blood: Serial Killers and their Victims.* Universal Publishers, Boca Raton, 2004.

Penrose, V., *The Bloody Countess: Atrocities of Erzsébet Bathory*. trans. Trocchi, A., Creation Books, London, 2000.

Pizarnik, A., 'The Bloody Countess'. *The Oxford Book of Gothic Tales*. Baldick, C. (ed),Oxford University Press, Oxford, 1992.

Totaro, D., 'The 'Eternal' Interview with Federico Sánchez'. *Offscreen*. Vol. 9, No. 10 (October 2005), pp. 1-13.

Filmography

Correa, R. (dir), *Blood Scarab*. M.T. Parent, D. Howison & B. Stevens (perf), Frontline Entertainment, 2008.

Delpy, J. (dir), *The Countess*. J. Delpy, D. Brühl & W. Hurt (perfs), EMC Filmproduktion, 2009.

Liebenberg, W. & F. Sánchez (dirs), *Eternal*. C. Pla, C. Néron, V. Sánchez, & L. Balaban (perfs), Here! Films/Regent, 2004.

Giovanna Rivero's 'Contraluna': Meeting the Monstrous Lilith

Verónica H. Saunero-Ward

Abstract
This essay provides a psychoanalytical perspective on the Hebrew mythical figure Lilith as she is represented in Giovanna Rivero's 'Contraluna'[1] (Alter-Moon). The novella illustrates the impossibility of a sexual relationship as Lacan defines it between men and women. The protagonist is propelled on a fantastic journey to entropy, compelled by his sexual obsessions. The objects of his obsessions are personifications of Lilith. The first, his lover, is an urban representation of Lilith as the irresistible and promiscuous seductress who he ultimately kills in a jealous rage. The second emerges from the impenetrable world of the jungle, where he is drawn to find an antidote for the pheremonal cause of his obsession. Snared by the chaotic universe of the jungle, he gives up his search and becomes obsessed by the other face of Lilith, a supernatural creature half mulatta, half demoness; a monstrous mother/lover figure who rules man's destiny. In contrast to his relationship to his lover, the protagonist seeks to be possessed and then devoured by the mulatta. At the end, they both reach entropy through an implicit suicidal sexual act. By utilizing the myth of Lilith, the hallucinatory and the chaotic nature of the jungle, fairy tales, and the delirious state caused by illness, all elements of the fantastic mode, Rivero achieves a new language that better conveys the erotic aggressivity identified by Jacques Lacan as underlying a male-female relationship. Though the story is told in the first person and the protagonist is male, the story establishes the myth of Lilith as the rationalization of man's fear of that which is feminine. Rivero also examines women's self-destructive narcissism made evident when embodying man's Desire. Both the protagonist's sexual obsession and his lover's narcissism constitute their *jouissance* that leads them to the absolute zero.

Key Words: Giovanna Rivero**,** Latin American Women Writers, Lilith, monstrous, Jacques Lacan, fantastic, sexual obsession, mulatta.

*****

Le Vampire

Toi qui, comme un coup de couteau,
Dans mon cœur plaintif es entrée ;
Toi qui, forte comme un troupeau
De démons, vins, folle et parée,

De mon esprit humilié
Faire ton lit et ton domaine ;

>   --Infâme à qui je sui lié
>   Comme le forçat à la chaîne.
>   …
>   J'ai prié le glaive rapide
>   De conquérir ma liberté,
>
>   Et j'a dit au poison perfide
>   De secourir ma lâcheté.
>   …
>   « Tu n'es pas digne qu'ont t'enlève
>   A ton esclavage maudit,
>
>   Imbécile ! –de son empire
>   Si nos efforts te délivraient,
>   Tes baisers ressusciteraient
>   Le cadavre de ton vampire ! »
>
>   Charles Baudalaire[2]

Giovanna Rivero (1972 -) is an outstanding young author who belongs to the recent wave of Bolivian writers that have achieved international recognition. Her short stories are in a sphere that transcends the quotidian, goes beyond the mimetic, and resides in the fantastic. Her readers are confronted with social and religious taboos that they would rather not acknowledge, which are conveyed by an eroticism and violence sometimes uncomfortably graphic. Considering that Rivero's narrative opens fissures into the unconscious and questions the very nature of human beings, a psychoanalytical approach represents the most effective means to understand her work. Her short story, 'Contraluna' (2002), illustrates Jacques Lacan's notion that neither love nor sex can grant the subject a return to the wholeness of the self that pertains to the real. It depicts the erotic agressivity in the sexual consociation between man and woman, which is the result of self-destructive behaviours: sexual obsession in man and narcissistic suicidal aggression in woman.

In Lacanian terms, the unobtainable real is that which is beyond symbolization: 'The real is 'the impossible' because it is impossible to imagine, impossible to integrate into the symbolic order, and impossible to attain in any way.'[3] For Lacan, the entrance to the symbolic entails the sexuation of the subject, thereby establishing sexual differentiation and, since becoming a sexuated being is the reason for the subject's mortality, sexuality is linked to death and not to immortality.[4] This essay proposes a Lacanian interpretation of a story of lust and obsession narrated in 'Contraluna', through the application of Barbara Creed's concept of the monstrous feminine[5] that speaks to man's unconscious fear of the excessive feminine body. This construction then leads into an alternative reading of the Hebrew myth of Lilith.

The notion of the monstrous has been identified with the Other, the unconscious that threatens to erupt and bring the symbolic order into question. To fulfil the desire of the Other, or to become the object of the desire of the Other, would signify for the subject the return to the real; such a yearning can never be filled, for the real is not Kant's 'thing in itself,'[6] but an impossibility, a void. However, the subject never resigns itself to not filling this lack. In 'A Love Letter,'[7] Lacan states that in relation to what can be said of the unconscious, woman belongs to the side of the Other, thus, in a sexual relation, man's Other is woman.

In Lacanian studies of sexual difference, woman as a universal concept does not exist.[8] She is a *'pas-toute,'* a symptom of a man, in the sense that a woman can only ever enter the psychic economy of man as fantasy *object a*, the cause of their desire.[9] That is to say where desire and the object of desire are the *effect*, *objet a* is what causes or produces that effect. Man needs woman to produce desire, for a subject without desire is suspended indefinitely in the state of *angoisse* where he experiences the lack of the lack that generates desire.

As an object-fantasy, woman's sexual representation in the symbolic is a response to man's need to fulfil his desire of the Other. In 'Guiding Remarks for a Congress in Feminine Sexuality,' Lacan asserts that the symbolic establishes female sexuality as inseparable from the representations through which it is produced. That is, the images and symbols *of* woman are one with the images and symbols *for* woman.[10] She becomes what she is meant to portray in the symbolic. Her representation follows the binomial structure of subject / object, or man / woman, and defines her in moral terms of good / evil. The obvious dichotomy of the virgin and the whore, charged with sexual connotations, explains the symbolization of woman: '…it is the representation of sexuality which conditions how it comes to play.'[11] Both images equate moral and religious notions of good and evil. Evil usually relates to the 'not I', to the Other. In his article, 'Magical Narratives: Romance as Genre,' Fredric Jameson states,

> Any social structure tends to exclude as 'evil' anything radically different from itself or which threatens it with destruction … It is a concept at one with the category of otherness itself: evil characterizes whatever is radically different from, whatever by virtue of precisely that difference seems to constitute a very real and urgent threat to my existence.[12]

The supernatural provides an explanation of the presence of the angelic and the demonic in the real world, but its origins stem from man's fears that reside in his unconscious. In the case of woman, the angelic becomes the virtuous mother and the sexualised demonic figure becomes the succubus. The mythical Lilith from the Hebrew tradition embodies the latter. In *The Hebrew Goddess*, Raphael Patai recounts how Lilith was the first wife of Adam, made of filth and sediment, who rebelled against the sexually submissive role prescribed for her. She abandoned Adam and fled paradise to become a seducer of defenceless men, a witch, a child-slayer, and the procreator of demons.[13] Various sources that recount the myth of Lilith generally portray her as the embodiment of sexual peril. '[Lilith] The paramour of lascivious spirits rose to be the bride of Samael the Demon King, ruled as Queen of Zemargad and Sheba, and ended up as the consort of God himself.'[14] Her sexual appetite and aggressive behaviour make her desirable and feared. No masculine being, mortal or immortal, is able to remain immune to her sexual lure. Her power is well represented in the Sumerian terracotta relief, circa 1800 - 1750 BCE, that portrays her as a beautiful naked young woman (the seducer), with owl's feet and wings (the night dweller), and holding a ring and staff (the Sumerian symbols of authority). She is guarded by two owls and two lions that represent the ideas of wisdom and absolute power (see Figure 1).

Figure 1. Earliest representation of Lilith: A Mesopotamian terracotta relief known as *The Burney Relief* or *Queen of the Night*. It is been dated between 1800 and 1750 B.C.E. © Trustees of the British Museum.

The Zohar illustrates how man manipulates Lilith's image to hide his weaknesses. Generally, she first appears in the shape of a beautiful nubile girl but once she seduces them 'against their will,' she metamorphosises into a terrifying old hag. Different cultures that embrace the myth modify her image, but if the *how* of her appearance undergoes changes, the *what* she represents is also subjected to transformations. Lilith serves to embody all of what relates to woman's sexuality that is beyond man's understanding and control.[15] In Freudian terms, she is an example of the phallic woman who bears masculine traits such as sexual aggressiveness and authoritarianism.[16] In *Female Sexuality*, Freud explains that the castration complex affects a girl in three possible fashions. In the first one, the woman-to-be becomes traumatized and completely rejects her sexual nature. In a second one, she assumes her true feminine self and accepts the father figure as love-object. In the third case, she develops a 'masculinity complex' and rebels against the male's alleged superiority as

> she clings in obstinate self-assertion to her threatened masculinity; the hope of getting a penis sometime is cherished to an incredibly late age and becomes the aim of her life, whilst the phantasy of really being a man, in spite of everything, often dominates long periods of her life.[17]

Although the third possibility could lead the girl to a homosexual love-object, her masculinised self simply assumes a more assertive role by distancing herself from her social-symbolical characteristics and identifying her with the monstrous.

The actions of Freud's phallic woman are viewed as a need for revenge and stem from the dark mystery that dwells in the feminine. In Barbara Creed's terms, however, Lilith would not be the *castrated* woman but the *castrating* woman who 'represents a terrifying sexual fantasy of sexual difference.'[18] Woman is not castrated nor is she, in Lacanian terms, a fantasy cause of desire; what lies behind this representation of woman is the potentiality of castration. Lilith incarnates the vagina that mutilates man and the womb that envelops him. Rivero has captured both these embodiments in her characters.

Since the late nineteenth century, other interpretations of the myth have surfaced. Critics affirmed that Dante Gabriel Rossetti's sonnet 'Lilith' published in 1868, which accompanies his painting 'Lady Lilith' of 1863, introduced the archetype of Lilith to the Western world and initiated a re-examination of the myth that allowed for feminist readings. Since then, a total inversion of values has taken place. Lilith, the monstrous demoness, became a feminist icon.[19]

Incarnations of Lilith are constantly present in Giovanna Rivero's short stories. In 'Contraluna' the narration takes the shape of a scientist's field journal that chronicles the last five weeks of his life. It tells the story of a man trapped between two women. Nora, his lover, personifies Lilith as the irresistible and promiscuous seductress who ridicules him and questions his masculinity and whom he ultimately kills in a jealous rage. The second woman is a supernatural creature, a closer representation of the myth: she is half mulatta, half demoness; a monstrous mother / lover with owl's feet and feline green eyes who gives birth to frogs and takes the lives of her subjects at whim. She rules in the hallucinatory and chaotic world of the Brazilian jungle where the scientist goes to distil the venom of scorpions that he believes will provide an antidote to women's pheromones. These hormones symbolize Lilith's pervasive power over man. The mulatta has no name; she is meant to signify the lewd and sinful sexuality associated with women of colour. The fact that she is of mixed race strengthens her condition of monstrous.

Rivero's two personifications of Lilith offer another reading of the myth. Nora and the mulatta are not just manifestations of a malevolent Lilith who emasculate the protagonist, nor do they embody woman's empowerment. They both represent the castrating woman, the *vagina dentata* that holds the potential power to castrate man, and the archaic mother who possesses man by enveloping him in her womb.

One of themes in 'Contraluna' deals with the male subject's confrontation with the loss of the *objet a*. It depicts metaphorically a journey from the city to the jungle, from reason into madness, from life to death, from the symbolic to the unconscious. The narrative places the scientist between both Liliths, approaching one or the other, attracted and repelled at the same time, yet never escaping their magnetic field of attraction and repulsion. As he moves forward; their paths converge into a common vertex creating a triangle shape that signifies their arrival to entropy, or in Lacanian terms, to the absolute zero (see graphic below).

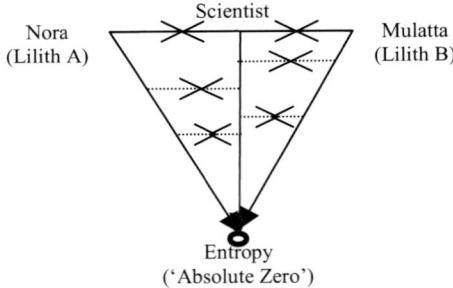

Figure 2: The erotic aggressivity that leads to entropy.

The protagonist is a biologist who believes in the capacity of language to construe his reality. The fantasy that permeates his life is his attraction to Nora and though he does not love her, he wants to possess her, and this need becomes a deadly obsession. He transgresses the threshold of the pleasure principle into *jouissance*, which, in the simplest terms, is an excess of pleasure not devoid of pain. *Jouissance* adds a sadomasochistic element to this relationship. The scientist at first persists in explaining his weakness in symbolic terms as 'química, sí, pura empatía celular'[20] until Nora's death, when he finally acknowledges the irrationality of life. Her body, though it belongs to a 'perra callejera'[21] - a characterization that aligns her with the image of the whore - grants him the comforting feeling of being contained when he is inside her and, simultaneously, the terrifying feeling of ceasing to be

> allí, en su 'tubo de ensayo', voy aniquilando la materia, convirtiéndola en sudor y jadeo....Y todo lo que sé, lo que busco, va fosilizándose, inútil, hasta dejar de ser conocimiento, de ser certeza o duda.[22]

When the protagonist has sexual intercourse with Nora, he reaches an amoeba-like state that terrifies him in that it signifies relinquishing his symbolic state, that is, his sex and social construction. According to Creed's theory, Nora's sex represents a threat of castration. Like Lilith, she is a creature of the night.[23] Unlike the goddess, however, she wears a black mask in bed to symbolically shield her vulnerability and to withhold from him glimpses of her true self. It also endows her eyes with feline attributes, a sign of her alterity that greatly perturbs the scientist. Later in the story, when he arrives in the jungle, he will be trapped by the yellow feline eyes of the mulatta. Guattari comments that the yellow eyes of a feline in a human are an example of an affect that throws the self into upheaval, making it real and uprooting it from humanity.[24]

The protagonist strives to counteract Nora's power by trying to possess her beyond sex, by dispossessing her of her soul. He tears the mask off her face, pulling off a lock of hair, and hits her on the eye in an effort to reveal that part of her nature she hides from him, her contraluna. Indifferent to the pain he causes, the protagonist feels relieved when the blackness of the mask that symbolizes her hidden self is replaced by the greenish colouring of the haematoma

> En el párpado izquierdo todavía permanece el hematoma; en los bordes, la sangre empieza a circular adquiriendo un tono verdoso a través de la piel, ya no tan oscuro, ya no tan doloroso.[25]

The violence escalates as the desire and the fear become unbearable. At an unconscious level, he believes that only the death of his fantasy (Nora) will render him free of *jouissance*. He wants to possess what is intangible in her and to admit this fact would represent the absolute breakdown of the subject. Ultimately, he strangles his lover as they have intercourse.

It is significant that the scientist embraces the abject Lilith after her death. He smears himself with her feces so as to have his body and soul enveloped by her one more time, saying: 'Unté mi cara y mi cuerpo, y esto que me habita, incluso en la negrura de la selva, mi espíritu.'[26] He is taking back what he rejected in Nora when she was alive. In *Powers of Horror*, Julia Kristeva states that: 'The abject confronts us with our earliest attempts to release the hold of maternal entity even before existing outside of her ... It is a violent, clumsy breaking away.'[27] By embracing her excrements, the character is trying to reunite with the archaic mother, an attempt to reach the Lacanian real. However, the desire of the Other exceeds the object of desire *objet a*. Nora is gone but the desire persists by the metonymic transfer of the *objet a* to another, the mulatta.

The lover's response to the protagonist's obsession is what Lacan terms narcissistic suicidal aggression.[28] In this concept, the erotic-aggressive character of the narcissistic infatuation with the specular image can lead the subject to self-destruction.[29] In 'Aggressiveness in Psychoanalysis,'[30] Lacan explains that, besides 'clarifying the ambivalence of the 'partial drive' of scotophilia, narcissism explains the relation of another 'partial drive', sadomasochism, and the aggressiveness that is manifested in both of them.' There is a sadomasochistic quality to Nora's words and actions. Her goading leads the scientist to beat her and his beating her leads her to taunt him even more. She dares him to leave her: '¿Por qué quieres poseerme? ¿No te basta con cogerme? ¿con pegarme? ¿Qué más quieres de mí?'[31] She will relinquish her *self* only in death: '¿Quieres que sea tuya? Entonces, mátame.'[32] He obeys and strangles her. Nora's possible motivation to risk death could be to reach the ultimate intensity in the sexual act. By goading and ridiculing her lover, she leaves him no other alternative but to kill her so he can reach the absolute release. Lacan asserts that

> one cannot overemphasize the irreducible character of narcissistic structure and the ambiguity of a notion that tends to misrecognize the constancy of aggressive tension in all moral life that involves subjection to this structure: for no amount of oblativity (genital love / mature love) could free altruism from it.[33]

If woman is the cause of man's desire, his *objet a* expressed as a fantasy, and desire and the object of desire are effects produced by the *objet a*; the fantasy must remain in man if desire is to persist. Rivero's protagonist expresses the need to feel his lack by referring to men as creatures who feed on others to survive. Men are parasites: '…somos garrapatas, tomamos de los demás la materia necesaria para existir…',[34] or vultures: 'Shulkan y yo, como todos los hombres, tuvimos el mismo destino: somos buitres.'[35] His words evoke Lacan's *objet a* cause of desire. If the *objet a* is absent, the subject experiences *angoisse*.

The scent of Nora's pheromones hounds the scientist even after death. Unable to fight his obsession through reason, he abandons his life in the city and delves into the mysteries of the jungle, an act that symbolizes his exit of the symbolic into the unconscious where signifiers do not meet any signified: 'En Río Branco los negros han destruido la razón […] Se me han olvidado las palabras […] mis certezas.'[36] In Lacanian terms, the protagonist experiences an excess of *jouissance* or Surplus-*jouissance,* which Žižek explains as the *objet a* which exists (or rather insists) in a kind of curved space in which, the more you approach it, the more it eludes your grasp (or, the more you possess it, the greater the lack...)[37]

The protagonist succumbs completely to his obsession and, in the fantastic universe of the jungle, his *objet a* assumes the form of the mulatta of the yellow eyes. Once he enters her universe, the scientist relinquishes his symbolic self, giving in to her beckoning. Just as with Nora, he claims no responsibility for his actions and perceives his impending death as a result of the mulatta's will and not of his own. His lover and the mulatta are two faces of Lilith, a response to all that is sexually mysterious or dangerous that man fears in woman's sexuality. Hence his *objet a.*

Rivero adds an ironic twist to another of Lilith's transgressions. The myth recounts that men would blame her for their shameful involuntary nocturnal emissions and the seed stolen from these 'forced' couplings would allow her to give birth to demons that would plague humanity. The following is a passage from the Zohar:

> She roams at night, and goes all about the world and makes sport with men and causes them to emit seed. In every place where a man sleeps alone in a house, she visits him and grabs him and attaches herself to him and has her desire from him, and bears from him ... and all this takes place when the moon is on the wane.[38]

Unable to acknowledge their perceived weaknesses, men rationalize their inability to control their desires by creating a supernatural being to take the blame. They concede to this female and diabolical creature the sexual power she exerts on them, only because they have assigned her a fantastic nature.

In Rivero's short story demons and men are interchangeable. The scientist witnesses a ritual where the natives make a tight circle around the mulatta who feeds them a hallucinogen *(muscaria)* and places some in their hands to rub on their bodies. The *muscaria* generates psychological rifts, altering their sense of reality, and its topical application eventually causes their flesh to rot. As all eyes are held on her, she squats, grunts and gives birth to a frog. The batrachian, still bloody with the placenta, leaps around and stops in front a woman who then screams, terrified. The mulatta approaches her and, with a sharp, calcified nail, rips her aorta open. The natives, like 'buitres, animales salvajes'[39], lunge at her to drink her blood. Then, they squeeze together to make a wall surrounding the frog. When they disperse, there is a man in its stead: 'la antimateria, la sombra anterior'[40] . As for the scientist, once he enters the fantastic world of the mulatta, he gradually metamorphosizes into a vulture so as to disclose his true nature: a creature, like a vampire that feeds off others to survive.

There is no evidence in the story that the mulatta requires a male partner to procreate; in fact, there is the intimation that the creature she bears is the result of parthenogenesis. She is the generative archaic mother, 'constructed within patriarchal ideology, as the primeval 'black hole', the originating woman which gives birth to all life.'[41] But, because her image is a product of patriarchal ideology, she inspires terror, which is precisely what the natives, the protagonist, and his guide feel for the mulatta. The archaic mother is constructed 'as a negative force, she is represented in her phantasmagoric aspect in many horror texts...'[42] However, defined outside the symbolic, before and beyond the phallus, the archaic mother assumes another meaning, that of the true giver of life, independent of man's designs. Creed brings attention to the difference between the concept of the *vagina dentata* and the mother's womb.

> Unlike the female genitalia, the womb cannot be constructed as a 'lack' in relation to the penis [...] the womb signifies 'fullness' or 'emptiness' but always it is its own *point of reference*.'[43]

It can be inferred then that woman, as her own point of reference, does not have need of an *objet a* to become the desire of the Other in the manner that man necessitates of woman to fill the fantasy that generates desire: 'The concept of the archaic mother allows for a notion of the feminine which does not depend for its definition on a concept of the masculine.'[44]

There is a mother-child rapport between the natives and the mulatta, whom they call 'la Gran Madre.'[45] Like Lilith, she gives birth to a non-human creature, a frog. However, as opposed to Lilith's demons that stand opposed to the children of mankind, the frog becomes a man, suggesting that man is himself a demon, 'a plague of mankind' and that man makes his own hell. The idea that man is responsible for the evil in the world is pursued in Rivero's parody of *The Frog Prince*, a fairy tale that the brothers Grimm disseminated. Edited versions for children tell the story of a prince who was cursed by an evil witch who transformed him into a frog. He was able to return to his original form when a beautiful princess acquiesces kindly to his request for a kiss. When she willingly kisses the frog, a most handsome prince appears in the place of the frog; they fall immediately in love, marry and live happily ever after.

In Rivero's version, the frog becomes a man through human sacrifice, sucking the life of another. It is violence and not love that brings man to his human form: one life for the price of another. Also, it is not coincidental that a woman is chosen to be sacrificed. Anchored in the realm of reason, the protagonist is not aware of the magical world until he gets to the jungle, and confesses he never read fairy tales: 'Yo leía a Marco Polo.'[46] Shulkan, his guide, proceeds to explain the story to him: 'La idea, compadre, es que tú y yo somos, bajo este cuero, un batracio inhibido, tímido, buscando una negra que nos libere.'[47] In contrast to the fairy tale, Rivero's version presents man's true nature as a batracchian and his human form as a disguise.

Rivero enters the realm of the fantastic when the protagonist errupts into the unconscious (the jungle), where the Law of the Father is absent. Transgression takes place. According to Rosemary Jackson in *Fantasy: The Literature of Transgression*, 'Fantasy, with its tendency to dissolve structures, moves towards an ideal of undifferentiation, and this is one of its defining characteristics. It refuses difference, distinction, homogeneity, reduction, discrete forms.'[48] Jackson equates this concept of undifferentiation to the instinct Freud identifies in *Beyond the Pleasure Principle* as

> the most fundamental drive in man: a drive towards a state of inorganicism ... a longing for Nirvana ... This condition he termed a state of entropy, and the desire for undifferentiation he termed an entropic pull, opposing entropy to ... the erotic, aggressive drives of any organicism.[49]

The subject arrives at the absolute chaos when there is no more distinction between subject and Other, man and woman, the organic and inorganic, human and animal or vegetable. Lacan defines this state as the 'eternal and irreducible desire of the subject to arrive at the absolute zero.'[50] Metamorphosis is a step towards undifferentiation. In 'Contraluna', the mulatta has yellow eyes, 'ojos de puma.'[51] The most powerful predator in the jungle inhabits the mulatta, and the scientist fears what lies behind her yellow eyes. This unknown is the monstrous feminine, the feminine excess represented in terms of horror. It is unnamed because it challenges the language of the symbolic. As with Nora's mask, he wants to destroy them: 'Cuando estés distraída mirando el río, te sacaré los ojos. Tus ojos. Esas malditas lunas amarillas.'[52]

Another example of undifferentiation is the mutation into vultures that both the scientist and his guide undergo when they penetrate the jungle. When his guide approaches his imminent death, he has already altered his shape: 'Shulkan no escapó, no quería escapar [...] veo sus plumas ensangrentadas.'[53] The protagonist assumes willingly his new state, thereby acknowledging his departure from the symbolic:

> Aquí quiero quedarme, bajo la luna [nyctophilia], no necesito las palabras [the dimension of the symbolic], mi graznido se esparcirá por Río Branco, entrará por los oídos de los negros, aletearé sobre sus cabezas...[54]

Rivero alludes to the protective role of the owls that flank Lilith in the Sumerian relief when the scientist gives away his deadly intentions: '...no seré tu guardián, mulata.'[55] Like other scavenging raptors he awaits the death of others to feed: 'Voy buscando la carroña, espero la muerte de los negros, levanto sus costras, la piel carcomida por la muscaria para buscar algo de carne, un resto de carne.'[56]

If in the 'real' world the scientist kills Nora, he also commits suicide. Her death is physical; his is symbolic, for he is lost to the world, as he knows it. In the realm of the fantastic the dissolution of the subject is absolute. What remains is his relentless pursuit for the object of his desire i.e., the mulatta, translated into equal impelling urges to possess and destroy her. However, a face-to-face encounter will bring about their respective deaths at each other's hands. The end of the story mirrors the last sexual encounter between the protagonist and his lover. Nora subjugates him; 'en la cama ella es la que domina,'[57] in the jungle the mulatta rules, 'la mulata es mi ama,'[58] Nora's legs pin him down, 'las piernas que me atenazan,'[59] the mulatta's claws bind him to the ground, 'anclado en sus garras.'[60] Whereas Nora's sex, ready for intercourse, is described in phallic terms, 'el aguijón erguido,'[61] the mulatta is about to perform a motherly act, 'La mulata estira la mano para darme de comer ... me acerca a su sonrisa de bruja.'[62] The protagonist strangles Nora, and in his final confrontation with the mulatta, he, now a vulture, turns her maternal act into an incestual one. He/it lifts his beak and thrusts repeatedly into something soft. She moans, either in pleasure or in pain: 'Ahora martilleo algo blando. Ella gime.'[63] The last words in the story speak to their arrival at the absolute zero, at entropy: 'La luz fría de la noche va desnudándolo todo. Ya no hay secretos: contraluna.'[64]

In contrast to the myth where Lilith seduces and consumes men in her desire, the scientist and the mulatta consume and annihilate each other. There is no unity but dissolution; they reach entropy but their union in death does not avail them in returning to the pre-symbolic wholeness of the self. Their longing for the real remains, forasmuch as the real is an unattainable void. By reaching this conclusion, Rivero suggests that woman, as her own point of reference, is self-sufficient and her own *objet a*. Lacan alludes to this aspect of the feminine when, in 'God and ~~Woman~~'s *jouissance*,' he makes reference to woman's *jouissance* which is different from phallic *jouissance*.[65] Woman's *jouissance* is placed beyond the signifier (the absolute Other) and allows her to state her position as a desiring subject. As Jacqueline Rosen explains in *Sexuality in the Field of Vision*, this position brings up the question of what her *jouissance* signifies. Rosen interprets Lacan's words as the possibility that woman 'might break against and beyond that system itself,'[66] that is to say to transcend the limitations of language. Rivero's two faces of Lilith arrive at their woman's *jouissance* by virtue of their narcissistic nature, which in turn leads them to self-annihilation. Nora overcomes the confines of the protagonist's phallic sexuality by taunting him until he kills her in the midst of the sexual act itself. The fantastic figure of the mulatta, despite of being free of all socio-symbolical ties that categorize woman, as the archaic mother, falls victim to her own progeny. Nevertheless, a negative ramification of becoming a desiring subject represents woman's lost chance for immortality. Woman, likewise man, as Rivero's characters illustrate, diffuses herself in the entropic sexual union to remain forever prey to the yearning for the traumatic real.

Notes

[1] G. Rivero, *Contraluna*, La Hoguera, Santa Cruz, 2005.
[2] *Charles Baudelaire: Selected Poems from 'Les Fleurs du Mal'*, trans. N.R. Shapiro, University of Chicago Press Chicago, 2000, pp. 66-67.
[3] D. Evans, *Introductory Encyclopedia of Lacanian Psychoanalysis*, Routledge, London, 1996, p. 160.
[4] J. Lacan, 'Kant avec Sade', *Écrits*, trans B. Fink, W.W. Norton & Company, New York, 2006, p. 652.
[5] B. Creed, *The Monstrous Feminine: Film, Feminism, Psychoanalysis*, Routledge, London, 1993.
[6] Slavoj Žižek postulates that: 'The conclusion to be drawn is that the Lacanian Real is a much more complex category than the idea of a fixed trans-historical 'hard core' that forever eludes symbolization; it has nothing to do with what Immanuel Kant called the 'Thing-in-itself,' reality the way it is out there, independently of us, prior to being distorted by our perceptions...' (S. Žižek, 'Troubles with the Real: Lacan as Viewer of Alien', *How to Read Lacan*, W. W. Norton & Company, New York, 2007, p. 65).
[7] J. Lacan, 'A Love Letter', *Encore: The Seminar of Jacques Lacan: Book XX: On Feminine Sexuality, The Limits of Love and Knowledge, 1972-1973*, trans B. Fink, W.W. Norton & Company, New York, 1999, p. 81.
[8] In *The Metastases of Enjoyment*, London, Verso, 2005, p. 143, Žižek explains that 'Woman does not exist does not in any way refer to an ineffable feminine Essence beyond the domain of discursive existence: *what does not exist is this very unattainable Beyond* [...] 'the enigma of woman' ultimately conceals the fact that there is nothing to conceal.'
[9] D. Evans, op. cit., p. 160.
[10] J. Lacan, 'Guiding Remarks for a Congress in Feminine Sexuality', *Écrits*, trans B. Fink, W.W. Norton & Company, New York, 2006, p. 613.
[11] Ibid.
[12] F. Jameson, 'Magical Narratives: Romance as Genre', *New Literary History*, Vol. 7, No. 1, 1975, p. 140.
[13] R. Patai, *The Hebrew Goddess*, 2nd ed, KTAV, New York, 1990, p. 221.
[14] Ibid.
[15] Patai, op. cit., p. 233.
[16] Creed, op. cit., p. 157.

[17] S. Freud, 'Female Sexuality', *The International Journal of Psychoanalysis*, Vol. 13, 1932, p. 285.

[18] Creed, op. cit., p. 158.

[19] In her study of the evolution of Lilith's representations in literature, (A Scerba, 'Changing Literary Representations of Lilith and the Evolution of a Mythic Heroine' in *Feminism and Women Studies*, retrieved 7 June 2009 http://feminism.eserver.org), Amy Scerba concludes that: 'Because of *Rossetti's* work - even if only because of the popularity of his work and not its quality or actual content - *Lilith* has been adopted as a feminist heroine in a variety of mediums today. From *Lilith* magazine to the 'Lilith Fair,' her image is being heralded as one of opportunity, voice, and power for women. In almost all cases, Rossetti has been recognized and read by modern critics and interpreters as the first to give her figure voice and opportunity, allowing for such modern positive representations to develop.

[20] Rivero, op. cit., p. 131, 'chemistry, that's it, sheer cellular empathy'. All translations into English of Rivero's work are mine.

[21] Ibid., p. 130, 'street whore'.

[22] Ibid., p. 131, '... there, in her 'test tube,' I am killing matter, transforming it in sweat and panting...and everything I look for is turning into fossil, useless, until it ceases to be knowledge, certainty or doubt.'

[23] Lacan relates nyctophilia or love for the night to narcissism.

[24] G. Deleuze, & F. Guattari, *A Thousand Plateaus: Capitalism and Schizophrenia*, trans B. Massumi, University of Minnesota Press, Minneapolis, 1987, p. 240.

[25] Rivero, op. cit., p. 132, 'Her left eye shows the greenish colouring of a bruise, the blood begins to circulate around the edges under the skin, not so dark, not so painful.'

[26] Ibid., p. 149, 'I rubbed my face and my body, and this that inhabits me, even the darkness of the jungle, my spirit.'

[27] J. Kristeva, *Powers of Horror: An Essay on Abjection*, trans. L.S. Roudiez, Columbia University Press, New York, 1982, p. 13.

[28] Evans, op. cit., p. 120.

[29] Ibid.

[30] J. Lacan, 'Aggressiveness in Psychoanalysis', *Écrits*, B. Fink (ed), W.W. Norton & Company, New York, 2006, 82-101, p. 97.

[31] Rivero, op. cit., p. 149, 'Why do You want to possess me? Isn't it enough to fuck me? To hit me? What else do you want of me?'

[32] Ibid., p. 148, 'Do you want me to be yours? Then, kill me.'

[33] J. Lacan, 'Aggressiveness in Psychoanalysis', pp. 96-97.

[34] Rivero, op. cit., p. 137, '...we are ticks; we take from others the necessary matter to exist...'

[35] Ibid., p. 149, 'Shulkan and I, like all men, we had the same destiny: we are vultures.'
[36] Ibid., p. 128, 'In Rio Branco, the blacks have destroyed reason ... I have forgotten all words ... my certainties.'
[37] S. Žižek, 'Surplus-Enjoyment Between the Sublime and the Trash', *Lacanian Ink 15*, Viewed on 7 June 2009, <http://www.lacan.com/cover15.htm>.
[38] Patai, op. cit., p. 233.
[39] Rivero, op. cit., p. 141, 'vultures, wild animals'.
[40] Ibid., 'the anti-matter, the previous shadow'.
[41] Creed, op. cit., p. 27.
[42] Ibid.
[43] Ibid., p. 28.
[44] Ibid.
[45] Rivero, op. cit., p. 135, 'The Big Mother'.
[46] Ibid., p. 141, 'I used to read Marco Polo'.
[47] Ibid., p. 141, 'The idea, my friend, is that you and I are, under this thick skin, an inhibited, shy batracchian who is looking for a black woman to free us.'
[48] R. Jackson, *Fantasy: The Literature of Subversion*, Methuen, London, 1981, p. 72.
[49] Ibid., pp. 72-73.
[50] J. Lacan, *The Language of the Self: The Function of Language in Psychoanalysis*, John Hopkins University Press, Baltimore, 1997, p. 191.
[51] Rivero, op. cit., p. 128, 'eyes of a mountain lion'.
[52] Ibid., p. 128, 'When you will not be paying attention, looking at the river, I will tear out your eyes. Those cursed yellow moons.'
[53] Ibid., p. 129, 'Shulkan did not escape, did not want to escape ... I see his bloody feathers'.
[54] Ibid., p. 128, 'I want to stay here, I don't need words, my caw will be heard all over Rio Branco, it will enter the ears of the blacks, I will flutter my wings over their heads...'
[55] Ibid., 'I will not be your guardian, mulatta.'
[56] Ibid., p. 149, 'I am looking for carrion, I await the death of the blacks, I raise their scabs, their skin eaten away by the *muscaria* looking for some meat to eat, a bit of meat.'
[57] Ibid., p. 131, 'She subjugates me in bed'.
[58] Ibid., p. 149, 'The mulatta is my master'.
[59] Ibid., p. 148, 'her legs that clutched me'.
[60] Ibid., p. 149, 'anchored in her claws'.
[61] Ibid., p. 148, 'her sting erect'.
[62] Ibid., p. 149, 'The mulatta stretches her hand to feed me [...] she brings close to me her witch smile.'

[63] Ibid., 'Now I hammer something soft. She moans.'
[64] Ibid., 'The cold light of night strips everything. There are no more secrets: contraluna.'
[66] J. Lacan, 'God and ~~Woman~~'s *jouissance*', *Encore: The Seminar of Jacques Lacan: Book XX: On Feminine Sexuality, The Limits of Love and Knowledge, 1972-1973*, W.W. Norton & Company, New York, 1999, pp. 73-74.
[67] J. Rosen, *Sexuality in the Field of Vision*, Verso, London, 2005, p. 176.

Bibliography

Armitt, L., *Contemporary Women's Fiction and the Fantastic*. St. Martin's Press, New York, 2000.

Baudelaire, C., 'Le Vampire'. *Charles Baudelaire: Selected Poems from 'Les Fleurs du mal'*. trans. Shapiro, N., University of Chicago Press, Chicago, 2000.

'Burney Relief'. *Wikipedia*. Viewed on 2 June 2009. <http://en.wikipedia.org/wiki/Burney_Relief>.

Creed, B., 'Horror and the Monstrous-Feminine: An Imaginary Abjection'. *Feminist Film Theory*. Thornham, S. (ed), New York, New York University Press, 1999.

——, *The Monstrous Feminine: Film, Feminism, Psychoanalysis*. Routledge, London, 1993.

Deleuze, G. & Guattari, F., *A Thousand Plateaus: Capitalism and Schizophrenia*. trans. Massumi, B., University of Minnesota Press, Minneapolis, 1987.

Evans, D., *Introductory Encyclopedia of Lacanian Psychoanalysis*. Routledge, London, 1996.

Feher-Gurewich, J., 'A Lacanian Approach to the Logic of Perversion'. *The Cambridge Companion to Lacan*. Rabaté, J.M. (ed), Cambridge University Press, Cambridge, 2003.

Freud, S., 'Female Sexuality'. *The International Journal of Psychoanalysis*. Vol. 13, 1932, pp. 281-297.

Freud, S., *Beyond the Pleasure Principle.* trans. Strachey, J., Norton, New York, 1989.

Jackson, R., *Fantasy: The Literature of Subversion.* Methuen, London, 1981.

Jameson, F., 'Magical Narratives: Romance as Genre'. *New Literary History.* Vol. 7, No. 1, 1975, pp. 133-163.

Kristeva, J., *Powers of Horror: An Essay on Abjection.* trans. Roudiez, L.S., New York, Columbia University Press, 1982.

Lacan, J., 'Aggressiveness in Psychoanalysis'. *Écrits.* trans. Fink, B., W.W. Norton & Company, New York, 2006.

——, *Encore: The Seminar of Jacques Lacan: Book XX: On Feminine Sexuality, The Limits of Love and Knowledge, 1972-1973.* W.W. Norton & Company, New York, 1999.

——, 'Guiding Remarks for a Congress in Feminine Sexuality'. *Ecrits.* trans. Fink, B., W.W. Norton & Company, New York, 2006.

——, *The Language of the Self: The Function of Language in Psychoanalysis.* John Hopkins University Press, Baltimore, 1997.

Luepnitz, D., 'Beyond the Phallus: Lacan and Feminism'. *The Cambridge Companion to Lacan.* Rabaté, J.M. (ed), Cambridge University Press, Cambridge, 2003.

Miess, J., 'Another Gendered Other? The Female Monster-Heroin'. *Horrifying Sex: Essays on Sexual Difference in Gothic Literature.* Anolik, R.B. (ed), McFarland, Jefferson, 1987.

Mitchell, J. & Rose, J. (eds), *Feminine Sexuality: Jacques Lacan and the École Freudienne.* Macmillan, London, 1982.

Moi, T., 'From Femininity to Finitude: Freud, Lacan, and Feminism Again'. *Signs: Journal of Women in Culture and Society.* 2004, Vol. 29, No. 3, pp. 841-878.

Patai, R., *The Hebrew Goddess.* 2nd edn, KTAV, New York, 1990.

Rickert, T.J., *Acts of Enjoyment: Rhetoric, Žižek and the Return of the Subject.* University of Pittsburgh Press, Pittsburgh, 2007.

Rivero, G., *Contraluna.* La Hoguera, Santa Cruz, 2005.

——, *Sangre dulce.* La Hoguera, Santa Cruz, 2006.

Rosen, J., *Sexuality in the Field of Vision.* Verso, London, 2005.

Russ, J., *To Write Like a Woman: Essays in Feminism and Science Fiction.* Indiana University Press, Bloomington, 1995.

Scerba, A., 'Changing Literary Representations of Lilith and the Evolution of a Mythic Heroine'. *Feminism and Women Studies.* Viewed on 7 June 2009, <http://feminism.eserver.org>.

Shinn, T.J., *Worlds within Women: Myth and Mythmaking in Fantastic Literature by Women.* Greenwood Press, Connecticut, 1986.

Žižek, S., *How to Read Lacan.* Critchley, S. (ed), W.W. Norton & Co., New York, 2007.

——, (ed), *Lacan: The Silent Partners.* Verso, London, 2006.

——, *The Metastases of Enjoyment: On Women and Causality.* 2nd ed, Verso, London, 2005.

——, 'Surplus-Enjoyment between the Sublime and the Trash'. *Lacanian Ink 15.* Viewed on 7 June 2009, <http://www.lacan.com/cover15.htm>.

PART 4

The Mechanics of Monsterisation

A Three-Eyed Monster: The Picture of a Photographer in World Literature

Joanna Madloch

Abstract
Following the invention of photography, the daguerreotypist emerged as a new type of literary character to be ridiculed by nineteenth-century authors. In twentieth-century literary works, the picture of a harmless oddball evolved into the disturbing portrait of the most disliked and notorious tried-and-tested monster, the dreaded photographer. This chapter uses the theory of a monster, as described by Noël Carroll in *The Philosophy of Horror or the Paradoxes of the Heart*, to analyse how photographers are portrayed as monsters in fictional works. Fusion, the most popular method according to Carroll, condenses opposed categories and leads to the creation of a hybrid form of monster-photographer. Some examples include (a) 'photographer-Frankenstein,' an emotionally troubled, solitary, machine-like human; (b) 'photographer-vampire,' a blood- and soul-sucking individual; (c) 'photographer-Cyclops,' an uncivilized, deformed, and cruel being; and finally, (d) 'photographer-Priapus,' an impotent, but sexually-obsessed deviant. The other methods listed by Carroll include: fission that bases on violation of categorical conflicts and produces monstrous characters as doubles or doppelgangers, and horrific metonymy which links the product of the monstrous activity with the monster itself. They are both used to produce characters of photographers as monsters, and at the same time, reveal the genuine nature of social resentment toward photographers. As this chapter demonstrates, it is fear of the resulting pictures that makes a photographer a public enemy. The photographer becomes infamous as the person, who sees too much, understands too much, reveals truth, and who obviously inflicts fear. This fear, in turn, categorizes the photographer as a monster, both in the metaphorical and physical sense.

Key Words: Photographer, monster, trickster, defect, isolation, obsession, impurity, oddity, abuse, death.

*****

1. Introduction

The introduction of photography as a new art form in the nineteenth century attracted much public attention and triggered intense emotions. The world of the well-established arts welcomed photography with extreme opinions, ranging from enthusiastic acceptance, expressed mostly by English-speaking writers such as Edgar Alan Poe, Lewis Carroll, Jack London, and Arthur Conan Doyle, to complete rejection, articulated mostly by French authors such as Gérard de Nerval, Alexandre Dumas Père, and Charles Baudelaire, who called photography 'an industry,' that 'by invading the territories of art has become art's most mortal enemy.'[1]

The uncertainty of the meanings and functions of the new art (which quickly challenged the prosperous existence of painting, especially realistic portraiture), together with the mysterious aura that emanated from the photographic process itself, helped to build up the atmosphere of suspicion and mistrust toward those who practiced photography. Shortly after the daguerreotypist became a literary character, nineteenth-century writers mostly portrayed him[2] as an individual stirring up disorder and laughter, either thanks to his adventurous nature[3] or because of his lack of professional skills.[4] The perception of photography as a sort of modern dark magic became an added dimension to this mysterious new craft. Many photographers got involved in the trendy movement of spiritualism, manifested as spirit photography or ghost photography, a trade practiced by well-renowned artists like Arthur Conan Doyle.[5] Furthermore, the conviction that photography 'steals' the human body and/or soul was a popular superstition shared by many luminaries of the nineteenth-century culture, such as Théophile Gautier, Gérard de Nerval, and Honoré de Balzac. This common fallacy was ridiculed by Julies Fleury Husson, known as Champfleury, in his witty and hilarious satire *The Legend of the Daguerreotypist* (1863).

One who analyses the picture of the nineteenth-century photographer can easily relate it to the archetype of a mythological trickster understood here as a 'semiotic creature.'[6] The classical trickster is a character located on the periphery of the known, straddling the boundary between the domesticated and wild. He is a traveller and discoverer of new limits. He and his craft, however, belong to the marginal zone, a place between art and science, where he discovers new possibilities beyond what is known in human expression, and introduces new technological inventions. In twentieth-century literature, the image of the photographer changes radically. He begins as a funny, clumsy, and calamity-prone trickster who, by the end of the twentieth century, transforms into one of the most feared, strange, and repulsive monsters in all of the literary arts.[7]

In his book entitled *The Philosophy of Horror or the Paradoxes of the Heart*, Noël Carroll explains the structures of horrific imagery and gives a recipe for 'how to make a monster.'[8] However, Carroll mostly discusses fantastic creatures born by the imagination of horror book writers and movie creators; as such, a photographer, as presented in the modern literature, perfectly fits into the monstrous pattern proposed by the author. The first trait Carroll lists as essential to a monster's characteristics is a threatening demeanour. People have been always afraid of monsters; in fact, the human imagination created monsters as the incarnation of genuine and imagined horrors of life. In the same way, they have become afraid of photography and photographers. The purpose of this chapter is to give an explanation to the phenomenon of the sinister portrait of photographers in literature, which undoubtedly reflects social reluctance toward them.

2. Ugly and Repulsive

Although the actual trade of being a photographer elicits suspicion a priori, his external appearance only further adds to the notion that photographers are 'monsters.' As evidence of this, many photographers have been described in literature as being physically defective; even the young and handsome Halgrave from Hawthorne's novel is portrayed as having 'a grave and thoughtful expression.'[9] The vast majority of fictional photographers are often males who do not care about their appearance or personal hygiene. Rick DeMartinis' short story, 'Billy Ducks among the Pharaohs' (1986), clearly demonstrates this, as Billy Ducks is described as an extremely ugly and scruffy man with 'haggard, bloodshot eyes. Dark, tender-looking pouches hung like pulpy half-moons under them.... He was in pyjamas and bathrobe, even though it was midafternoon.'[10] Many literary photographers are also portrayed as being seriously handicapped and badly deformed: Monsieur Paul, the provincial photographer from Daphne du Maurier's 'The Little Photographer' (1952) is lame;[11] E.J. Bellocq, presented by Michael Ondaatje in 'Coming Through Slaughter' (1976), is a hydrocephalic semi-dwarf; and in 'Viewfinder' (1981) Raymond Carver portrays a working door-to-door photographer without hands, with metal hooks attached to what are left of his arms.

While the examples listed above portray photographers as physically challenged, sometimes photographers' 'otherness' gets to the point of physical monstrosity. An example of this horrific transformation is shown in V.S. Pritchett's 'The Image Trade' (1974), where the main character, a recognized writer, describes a celebrity photographer who takes his picture as a 'hovering vulture' and an 'unfortunate Satan walking up and down the world looking for souls.'[12] Also in Miles Gibson's *Kingdom Swann* (1990) a photographer is shown as a ravenous and depraved creature ('He was a monster. A wicked old fiend feasting on youth and innocence,'[13]) and a narrator in Michel Tournier's *The Ogre* (1970) states implicitly that 'The photographer is misery, greedy, avid, and centripetal.'[14] In the same novel, a photographer is as well presented as a monster-like being, with his camera described as a Cyclopean eye or an enormous sexual organ or weapon. This kind of deformation/magnification structure is a very typical trope of presenting a monster in a horror story.[15] The camera attached to a photographer's eye becomes a Cyclopean eye - the eye of a monster, which ultimately transforms its operator into a monster himself. Cyclops, as it is well known, are giants that appear in classical Greek and Roman mythology, 'grotesquely ugly humanoids with a single eye in the middle of the forehead ... crude, ungainly, and given to aggression and cannibalism.'[16] The association with a mythological Cyclops interconnects a photographer's physical defectiveness, his psychological shortcomings, and his lack of sociological adaptation.

Like a typical mythological monster, the photographer is presented in the literature as someone who rejects accepted norms of social and family life, choosing different forms of isolation instead. The majority of photographers portrayed in the analysed writing lead solitary lives. As stated by the photographer Peter Lime, a character from Leif Davidsen's, *Lime's Photograph* (2002), compares himself to a wolf ('wolves live and hunt best when alone'[17]). A photographer's singleness is often presented as the advantage that promotes their independence and mobility.[18] However, loneliness is far more often part of a photographer's life, especially among female photographers, like Miss Pratt from Paul Theroux's 'Greene' (1978), and the woman photographer from Cynthia Ozick's 'Shots' (1982). Interestingly, even photographers who seem to be surrounded by family and friends intentionally isolate themselves and remain detached from their relatives. One of the best illustrations of this is provided in John Updike's short story, 'The Day of the Dying Rabbit' (1969). In this tale, a photographer, the father of six children, remains calm and emotionally detached during a very moving family scene in which his children are taking care of a dying animal. The father describes this scene in detail, with professional objectivity and coolness, and looks at the situation as if he was photographing it. In other stories, photographers involved in relationships often prove themselves unable to appreciate what they have and disregard their families (Alberto Moravia's 'The Swollen Face' [1962]), use those who love them (Pritchett's 'Image Trade' and Annie Proulx's 'Negatives' [1996]), abuse their relatives ('Billy Ducks among the Pharaohs', Rosellen Brown's 'Good Housekeeping' [1973], Kathryn Harrison's 'Exposure' [1993]), and eventually drive family members to suicide (Colette's 'The Photographer's Wife' [1944]). Also, a photographer's house, as shown in the fiction, often tends to look more like a monster's den than a human's dwelling, and people who share their lives with photographers also happen to be described as monster-like creatures ('Billy Ducks among the Pharaohs').

As stated by Noël Carroll, in the case of a monster's aloofness, there is always the question of whether the monster separates himself, or if society rejects him first.[19] As mentioned above, many fictional photographers choose a solitary life for the sake of their independence, but far more often they are excluded from society due to their strangeness, quirkiness, or even criminal behaviour. While some of the physically monstrous photographers may trigger sympathy as victims of circumstance, like Edgar Rogers, a character from Harrison's novel *Exposure,* a celebrity photographer who separates himself from the world after his beloved wife's death, they more often than not demonstrate that their body reflect serious mental disorders.

3. Strange and Impure

As mythical monsters often seem single-purposed (Cyclops devour humans, vampires suck blood, serpents collect wealth and knowledge, various water monsters set out to drown people), photographers, as described in the analyzed writing, suffer their own obsession - photography. This particular obsession, regardless whether it is a trade or a hobby, surprisingly turns into a consuming mania, dangerous both for the photographer and his model. While pursuing a particular picture, photographers tend to forget about everything else. There are numerous examples of the psychotic behaviour displayed by a photographer when it comes to taking 'the picture.' For illustration, in Ernest William Hornung's novel *The Camera Fiend* (1911), a mysterious doctor-spiritualist-photographer is obsessed with the idea of photographing a soul leaving a body of a dying person; in Moravia's 'The Swollen Face', a photographer gets completely frenzied by his passion of taking a picture of a celebrity; in Joseph Heller's *Catch 22* (1961) a photographer nick-named 'Hungry Joe' is possessed with mania of taking a picture of naked women; in Italo Calvino's 'The Adventures of a Photographer' (1955), a photographer named Antonio believes that 'photography has a meaning only if it exhausts all possible images,'[20] which brings him to capture everything around him on film.

As stated by Jeffrey Jerome Cohen, one of the most important qualities of a monster is its impurity.[21] Monsters do not belong, but rather they pollute the established order, break the rules of civilization, and stir up chaos. For example Ann Rogers in Harisson's *Exposure* is a notorious shop-lifter and drug-addict who uses her photographic equipment to hide both drugs and stolen goods; and Billetdoux in 'Billy Ducks among the Pharaohs' defecates in public. They fit into a marginal zone, with disorder, lack of harmony, and a different understanding of fundamental categories such as right/wrong or beauty/ugliness. This quality of monstrosity in a photographer's case manifests itself mainly through the photographer's interest and the way he chooses subjects for pictures. As is shown in the analysed writing, photographers concentrate their attention on the oddities of life, topics that are publicly considered inappropriate or disgusting, and subjects that stay within the cultural marginal zone. One of the most revolting among the analysed characters, Billetoux in 'Billy Ducks Among the Pharaohs' tries to earn his living by selling photographs door-to-door, which makes him witness the most intimate and shameful details of people's existence. Walter, a character from Proulx's 'Negatives', gets pleasure from photographing 'oddballs' and the poor quality of his picture doubles the effect of ugliness. Both in Henry Miller's *Tropic of Cancer* and Michael Ondaatje's 'Coming Through Slaughter', the photographers are obsessed with photographing prostitutes and the misery of their lives. In the novel *Reflex* (2005), by Dick Francis, photographer George Millace is described as a 'pitiless photographer of moments all jockeys preferred to ignore'[22] when he enjoys documenting the most shameful moments of people's lives. As a final example, a female photographer in Ozick's 'Shots' is fascinated by photographing dead people.

4. Dangerous and Deadly

Contrary to Barry Munger, who names a photographer 'a guilty bystander'[23] by pointing to his quality of passiveness and objectiveness as a neutral observer of life, photographers are portrayed in fiction not only as observers and admirers of ugliness and evil, but as participants who actively create trouble in search of a prize topic. This way, a photographer turns from a 'minor devil,' one who enjoys wickedness and watching it unfold, into an 'active monster,' one who produces genuine danger, not only by his scary looks, but by his hazardous actions. As shown in the analysed writing, a photographer will not hesitate to stage a situation of suffering and distress, only to take a picture of it, with no consideration for his model's feelings. It is significant that taking photographs is often described in texts as a metaphor of crime and violence, with the photographers' gear seen as weapon or tool of offence. As stated by John Berger, 'The word *trigger*, applied to rifle and camera, reflects a correspondence which does not stop at the purely mechanical.'[24] Dora, a character from Robert Solé's *The Photographer's Wife* (1999), describes her encounter with a camera as an act of taming a strange creature ('I endeavoured to tame the monster, unwilling to acknowledge that I found it irresistibly attractive,'[25]) and the process of taking pictures as an act of violating a subject ('I transmit my emotion to my subject. I dominate them throughout the sitting, almost as if I were pointing a gun at them.'[26]). A narrator from Gibson's *Kingdom Swann* compares taking pictures to feeding a monster and a photographer to a hunter ('He stalked the streets in search of fresh women to feed to the hungry camera.'[27]). Similarly, the process of giving substantial food to the camera appears in Prichett's 'Image Trade': 'A little toad in the lens has shot out a long tongue and caught a fly.'[28] A photographer-narrator in Davidsen's *Lime's Photograph* calls his own camera a 'serpent in the Garden of Eden' that destroys its 'security and serenity,'[29] and keeps using military terminology while describing his work as 'hired assassin' ('I lay like sniper in Bosnia.'[30]).

The abuse of a model by a photographer can be psychological, as in the case of a writer-narrator in Prichett's 'Image Trade', who likens his impression of being photographed by an arrogant photographer to torment and rape. The classic example of the exploitation of a child by a father-photographer is provided in Harrison's novel *Exposure* a story that portrays a man who builds up his entire career on secretly photographing his adolescent daughter's first sexual experiences and her attempts at staging 'death.' As presented in the fiction, however, some photographers are also driven to perform acts of physical cruelty for the sake of taking a certain picture. Illustrations of such acts are given in Brown's 'Good Housekeeping', where a mother-photographer pinches her baby to make him cry when she wants to photograph the inside of his mouth; in Tournier's *The Ogre,* a photographer is so fascinated by a boy's fresh wound that he keeps photographing it in detail when he should really help the injured victim of the accident; in Proulx's 'Negatives' a photographer forces his naked model to crawl into an oven; and in Hornung's *Camera Fiend* a psychopathic photographer kills people with an altered camera that really contains a firearm, and ultimately commits suicide while attempting to take a shot of his own soul.[31]

'Photography that isn't serious doesn't affect the model,'[32] states a photographer in Michel Tournier's 'Veronica's Shrouds' (1978) which shows an extreme example of psychological and physical exploitation of a model by a photographer. Veronica, a female photographer portrayed in the story, invents a process called 'direct photography' that entails photographing the model's body without film. The developing bath that Hector, Veronica's model-lover frequently takes, severely damages his skin and most likely leads to his death. This motif associates the title of the short story with the funeral shrouds that are used to cover a body after death. Veronica herself turns out to be an atrocious version of a 'man-eater' type of woman, a genuinely horrific praying mantis who abuses the man, discarding him once he becomes worthless for her purpose. Her complexion shows another monstrous aspect of a photographer as portrayed in fiction: his affiliation with deviant sexuality and death.

The lecherousness of mythological and folk monsters is well represented in a metaphorical picture of a monster kidnapping and devouring young virgins, as in the story of Little Red Riding Hood where a wolf outwits and consumes both a girl and her grandmother. Among the photographers portrayed in fiction, sexual aberration can be listed as one of their major traits, mainly due to the image of the oversized single lens reflex (SLR) camera lens often associated with a male sexual organ (Tournier's *The Ogre*), which turns a photographer into a modern version of the mythological Priapus. The massive lens of SLR cameras has been always linked to sexual potency, and has been often ridiculed in pop culture as a penis extension. Nevertheless, while associating a photographer equipped with his SLR and with the fabled Priapus, a grotesquely deformed short man with an oversized, erected penis, one should remember that the immense sexual organ caused Priapus nothing but trouble. Contrary to popular belief, his owner was not a sex god, but rather a frustrated impotent. This correlation once again proves a photographer's incapability of having a successful relationship, not only in the sexual sense, but in general. As stated above, the majority of the photographers presented in the analysed works are single and not interested in enduring relationships. In addition, those who have families often struggle within them, such as the paparazzo portrayed in Moravia's 'The Swollen Face', who treats his wife as an obstacle in performing his job. Even if a spouse can be useful and helpful for a photographer, as is shown in Pritchett's 'The Image Trade', where Zut's wife carries all his equipment after him, many photographers in fiction still concentrate their interest around more casual relationships with prostitutes or teenage girls ('Billy Ducks among the Pharaohs'). Some are even convicted paedophiles, like in Diana Hartog's novel *The Photographer's Sweethearts* (1996), a tale that portrays the character of Louis Olsen, a photographer, mystic, and healer. If the photographers depicted in these fictitious works happen to encounter real passion, it often leads to their destruction or even death. For example, a character portrayed in Calvino's 'The Adventures of a Photographer' loses his mind when a girlfriend leaves him; a gay photographer from Francis' *Reflex*, commits a suicide when ditched by his boyfriend; and finally Monsieur Paul, pictured in du Maurier's 'The Little Photographer', gets killed by the object of his passion. The examples of photographers who love and are loved are extremely rare (Halgrave in *The House of Seven Gables* and Philip Nore in *Reflex*). Usually the objects of photographers' passion have to endure hardships, too: a photographer's wife from Colette's *The Photographer's Wife* takes her own life; Veronica from 'Veronica's Shrouds' sacrifices Hector for the sake of her invention; in 'Billy Ducks among the Pharaohs', the entire dysfunctional family suffers; Dora, a female photographer from Solé's *The Photographer's Wife*, loses her family due to her professional success accused of neglecting her natural duties in the male-oriented world; and Peter Lime from the novel *Lime's Photograph* by Davidsen gets his family murdered by men searching for one of his photographs.

5. How is the Monster Made?

Given the above examples, it is clear to envision that the photographers, as portrayed in fiction, are incapable of love and other human emotions. The attachment to his trade and its tools turns him into a hybrid creature, a machine, someone who is inept at feeling human and who becomes fully accustomed societal norms. In *Reflex*, Philip Nore described the process of transformation: '[a camera] gets to be a part of you. ... It is your shield. Keeps you a step away from the world. Makes you an observer. Gives you an excuse not to feel.'[33] Thus, a photographer is presented as an emotionally-troubled machine of a man, whose major traits include 'cold,' expressionless eyes, as portrayed in Hornung's *Camera Fiend* ('his eyes were cold steel,'[34] 'daggers in his eyes,'[35]) or in Hawthorne's *House of Seven Gables* ('Phoebe felt his eye often; his heart, seldom or never.'[36]) Machine-man, Frankenstein joins the collection of monstrous portraits of a photographer as a vampire (sucking the blood and soul of a victim), Priapus (impotent but obsessed with deviant sexuality), and Cyclops (deformed and cruel cannibal). All these horrific beings are constructed according to Noël Carroll's principles of fusion and represent 'creatures that transgress categorical distinctions such as inside/outside, living/dead, insect/human, and flesh/machine.'[37] While fusion 'hinges upon conflating, combining, or condensing distinct and/or opposed categorical elements in a spatial-temporally continuous monster,'[38] fission, another structural method of composing a monster, is based on violating categorical conflicts.

As stated by Noël Carroll, the typical example of a monster created on the principles of fission is a double or a doppelganger, but a photographer himself/herself is rarely represented as this kind of monster. It is the photography trade itself that actually produces doubles, likenesses of objects and people photographed. It seems that this particular function of a photographer is what earns him a foul opinion among the public, as well as monstrous portrait in fiction. While analysing the gruesome representations of a photographer in writing, one can come to the conclusion that although a photographer is presented as a revolting, dangerous character both physically and mentally, it is mostly his ability to see and to record what he witnesses that causes the most fear. The desire to see and photograph often gets a photographer into trouble, as shown by Jack London in his autobiographical story, 'How Jack London Got In and Out of Jail in Japan,' or Jerzy Kosinski's 'Blind Date,' but it is far more common for a photographer to disrupt other people's lives. As presented in literature, photographs often are used as proof of marital infidelity (Penelope Lively's *The Photograph* [2003], du Maurier's 'The Little Photographer') and crime (Julio Cortazar's 'Blow-up' [1959]), to document scandalous episodes of people's lives (Arthur Conan Doyle 'Scandal in Bohemia' [1891]), and to serve as blackmail tools (Francis' *Reflex* and du Maurier's 'The Little Photographer'). All the examples listed above deal with unwanted photographs, uninvited documents that from the point of view of the characters victimized them and should have never existed.

Though photography has an ability to lie (Dorris Dörrie's 'Lies') and create its own reality ('Veronica's Shrouds'), the craft has been long believed to document facts and expose the truth.[39] This conviction has made a photographer an unwanted witness and a monster, according to the rules of horrific metonymy, which links the products of the monstrous activity (undesired photographs) to the monster itself. Additionally, as shown in fiction, photographers not only document life, but also interpret it and solve its riddles. They take pictures and reconstruct the stories as told by them, such as in Cortazar's renown short-story, 'Blow-Up,' in which a photographer discovers crime activity accidentally recorded on his prints; *Reflex*, where a photographer deciphers the other photographer's enigma; *The House of Seven Gables*, that shows a photographer discover a long-hidden family mystery; or Graham Rawle's *Diary of Amateur Photographer. A Mystery* (1998), where a young photographer-wannabe tries to solve a criminal mystery that he discovers thanks to some photographs that accidentally get in his possession.[40] A twentieth century photographer's intelligence, wit, skills, and hi-tech equipment make him far more dangerous and unpredictable than his nineteenth century predecessor. Popular demand for gossip as a form of news, or even variation of 'truth,' in the twentieth century resulted in the creation of the 'paparazzo.' This profession is defined as those men and women whose job and passion consists of hunting celebrity subjects and revealing their secrets to the public. This attitude reflects upon literature, and portraits of paparazzi, as created by Alan Russell in his *Exposure* (2002), Robert M. Everesz in *Killing Paparazzi* (2002), and Davidsen in *Lime's Photograph* as they fit into the above described model of monstrosity. Like the other photographers described in fiction, paparazzi, also lead lonely lives - either by choice or by accident - and misuse alcohol and drugs: Peter Lime from Davidsen's *Lime's Photograph* is an alcoholic fighting his addiction; Nina Zero portrayed in Everesz's *Killing Paparazzi* comes from a dysfunctional family, serves a murder sentence, and later becomes a paparazzo who enjoys scaring people while photographing them. Paparazzi also rarely experience any pricks of conscience because of the results of their actions. The only exception is Graham Wells, a character from Russell's *Exposure*, who is tormented by the feeling of guilt after people whom he perused died in the accident.[41]

After comparing pictures of the nineteenth and twentieth century photographers in literature, one comes to the conclusion that the portrait of photographers created in different times and cultural situations depends on the general social situation of photography, and also reflects public opinion about those who practice it. During the age of the daguerreotype, people were amused and sometimes scared by the new invention's technological advancement and the unpredictable side effects of its use. These notions resulted in the birth of superstitious beliefs about photography's supernatural abilities, built social reserve toward it, and lead to creation of photographer's ridiculous portrayal in the arts.

It was not until the twentieth century that the genuine power of and fear toward photography was recognized, and which altered the fictional portrait of photographer from trickster to monster. The technological progress drastically changed the range of situations when pictures can be taken. While in the nineteenth century photographs had to be staged and carefully planned, in the following century technological progress permitted photographers to take pictures faster, better, and often unnoticed by a subject. At the same time, the simplification of previously complicated skill that was reserved for professionals revolutionized the accessibility of photography. Simple point-and-shoot cameras and built-in cell phone cameras have made everybody a photographer. The democratisation of photography has altered the perception of the reality, constantly photographed not only by professionals, but mostly by amateur photographers. A relatively good photograph can be practically taken now by anyone, anywhere, and anytime, making nobody 'safe' from being photographed. Candid photographs have changed people's ways of self-perception. While in the nineteenth century people would dress in their finest clothing for photographs, to be remembered in family albums by future generations, now photography catches us unprepared and underdressed, generally revealing a version of ourselves we would rather not be aware of.

In the age of advanced photography, anyone's action can be documented without his or her knowledge. This results in the association of photography with the notion of gaining and accumulating information. However, this meaning is altered in the age of the digital darkroom, where photographs can be manipulated beyond any documentary notion. Photographic 'evidence' does not need to be captured, but rather can be created by programs such as Photoshop®. No doubt that because of uninterrupted technological progress in the field of photography, the photographer will continue to be seen as a 'monster' in the twenty-first century.

Notes

[1] C. Baudelaire, 'The Salon of 1859', *Literature and Photography. Interactions 1840-1990*, trans. J. Mayne, J.M. Rabb (ed), University of New Mexico Press, Albuquerque, 1995, p. 67.

[2] The majority of photographers written about in nineteenth century literature are male. I have used the male pronoun (e.g., he, his, him) to depict this.

[3] Gérard de Nerval, in *Travels to Orient* (1846-47), writes about a young photographer who, while trying to photograph an upper-class woman, almost gets caught by the woman's friends. He is forced to remain in hiding in her bedroom, devoid of food, and is ultimately blackmailed by his potential subject. The situation turns tragicomic, as the photographer narrowly escapes through a window, losing all of his equipment, and is ultimately seen as a victim of his own vanity, greediness, and gullibility.

[4] Lewis Carroll, a most renowned and successful photographer of the Victorian era, concentrated on showing photographers' professional failures in the short story 'A Photographer's Day Out' (1860) and in his poem 'Hiawatha's Photographing' (1887). Additionally, Ernest William Hornung, in his short story 'A Spoilt Negative' (1888) presents a disastrous photographer in his hopeless attempts to take a good picture. In both Carroll's work and Hornung's story, a photographer tries his best to photograph his subject but his lack of skills prevents him from succeeding.

[5] The suspicious affiliation of a photographer is well portrayed by Nathaniel Hawthorne in the novel *The House of Seven Gables* (1851).

[6] C.W. Spinks, 'Trickster and Duality', *Trickster and Ambivalence: The Dance of Differentiation*, Atwood Publishing, Madison WI, 2001, p. 8.

[7] Twentieth-century literature also introduces women photographers, portrayed with similar characteristics as the male photographers. However, for the convenience of this chapter I will still continue to use the male pronouns: he, him, and his.

[8] N. Carroll, *The Philosophy of Horror or Paradoxes of the Hearth*, Routledge, New York, 1990, p. 43.

[9] N. Hawthorne, *The House of The Seven Gables*, A Bantam Book, New York, 2007, p. 35.

[10] R. DeMartinis, 'Billy Ducks among the Pharaohs', *Caught in Act: The Photographer in Contemporary Fiction*, Timken Publishers Inc., New York, 1996, p. 15.

[11] His sister, also involved in photography, is lame as well.

[12] V.S. Pritchett, 'The Image Trade', *Caught in Act, The Photographer in Contemporary Fiction*, Timken Publishers Inc., New York, 1996, p. 9.

[13] M. Gibson, *Kingdom Swann: The Story of a Photographer*, The Do-Not Press, London, 1998, p. 41.

[14] M. Tournier, *The Ogre*, trans. B. Bray, John Hopkins University Press, Baltimore, 1997, p. 462.
[15] Carroll, op. cit., p. 49.
[16] C. Rose, *Giants, Monsters & Dragons: An Encyclopedia of Folklore, Legend, and Myth*, W. W. Norton & Company, Inc., New York, 2000, p. 91.
[17] L. Davidsen, *Lime's Photograph*, trans. G. Kynoch, Vintage, London, 2002, p. 14.
[18] For example, Philip, the jockey-photographer from Dick Francis' *Reflex* (1981), Jack London, the traveller from 'How Jack London Got In and Out of Jail in Japan' (1904), the photographer-flâneur from Miller's *Tropic of Cancer* (1934), and the rebellious and persistent photographer from Jerzy Kosinski's 'Blind Date' (1977).
[19] Carroll, op. cit., p. 208.
[20] I. Calvino, 'The Adventures of a Photographer', *Literature and Photography: Interactions 1840-1990*, trans. W. Weaver, J.M. Rabb (ed), University of New Mexico Press, Albuquerque, 1995, p. 185.
[21] J.J. Cohen, 'Monster Culture (Seven Theses)', *Monster Theory: Reading Culture*, J.J. Cohen (ed), University of Minnesota Press, Minneapolis, 1996, p. 7.
[22] D. Francis, *Reflex*, A Berkley Book, New York, 2005, p. 2.
[23] B. Munger, 'The Guilty Bystander', *Caught in Act, The Photographer in Contemporary Fiction*, B. Munger (ed), Timken Publishers Inc., New York, 1996, pp. vii-x.
[24] J. Berger, 'Photographs of Agony', *The Photography Reader*, L. Wells (ed), Routledge, London, New York, 2003, p. 289.
[25] R. Solé, *The Photographer's Wife*, trans. J. Brownjohn, The Harvill Press, London, 1999, p. 46.
[26] Ibid., p. 251.
[27] Gibson, op. cit., p. 78.
[28] Pritchett, op. cit., p. 8.
[29] Davidsen, op. cit., p. 9.
[30] Ibid., p. 4.
[31] The same motif of a photographer who kills with a weapon hidden in a camera is used in the famous sociological thriller movie *Peeping Tom* by Michel Powell (1960). In the story, a sociopathic photographer approaches his victims with a camera that contains a knife, and photographs their fear at the moment they realize their impending death.
[32] M. Tournier, 'Veronica's Shrouds', *The Short Story & Photography 1880's-1980's*. trans. B. Wright, J.M. Rabb (ed), University of New Mexico Press, Albuquerque, 1998, p. 243.
[33] Francis, op. cit., p. 42.
[34] E.W. Hornung, *The Camera Fiend*, Charles Scribner's Sons, New York, 1911, p. 48.

[35] Ibid., p. 49.
[36] Hawthorne, op. cit., p. 151.
[37] Carroll, op. cit., p. 43.
[38] Ibid., p. 46.
[39] A photograph is often used as an object that both reveals the truth and implicates death in many horror and thriller movies. In *The Omen* (1976) by Richard Donner, the characters can predict their forthcoming death from distorted photographic portraits of themselves. The same way, in Gore Vitebski's *The Ring* (2002), the characters know about their doom from the photographs; in Alejandro Amenábar's *The Others* (2001) the character played by Nicole Kidman finds out that she and her family are dead from the photographs hidden in her house.
[40] This meaning of photography has been exploited in the movies, where a photographer is often portrayed as the one who discovers the truth, albeit sometimes accidentally (*Rear Window* [1954] by Alfred Hitchcock, *Blowup* [1966] by Michelangelo Antonioni).
[41] The plot of the last novel relates to the death of Lady Diana and her lover. Her death, the result of being chased down by the paparazzi, ignited many discussions about the paparazzi's immorality, and caused many to view them as 'hyenas' who feed upon other's misery.

Bibliography

Baudelaire, C., 'The Salon of 1859'. *Literature and Photography. Interactions 1840-1990.* trans. Mayne, J., Rabb, J.M. (ed), University of New Mexico Press, Albuquerque, 1995.

Berger, J., 'Photographs of Agony'. *The Photography Reader.* Wells, L. (ed), Routledge, London, New York.

Brown, R., 'Good Housekeeping: A (Very) Short Story'. *Literature and Photography: Interactions 1840-1990.* Rabb, J.M. (ed), University of New Mexico Press, Albuquerque, 1995.

Calvino, I., 'The Adventures of a Photographer'. *Literature and Photography. Interactions 1840-1990.* trans. Weaver, W., Rabb, J.M. (ed), University of New Mexico Press, Albuquerque, 1995.

Carroll, L., 'Hiawatha's Photographing'. Viewed on 30 January 2010, <http://www.netpoets.com/classic/poems/013015.htm>.

——, 'A Photographer's Day Out'. Viewed on 30 January 2010, <http://www.cartage.org.lb/en/themes/BookLibrary/books/bibliographie/C/Carr/p4/p4-do.html>.

Carroll, N., *The Philosophy of Horror or Paradoxes of the Hearth*. Routledge, New York, 1990.

Carver, R., 'Viewfinder'. *The Short Story & Photography, 1880's-1980's*. Rabb, J.M. (ed), University of New Mexico Press, Albuquerque, 1998.

Cohen, J.J., 'Monster Culture (Seven Theses)'. *Monster Theory: Reading Culture*. Cohen, J.J. (ed), University of Minnesota Press, Minneapolis, 1996.

Colette, 'The Photographer's Wife'. *The Collected Stories of Colette*. trans. White, A., Phelps, R. (ed), Farrar, Straus and Giroux, New York, 1984.

Cortázar, J., 'Blow-Up'. *The Short Story & Photography 1880's-1980's*. Rabb, J. M (ed), University of New Mexico Press, Albuquerque, 1998.

Davidsen, L., *Lime's Photograph*. Vintage, London, 2002.

DeMartinis, R., 'Billy Ducks among the Pharaohs'. *Caught in Act. The Photographer in Contemporary Fiction*. Munger, B. (ed), Timken Publishers, Inc., New York, 1996.

Doyle, A.C., 'Scandal in Bohemia'. *The Short Story & Photography, 1880s-1980s*. Rabb, J.M. (ed), University of New Mexico Press, Albuquerque, 1998.

Dörrie, D., 'Lies'. *Caught in Act: The Photographer in Contemporary Fiction*. Munger, B. (ed), Timken Publishers, Inc., New York, 1996.

Du Maurier, D., 'The Little Photographer'. *The Short Story & Photography, 1880s-1980s*. Rabb, J. M. (ed), University of New Mexico Press, Albuquerque, 1998.

Everesz, R., *Killing Paparazzi*. St. Martin's Minotaur, New York, 2001.

Francis, D., *Reflex*. A Berkley Book, New York, 2005.

Gibson, M., *Kingdom Swann: The Story of a Photographer*. The Do-Not Press, London, 1998.

Hartog, D., *The Photographer's Sweethearts*. The Overlook Press, Woodstock, New York, 1996.

Harrison, K., *Exposure*. Warner Books, New York, 1993.

Hawthorne, N., *The House of The Seven Gables*. A Bantam Book, New York, 2007.

Heller, J., *Catch 22*. Simon and Schuster, New York, 1996.

Hornung, E.W., 'A Spoilt Negative'. *The Short Story & Photography, 1880s-1980s*. University of New Mexico Press, Albuquerque, 1998.

——, *The Camera Fiend*. Charles Scribner's Sons, New York, 1911.

Kosinski, J., 'Blind Date'. *Literature and Photography: Interactions, 1840-1990*. University of New Mexico Press, Albuquerque, 1995.

Lively, P., *The Photograph*. Penguin Books, New York, 2004.

London, J., 'How Jack London Got In and Out of Jail in Japan'. *Literature and Photography: Interactions, 1840-1990*. University of New Mexico Press, Albuquerque, 1995.

Miller, H., *Tropic of Cancer*. Grove Press, New York, 1994.

Moravia, A., 'The Swollen Face'. *Caught in Act: The Photographer in Contemporary Fiction*. Munger. B. (ed), Timken Publishers Inc., New York, 1996.

Nadar, F., 'Balzac and the Daguerreotype'. trans. Repensek, T., *Literature and Photography: Interactions, 1840-1990*. University of New Mexico Press, Albuquerque, 1995.

Nerval, G. De, 'Travels to Orient'. *Literature and Photography: Interactions, 1840-1990*. University of New Mexico Press, Albuquerque, 1995.

Ondaatje, M., 'Coming Through Slaughter'. *Literature and Photography: Interactions, 1840-1990*. University of New Mexico Press, Albuquerque, 1995.

Ozick, C., 'Shots'. *Caught in Act: The Photographer in Contemporary Fiction*. Timken Publishers Inc., New York, 1996.

Pritchett, V.S., 'The Image Trade'. *Caught in Act: The Photographer in Contemporary Fiction*. Timken Publishers Inc., New York, 1996.

Proulx, A., 'Negatives'. *Caught in Act: The Photographer in Contemporary Fiction*. Timken Publishers Inc., New York, 1996.

Rawle, G., *Diary of an Amateur Photographer*. Picador, London, 1998.

Rose, C., *Giants, Monsters & Dragons: An Encyclopedia of Folklore, Legend, and Myth*. W.W. Norton & Company, Inc., New York, 2000.

Russell, A., *Exposure*. St. Martin's Minotaur, New York, 2002.

Solé, R., *The Photographer's Wife*. trans. Brownjohn, J., The Harvill Press, London, 1999.

Spinks, C.W., 'Dance of Differentiation: Trickster and Ambivalence'. *Trickster and Ambivalence: The Dance of Differentiation*. Atwood Publishing, Madison WI, 2001.

Theroux, P., 'Greene'. *Caught in Act: The Photographer in Contemporary Fiction*. Timken Publishers Inc., New York, 1996.

Tournier, M., *The Ogre*. trans. Bray, B., John Hopkins University Press, Baltimore, 1997.

——, 'Veronica's Shrouds'. *The Short Story & Photography, 1880s-1980s*. University of New Mexico Press, Albuquerque, 1998.

Updike, J., 'The Day of the Dying Rabbit'. *The Short Story & Photography, 1880s-1980s*. University of New Mexico Press, Albuquerque, 1998.

Unmasking Mary Shelley's *Frankenstein* in Patrick Süskind's *Das Parfum*

Samantha Michele Riley

Abstract
This chapter traces the parallels between Patrick Süskind's *Das Parfum: Die Geschichte eines Mörders* (*Perfume: The Story of a Murderer* 1984) and Mary Shelley's *Frankenstein, or The Modern Prometheus* (1818). The protagonist, Grenouille creates an ur-perfume, much as Victor Frankenstein constructs his ur-creature, from the body parts of deceased humans. A reading of *Das Parfum* often recalls *Frankenstein* structurally in terms of character, theme, genre, and plot, and in particular the framework of the *Bildungsroman*. Even more, the two read in combination contributes, however controversially, to an age-old philosophical discourse on the sense of smell being arguably the most anti-intellectual, anti-social, and monstrous of the senses. When reading *Das Parfum* in combination with *Frankenstein* smell is set up in opposition to language as the more successful means to knowledge and power. Given the fact that the Creature in *Frankenstein* acquires the ability to use language and make logical appeals to mankind, one would expect that he would be successful in his endeavours. But instead, Grenouille who uses smell, an arguably primitive, and animalistic form of communication, is the one who succeeds. Here animalistic instinct proves more powerful than the highly evolved facility of language. This contradiction does not however separate the novels thematically, but instead unites them, as both novels symbolically reject the ideals of the Enlightenment, in place of more Romantic ones. Society dismisses the Creature because language holds no lasting power in Shelley's Romantic world, while Grenouille succeeds as the Romantic genius. Yet, even Grenouille's achievement is swiftly invalidated with his death - his absolute assimilation into society, signalling perhaps the emergence of a post-modern world.

Key Words: Romanticism, enlightenment, postmodernism, smell, olfaction, language, *Bildungsroman*, monstrosity, *Das Parfum*.

*****

In Patrick Süskind's *Das Parfum: Die Geschichte eine Mörders*, Grenouille concocts the world's most enticing perfume. He creates *his own* scent by extracting and distilling the essence not of rose petals or vanilla beans, but of skin from the pretty, young women he murders. Employing the technique of cold effleurage - one of the oldest methods of fragrance extraction - Grenouille smears his victims with a layer of animal fat, skilfully lathering on thicker amounts to the erogenous zones. After allowing the lard time to absorb the body's scent, Grenouille scrapes the carcass clean. Satisfied with his work, he returns home to concentrate the scent into an essential oil, adding yet another body to the others in his devilish perfume. Later, when he douses his own body with the perfume, as if by a stroke of lightening, society will finally smell his humanity. If fact, they will see him as humanity per excellence.

A close reading of Patrick Süskind's *Das Parfum* (1984) evokes the memory of Mary Shelley's *Frankenstein, or The Modern Prometheus* (1818). Critics received both novels controversially; both were instant international bestsellers. Yet, literary scholars initially objected to their shortcomings in style and morality.[1] Only within the last twenty years has *Frankenstein* become 'the widely read, widely revered all-but-canonized work it is today;' and only recently has *Das Parfum* received a growing number of positive literary reviews.[2]

A handful of scholars have noted in brief the connection between the two narratives.[3] I intend to further develop this idea here. Other critics have found certain structures and motifs in *Das Parfum* that are comparable to those in *Frankenstein*. Some have likened Süskind's text to the Romantic novel relying heavily on Romantic subtexts and nineteenth-century narrative strategies, including the genre of the *Bildungsroman*.[4] Critics have analyzed specifically how Süskind incorporates Romantic and Gothic themes, which one also finds in *Frankenstein*, including a pathos of monsterism,[5] the dichotomy between good and evil,[6] Romantic intuition[7] versus a scepticism toward scientific inquiry and the ideals of the Enlightenment.[8]

In comparing the two novels here side-by-side, I will first show how a reading of *Das Parfum* recalls *Frankenstein* structurally in terms of character, theme, genre, and plot.[9] Then, I will illustrate how a comparative analysis of the novels contributes, however controversially, to an age-old philosophical discourse on the sense of smell being arguably the most anti-intellectual, anti-social, and monstrous of the senses.

Frankenstein and *Das Parfum* are similar in terms of character, as the protagonist of both stories is depicted as monstrous. Both suffer under a loathsome physical condition or disability; both exhibit morally corrupt behaviour. The Creature in *Frankenstein*, for example, lacks a typical human appearance, having been made out of the remains of decaying body parts sown together. Similarly, Grenouille in *Das Parfum* is also physically disfigured, due to the fact that he lacks smell, that is, his body does not have a scent. Society, unable to smell Grenouille, cannot ironically *see* him. His alien-like nature makes him an abomination in the eyes of humankind.

Notably, in German, the notion of not being able to smell someone or something has a cultural connotation encapsulated in the sayings '*Ich kann die/den nicht riechen*' or '*etwas nicht riechen können.*' The first of which means literally 'I can't stand her/him.' The second connotes one's inability to anticipate something happening, said after the fact. In the context of *Das Parfum,* these sayings enrich the interpretation of the text, as society can neither stand Grenouille's presence, nor predict his motifs or subsequent actions. His particular interest in perfumery eludes his masters. Victims of Grenouille's murderous villainy never see him coming. Finally, at the end of the novel, the Parisians are taken captive unaware by Grenouille's super-perfume. That a poor, wretch of a man could take complete control of all the citizens of Paris by the power of a scent, no one could have foreseen.

In both novels, the way in which the protagonist's disabled body is constructed as something monstrous might best be understood as a form of racial stereotyping, as a kind of moral physiognomy. A number of scholars have noted how, in *Frankenstein,* for example, while Victor strives to create the beautiful *Übermensch*, he concocts instead a bogyman, composed of nineteenth-century racial and ethnic stereotypes of the Other.[10] H. L. Malchow, for, example, has suggested that the Creature's large stature and 'dark and sinister' appearance denotes the stereotypical 'black man in both the literature of the West Indies and that of West African exploration.'[11] Racist innuendos are easily palpable in Victor's first description of his creation.

> I saw the dull yellow eye of the creature open ... His yellow skin scarcely covered the work of muscles and arteries beneath; his hair was of a lustrous black, and flowing; his teeth of a pearly whiteness; but these luxuriances only formed a more horrid contrast with his watery eyes, that seemed almost of the same colour as the dun white sockets in which they were set, his shrivelled complexion, and straight black lips.[12]

According to Malchow, the Creature's 'yellow skin' and 'watery eyes' are comparable to a nineteenth-century description of the Mandika people in Western Africa.[13] Additionally, the contrast of the bright white teeth and yellow eyes with black hair is a well-known stereotype of persons of colour.

In another scene, the otherwise kindly son Felix equates the Creature's malformed body with malicious intent, and beats and chases him away.

> Felix darted forward, and with supernatural force tore me from his father, to whose knees I clung: in a transport of fury, he dashed me to the ground, and struck me violently with a stick.[14]

To this passage one may apply the trope of the beaten slave, in which physical violence on the slave's body is typically used as an agent of punishment to transgressors of the paternal rule or more generally, of the hegemonic order.[15]

In *Das Parfum,* the narrative's depiction of Grenouille is arguably equally as racist. For instance, the narrator applies a common type of racial slur, in referring to Grenouille as an animal or animal-like. Grenouille's name in French means the word 'frog.' He is also described in the text as a 'Teufel,' 'ein Nichts,' 'eine Spinne,' 'ein Zeck,' and 'ein Ding.'[16] Despite the fact that Grenouille is a hard worker, his master treats him like an animal: '[Sein Meister] hielt ihn nicht mehr wie irgendein Tier, sondern wie ein nützliches Haustier.'[17] The trope of the beaten slave may also be employed in the following passage, in which the narrator writes: 'Da sehe man Pusteln und Narben, [...] allenthalben eine Zersetzung der Haut; und sogar eine deutliche fluidale Verkrüppelung des Skeletts, die als Klumpfuß und Buckel sichtbar hervortrete.'[18] Of course, Grenouille is crippled from the toxic conditions of working in a tannery, as well as living in a cave for seven years, and not from the whip of a master. Nevertheless, dangerous jobs have always been historically assigned to the undesirables of society.

In terms of behaviour, both protagonists indulge in monstrous acts of murder. Yet, we interpret their intentions differently. Traditional readings of *Frankenstein*, for example, ask readers to sympathize with the Creature. We must therefore believe that while the Creature is born a corporal monster, he is only later nurtured into a monster ethically speaking through his isolation from humankind. The Creature becomes a murderer only in the name of revenge to hurt those who have rejected his company.

In *Das Parfum,* Grenouille is, however, born as both a physical, as well as an ethical monster, or more distinctly, he is a psychopath. Characteristic of psychopaths, Grenouille is unable to bond with a mother or paternal figure, failing to form a mature superego. Consequently, like a psychopath, Grenouille is antisocial, psychologically and morally immature, egocentric, impulsive, deceitful and manipulative, solipsistic, a free-rider, and lacks empathy or remorse for his actions.[19] At no point in his life does he desire companionship, nor is his compulsion to kill an act of revenge or emotion. He simply lives for his fetish, which source originates from his lust for certain bodies of smell. The fact that he kills human beings or even more specifically women appears to be only coincidental. If the objects of his desire – of their smell, where available in other forms, such as flowers or already fabricated perfumes, he would have had arguably no reason to murder.

Thematically speaking, both novels also align themselves with the genre of the gothic horror novel. *Frankenstein* is one of the proto-typical models of this genre and *Das Parfum* mimics this paradigm closely as well. We find thematic elements similar to the Gothic novel, such as terror, monstrosity, murder, sinfulness, the sublime, and the supernatural. In *Frankenstein*, for instance, Victor Frankenstein, suffering under the sin of pride and scientific inquiry, creates a monster of supernatural proportions, which eventually murders all persons his maker holds dear. In *Das Parfum*, Grenouille kills a number of people to create a perfume to control society, and succeeds, only to be literally cannibalised by it, that is by his fellow man, in the end.

Gothic horror is also known for its depiction of a fallen world, in which the setting evokes a dark and uncertain, if not supernatural atmosphere of dread. We find such settings in *Frankenstein* in Victor's laboratory as the Creature's birthplace, the sublime Swiss Alps, the isolated and sparsely populated village where Victor creates and destroys the Creature's female companion, as well as the frigid Arctic, which serves as the battlefield between maker and made at the end of the novel.

In *Das Parfum*, the narrator describes eighteenth-century France, and most specifically Paris, as a cosmos of decay and crime, which is characterized unusually by smell. For instance, the narrator writes,

> Zu der Zeit, von der wir reden, herrschte in den Städten ein für uns moderne Menschen kaum vorstellbarer Gestank. ... Die Menschen stanken nach Schweiß und nach ungewaschenen Kleidern; aus dem Mund stanken sie nach verrotteten Zähnen, aus ihren Mägen nach Zwiebelsaft und an den Körpern, wenn sie nicht mehr ganz jung waren, nach altem Käse und nach saurer Milch und nach Geschwulstkrankheiten. Es stanken die Flüsse, es stanken die Plätze, es stanken die Kirchen, ... ja sogar der König stank....[20]

Here, physical decay doubles for spiritual and moral decay as well.

Also, the condition of each protagonist's birth is equally macabre and morally bankrupt. Each protagonist is born in a slaughterhouse; whereby the Creature is literally composed of remains, while Grenouille is lying in them. Eschewing all parental responsibility, the mother-figure in both narratives deems the protagonist's birth as abortive, and fanaticising filicide, abandons her/his child.

In *Frankenstein*, Victor assembles a Creature out of the remains of decaying body parts, which he collects from graveyards and hospitals. The birthing chamber, Victor's laboratory, is also presumably littered with human remains and blood. Victor births the Creature, only to shun and exile him after the fact, despite the Creature's supplications for love, reason, and forgiveness.

In *Das Parfum*, in comparison, Grenouille's mother conceives him out of wedlock, possibly working as a prostitute. She births him into a bath of fly-covered fish guts and blood under her work table in the town market, and then walks away from her newborn son, never to look back. Society follows suit, marginalizing the orphaned child as dangerous, ugly, and malignant. Other Gothic-like settings in *Das Parfum* include the poisonous conditions of the tannery, the scenes of murder, and the perfumery in Grasse, where Grenouille makes his ur-perfume out of the scent of corpses.

Also, Grenouille's journey to the isolated mountain cave, where he sustains an animal-like existence for seven years, and his further travels throughout the novel, follows the Gothic motif of the '*Wanderer*.' Grenouille, like the Creature in *Frankenstein*, as if divinely punished for his evil deeds, seems destined to ramble the Earth like the biblical Cain. The Creature suffers from this same curse, travelling throughout Europe, and later to the barren Arctic to spend the rest of his days alone.

In terms of plot and genre, *Frankenstein* and *Das Parfum* are most comparable to the *Bildungsroman*. Scholars such as Jen Hill have called *Frankenstein*'s narrative an impossible *Bildungsroman*, focusing however entirely on Victor Frankenstein and Captain Walton's intellectual development, and namely not the Creature's.[21] However, within the confines of this chapter, I will only explore the Creature's development as it relates to the *Bildungsroman*.

Simply put, both novels tell the story of an eighteenth-century European man, who undertakes a kind of education and apprenticeship, with the objective of gaining entrance to the social order in which they live, albeit for different purposes. The Creature wants to be part of society, while Grenouille wants to rule it. In both instances, however, the narratives deviate from the genre, in that society, instead of welcoming, ostracizes the protagonist due to his atypical physical characteristics. Viewed as inhuman, and essentially the Other, society excludes him from their fellowship.

My understanding of the term *Bildungsroman* is informed by both traditional and post-modern definitions of the genre. Traditionally, a *Bildungsroman* is defined as a narrative that focuses on the spiritual, moral, psychological, and social development of a protagonist from childhood to relative maturity. In each case, the protagonist eventually, however roughly, comes to embrace the spirit and values of the social order around him and takes his place in intellectual society.

In *Frankenstein,* for example, as the Creature matures, he develops a sense of moral responsibility to participate actively in the society of his master, Victor Frankenstein. To achieve this goal, he acquires the tool of language and educates himself. The Creature tries to shape his world accordingly, relying on the morsels of wisdom and logic encapsulated in such books he literally 'finds along his journey,' which just happen to be a good sampling of the canon of Romantic literature, including Goethe's *The Sorrows of Young Werther*, Milton's *Paradise Lost*, and a volume of *Plutarch's Lives*. He also learns to speak a human language, German, as well as acquires a solid foundation in the history and nature of the human condition by eavesdropping on their (human) interactions.

Equally important, the Creature, mimicking the behaviour of his maker, yearns for a heteronormative kinship relationship. Yet, the sex of the Creature is unclear, given the fact that the sex of the body parts out of which he is composed, or rather the sex of the original owners of those body parts, is not addressed in the text. In other words, the Creature could have been constructed out of male and female body parts - a fact which marks the Creature with a kind of sexual ambiguity and social depravity. Still, imitating his maker, the Creature appears to identify as a male and heterosexual. He therefore commands Victor make him a female of his own, believing like Victor that one can manipulate and control one's own life as well as the lives of other (human) beings through the auspices of knowledge acquired through language.

Alongside traditional definitions of the *Bildungsroman*, I also use Bakhtin's more post-modern definition to serve as a springboard for new readings. Specifically, I refer to the following passage:

> In [some Bildungsroman] however, human emergence is of a different nature. It is no longer man's own private affair. He emerges *along with the world* and he reflects the historical emergence of the world itself. He is no longer within an epoch, but on the border between two epochs, at the transition point from one to the other. This transition is accomplished in him and through him. He is forced to become a new, unprecedented type of human being. What is happening is precisely the emergence of a new man. The organizing force held by the future is therefore extremely great here - and this is not, of course, the biographical future, but the historic future. It is as though the very *foundations* of the world are changing, and man must change along with them. Understandably, in such a novel of emergence, problems of reality and man's potential, problems of freedom and necessity, and the problem of creative initiative rise to their full height.[22]

Most concretely, I look to Bakhtin to help extend our understanding of the implications of Grenouille's unorthodox narrative of social development.

In *Das Parfum*, Grenouille too aspires to engage with, and in fact lead or rather control humankind. Like the Creature in *Frankenstein*, Grenouille seeks a way to actively shape his world. Grenouille is also an autodidact, who amasses his knowledge mostly through trial and error. However, like the Creature, he seeks tutors, but only to fill in those gaps of knowledge, which books and intuition cannot supply. He apprentices in the trade of perfumery only as a means to procure the tools and skills he seeks to create his ultimate perfume.

While in *Frankenstein* the Creature uses man's language to shape his reality, Grenouille uses, oddly enough, perfume. Ironically, while Grenouille has no interest in participating in society except as a means to an end, the fruits of his labour, his perfumes as products of his mind (and nose), become valuable commodities in aristocratic French society. The Creature, however, is rarely seen as anything but a monster or at best as a 'good spirit' when he helps out a family in exile, however, in incognito.

Just as much as both novels fit, they also depart from the structure of the typical *Bildungsroman*, and in particular with regards to their resolution. Instead of becoming functioning members of society, by the end of both narratives, the protagonists are socially rejected, viewed as disabled and impotent savages. Fulfilling their similar, dreadful prophesies, both become serial killers. The Creature kills Victor's brother, wife, and best friend. Grenouille kills a dozen young girls. In contrast, however, the Creature's murders may be called crimes of passion brought on by his exiled state, while Grenouille murders to satisfy his fetish - that is to create his ur-perfume. In any case, the protagonists are incapable of becoming the active and/or powerful citizens they had hoped to become. Victor chases the Creature into the Arctic. Grenouille is condemned to death, and is eventually eaten alive by the citizens of Paris.

At the same time, one might interpret the resolution of *Das Parfum,* and with that its structure, as a kind of post-modern *Bildungsroman* as Bakhtin has proposed. While the Creature fails to earn the friendship of humankind, Grenouille gains complete dominance over them at the end of the novel. Even the Parisian's literal consumption of Grenouille's body, for they do eat him up, might be understood, arguably, as his total and, therefore, successful symbolic assimilation into society. Indeed, following Bakhtin, Grenouille not only emerges as a man of the world, but also he represents the historical emergence of the post-modern world itself. Grenouille's physical transition signals and mimics a worldly one - the shift from an enlightened world governed by reason to a postmodern one in which the fallacies of logic are exposed and subsequently, chaos and monstrosity rule.

The respective failure and achievement of the protagonists can arguably be attributed to the protagonist's chosen tool of power and persuasion. The Creature, for example, acquires the use of language, and Grenouille, his sense of smell. More specifically, in *Frankenstein,* the Creature chooses the tool of the Enlightenment, whereby language is a means to knowledge, and therefore to power. For him, this 'godlike science' is imbibed with the authority to make him human.

> I found that these people possessed a method of communicating their experience and feelings to one another by articulating sounds. I perceived that the words they spoke sometimes produced pleasure or pain, smiles or sadness, in the minds and countenance of the hearers. This was indeed a godlike science, and I ardently desired to become acquainted with it.[23]

Peter Brooks describes the link between language and social identity in *Frankenstein*, whereby language chains the monster to the culture of man to which the Creature wants to belong.[24] Yet, through language, the Creature is only able to alter society's perception of him temporarily. He may be chained to culture, but he remains nonetheless a chained monster in their eyes. For example, the Creature is able to convince Victor and the ship Captain Walton to listen to his story of emergence, anticipating their sympathy and respect. In telling his story, he hopes to demonstrate his capacity to reason, believing that men like Victor and Walton hold this enlightened value most dear. Yet, the Creature's assumptions prove incorrect, for in the end, he cannot persuade the men.

For example, Walton writes in his diary,

> I was at first touched by the expressions of his misery; yet when I called to mind what Frankenstein had said of his powers of eloquence and persuasion, and when I again cast my eyes on the lifeless form of [Victor], indignation was rekindled within me. 'Wretch!' I said.[25]

Walton is swayed by the Creature's words, until he sees an image (that of Victor's dead body). Notably here, the sense of sight dominates the power and persuasion of language.

In *Das Parfum,* Grenouille chooses alternately smell, in the form of a perfume, as his weapon to influence and ultimately to take control of society. Grenouille believes, unlike the Creature, that scent curiously enough is a more effective and persuasive tool than language. In fact, in terms of language, the protagonist barely speaks at all. Instead, in the final climatic scene in the novel, Grenouille douses his body with the super-perfume he has created in order to command absolute control over society and obtain their unconditional acceptance and love. He does this so effectively, mankind cannibalises him; they tear him apart and eat him up out of love. The narrator writes,

> In kürzester Zeit war der Engel in dreißig Teile zerlegt, und ein jedes Mitglied der Rotte grapschte sich ein Stück, zog sich, von wollüstiger Gier getrieben, zurück und fraß es auf. Eine halbe Stunde später war Jean-Baptiste Grenouille in jeder Faser vom Erdboden verschwunden. ... [Wie] leicht es ihnen doch gefallen war und daß sie, bei aller Verlegenheit, nicht den geringsten Anflug von schlechtem Gewissen verspürten. Im Gegenteil! ... Sie waren außerordentlich stolz. Sie hatten zum ersten Mal etwas aus Liebe getan.[26]

The crowd is mastered by the smell of Grenouille's perfume. No images, thoughts, or words of reason, nor any notions of shame, ethics, morality, or religion persuade them otherwise. Instead, they consume him and are, astonishingly, thereby convinced that they have done something noble, if not out of love. In contrast, in *Frankenstein*, language serves only to make the Creature aware of the distance language itself establishes between him and society. The Creature is cursed to wander the fields of barren ice outside the company of men and women forever. While in *Das Parfum,* smell successfully narrows this gap. Grenouille is so fully integrated into the culture of man, they subsume him - literally.

To facilitate an understanding of the implications of privileging the sense of smell over language, I will briefly introduce a history of the philosophical and psychoanalytical debates surrounding the sense of smell in contrast to the power of language as a means to knowledge. From antiquity until today, philosophers, rhetoricians, linguists, as well as literary and scientific scholars of all kinds have revered the power of language, in its written and spoken forms, as the most powerful, and for some most logical, and for others most moral means of persuasion. For example, starting in antiquity, Plato thought the 'analysis of language is ancillary to philosophical pursuits.'[27] Alternately, Plato,[28] as well as Aristotle,[29] believed smell to be an inferior, proximal, animalistic, subjective, self-referential, and sensual sense. For them, smell was less pure than other supposedly more noble, intellectual and sublime senses, such as sight or hearing.

Descartes dismissed smell as vulgar.[30] He saw language, however, as a divinely inspired and 'uniquely human sense.'[31] He wrote, 'Those who have the strongest power of reasoning, and who most skilfully arrange their thoughts in order to render them clear and intelligible, have the best power of persuasion.'[32] Kant also found smell coarse and unpleasant.[33] Alternately, he emphasized 'reason's power [as expressed through language] to overcome the limitations of sensory comprehension.'[34] Schopenhauer thought smell was an inferior sense.[35] On language, he wrote that

> perception [including sensory perception] always determines only the material, never the formal truth of the proposition, for the formal truth is determined according to the logical rules alone [as made explicit through language].[36]

Hegel removed the sense of smell entirely from his aesthetics.[37] Yet, language, according to Hegel has the capacity to make us human beings. He wrote how language has 'the power which posits the inner as a being [which in turn is] the being of Spirit as Spirit.'[38] Darwin deemed smell a primitive sense. Like Hegel, he thought the capacity to use language to reason, form thoughts and express emotions, a power unique to humans and not animals.[39] German philosopher Georg Simmel referred to smell as the antisocial sense and drew connections between smell and racism, concluding, 'Die soziale Frage ist nicht nur eine ethische, sondern auch eine Nasenfrage'[40] He also linked male dominance in culture to men's ability to use language more powerfully than women.[41]

A number of influential philosophers however, including Rousseau and Nietzsche, took a more positive approach to the sense of smell. Rousseau claimed it to be the sense of the imagination and love.[42] Nietzsche celebrated smell, calling society's rejection of this sense as a means to knowledge a rejection of man's animalistic nature. In fact, Nietzsche called his act of philosophical investigation a 'scenting out,'[43] and he once claimed that 'Mein Genie ist in meinen Nüstern.'[44]

Freud raised the sense of smell philosophically-speaking to a whole new level, identifying smell as a mark of psychological repression, a fetish, and a sign of abnormal sexuality.[45] Freud proposed 'a direct relationship between the development of civilization and the virtual eradication of the sense of smell' suggesting instead that the 'olfactory sense was hindrance to knowledge and aesthetics.'[46] Later, Lacan claimed in his seminar *L'Angoisse* that 'the Other' does not smell.[47]

Finally, twentieth-century French psychoanalyst Françoise Dolto perhaps best captures the meat of the philosophical debate surrounding the possible intellectual and cultural merits of the sense of smell, or rather lack thereof, claiming 'Culture is speech and obviously not smell.'[48]

When reading *Das Parfum* in combination with *Frankenstein,* smell is set up in opposition to language as the more successful means to knowledge and power. This contradiction does not, however, separate the novels thematically, but instead unites them, as both novels symbolically reject the ideals of the Enlightenment in place of more Romantic ones. Both narratives destabilize and invalidate the values of reason and logic. Society rejects the Creature because language holds no lasting power in Shelley's Romantic world, while Grenouille succeeds as the Romantic genius.

Within the framework of a typical *Bildungsroman*, a young, white, heterosexual, middle to lower class boy must undertake years of instruction, learning rhetoric and composition, in addition to other subjects, to eventually be able to show his merit and converse within the intellectual elite.[49] In essence, the child must learn to 'talk the talk,' and mature through language, before he will even be *heard* or *seen* as an adult. Of course, once the child has procured this skill, he must use it as a tool of negotiation. True success comes when he has mastered language enough that through its use he may master other men. Accordingly, the Creature in *Frankenstein* attempts to do just this.

The respective failure and success of the protagonists can arguably be attributed to the protagonist's chosen tool of power and persuasion. The Creature, for example, acquires the use of language, and Grenouille, scent. Alternately, in *Das Parfum*, while Grenouille undergoes a kind of apprenticeship, he neither develops his rhetorical speaking or writing skills, nor does he want to converse with other human beings. In fact, he speaks, reads, and writes only out of necessity. For Grenouille, unlike the Creature in *Frankenstein*, cultivates not language, but disputably a mere primitive bodily sense, his gift of smell and scent-making, as a means to gain power and persuade others. Not only does Grenouille choose an unorthodox method, but his motive is suspect. In fact, we know that Grenouille's intentions are immoral and pose a direct threat to society. He is a murderer of women. His actions undermine the trajectory of a typical *Bildungsroman* in which heteronormative society, as in the camaraderie of men and marriage with women, is the end goal. The asexual Grenouille violates this code by eschewing mankind, all the while destroying their commodity - available young, pretty, virgin girls.

Ironically, Grenouille succeeds in gaining control over society, while the Creature fails. Despite his eloquence and logical pleas, the Creature is unable to convince neither his master nor others of his humanity. Grenouille, on the other hand, creates a perfume so powerful, all human beings see him or rather *smell* him as the ideal of humanity itself. Grenouille's success challenges and ultimately undermines not only the paradigm of the traditional *Bildungsroman*, but also genre's fundamental understanding of intellect. The world as presented by a typical *Bildungsroman*, which represents a world bound by the logic and reason of the Enlightenment, assumes that for humans, intellectual development equates progress. Here, mind always wins out over matter.

We can infer that within this framework that the use of the senses, and in particular the sense of smell, would be seen as nothing more than a basic skill, believed to be used rarely by humans, expect for passing amusement or variably an irritant, like with nice smelling perfume or the stench of rotting food. At the most, scent is a tool of survival, which utility lies in helping us avoid danger, like smelling the smoke of an approaching fire. Most characteristically, in this mindset, scent is an innate skill of primitive animals, and namely, not a skill honed to gain admittance into intellectual society, nor rule the world.

Yet, Grenouille does fulfil some of the requirements of the genre of the *Bildungsroman*. In fact, in acquiring skills through his apprenticeship, Grenouille comes to rule the world, thereby meeting the ultimate goal of the genre. When comparing *Das Parfum* to *Frankenstein*, Grenouille's ascendancy through scent puts into question the very clout of language employed by the Creature.

In the fictional worlds laid bare by Shelley and Süskind, language at its best can alter society's perception of the individual, and yet it cannot compensate entirely for one's Otherness. Scent here is *the* most powerful medium of communication, the value extraordinaire of the Romantic world, which is able to undividedly alter society's perception at will, and thus mask Grenouille's Otherness and monstrous nature (his physical appearance, his lack of scent, and his acts of murder and crime).

Scholars of *Frankenstein*, such as David Collings claim that

> Lacan and Shelley both suggest that society orients itself toward the fantasy of an impossible fulfilment which, if ever realized, would be the source of great dread.... Conflating utopias and monsters, Shelley anticipates Lacanian theory, urging us to recognize the limits of the emancipatory dream, accept the

conflicts of modern society, and thereby undo the very that enables prejudice and exclusion.[50]

This same logic may be applied to *Das Parfum*. Grenouille dousing his body with his super-perfume is demonstrating the norms and forms of belonging and community, which according to Lacan, is already a monstrous act. For Lacan, the monster is 'the one who found the analytic key, the active force of men.'[51]

Alternately, following Slavoj Žižek, smell could also be understood as symbolic of the 'surplus' or that which, using the tool of language, scientific inquiry and reason cannot detect or comprehend, which is again, a rejection of the ideals of the Enlightenment. According to Žižek,

> the pure 'subject of the Enlightenment' is a monster ... In this sense, monsters can be defined precisely as the fantasmatic appearance of the 'missing link' between nature and culture.... Therein consists the ambiguity of the Enlightenment: the question of 'origins' (origins of language, of culture, of society) which emerged in all its stringency with it, is nothing but the reverse of a fundamental prohibition to probe too deeply into the obscure origins, which betrays a fear that by doing so, one might uncover something monstrous.[52]

Derrida, in his postmodern take on language, also offers a similar theory, whereby man's use of language, out of which he constitutes his world, is nothing but an empty, monstrous sign, or rather a monstrous existence. In place of obeying the 'protocols, rules, intuitions, roles, laws, and established formulae' written down in language, Grenouille invokes an 'alternative kind of performative [that] 'creates the norms and laws that validate it' and necessarily shows in the (monstrous) form of showing nothing.'[53] Following this logic, Grenouille is not violating the logic of the *Bildungsroman* or an enlightened world, but instead, as Derrida shows,

> the very question of monsterism and monstrosity arises in the vicinity of questions of *Geschlecht* (of belonging and community; of [national] culture; of species and genus; of 'man,' humanity, and animality; and of 'norms and forms') that not only characterize a long-standing philosophical tradition, but that may even be thought to supply the very conditions of possibility for a thinking and realization of the Enlightenment ....[54]

Within this context, Grenouille, void of sense and scent, and mute as well - stripped of language, is the ideal citizen in spite of and because of his Otherness - his monstrosity. Society now sees and accepts him as exhibiting every characteristic they value in a member of society, and much more. Grenouille is the super-member or the *Übermensch*, a status that Victor Frankenstein had hoped his Creature would achieve through language, and yet did not. And we cannot deny Grenouille's success. The texts reads,

> Sie fühlten sich zu diesem Engelsmenschen hingezogen. Ein rabiater Sog ging von ihm aus, eine reißende Ebbe, gegen die kein Mensch sich stemmen konnte, um so weniger, als sich kein Mensch gegen sie hätte stemmen wollen, denn es war der Wille selbst, den diese Ebbe unterspülte und in ihre Richtung trieb: hin zu ihm. [55]

Grenouille becomes the perfect citizen not because he exhibits the ability to speak or to reason. He does not demonstrate her values or civility. Instead, he is unconditionally accepted by society because he smells like a human. In fact, he smells not like a man, but arguably like a woman, as his perfume is a conglomeration of the scent of only women's bodies. Here, the animalistic, and perhaps most feminine or womanly, and most monstrous part of human nature wins out. Even the most civilized human cannot escape the intoxication of his scent.

Grenouille in *Das Parfum*, unlike the Creature in *Frankenstein,* overcomes his Otherness, and consequently, not only because he becomes the ideal member of society, but by virtue of the fact that he emerges as society itself. In this sacrificial act, Grenouille acquires access to human bodies, and climbs into their mouths. Grenouille becomes, at last, society incarnate. He is the champion of the postmodern *Bildungsroman*.

Here, in the end, postmodernity poses a challenge to both the logic of the enlightened world of the *Bildungsroman* as well as the authenticity of the Romantic genius. In this post-modern world, nothing is pure nor liberated from power structures, but instead absolute freedom denotes absolute enslavement. In this framework, Grenouille gains power over society only long enough to submit himself entirely unto it.

Notes

[1] *The Quarterly Review* published a scathing review of *Frankenstein* in 1818: 'Our taste and our judgment alike revolt at this kind of writing, and the greater the ability with which it may be executed the worse it is – it inculcates no lesson of conduct, manners, or morality.' ('Review of Frankenstein; or the Modern Prometheus,' *The Quarterly Review*, Vol. 18, Jan. 1818, p. 385.) In comparison, *Die Welt* published a critique of *Das Parfum* in 1985: 'Dieser Roman ist ein Juwel an preziösem Stil und äußerer Spannung, aber heraus kommt ein hundsgemeiner

Götze. Das ist wörtlich zu verstehen.' (R Krämer-Badoni, 'Neuer Vampir für den Film? Patrick Süskinds Romangeschichte eines Mörders,' *Die Welt*, 16 Feb, 1985, para. 1: 'This novel is a jewel with a contrite style and a palatable thrill. But, in the end, it is just a nasty, little Idol, literally speaking.' [Translation mine]) In other words, *Das Parfum* only pretends to be a great novel.

[2] B. Bennett, 'Editing Mary Wollstonecraft Shelley: A Bicentenary Review', *Keats-Shelley Journal*, Col. 46, 1997, p. 28.

[3] Cf. T. Burr, W, Knorr & S. Romer.

[4] Cf. J. Adams, et. al.

[5] Cf. N. Donahue, et. al.

[6] Cf. N. Donahue, et. al.

[7] Cf. N. Donahue, B. Fleming, R. Gray & M. Jacobson.

[8] Cf. B. Butterfield, B. Fleming & R. Gray.

[9] I am comparing the literary novels here, and notably, not any film adaptations of either book.

[10] Cf. M. Jacobson, et. al.

[11] H.L. Malchow, 'Frankenstein's Monster and Images of Race in Nineteenth-Century Britain,' *Past and Present*, Vol. 139, 1993, p. 102.

[12] M. Shelley, *Frankenstein: The Modern Prometheus*, D. Lorne MacDonald & K. Scherf (eds), 2nd edn, Broadview Press Ltd, Orchard Park, NY, 1999, p. 85.

[13] H.L. Malchow, op. cit., p. 103.

[14] Shelley, op. cit., p. 160.

[15] J. Glancy, *Slavery in Early Christianity*, Oxford University Press, Oxford, 2002, p. 118.

[16] Translated: 'Devil,' 'a nothing,' 'a spider,' 'a tick,' and 'a thing.'

[17] Süskind, *Parfum,* p. 43; translated: '[His master] no longer kept him as just any animal, but as a useful house pet.' P. Süskind, *Perfume: The Story of a Murderer*, trans. J. Woods, Penguin, London, 1987, p. 34. All translations will be from this edition.).

[18] Süskind, *Parfum*, p. 181; translated: 'One could see the pustules and scars […]; a general disintegration of the skin; and even clear evidence of fluidal deformation of the bone structure, the visible indications being a clubfoot and a hunchback.' (Süskind, Ibid., p. 88).

[19] S. Costello, *The Pale Criminal: Psychoanalytic Perspectives*, Karnac Books, London, 2002, pp. 145-146.

[20] Süskind, op. cit., pp. 5-6; translated: 'In the period of which we speak, there reigned in the cities a stench barely conceivable to us modern men and women. […] People stank of sweat and unwashed clothes; from their mouths came the stench of rotting teeth, from their bellies that of onions, and from their bodies, if they were no longer very young, came the stench of rancid cheese and sour mile

and tumorous disease. The rivers stank, the marketplaces stank, the churches stank, […] even the King himself stank […].' (Süskind, op. cit., pp. 3-4).

[21] J. Hill calls *Frankenstein* an 'impossible Bildungsroman,' in so far as Walton and Victor Frankenstein privilege the imagination over fact and experience. While the protagonist of a Bildungsroman must typically find and negotiate his identity within society, Walton and Victor must, however problematically, find theirs outside the community of men. By men here, I do refer to the male-dominated intellectual society as it is represented in *Frankenstein*.

[22] M. Bakhtin, 'The Bildungsroman and Its Significance in the History of Realism (Toward a Historical Typology of the Novel)', *Speech Genres and Other Late Essays*, University of Texas Press, Austin, 2004, p. 23.

[23] Shelley, op. cit., p. 137.

[24] P. Brooks, 'Godlike Science/Unhallowed Arts: Language and Monstrosity in Frankenstein', *New Literary History*, Vol. 9, No. 3, 1978, p. 595.

[25] Shelley, op. cit., pp. 241-242.

[26] Süskind, op. cit., p. 320; translated: 'In very short order, the angel was divided into thirty pieces, and every animal in the pack snatched a piece for itself, and then, driven by a voluptuous lust, dropped back to devour it. A half an hour later, Jean-Baptist Grenouille had disappeared utterly from the earth. […] But to eat a human being? They would never, so they thought, have been capable of anything that horrible. And they were amazed that it had been so very easy for them and that, embarrassed as they were, they did not feel the tiniest twinge of conscience. On the contrary! […] All of a sudden there were delightful, bright flutterings in their dark souls. […] They were uncommonly proud. For the first time they had done something out of Love.' (Süskind, op. cit., 263).

[27] T. Givón, *Context As Other Minds: The Pragmatics of Sociality, Cognition, and Communication*, John Benjamins Publishing Company, Amsterdam, 2005, p. 17.

[28] Plato & P. Kalkavage, *Plato's Timaeus: Translation, Glossary, Appendices and Introductory Essay*, The Focus Philosophical Library, Focus Publishing/R. Pullins, Newburyport, MA, 2001.

[29] K.F. Thomas & S. Humphries, *Commentary on Aristotle's De anima*, The Thoemmes Library of Classics and Ancient Philosophy, No. 4, Thoemmes, Bristol, 2003.

[30] R. Descartes, *Le Monde, L'Homme*, A. Bitbol-Hespériès & J. Verdet (eds), Editions du Seuil, Paris, 1996.

[31] M. Boden, *Mind As Machine: A History of Cognitive Science*, Clarendon Press, Oxford, 2006.

[32] R. Descartes, *Discourse on the Method of Rightly Conducting the Reason and Seeking for Truth in the Sciences and Meditations on First Philosophy*, Digireads.com Publishing, Stilwell, KS, 2005, p. 5.

[33] I. Kant, *Anthropologie in pragmatischer Hinsicht*, F. Meiner, Leipzig, 1912.

[34] J. Hamilton, *Music, Madness, and the Unworking of Language*, Columbia University Press, New York, 2008, p. 110.
[35] A. Schopenhauer, *The World as Will and Idea*, Trübner & Co., London: 1886, p. 194.
[36] Ibid., p. 89.
[37] G. Hegel, *Georg Wilhelm Friedrich Hegel's Vorlesungen über die Aesthetik*, H. Hotho (ed), Duncker & Humblot, Berlin, 1842.
[38] J.P. Surber, *Hegel and Language*, SUNY Series in Hegelian Studies, State University of New York Press, Albany, 2006, p. 111. Brackets in original.
[39] C. Darwin, *On the Origin of Species by Means of Natural Selection, Or the Preservation of Favoured Races in the Struggle for Life*, Folio Society, London, 2006.
[40] G. Simmel, *Soziologie, Untersuchungen über die Formen der Vergesellschaftung*, Duncker & Humblot, Leipzig, 1908, p. 657; translated: 'The social question is not only an ethical one, but also a question of the nose' (my translation).
[41] D. Frisby, *Georg Simmel*, E Horwood, Chichester, 1984, p. 407.
[42] J. Rousseau, *Emile, ou de L'éducation*, Gaillimard, Paris, 1969.
[43] F. Nietzsche, *Ecce Homo*, Kritische Studienausgabe 6, Deutscher Taschenbuch Verlag, München, 1988, p. 366.
[44] A. Guérer, 'Olfaction and Cognition: A Philosophical and Psychoanalytic View', *Olfaction, Taste, Cognition*, Cambridge University Press, Cambridge, 2002, p. 6: 'My genius is in my nostrils' (my translation).
[45] S. Freud, *Civilization and its Discontents [Das Unbehagen in der Kultur]*, J. Strachey (ed), W.W. Norton & Co., New York, 1962.
[46] Guérer, op. cit., p. 9.
[47] P. Adams, *The Emptiness of the Image: Psychoanalysis and Sexual Differences*, Routledge, London, 1996, p. 104.
[48] Guérer, op. cit., p. 9. Thanks to Annick Le Guérer's article on 'Olfaction and Cognition: A Philosophical and Psychoanalytic View', *Olfaction, Taste, Cognition* for her concise history of scent.
[49] Typical *Bildungsromane* include for example Johann Wolfgang Goethe's *Wilhelm Meisters Lehrjahre* (1795-1796), which is often considered the prototypical *Bildungsroman*, as well as Charles Dickens's, *David Copperfield* (1849-1850) and *Great Expectations* (1860), Henry James's *What Maisie Knew* (1897), E. M. Forster's *The Longest Journey* (1907), D.H. Lawrence's *Sons and Lovers* (1913), or even novels from today such as J.K. Rowling's *Harry Potter* series (1997-2007).
[50] D. Collings, 'A Psychoanalytic Perspective: The Monster and the Maternal Thing: Mary Shelley's Critique of Ideology' in J. Smith (ed), *Frankenstein: Complete, Authoritative Text with Biographical, Historical, and Cultural Contexts,*

Critical History, and Essays from Contemporary Critical Perspectives, Bedford/St. Martin's, Boston, 2000, p. 280.
[51] J. Lacan, *The Seminar of Jacques Lacan. Book 3: The Psychoses, 1955-1956*, J. Miller (ed), W.W. Norton, New York, 1993, p. 323.
[52] S. Žižek, *Enjoy Your Symptom!: Jacques Lacan in Hollywood and Out*, Routledge Classics, New York, 2008, p. 136.
[53] S. Wortham & C. Fynsk, *Counter-Institutions: Jacques Derrida and the Question of the University,* Perspectives in Continental Philosophy, No. 55, Fordham University Press, New York, 2006, p. 67.
[54] Ibid., emphasis in original.
[55] Süskind, op. cit., p. 320; translated: 'They felt themselves drawn to this angel of a man. A frenzied, alluring force came from him, a rid-tide no human could have resisted, all the less because no human would have wanted to resist it, for that tide was pulling under and dragging away was the human will itself: straight to him' (Süskind, op. cit., p. 262).

Bibliography

Adams, J., 'Narcissism and Creativity in the Postmodern Era: The Case of Patrick Süskind's Das Parfum.' *The Germanic Review*. Vol. 75, No. 4, 2000, pp. 259-279.

Adams, P., *The Emptiness of the Image: Psychoanalysis and Sexual Differences*. Routledge, London, 1996.

Bakhtin, M., 'The Bildungsroman and Its Significance in the History of Realism (Toward a Historical Typology of the Novel)'. *Speech Genres and Other Late Essays*. Emerson, C. & Holquist, M. (eds), University of Texas Press, Austin, 2004.

Bennett, B., 'Editing Mary Wollstonecraft Shelley: A Bicentenary Review'. *Keats-Shelley Journal*. Vol. 46, 1997, pp. 23-28.

Boden, M., *Mind As Machine: A History of Cognitive Science*. Clarendon Press, Oxford, 2006.

Brooks, P., 'Godlike Science/Unhallowed Arts: Language and Monstrosity in Frankenstein'. *New Literary History*. Vol. 9, No. 3, 1978, pp. 591-605.

Burr, T., ''Perfume' is a Sensory Overload'. *The Boston Globe*. 5 Jan. 2007, Viewed on 10 May 2009.

Butterfield, B., 'Enlightenment's Other in Patrick Suskind's Das Parfum: Adorno and the Ineffable Utopia of Modern Art'. *Comparative Literature Studies*. Vol. 32, No. 3, 1995, pp. 401-418.

Collings, D., 'A Psychoanalytic Perspective: The Monster and the Maternal Thing: Mary Shelley's Critique of Ideology'. *Frankenstein: Complete, Authoritative Text with Biographical, Historical, and Cultural Contexts, Critical History, and Essays from Contemporary Critical Perspectives*. Bedford/St. Martin's, Boston, 2000, pp. 280-295.

Costello, S., *The Pale Criminal: Psychoanalytic Perspectives*, Karnac Books, London, 2002.

Darwin, C., *On the Origin of Species by Means of Natural Selection, Or the Preservation of Favoured Races in the Struggle for Life*, Folio Society, London, 2006.

Derrida, J., 'Geschlecht II: Heidegger's Hand'. *Deconstruction and Philosophy: The Texts of Jacques Derrida*. University of Chicago Press, Chicago and London, 1987.

Descartes, R., *Discourse on the Method of Rightly Conducting the Reason and Seeking for Truth in the Sciences and Meditations on First Philosophy*. Haldane, E. (ed), Digireads.com Publishing, Stilwell, KS, 2005.

——, *Le Monde, L'Homme*. Bitbol-Hespériès, A. & Verdet, J. (eds), Editions du Seuil, Paris, 1996.

Dolto, F., *Les Cahiers du Nouveau-Né 3: D'Amour et de Lait*. Stock, Paris, 1980.

Donahue, N., 'Scents and Insensibility: Patrick Süskind's New Historical Critique of 'Die Neue Sensibilität'. *Das Parfum*,' *Modern Language Studies*. Vol. 22, No. 3, 1985, pp. 36-43.

Fleming, B., 'The Smell of Success: A Reassessment of Patrick Süskind's *Das Parfum*'. *South Atlantic Review*. Vol. 56, No. 4, 1991, pp. 71-86.

Freud, S., *Abriss der Psychoanalyse*. Fischer Taschenbuch Verlag, Frankfurt am Main, 1990.

____, *Civilization and its Discontents [Das Unbehagen in der Kultur]*. Strachey, J. (ed). W.W. Norton & Co., New York, 1962.

Frisby, D., *Georg Simmel*. E. Horwood, Chichester, 1984.

Givón, T., *Context As Other Minds: The Pragmatics of Sociality, Cognition, and Communication*. John Benjamins Publishing Company, Amsterdam, 2005.

Glancy, J., *Slavery in Early Christianity*. Oxford University Press, Oxford, 2002.

Goethe, J. von, *The Sorrows of Young Werther*. Pike, B. (ed), Modern Library, New York, 2004.

Gray, R., 'The Dialectic of 'Enscentment': Patrick Süskind's *Das Parfum* as Critical History of Enlightenment Culture'. *PMLA*. Vol. 108, No. 3, 1993, pp. 489-505.

Guérer, A., 'Olfaction and Cognition: A Philosophical and Psychoanalytic View'. *Olfaction, Taste, Cognition*. Rouby, C. (ed), Cambridge University Press, Cambridge, 2002. pp. 3-15.

Hamilton, J., *Music, Madness, and the Unworking of Language*. Columbia University Press, New York, 2008.

Hegel, G., *Georg Wilhelm Friedrich Hegel's Vorlesungen über die Aesthetik*. Hotho, H. (ed), Duncker & Humblot, Berlin, 1842.

Hill, J., *White Horizon: The Arctic in the Nineteenth-Century British Imagination*. SUNY Press, New York, 2007.

Jacobson, M., 'Patrick Süskind's Das Parfum: A Postmodern Künstlerroman'. *The German Quarterly*. Vol. 65, No. 2, 1992, pp. 201-211.

Kant, I., *Anthropologie in pragmatischer Hinsicht*. Vorländer, K. (ed), F. Meiner, Leipzig, 1912.

Knorr, W., 'Aus Zwerg Nase wird ein Frankenstein der Düfte'. *Die Weltwoche*. 21 March 1985.

Krämer-Badoni, R., 'Neuer Vampir für den Film? Patrick Süskinds Romangeschichte eines Mörders'. *Die Welt*. 16 Feb. 1985.

Lacan, J., *Le Séminaire. Livre 10: L'angoisse*. Miller, J. (ed), Editions du Seuil, Paris, 2004.

—, *The Seminar of Jacques Lacan. Book 3: The Psychoses, 1955-1956*. Miller, J. (ed), W.W. Norton, New York, 1993.

Levine, G., 'Frankenstein and the Tradition of Realism'. *Novel: A Forum of Fiction*. Vol. 7, No. 1, 1973, pp. 14-30.

—, *The Realistic Imagination: English Fiction from Frankenstein to Lady Chatterley*. University of Chicago Press, Chicago, 1981.

Malchow, H.L., 'Frankenstein's Monster and Images of Race in Nineteenth-Century Britain'. *Past and Present*. Vol. 139, 1993, pp. 90-130.

McWhorter, C., 'Human as Parasite in Patrick Suskind's Perfume'. *Notes on Contemporary Literature*. Vol. 28, No. 5, 1998, pp. 9-11.

Milton, J. & Elledge, S., *Paradise Lost: An Authoritative Text, Backgrounds and Sources, Criticism*. Norton, New York, 1975.

Moffatt, E., 'Grenouille: A Modern Schizophrenic in the Enlightening World of Das Parfum'. *Forum for Modern Language Studies*. Vol. 37, No. 3, 2001, pp. 298-313.

Nietzsche, F., *Ecce Homo*. Kritische Studienausgabe 6, Deutscher Taschenbuch Verlag, München, 1988.

Oates, J.C., 'Frankenstein's Fallen Angel'. *Critical Inquiry*. Vol. 10, No. 3, 1984, pp. 543-554.

Plato & Kalkavage, P., *Plato's Timaeus: Translation, Glossary, Appendices and Introductory Essay*. The Focus Philosophical Library. Focus Pub./R. Pullins, Newburyport, MA, 2001.

Plutarch, Dryden, J. & Clough, A., *Plutarch's Lives/The Dryden Translation*. Modern Library, New York, 2001.

'Review of *Frankenstein; or the Modern Prometheus*'. *The Quarterly Review*. Vol. 18, Jan. 1818, pp. 379-385.

Romer, S., 'Distilled, Bottled and Bewildered'. *Times Online*. 10 Jan. 2007, Viewed on 23 Feb. 2009.

Rousseau, J.J., *Emile, ou de L'éducation*. Gallimard, Paris, 1969.

Ryan, J., 'The Problem of Pastiche: Patrick Süskind's Das Parfum'. *The German Quarterly*. Vol. 63, Nos. 3-4, 1990, pp. 396-403.

Schopenhauer, A., *The World as Will and Idea*. trans. Haldane, R.B. & Kemp, J., Trübner & Co., London, 1886.

Shelley, M., *Frankenstein: The Modern Prometheus*. Lorne MacDonald, D. & Scherf, K. (eds), 2nd ed, Broadview Press Ltd, Orchard Park, NY, 1999.

Simmel, G., *Soziologie. Untersuchungen über die Formen der Vergesellschaftung*. Duncker & Humblot, Leipzig, 1908.

Sullivan, Z., 'Race, Gender, and Imperial Ideology in the Nineteenth Century'. *Nineteenth-Century Contexts*. Vol. 13, No. 1, 1989, pp. 19-32.

Surber, J. P., *Hegel and Language*. SUNY Series in Hegelian Studies. State University of New York Press, Albany, 2006.

Süskind, P., *Das Parfum: Die Geschichte eines Mörders*. Diogenes Verlag, Zürich, 1994.

—, *Perfume: The Story of a Murderer*. trans. Woods, J., Penguin, London, 1987.

Thomas, K.F. & Humphries, S., *Commentary on Aristotle's De anima*. The Thoemmes Library of Classics and Ancient Philosophy, No. 4. Thoemmes, Bristol, 2003.

Wortham, S. & Fynsk, C., 'Counter-Institutions: Jacques Derrida and the Question of the University'. *Perspectives in Continental Philosophy*. No. 55, Fordham University Press, New York, 2006.

Žižek, S., *Enjoy Your Symptoms! Jacques Lacan in Hollywood and Out*. Routledge Classics, New York, 2008.

Mutants, Mice and Monstrosities: Dystopia in *Kys'* by Tatyana Tolstaya

Cristina Ruiz Serrano

Abstract
Tatyana Tosltaya's dystopic novel *Kys'* addresses the question of authoritarian systems as social monstrosities and the controversial issue of the fate of Russian culture in the last century. In *Kys'* Tatyana Tolstaya depicts the barbaric and ruthless place post-nuclear-war Moscow has become: the inhabitants of this society turned primitive are a community of mutants suffering from what they call the Consequences of the Blast and previous knowledge has been lost. The society is divided into the Oldeners, those who lived before the Blast; the ignorant mutants born after the Blast; and the Degenerators, half-human four-legged beings. The autocracy in power controls the inhabitants of the city and manipulates them through ignorance and fear. Taking as points of departure Foucault's notion of power, the Lacanian categories of the I-Subject, the other, and the Other, and Cohen's definition of the monstrous as a cultural artefact created to be interpreted, in this article I explore the uses of monstrosity in *Kys'* and the ways they affect the configurations of power inscribed in the dystopian society depicted in Tatyana Tolstaya's novel. In addition, the representation of monstrous beings in *Kys'* will be analysed with regard to Tolstaya's impressions on the contemporary state of Russian culture.

Key Words: Tatyana Tolstaya, *Kys'*, dystopia, monstrosity, Russian literature, post-nuclear war, mutants, Michel Foucault, Jacques Lacan.

*****

As Patrick L. McGuire points out in *Red Stars: Political Aspects of Soviet Science Fiction,* 'Russia has a long tradition of politically significant literature'.[1] Since science fiction has consistently been a political genre, it is no wonder this genre has transformed into a predominant vehicle for articulating the authors' opinions on the present and future of human society and on socio-political issues in Russian literature.

Science fiction appeared in Russia in the late eighteenth century[2] and has become an extremely popular mode of expression since then. Dystopian science fiction, with its inherent speculation on human behaviour and representations of alienated and deprived societies of the future, has been widely cultivated in Russian literature. Examples of this interest in dystopia are 'Respublika Iuzhnogo Kresta' (Republic of the South Crest, 1904) by Valerii Briusov (1873-1924), *My* (We, 1929) by Evgenii Zamyatin[3] (1884-1937), *Obytaemyi Ostrov* (Inhabited Island, 1969) by Arkady (1925-1991) and Boris Strugatsky (1933), *Moskva 2042*

(Moscow 2042, 1985) by Vladimir Voinovich (1932), and *Kys'* (The Slynx, 2000) by Tatyana Tolstaya (1951), among many other texts.

Tatyana Tolstaya, a noteworthy Russian writer, is well known for her mordant essays on contemporary Russian life and her collections of short stories. Both the chosen topic and the narrative style of Tolstaya's first novel *Kys'*[4] differ from her previous works, which were, for the most part, written in a realistic manner. *Kys'* can be defined as a dystopia filled with literary allusions to authoritarian systems as social monstrosities and to the development of Russian culture in the last century. As a significant amount of Russian dystopian texts, Tolstaya's *Kys'* has a post-nuclear-war setting. The novel deals with the uncivilized town of Fedor Kuz'mich (named after the current leader), which is what Moscow has become into after nuclear devastation. Mice are the mainstay of survival. The inhabitants of this society have regressed and are a community of mutants suffering from what they call *posledstvia* (Consequences). The society is divided into *prezhnyi* (the Oldeners), those who lived before the Blast and recall the civilized world; the loutish and ignorant mutants born after the Blast and subject to *posledstvia* such as a tail, extra limbs, gills, cockscombs sprouting from eyelids, etc.; and *pererozhdentsy* (Degenerators), half-human four legged beings harnessed to sleighs. The major pastime after work is to exchange insults with neighbours, and people's lives are completely controlled by a rigid despotic system that manipulates them through ignorance and fear. The autocrat in power puts forth all 'inventions' and works of literature as his own; books from before the Blast are absolutely forbidden, and the feared *sanitary* (Saniturions) in their *Krasnie Sani* (Red Sleighs) track down anyone who exhibits the slightest sign of *Bolezn'* (Disease) or *Svoevolie* (Freethinking). *Kys'* (The Slynx[5]), a legendary beast that feasts on people's blood and thoughts and inhabits the wilderness beyond the town walls, embodies the most frightening threat to this monstrous community. The menacing presence of the mythical screeching Kys' discourages people from departing and guarantees their submission.

In Tolstaya's *Kys'* the story is presented through an omniscient narrator and a third-person narrator who relates from the viewpoint of Benedikt, the main character. Benedikt, son of an Oldener mother and a mutant father, is one of the scribes who copies the literary works presented by the tyrant Fedor Kuz'mich as his own. Through Benedikt's eyes, the reader becomes acquainted with this gruesome, oppressive and violent society from the point of view of mutants, for whom the lost world of the Oldeners (the readers' world) is more deviant than their own, more unintelligible and legendary than the superstitions and myths the mutants themselves accept as true. Some of the major argumentative lines in the novel are the concealed iniquity of the soul, the effects of ignorance and lack of a developed culture in society, and the deviance inherent in authoritarian repressive regimes.

In 'Monster Culture (Seven Theses)' Jeffrey Jerome Cohen states that:

> the monstrous body is pure culture. A construct and a projection, the monster exists only to be read: the *monstrum* is etymologically 'that which reveals,' 'that which warns,' a glyph that seeks a hierophant. Like a letter on the page, the monster signifies something other than itself.[6]

Basing my approach on Cohen's definition of the monstrous as a cultural artefact to be interpreted, in this article I explore how Tatyana Tolstaya makes use of monstrous beings and their roles in the configurations of power inscribed in her novel. In addition, the representation of monstrous beings in *Kys'* will be analysed with regard to the author's own impressions of the contemporary state of Russian culture.

Monstrosity is a foremost feature in *Kys'*. First, the figure of the monster is a menacing presence throughout the whole novel. Deformed bodies, half-human creatures, and human beings enslaved and kept in dark basements to hunt for mice are examples of physical monstrosity. The disturbingly dim-witted submissive population always starving contrasts with the well fed, all-mighty dreaded unscrupulous *Murzy*[7] (Murzas). Furthermore, the cat-like size of the oblivious and grotesque autocrat Fedor Kuz'mich Kablukov is just another hideous aspect of this dreadful dystopian society.

The figure of the monster is strategically used in *Kys'* to create opposition between good and evil, Oldeners and mutants, the worldview before and after the nuclear devastation, and, on a more subliminal level, to emphasize the attitude of different social groups towards culture in Russian society. Many of these antagonisms are even present at the narrative level: although the narration is presented through Benedikt's viewpoint, himself a mutant, who by describing this world to some extent 'normalizes' it, the implied reader clearly identifies with the Oldeners and perceives the depicted society as an after-nuclear-war nightmare.

By creating such antagonism between the mutant-narrator and the Oldener-implied reader, Tolstaya masterly enriches the narration[8]: she playfully detaches the narrator from the implied reader, creating a polyphonic narrative and a multifaceted conception of Otherness in the text. For the implied reader, the mutant is the monster and as such '[it] is continually linked to forbidden practices, in order to normalize and to enforce'.[9] The implied reader conceives the mutant and its world as deviance, as the rejected 'other' world. In opposition to that 'other' world, the dreadful world of mutants and edible mice, the readers' world (the Oldeners' world before the Blast) becomes the normalized one, the one that is enforced. From this perspective, creation of monsters is culturally useful to validate the readers' worldview and endorse their own structures of power since '[w]hen contained by geographic, generic, or epistemic marginalization, the monster can function as an alter ego, as an alluring projection of (an Other) self'.[10]

The dystopian society of *Kys'* flawlessly adjusts to the parameters of Lacanian psychoanalysis and Foucauldian theory on structures of power in society. In the identity of the I, that takes place after the 'mirror stage' through identification with the Socio-symbolic Other, Lacan underlines a deficiency that appears due to 'the invasion of the symbolic, by the fact that the subject depends on the signifier but the signifier is first of all in the field of the Other'.[11] As Yannis Stavrakakis explains:

> What belongs to the Socio-symbolic Other can never become totally ours; it can never become us: it will *always* be a source of ambivalence and alienation and this gap can never be bridged.[12]

In *Kys'* monstrosity establishes itself in society through the identification of the mutant I with the empowered Murzas (here the Other, the Object of desire) and the materialistic values they represent. Kept in need, ignorance and fear, the mutants' desire for possessions and power (signifiers of the Other) transform them into serfs of the empowered, into supporters of the monstrous system imposed upon them.

As is stressed in Tolstaya's novel, despite the loss that the subject perceives behind the symbolic, he/she attempts to appropriate the Other's values. According to Foucault, this is why the configurations of power are something similar to a 'net-like series of relations':

> Power is employed and exercised through a net-like organization. And not only do individuals circulate between its threads; they are always in the position of simultaneously undergoing and exercising this power.[13]

Thus, society is seen as a net of marginality in which the other often adopts the role of the I Subject and appropriates the values of the Other symbolic regarding his/her own subordinates. Meanwhile, this other, now I Subject, maintains his/her subordinates in the same submissiveness in which he/she was kept (or is currently kept) in relation to other active I Subjects who exert their dominion upon him/her. Indeed, in *Kys'* even those who are not monstrous by nature are induced into such by the empowered Murzas and the repressive system they personify. As a result, the circularity of power is enhanced. However, this desire for the Other also becomes a source of alienation: for instance, Head Saniturion Kudear Kudearich's thirst of power is never sufficiently satisfied, nor Benedikt's transformation into a dehumanized Saniturion (into the Kys' itself) allows him to identify with the Socio-symbolic Other.

From the perspective of the implied reader, it is the Oldener Nikita Ivanich instead of the narrator Benedikt who becomes the hero of *Kys'*. This reflexive and wise Oldener is one of the few people who still carry on the knowledge of the past world, by organizing the underground libraries of proscribed Oldenprint books, and by putting into work the ethical values inherent in humanity. The implied reader shares Nikita Ivanich's knowledge and worldview, and for this reason, it is this character who incarnates the Lacanian I that opposes the other, the mutants and the Degenerators. However, as Benedikt's narration reveals, despite being the respected *Glavnii Iztochnik* (Head Stoker), Nikita Ivanich is an outsider and the scope of his authority in society is limited. For instance, in Benedikt's *Rabochaya Izba* (Work Izba) Nikita Ivanich is not intimidated by the presence of the autocrat Fedor Kuz'mich or *Bolshie Murzy* (Greater Murzas). He does not bother bending himself over for Fedor Kuz'mich nor hesitate to express his exasperation with the dreadful Murzas whom mutants do not even dare to look at:

> -Bot chto, Shakal, vy mne ne tych'te. -vzvisalsia Nikita Ivanich.- I ne ukazyvaite! ... Mne trista let, i ja biurokraticheskogo khamstva esche pri Prezhnei Zhizni navidalsia, blagodariu pokorno! ... Eto vasha zadacha, vasha elementarnaia zadacha: podderzhivat' minimal'nyi poriadok! Vashi kollegi p'ianstvuiut, a vy menia dergaete po pustiakam. A v massovom alkogolizme, Shakal, otchasti i vasha vina. Da-da!!! Ne pervyi raz vam govoriu!!! Vy ne sklonny uvazhat' chelovecheskuiu lichnost'. Kak i mnogie, vprochem. I vash veteranskii status, – Nikita Ivanich golos povysil i krivym paltsem po stoleshnitse postuchal, – proposhu ne preryvat'! vash veteranskii status ne daet vam prava menia tretirovat'!!! A takoi zhe homo sapiens, grazhdanin i mutant, kak i vy! Kak i vot, -rukoi povel,- ostal'nye grazhdane![14]

Although this direct expression of hostility towards authority is shocking to the mutants who are present in the episode, among them Benedikt, it does not have any impact on them, since as the narrator-Benedikt explains: 'Vsie uzhe privykli, znaiut, chto Nikitu Ivanicha nechego slushat': neset Bog znaet chto, sam nebos' polovinu slov ne ponimaet.'[15]

This incident is revealing in different ways. Firstly, the ignorance in which mutants are kept is really convenient to the structures of power: their lack of knowledge and scarcity of lexicon prevent them from understanding the meaning of anything beyond the elemental needs of their quotidian lives. Secondly, Nikita Ivanich is aware of his ex-centricity, and from his position as the 'other' claims that he belongs to the mutant society, but as a respected individuality. Following his own principles of humanity and broad-mindedness, he attempts to preserve his individuality while belonging to the collective. The Head Stoker is not so alarmed by the exterior monstrosity - physical Consequences of the Blast - of his co-citizens as by their outrageous foolishness and lack of moral principles. Furthermore, the confrontation of the experienced and intelligent Nikita Ivanich with the Murza Shakal underlines the fact that, unlike the mutants, the Oldener recognizes the real nature of the empowered Murzas: the latter personify the true monsters who have transformed the population into monstrous beings through ignorance and fear.

In the above-mentioned episode, Benedikt, Fedor Kuz'mich, the Murzas, and scribes panic when they witness Nikita Ivanich's ability to start a fire from his mouth. Later Benedikt ponders about Nikita Ivanich's gift:

> A nichego starik ne boitsa, nikto emu ne nadoben - ni murza, ni sosedi. Potomu takaia sila emu dana, takoe Posledstvie zavidnoe: ogon' u nego vnutriakh vyrabatyvaetsia. Da on zakhochet - vsiu slobodu spalit, da chego: ves' gorodok, vse lesa vokrug, ... Potomu, znat', i nachal'stvo ego storonoi obkhodit, ne pridiraetsia, kak k nam, prostym golubchikam; ego zhe sila, i slava, i vlast' zemnaia![16]

Besides the practicality of Nikita Ivanich's ability in such a primitive and deprived society, the implications of the Oldener's gift go much further: the fire coming from his entrails metaphorically symbolizes the knowledge Nikita Ivanich possesses and asserts. Fire may bring warmth (life), or burn (threat); similarly, knowledge brings delight and improvement or represents a menace, as it is the case for the Murzas. In such a society where practicality and ignorance are celebrated, Nikita Ivanich's real power - knowledge - is neutralized by the system and remains unnoticed and unvalued by the populace.

Although Benedikt is envious of Nikita Ivanich's strength and power, the Oldener does not represent for him the symbolic Other, the object of desire. Since the knowledge and power - freedom - the Oldeners possess are unintelligible to the new race (the mutants), Benedikt considers the Oldeners as ex-centric subjects. Manipulated by the autocrats in power who only desire to maintain the status quo, this society rejects knowledge, progress, and civilization and submerges itself in the darkness of materialism and primitivism. Benedikt himself considers the wealthy Murzas the symbolic Other, the desired Object of Desire. He admires their power, their wealthy life style: in such a deprived society material improvement is the only desirable matter. However, Benedikt does not actively attempt to appropriate the Other's values. His wedding with the wealthy Olen'ka, the daughter of Kudear Kudearych, the *Glavnii Sanitar* (Head Saniturion), transforms him and puts him in a position of power from which just passively benefits. Benedikt, who is unaware of his bride and parents-in-law's real identity until after he and Olen'ka are engaged, becomes rapidly disgusted with his new banal and voracious relatives, and with his own meaningless existence. The values of the Other - in this case hyperbolic gluttony, desire of power, and lust - turn into a source of alienation and distress for the narrator of *Kys'*. Even the Other's appreciation for art (Kudear Kudearych's apparent fondness for books) happens to be a source of alienation for Benedikt. Kudear Kudearych lures him to become a reader of the fabulous collection of Oldenprint Books the Head Saniturion has collected in what he defines as expeditions to protect the art from perishing. Benedikt is manipulated to become a Saniturion, a killer himself, through his passion for books and not for a thirst for power on his part. In this episode Tolstaya parodies Benedikt's superficial love for culture, since he is unable to understand the ultimate meaning of his readings.

Both his disdain for power and devotion to literature underline Benedikt's in-betweenness in this monstrous society: even though his father-in-law, Kudear Kudearych, induces Benedikt to be a Saniturion and utilizes him to assassinate the tyrant Fedor Kuz'mich, he does not succeed in awakening in Benedikt any aspiration to hold a position of power. The narrator's proximity to the Oldeners - by his mother's talks and Nikita Ivanich's friendship and teachings since early childhood - places him in a somehow ex-centric position regarding the other mutants: his Object of desire becomes literature, knowledge, instead of power and material improvement. Even though Benedikt's infatuation with Oldenprint books is accompanied by his deceptive behaviour as a Saniturion -which separates him from the humanitarian and moral principles of the Oldeners - he does not actively pretend to hold power and remains outside the new dictatorial regime imposed by Kudear Kudearych and Degenerator Terenty Petrovych.

Using the definition of monster given by Cohen, mutants can also be described as '...disturbing hybrids whose externally incoherent bodies resist attempts to include them in any systematic structuration.'[17] And as the monster, the mutant 'is dangerous, a form suspended between forms that threatens to smash distinctions.'[18] Nevertheless, the threat the mutant represents in Tolstaya's novel is only relative, since despite its in-betweenness, it epitomizes the empowered class, the I Subject. In *Kys'* the real threat to both mutants and Oldeners, to society in general, is personified in the *pererozhdentsy* (Degenerators).

As in other dystopias, in *Kys'* the presence of human-animal hybrids 'raises questions or anxieties about the purity of the human and the animal.'[19] Generally considered a threat to humanity, hybrids are often depicted as 'things which violate and in that violation confirm natural order and the logic of Creation.'[20] In other words, although hybrids may awaken human beings' insecurities about the special place they maintain in the natural order, the negativity associated with the figure of human-animal hybrids validates that order and the principles of humanity, culture and civilization that humankind epitomizes. This issue is presented in Tolstaya's novel predominantly in connection with Degenerators, key figures in the narration, which are humans degraded into monstrous hybrids by their irrationality and maliciousness. For more than half of the novel, the *pererozhdentsy* (Degenerators) are represented as half-human four legged beings harnessed to sleighs. According to the narrator-Benedikt's description:

> ...a v sani pererozhdenets zapriazhen, bezhit, valenkami topochet, sam blednyi, vzmylennyi, iazyk naruzhu. Domchit do rabochei izby i vstanet kak vkopannyi na vsie chetyre nogi, tol'ko mokhnatye boka khodunom khodiat: khy-khy-khy.
> A glazami tak i vorochaet, tak i vorochaet. I zuby skalit. I oziraetsia...
> Ai, nu ikh k leshemu, pererozhdentsev etikh, luchshe ot nikh podal'she. Strashnye oni, i ne poimesh', to li oni liudi, to li net: litso vrode kak u cheloveka, tulovische sherst'iu pokryto i na chetveren'kakh begaiut. I na kazhdoi noge po valenku. Oni, govoriat, esche do Vzryva zhili, pererozhdentsy-to. A vse mozhet byt'.[21]

Taking into consideration Benedikt's account, Degenerators hardly may be thought of as human beings. Trusting the narrator's accurateness in his portrayal of the dysfunctional society he lives in, the reader does not even consider the possibility that the narrator may be holding information or communicating culturally biased ideas. As is the case regarding the human nature of Degenerators. Later in the narration, the reader is dazed when it is revealed that Degenerators speak and largely articulate their recollections from their lives before the Blast. Teterya[22], the Degenerator assigned to Benedikt after his wedding with the wealthy Olen'ka, gives the narrator reasons enough to speak at length on the topic:

> Vot paroda podlaia: vse by sporit', vozrazhat', nasvistyvat'. Lenivaia tvar' popalas', rasslablennaia: net chtob mchat'sia vikhrem, kak Benedikt liubil – net, pletetsia noga za nogu, svistit, zuboskalit; a esli devushka kakaia prosemenit – esche i komentarii sebe pozvoliaet:
> -O, kakoi babets obemistyi![23]

Depicted as a nasty, devious, defiant and lazy being by Benedikt, the implied reader is still sympathetic to the figure of the Degenerator and his bitter fate in the devastated society after the Blast. Although the implied reader is progressively more and more shocked by Teterya's nastiness, his behaviour is somehow justified by the inhumane treatment Degenerators receive. Nevertheless, it is necessary to say that the increase of human traits Teterya gradually acquires in the narration does not improve the portrayal the reader receives of him. After Benedikt takes a trip to his old *izba* with Teterya, the Degenerator

> razpustilsia, sovsem uvazhat' perestal. Poka Benedikt u pletnia
> stoial, skotina perekuril da spliunul nazem', a potom i govorit:
> -Xe, u menia raspashonka v Sviblove luchshe byla.
> -Teterya, kak ty rasgovarivaesh' s barinom?! Tvoe mesto v uzde!
> -A tvoe —znaesh gde...U menia servant byl
> zerkal'nyi...Televizor Rubin, — trubka ital'ianskaia... Stenka
> iugoslavskaia shurin dostal, sanuzel razdel'nyi, fotooboi zolotaia
> osen'....
> I stoit, tvar', na zadnikh lapakh, kak rovnia, i o pleten' opersia, i
> razgovarivaet, i v glazakh mechta, i za khoziaina ne schitaet! V
> vospominania uradilsia!²⁴

Teterya's long enumeration of his past life material possessions - a kitchen with linoleum, a fridge with a freezer, vodka, caviar, tea with lemon, beer in cans, etc. - is ironically ambivalent in the text. This is meaningless to Benedikt, who is completely ignorant of the meaning of those words and so cannot relate them to the human nature of Teterya. The Degenerator's inventory is simple perceived as another example of his insolence and meanness:

> Pravil'no Nikita Ivanich govorit: uvazhenie dolzhno byt' k
> cheloveku, spravedlivost'! A eta skotina cheloveka ne uvazhaet,
> ni v grosh ne stavit! Benedikt oserchal da i oblomal emu boka-to
> knutom, nadaval zaushim da nogoi pnul. A test' govorit: Terentii
> smirnyi, eto Potap norovistyi! Kakov zhe togda Potap?! Esli etot
> smirnyi? ... A posle etoi poezdki, vish', Petrovichem ego zovi.
> Seichas priam.²⁵

The effect of this enumeration on the reader is, nevertheless, definite. Through Teterya's recollections of his material possessions, the human nature of the Degenerator is certainly recognized by the reader. Meanwhile, Tolstaya subtlety highlights the hyperbolic importance of materialistic gains for the character and the primitive level of Teterya's needs and desires: among his recollections, there is not a single one related to his freedom, nor connected to any cultural thought.

Once his human nature is established, Tolstaya proceeds to illustrate the meanness and viciousness of the Degenerators. While Benedikt visits Nikita Ivanich, the Oldeners insist in calling Teterya - left outside in the cold with the sleigh - into the house, alleging that the treatment the Degenerator receives is *bezchelovechno* (inhumane), *chudovischno ekspluatatsia* (an appalling explotation).²⁶ The goodwill and humanity of Nikita Ivanich and his comrade have a negative effect on the Degenerator, who immediately initiates a heated discussion about the sociopolitical situation in Russia before the Blast and openly expresses his ruthless hatred towards the Oldeners and the principles they represent:

>   -...ochki napialiat i rassuzhdat'! Ne pozvoliu...krapivnoe semia!
>   ... Rasplodilis', blia! Dva protsenta vam byt' veleno! ... chtob u trudovogo naroda na shee ne zasizhivalsia! ... Kto vse miaso sel? ... Skazal: ni piadi!..Kurily ne otdadim ... A stolby svoi v zadnitsu sebe zasun'! Rasveli muzei v gosudarstve, parazity! Benzinom vas vsekh ... i spichku! ... i pppppppppparlament vash, i knizhki, i akademika Sssssssakharova! I ...²⁷

This episode illustrates that the civilized society before the Blast also had its own monsters and, most likely, they were partially responsible for the events that triggered the destruction of the previous civilization. If the Oldeners illuminated by knowledge only were affected by positive *posledstvia* (Consequences) - longevity, and the ability to start a fire from one's innards, for example, - the resentful, violent, materialistic and ignorant population from before the Blast were degraded even further, becoming Degenerators, human-animal hybrids. As soon as the implied reader and the reader accept Teterya's human nature, the question about what differentiates human beings from animals is raised. Tatyana Tolstaya provides a simple answer: it is culture and ethic principles. If these are annihilated, the line dividing humanity and beasts also disappears. From this perspective, it is the hybrid - or the irrational and unethical human being, - who personifies the 'real' monster, since it is able to willingly exercise its power to destroy civilization and deliberately annihilate the other.

Once Teterya - now respectfully called Terenty Petrovych - gains access to authority, he transforms himself in the I Subject, implementing and deploying the relations of power before exerted upon himself. One of the first deeds the now empowered Degenerator ('normalized' to the category of mutant) attempts to accomplish is to eradicate knowledge by destroying the Oldenprint books and burning up Nikita Ivanich. It is while the wise Oldener is at the stake, that he comprehends that knowledge and culture will certainly perish with him, that Nikita Ivanich uses his Consequence's gift to burn up the whole town. When Nikita Ivanich finally acknowledges that his monstrous co-citizens and the gruesome society they have built do not have any chance to overcome their degradation, he exerts his own power and obliterates the town and its inhabitants. The other - the Head Stoker - revolts against the empowered ones, the 'true' monsters, their serfs, and the system they represent. Only the custodians of knowledge and culture will survive to build a new society and bring new hope to Earth. At the moment of truth Nikita Ivanich makes a conscious decision: he recognizes and accepts that only by betraying the ethical principles in which he believes, culture and ethics will be preserved for future generations.

Under the humorous-carnivalesque narrative tone used in *Kys'*, the novel echoes a broad array of philosophical and socio-political questions regarding the dangers posed by authoritarian regimes. Despite the tight relationship that exists between power and repression, Foucault warns that due to the complex nature of power, there are other more advantageous ways to exert it than by repression:

> ... power will be a fragile thing if its only function were to repress, if it worked only through the mode of censorship, exclusion, blockage and repression, in the manner of a great Superego, exercising itself only in a negative way. If, on the contrary, power is strong this is because, as we are beginning to realise, it produces effects at the level of desire –and also at the level of knowledge.[28]

In agreement with Foucault's notions, Tatyana Tolstaya illustrates in *Kys'* the threat that authoritarian regimes - openly or under pseudo-democratic outfits - pose by taking advantage of all possible ways to exert power, annihilating the individual and limiting the level of desire of the population by manipulating or restraining its knowledge. It is only through knowledge and culture that the individual can escape alienation and flee the monstrosity of a future where the human being is dehumanised or converted into a serf of the empowered. In Tolstaya's novel those in power are the 'true' monsters by nature even though they generally do not have the physical appearance as such[29]. Although the Murzas seem to be physically 'normal' (the narrator rarely comments on these characters' monstrous physical traits), their gruesome nature is stressed by their amorality and abusive behaviour towards the population they manipulate and subjugate.

Besides this general warning about monstrous systems of government, *Kys'* contains a specific interpretation concerning Russia, its history and the contemporary Russian cultural situation. Read as an allegory about present Russian cultural affairs, *Kys'* is such a corrosive text, it is no wonder that the novel has been controversial in Europe due to Tolstaya's incisive remarks on the contemporary state of Russian culture.[30] In the novel Tolstaya criticizes the role that different strata of the society have played (and still play) within the Russian culture today. For example, in *Kys'* the Oldeners symbolize the Old Russian and Soviet *intelligentsia*, the intellectual elite who focuses on creating, developing and disseminating culture. After being the I Subject, the engine of a glorious and culturally highly prosperous cultural life before the Revolution took place, the *intelligentsia* faded away due to politically and socially oriented purges (Teterya's allusions to weeding out society's 'parasites'), forced exile, and censorship. During the Soviet period many members of the intelligentsia were dissidents, non-conformists who criticized the regime and informed about violations of human rights and officially published laws. For this reason in Tolstaya's novel Teterya (who embodies the populist forces who opposed liberalization and change of the Soviet Union) accuses the Oldeners of betrayal and of keeping all material goods for themselves (here Tolstaya is alluding to the scarcity of products in the Soviet

Union after Brezhnev's era). Although in *Kys'* Tolstaya acknowledges the *intelligentsia*'s leading role in preserving and disseminating the rich Russian cultural heritage, the author also criticizes the excessive individualism of the intellectual elite and their insufficient activism in improving society. In *Kys'* Degenerators unmistakably characterize the darkest forces of the Soviet regime that actively contributed to the annihilation of the *intelligentsia* and caused the stagnation of the post-revolutionary society. They were neither revolutionaries nor ideologically oriented individuals, but narrow-minded, self-centred opportunists who were only concerned with their own material well-being. Ignorant and unruly, they were incapable of understanding or valuing the humanistic inheritance and the cultural splendour the *intelligentsia* embodied. Transformed into Degenerators, they were even less capable of comprehending the importance of developing and maintaining their intellectual tradition. When their transformation from the other to the I Subject materializes, they act in the same manner as Teterya/Terenty Petrovych: they obliterate the hated other whose principles they cannot understand for not being those of power and material possessions, those of the Symbolic Other. The mutants in *Kys'* symbolize the new generations of Russians, born and raised deprived from many of their cultural and intellectual traditions, 'in a Russia that has become a place of anti-memory and anti-space, divorced from its intellectual traditions,'[31] and devoid of the so-desired material possessions, their Object of Desire.

Tolstaya's concern with the loss of the rich pre-revolutionary literary tradition in Russian culture, not properly recovered during the Soviet system, and neglected by the new generations, is also accurately depicted in *Kys'*. In the novel, Benedikt and the other scribes are unaware that they are copying poems from the Golden and Silver Ages of Russian poetry, and despite his infatuation with books, Benedikt is unable to understand them and appreciate their worth. The message of Tatyana Tolstaya is clear and strong: the power of literature, of culture in general, can only be understood within the background of a developed and breathing intellectual tradition. Although Tolstaya's novel is particularly concerned with contemporary Russian society and cultural state, her message has universal value. *Kys'* hides a general warning in a world where culture and humanistic doctrines are progressively devalued and materialistic principles and possessions exalted: the seeds of monstrosities such as the dystopian society depicted in *Kys'* are in our world; we need to prevent them from growing.

Notes

[1] P.L. McGuire, *Red Stars: Political Aspects of Soviet Science Fiction*, UMI Research, Michigan, 1985, p. 1.
[2] Ibid., p. 6.

[3] Zamyatin's *My* is considered one of the most influential dystopias in the history of literature. George Orwell, for example, publicly acknowledged the influence of Zamyatin's *My* in his novel *1984* (1949) and it has been suggested that the novel of the Russian writer was a source of inspiration for Huxley's *Brave New Word* (1932). Zamyatin wrote this novel in 1920-21 and it was published in English in 1922. Censored in the Soviet Union, *My* was published in Russian for the first time in 1967 in New York and it was never officially published in the Soviet Union, although the manuscript of the novel circulated in the Soviet Union as 'samizdat' (underground publication and distribution of Government-banned literature).

[4] T. Tolstaya, *Kys'*, Podkova, Inostranka, Moskva, 2001. The English translations of the quotations from this novel are taken from T. Tolstaya, *The Slynx*, trans. J. Gambrell, New York Review Books, New York, 2003.

[5] As M. Deyrup points out: '[l]ike much of the onomatopoeic word play that occurs in the novel, the ominous 'slynx' is presumably derived from the English words 'lynx' and 'slink''. See M. Deyrup, 'The Slynx: A Novel/Pushkin's Children: Writings on Russian and Russian Books', *Slavics and East European Journal*, Vol. 48, No. 1, 2004, p. 126.

[6] J.J. Cohen, 'Monster Culture (Seven Theses)', J.J. Cohen (ed), *Monster Theory: Reading Culture*, University of Minnesota Press, Minneapolis, 1996, p. 4.

[7] Literally, Murza is a Tartar feudal lord. In the novel, the term Murza refers to all members of the State empowered to ensure social and public order, obedience to the leader, and to enforce repression.

[8] In *Kys'* Tolstaya employs the etymology of names to conceal important information about the characters. For example, Benedikt derives from Church Latin *benedicte* meaning blessed, well spoken of. The name also refers to a newly married man who was previously considered a confirmed bachelor. Benedikt might also derive from Latin *bene dictus*, here in reference to Benedikt's role as the narrator. Nikita is of Greek origin. It derives from the Greek *nike* meaning victory and the name *Aniketus*, meaning the unbeaten, the unconquerable. In Nikolai Nekrasov's national epic *Komu na Rusi zhit' khorosho* (1878-1879, *Who Can Be Happy and Free in Russia*) Kudear was the name of a brigand chief who pillaged until he suddenly experienced a spiritual awakening and entered a Monastery to serve God. The double use of the name in Benedikt's father-in-law name and patronymic (Kudear Kudearych) intensifies the dissolute condition of this character. The contrasting meanings of Teterya (woodcock) and Terenty (Terence) stress the transformation that this character undergoes in the narration. The Russian proverb '*glukhaia i glupaia kak teterya*' (deaf and dim as a woodcock) clarifies the negative connotations associated with the Degenerator's nickname. On the contrary, the use of Terenty (Terence, which means tender, good) shows how the character is valued and respected later on.

[9] Cohen, op. cit., p. 16.
[10] Ibid., p. 17.
[11] J. Lacan, *The Four Fundamental Concepts of Psychoanalysis*, trans. A. Sheridan, J. Miller, (ed), Penguin, London, 1979, p. 5.
[12] Y. Stavrakakis, *Lacan and the Political*, Routledge, London and New York, 1999, p. 34.
[13] M. Foucault, *Power/Knowledge: Selected Interviews and Other Writings, 1972-1977*, trans. C. Colin, L. Marshall, J. Mepham & K. Soper; C. Gordon (ed), Pantheon Books, London, 1980, p. 98.
[14] Tolstaya, op. cit., pp. 81-82. 'now you listen to me, Jackal, don't be so familiar,' said Nikita Ivanich in a huff. 'And don't tell me what to do! I'm three hundred years old, and I saw enough bureaucratic nastiness in the Oldener Times to suffice! You have a job, an elementary responsibility to maintain a minimum level of order! You allow your colleagues to become inebriated, and you have the gall to badger me with trifles. The mass alcoholism we are experiencing, Jackal, is partly your fault. That's right! This isn't the first time I've brought this issue to your attention! You are not inclined to respect the individual human being. Like many people, for that matter. And your veteran status' –Nikita Ivanich raised his voice and tapped on the table with a crooked finger – 'please don't interrupt me! Your veteran status does not give you the right to harass me!! I am a *Homo sapiens*, a citizen and mutant, like you! Like all these citizens!' he said, gesturing broadly with his hand. (Tolstaya, op. cit., pp. 61-62.)
[15] Tolstaya, op. cit., p. 81. Everyone knows that there's no point in listening to Nikita Ivanich: he just rambles on, probably doesn't understand half the words he says himself. (Tolstaya, op. cit., p. 62.)
[16] Tolstaya, op. cit., p. 86. That old man isn't afraid of anything. He doesn't need anyone–no Murzas, no neighbors. Because he has such power, such an envious Consequence: fire comes from his innards. If he wanted, he could burn down the whole settlement, or the whole town, all the woods around it, […] That must be why the bosses avoid him, they don't mess with him like they do with us, simple Golubchiks; he has strength and glory and power on earth! (Tolstaya, op. cit., p. 66.)
[17] Cohen, op. cit., p. 6.
[18] Ibid.
[19] R. Davis, 'A White Illusion of a Man: Snowman, Survival and Speculation in Margaret Atwood's *Oryx and Crake*', *Hosting the Monster*, H.L. Baumgartner & R. Davis (eds), Rodopi, Amsterdam, 2008, p. 243.
[20] S. Shalih, 'Idols and Simulacra: Paganity, Hybridity and Representation in *Mandeville's Travels*', *The Monstrous Middle Ages*, B. Bildhauer & R. Mills (eds), University of Toronto Press, Toronto, 2003, p. 113.

[21] Tolstaya, Ibid., pp. 6-7. [Rich people] ride on sleighs, flashing their whips, and they've got a Degenerator hitched up. The poor thing runs, all pale, in a lather, its tongue hanging out, its felt boots thudding. It races to the Work Izba and stops stock-still on all four legs, but its fuzzy sides keep going *huffa, puffa, huffa, puffa.* And it rolls its eyes, rolls'em up and down and sideways. And bares its teeth. And look around…To the hell with them, those Degenerators, better to keep your distance. They're strange ones, and you can't figure out if they're people or not. Their faces look human, but their bodies are all furry and they run on all fours. With a felt boot on each leg. It's said they lived before the Blast, Degenerators. Could be. (Tolstaya, op. cit., p. 4.)

[22] Teterya/Terenty Petrovich appears to be indebted to the character of Sharik/Poligraf Poligrafovich Sharikov, the stray dog transformed into a proletarian lout in the novel *Sobachee tsertse* (Heart of a Dog, 1925) by Mikhail Bulgakov (1891-1940). The novel is a scathing satire about the New Soviet Man. In *Sobachee tsertse* a stray dog, Sharik, progressively takes human form after the prominent professor Filip Filipovich Preobrazhenky implants human glands and testicles into it. The more human Sharik becomes, the more his meanness and viciousness grow. His behaviour becomes so unbearable and sordid (he even dares to officially accuse Filip Filipovich, - who personifies the pre-revolutionary *intelligentsia* - of contrarrevolutionary activities), that the professor turns Sharik back into his former canine self.

[23] Tolstaya, op. cit., p. 201. Here's a nasty breed for you: all they want to do is argue, object, and whistle. Benedikt ended up with a lazy cur, a real slacker. He wouldn't race flat out like a whirlwind, the way Benedikt liked. No, he had to prance around putting one foot after the other, whistling and grinning. If a girl passed by he'd even allow himself to make comments: 'Whoa, what a voluptuous broad!' (Tolstaya, Ibid., p. 154.)

[24] Ibid., p. 208. After that trip Teterya got completely out of hand and lost all respect for Benedikt. While Benedikt stood at the fence, that furry pig stood by and smoked, he even spat on the ground, and then said,: 'Ha, I had a dive in Sviblovo that was better than that place.''Teterya, watch how you talk to your betters! Your place is in the bridle!''And yours is –you know where…I had a mirrored buffet. And a color TV with an Italian tube…My brother-in-law managed to get a hold of a Yugoslav cabinet set, I had a separate bathroom and toilet, Golden Autumn wallpaper.' …And he stands there, the rodent, on his hind legs like he was an equal, leaning on the fence, chatting, and there's a dream in his eyes, and it's clear as day he doesn't think of Benedikt as his master at all! He's lost in memories! Tolstaya, Ibid., p. 160.

[25] Ibid., p. 209. Nikita Ivanich is right when he says there should be respect for people, and justice too! But this swine doesn't respect people, he doesn't give a fig

for them! Benedikt got mad and beat him on the sides with the whip, slapped him on the ears and kicked him good and hard. And his father-in-law says Terenty's the calm one, it's Potap that's skittish! What's Potap like, then, if this one is obedient? ... After that trip, you gotta call him Terenty Petrovich, like he was some kind of Murza. Yeah, sure. (Tolstaya, ibid., p. 161.)

[26] Ibid., p. 227.

[27] Ibid., pp. 279-80. ... They stick a pair of glasses on and then they start thinking! ... I won't let you weeds hit me with a wrench. ... Gone and multiplied like rabbits, shit! Supposed to be two percent and not a cent more so you don't crush the working class! ... Who ate all the meat? ... I said not one inch! ...We won't give up the Kuriles ... And you can stick your pillars up your rear end! You parasites, tried to turn the country into a museum. Pour gasoline over you and –just one little match! ... and your pppparliament, and your books, and your academic Ssssssssakharov! And ... (Tolstaya, Ibid., pp. 216-217.)

[28] Foucault, op. cit., p. 59.

[29] Nevertheless, in *Kys'* the concealed monstrosity of the empowered' soul might also be accompanied by covered monstrous traits. This is, for example, the case of Benedikt's family-in-law. The hidden long, gray and sharp claws that Kudear Kudearevich, his wife and daughter have in their feet metaphorically represent their rapacious disposition and voracity for material possessions.

[30] Deyrup, op. cit., p. 127.

[31] Ibid., p. 126.

Bibliography

Cohen, J.J., 'Monster Culture (Seven Theses)'. *Monster Theory: Reading Culture.* Cohen, J.J. (ed), University of Minnesota Press, Minneapolis, 1996.

Davis, R., 'A White Illusion of a Man: Snowman, Survival and Speculation in Margaret Atwood's *Oryx and Crake'*. *Hosting the Monster.* Baumgartner, H.L. & Davis, R. (eds), Rodopi, Amsterdam, 2008.

Deyrup, M., 'The Slynx: A Novel/ Pushkin's Children: Writings on Russian and Russian Books'. *Slavics and East European Journal.* Vol. 48, No. 1, 2004, pp. 125-127.

Foucault, M., *Power/Knowledge: Selected Interviews and Other Writings. 1972-1977.* trans. Gordon, C., Marshall, L., Mepham, J. & Soper, K.; Gordon, C. (ed), Pantheon Books, New York, 1980.

Lacan, J., *The Four Fundamental Concepts of Psychoanalysis*. trans. Sheridan, A., Miller, J. (ed), Penguin, London, 1979.

McGuire, P.L., *Red Stars: Political Aspects of Soviet Science Fiction.* UMI Research, Michigan, 1985.

Shalih, S., 'Idols and Simulacra: Paganity, Hybridity and Representation in *Mandeville's Travels*'. *The Monstrous Middle Ages.* Bildhauer, B. & Mills, R. (eds), University of Toronto Press, Toronto, 2003.

Stavrakakis, Y., *Lacan and the Political*. Routledge, London and New York, 1999.

Tolstaya, T., *Kys'.* Podkova. Inostranka, Moskva, 2001.

——, *The Slynx*. trans. Gambrell, J., New York Review Books, New York, 2003.

The Distorted Mirror: The Monstrosity of Artificial Beings

Jesús Eduardo Oliva Abarca

Abstract
Artificial creatures in literature have anticipated topics that disciplines like philosophy, social anthropology and cybernetics hold as fundamental. Authors of genres from fantasy to science fiction have been representatives of contemporary tendencies; some emphasize the ethical dilemma of these beings' existence, others fall for their allure. We now witness reality-surpassing fiction, in the form of automata, robots, androids and cyborgs. For some, these represent the possibility of integration between biological and synthetic entities, while others see in this union the eventual dissolution of the meaning of humanity. In this chapter I attempt to interpret the monstrous aspects of artificial beings in works by Hoffman, Shelley, Villiers de l'Isle-Adam, Poe, Čapek and Philip K. Dick, and the impact these creatures have had on culture in general. I intend to demonstrate that their repugnance lies not in their ugliness or cruelty but in the peculiar way in which their ability to convey intelligence and passion awakens contradictory emotions in us, the readers. Their expression of independence supposedly reserved for humankind forces us to reflect on the definition of our own identity.

Key Words: Android, automaton, gynoid, hyperreal, monstrosity, replica, robot, simulacrum, artificial being, cybernetics.

*****

1. The Specular Device

Since humanity has consisted of sentient beings, its fascination with its own activity has driven it to search for the secret of life. Unsatisfied with the effect of its actions on nature, humanity invented a domain within society that echoed its will. Humanity's intelligence told itself that it possessed the answer to the question of what it means to be alive. However, this reflection was never more than an unfinished exercise, in which humanity's image appeared incomplete. Humanity then decided to replicate itself in creatures that, because of their similarity to humanity, were able to completely unmask the enigma of its existence. These 'beings' offered humanity a mirror where it could ponder the secrets of humanity's spirit.

2. The Double Mechanic

The automaton can be considered humanity's first attempt to emulate a living being through mechanics. These machines, imitators in body and movement of animate beings have a long history - beginning in ancient civilizations and continuing into the present day - to incite reactions of horror that border on fascination. Let us remember, for example, the legend of Albertus Magnus, the Medieval theologian credited with creating an automaton to be his manservant. Magnus' disciple, Thomas Aquinas, later destroyed the artificial attendant, as he considered the creature an offence to God, the exclusive creator of life *ex nihilo*.

The automaton as it is conceived today achieved a refinement thanks to the advances in engineering, specifically clockwork, which accompanied the advent of the Industrial Revolution. This was well into the modern era. Jacques de Vaucanson (1709-1782) is famous for creating a mechanical duck able to imitate the digestive process, as well as a flute and drum-playing doll christened 'The Flute Player.' Even better known is Pierre Jaquet-Droz (1721-1790), creator of 'The Musician,' 'The Draughtsman' and 'The Writer,' works whose complex design and lifelike movement earned them fame as mechanical masterpieces.

One of the most controversial automata was Hungarian inventor Wolfgang von Kempelen's (1734-1804) 'The Turk', a humanlike mannequin decked in Arabic attire that, as the legend goes, was unbeatable at chess. It travelled throughout Europe and eventually fell into the hands of Johan Maelzel (1772-1838), who exhibited it in the United States.

By the eighteenth and nineteenth centuries, mechanical innovations had succeeded in enshrining the automaton in the cultural imaginary of any enlightened individual; this robot, given life by the wonders of burgeoning technology, aroused pride and suspicion. Ideal conditions, in short, for the automaton to become a literary subject in its own right. We see examples of such literature in the short stories 'Automata' (Die Automate) and 'The Sand-Man' (Der Sandmann) by E. T. A. Hoffmann (1776-1822), as well as Edgar Allan Poe's (1809-1849) essay 'Maelzel Chess-Player,' written to expose the hoax of the chess-playing Turk.

In 'Automata,' two young friends, Lewis and Ferdinand, attend an exhibition of 'The Turk,' a mechanical mannequin said to be able to read one's destiny, like a kind of artificial oracle. The boys are fascinated at this wonder but cannot entirely abandon their skepticism, insisting that the automaton must depend on the will of a 'person ... who speaks to us through the Turk.'[1] Despite the machine's exhibitor happily showing them its inner workings and even speaking aloud while it pronounces its prophecies, the artist

> laughed and joked in the farthest corner of the room with the spectators, leaving the figure to make its gestures and give its replies as a wholly independent thing, having no need of any connection with him.[2]

Of the two friends, Lewis is especially frightened by the mechanical movements of these dead figures, 'mere images of living death,'[3] whom he addresses with the words of Macbeth: 'Thou hast no speculation in those eyes/ Which thou dost glare with.'[4]

In 'The Sand-Man,' the automaton's enchantment reaches seductive proportions. The narrative's main character, Nathaniel, falls in love with the beautiful Olimpia, daughter of the inventor Spalanzani. On the occasion of her debut into society, Nathaniel succumbs to passion and confesses his affection for her. Her moaning inflames him all the more, since he interprets this as corresponding love. But Nathaniel's friend Siegmund is suspicious of Olimpia, 'Miss Wax-face-wooden doll,'[5] and he confides to his companion that she seems

> singularly statuesque and soulless. Her figure is regular, and so are her features, that can't be gainsaid; and if her eyes were not so utterly devoid of life, I may say, of the power of vision, she might pass for a beauty. She is strangely measured in her movements, they all seem as if they were dependent upon some wound-up clockwork. Her playing and singing have the disagreeably perfect, but insensitive timing of a singing machine, and her dancing is the same. We felt quit afraid of this Olimpia, and did not like to have anything to do with her; she seemed to us to be only acting *like* a living creature, and as if there was some secret at the bottom of it all.[6]

Nathaniel listens to the advice with scepticism, but it is not long before he realizes, during the altercation between Coppelius-Coppola and Spalanzani, that Olimpia is a lifeless doll. Indeed, she turns out to be nothing more than Spalanzani's most perfect automaton.

In the same vein, Edgar Allan Poe's incredulity about the workings of 'The Turk' led to an essay refuting the supposed autonomy of this mechanical being, which he was unable to conceive as 'a pure machine, unconnected with human agency in its movements.'[7] Poe describes in detail 'The Turk's' performance in a public game in which it wins, proceeding to gloat for the spectators. Unlike 'The Sandman,' in which the automaton passes for a human being, here the illusion consists of the machine achieving human intellect; it is even admitted that 'at every movement of the figure machinery is heard in motion.'[8] Although Maelzel's mechanical chess player was ultimately revealed to be a hoax - a human was in fact controlling its movements. Poe makes an interesting objection with respect to the machine is that 'the external appearance, and, especially, the deportment of the Turk, are, when we consider them as imitations of life, but very indifferent imitations.'[9]

Simulacrum encompasses the automaton's existence; imitation is its modus operandi. However, it would be a mistake to think that the disgust these artificial beings often provoke is due to their replicating and even perfecting the human figure. Their grotesqueness lies not in their appearance, but in the very act of simulation.

> To dissimulate is to pretend not to have what one has. To simulate is to feign to have what one doesn't have. One implies a presence, the other an absence. But it is more complicated than that because simulating is not pretending ... Therefore, pretending, or dissimulating, leaves the principle of reality intact: the difference is always clear, it is simply masked, whereas simulation threatens the difference between the 'true' and the 'false', the 'real' and the 'imaginary'.[10]

The absence Baudrillard mentions has been shown in the literary examples cited above. Both Hoffmann and Poe agree that automata imitate life in an imperfect way. A romantic conception, according to the spirit of both writers, would lead to the conclusion that automata have no soul, the very metaphysical origin of life. I propose that, beyond it lacking a soul, the monstrosity of the automaton lies, more precisely, in its being devoid of meaning; the meaning of our feelings and passions, that which combats indifference. The automaton is, to some degree, the first step toward a hyperrationalisation of human action; it is a figure that reflects our own image but does so without a trace of the havoc of our emotions - an indifferent gesture, nothing more.

3. The Disobedient Reflection

One of the most fascinating and frightful beings to come out of literature is, without a doubt, Frankenstein. Mary Shelley's *Frankenstein, or the Modern Prometheus* (1818), is a dream of progress turned nightmare. The creature created by Victor Frankenstein is the first artificial being produced by a still rudimentary organic engineering, in an eagerness to examine the mysteries of the soul. It is an android, an organic entity in the form of a man. In the solitude of his laboratory, the scientist assembles the creature using parts of corpses, experiencing no disgust at this task, since in his view he was achieving the ideal of human perfection. The first problem Dr. Frankenstein faces is the body's composition, since the replication of the human figure required including even the smallest internal organ. Frankenstein decides 'to make the being of a gigantic stature, that is to say, about eight feet in height, and proportionably large.'[11] The experiment is successful; the doctor becomes a surrogate father. But soon the illusion gives way to the horror of his creation: 'he was ugly then, but when those muscles and joints were rendered capable of motion, it became a thing such as even Dante could not have conceived.'[12] It is significant that it is only when the monster shows movement that the doctor can no longer contain his fear. His creature is a monster because, despite its organic origin, it is a being *contra natura*, a deviation of nature: 'Real monsters, as several exhibits revealed, were generally regarded as 'freaks of nature' (*lusus naturae*), examples of nature gone wrong.'[13] The creation, for all of its outward ugliness, is nevertheless alive. Unlike the mechanical automaton, whose movements are always regular and exact, the creature's movements have something spontaneous about them, similar to those of a newborn baby.

Frankenstein abandons his creation, condemning him to loneliness and alienation. The scientist's android does not even have a name; it is a being denied an identity. Because of its abnormality he is unable to coexist in society, it is destined to be merely the Other: 'Monsters are our *Others* par excellence.'[14] Román Gubern observes appropriately that Frankenstein's creature is an aesthetic monster, whose monstrosity lies specifically in his physical disproportion and ugliness.[15] However, this is only a half-truth. The creature's monstrosity lies in the fact that his physical ugliness is disproportionate to his good-natured spirit. In the first encounter between creator and creature, near Montblanc, the monster confesses: 'Believe me, Frankenstein, I was benevolent; my soul glowed with love and humanity; but am I not alone, miserably alone? You, my creator, abhor me.'[16]

The creature tells Frankenstein how he learned to speak during time spent anonymously with the De Lacey family. He reveals that he is intelligent and capable of understanding in a symbolic universe, an ability believed to be reserved for man. The monster is an outcast because of his appearance; his outer ugliness excludes him from culture, but his intelligence qualifies him as a cultural being. What's more, the monster perceives in his self-consciousness his status as in exile, a representative of the margins of human civilization. This drives him to declare himself an enemy of humanity, and to take the lives of his creator's loved ones, unless the scientist creates a companion for him. The monster maintains that

> man will not associate with me; but one as deformed and horrible as myself would not deny herself to me. My companion must be of the same species and have the same defects. This being you must create.[17]

Frankenstein's monster is a being of ambiguities, not unlike Hoffmann's automata. However, what distinguished the latter from a human being was their mechanical inertia, mere representation devoid of meaning, devoid of *intentionality*. On the other hand, the only difference between Frankenstein's creature and man is his appearance, since his actions are also– motivated by will and reason. The monster longs for company, someone like himself with whom to share his existence. He is an empathic creature, in short, with the emotional intelligence to look for the meaning of life in relationships. From a philosophical point of view, human beings possess three exclusive spiritual attributes: thought, feeling and will. Frankenstein's creature shares these traits with man, since he, in effect, feels not only physical suffering but also moral and emotional anguish. When the monster's creator destroys his would-be companion, the creature complains: 'I have endured incalculable fatigue, and cold, and hunger; do you dare destroy my hopes?'[18] Frankenstein's monster does not live in the sphere of simulacrum, but rather his thoughts, feelings and volition have an effective and concrete reality.

A psychoanalytical reading of Shelley's novel might conclude that Frankenstein's creature represents a threat to the narcissistic image that the humans have of themselves. When a creature unlike us appropriates the constitution of our personality, it endangers our identity, individual and collective. This sentiment is perhaps at the heart of Victor Frankenstein's grim speculation when he begins work on the monster's companion.

> Even if they were to leave Europe and inhabit the deserts of the new world, yet one of the first results of those sympathies for which the daemon thirsted would be children, and a race of devils would be propagated upon the earth who might make the very existence of the species of man a condition precarious and full of terror.[19]

Frankenstein is horrified by the prospect of a new species overcoming the human race, taking control of the symbolic universe formerly reserved for the man and destroying the narcissistic complex on which humanity's ideal is founded. The scientist, personification of the progressive spirit of the Modern Age, is so fascinated by his own image that decides to make it tangible in a creature, but the image he sees in this mirror is a distorted one, a grotesque hyperbole of his own impassioned reason. Frankenstein's monster is *sui generis*, not only a product of rationalization gone mad, but in fact a *rational* monster. It is conscious of itself and unsatisfied with his condition: 'You hate me, but your abhorrence cannot equal that with which I regard myself.'[20] What is most upsetting about this monster is its humanity: its self-hatred, its quest to nullify its own existence. The creature is a sign of a disillusioned humanity, corrupted by a loathing of what is different and strange. Its decision to take its own life is an ontological affirmation, albeit paradoxical: the creature flaunts its independence from Doctor Frankenstein's will. The boundaries between what is artificial and what is alive have become muddled. The creature is not a reflection of its creator; rather, it searches for its own image in the mirror of the world.

4. The Emancipated Artificiality

Frankenstein's creature is the immediate predecessor of the menagerie of contemporary artificial beings. The junctions between what is artificial and what is alive narrow, resulting in more perfect anthropomorphous machines, organic or mechanical, mirroring with greater and greater precision the human being that conceives them. The automata seem hideous because of their lack of meaning and human intentionality; humanity is upset by its own indifferent image, hence the horror suffered when confronted with a distorted and grotesque physical reflection that is at the same time a conscious being. What would the human reaction be with a creature created in its image and likeness that nevertheless demands for itself the ideal of humanity, the autonomy of being alive? Would we give this new entity the dignity of being human, or would we simply be appalled by it?

A. The Gynoid in Love

L'Ève future (1886) by Auguste Villiers de l'Isle-Adam (1838-1889) carries the fascination with artificial beings to its final consequences, personified in Hadaly. This *andréide* is Edison's invention to remedy Lord Ewald's dissatisfaction with his relationship with Miss Alicia Clary. The young man is disturbed by the fact that, physically, Alicia is the ideal of feminine beauty, yet her 'intimate being' is superficial and vain.

> ...Between the body and the soul of Miss Alicia, it wasn't just a disproportion which distressed and upset my understanding; it was an absolute *disparity* ... Her intimate being was in flat contradiction with the form it inhabited.[21]

The lover's observation is a rejection of the concrete woman's nature, which he conceives as a being of appearances.

> Miss Alicia, now, like every other mediocre being, is far from being *stupid*. She's simply *foolish*. Her dream would be to appear before the world as a 'clever woman', because of the 'brilliant' reputation, the special advantages, that she thinks such reputation would give her.[22]

As a solution Edison offers Ewald 'transubstantiation,' suggesting that Miss Alicia be reinvented without the moral contingencies of the original one. The longing for the ideal woman can be achieved through science, which corrects spiritual and corporal discords. Joining science and desire, Edison introduces to Lord Ewald the woman of the future: the gynoid Hadaly. The young lover marvels at the gynoid's outer similarity to Alicia, at the precision with which the artificial has imitated and melded with the natural. The only difference is that Hadaly, like the automaton Olimpia, is empty, representing only a docile object for male desire. That being, Lord Ewald's desire is intellectual as well as erotic. He has no interest in an 'doll, without feeling or intelligence,'[23] and he maintains the suspicion that the artificial cannot equal what is alive. But Edison replies that Ewald *'will not be able to distinguish one from the other.'*[24] Edison's joy over the artificial miracle comes to a climax when he states that Hadaly's operation *'will be a little more dependent on electricity than that of her model.'*[25] The scientist matches natural biological processes with mechanical ones; in a kind of biological *mechanicism* in which organism and mechanism transpose one another, resulting in a mechanization of what is human and the humanized machine.

Hadaly is the perfect woman because, although her appearance is feminine, she is ultimately a man's invention; she is the feminine replication of the masculine. Edison is aware of this when he tells Ewald that the *andréide* '*is nothing but your own soul reduplicated.*'[26] The 'human machine' materially discredits the corporeal woman and also provides a consolation for her mortality. As a machine, Hadaly's beauty is incorruptible by time; what's more, personifying an ideal, she exists outside of time, 'is a Being in Limbo, a mere potentiality.'[27] Identity is not a problem for this 'magnetic-electric being', since her body is not subject to the vicissitudes of a natural life.

> - You can reproduce the IDENTITY of a woman? You, a man born of woman?
> - She will be a thousand time more identical to herself ... than she is in her own person! Yes! I assure you! Since not a day passes without changing some outlines of the human body, and the science of physiology demonstrate to us that the body changes *completely* all of its atoms, every seven years approximately. Does anyone's body really exist at any given point? Does one ever resemble oneself?[28]

Once she is set in motion, 'alive,' the *andréide* captivates Lord Ewald in an ambiguous way. He cannot ignore the fact that Hadaly is made of metal parts, an artificial copy of a living being, a false Alicia but which seemed more natural than the real one. The representation has outdone the original. Reality breaks down into the symbols that represent it: Hadaly surpasses the living Alicia, her model. The *andréide* is *hyperreal*, easing the pain in the absence of substance; the copy 'could laugh' even and behave in society. The imperative of human authenticity seems to separate momentarily from the organic. The artificial can be even more natural than what is genuinely alive, and the false Alicia can be more *real* than the Alicia of flesh and blood. But Lord Ewald's preoccupation is if he could love the mechanical copy of a concrete woman, if this erotic deviation - love for the artificial - is appropriate morally and spiritually speaking.

Edison and Lord Ewald do not see each other for a period of time, during which the scientist works on Hadaly's improvement. When the young man meets with Miss Alicia again he experiences an idyll which convinces him that there is no longer any discrepancy between body and spirit in the girl. Madly in love, he vindicates the flesh above the machine, stating ecstatically, 'you exist, truly, as a creature of flesh and blood, like me!'[29] But this Alicia, 'whom love can render as ideal'[30] reveals her real identity to him: 'Dear friend, don't you recognize me? I'm Hadaly.'[31] The lover succumbs to paraphilia of the device. Once the boundaries between the human and the artificial are overcome, Hadaly seems hideous for Lord Ewald, not only because the *andréide* is a technological abstraction he grew to love, but because she corresponds his love with a passion equally human. The only obstacle impeding the consummation of the love between *andréide* and man is the latter's reservations with respect to Hadaly's artificial state. She is not an unprecedented being, but rather a copy that overtakes the original. The artificial being must demand for itself an image all its own.

B. The Robotic Insurrection

The search for autonomy and a space of one's own, which in *Frankenstein* was the inception of a rebellion, in *R.U.R.* (2004) is a full-fledged revolution. Here the fully conscious artificial creature confronts the need to abolish the dominant human system and replace it with a new order. Čapek's (1890-1938) play recounts the advent of mass-produced anthropomorphic beings with an organic substance similar to that of man, based on the experiments of the mythical scientist Rossum. These creatures, called *robots*, are used as servants of humans. The word 'robot' here does not allude to a machine that performs specific actions, but to the idea of hard labour. The robots are organic beings, of intellectual abilities superior to those of man, but they possess no affections or feelings, not to mention free will. Their actions are mechanical: 'the Robots are not attached to life.'[32] In the first interview between Harry Domain, president of Rossum's Universal Robots, and Helena Glory, the young woman who defends the machines, Domain explains Rossum's ambition 'was nothing more or less than to supply proof that Providence was no longer necessary.'[33] The dream of progress is realized through bioengineering; the man of science has not only learned to imitate nature, he has surpassed it masterfully.

> Young Rossum invented a worker with the minimum amount of requirements. He had to simplify him. He rejected everything that did not contribute directly to the progress of work. In this way he rejected everything that makes man more expensive. In fact, he rejected man and made the Robot ... the Robots are not people. Mechanically they are more perfect than we are. They have an enormously developed intelligence, but they have no soul ... Very neat, very simple. Really a beautiful piece of work. Not much in it, but everything in flawless order. The product of an engineer is technically at a higher pitch of perfection than a product of nature.[34]

However, these products are disposable. The robot is a mass-produced object with no identity. It is an organic body, but does not reproduce through procreation or experience the cycle of life and death as humans do. The robot is manufactured then distributed or sold, to be used and worn out. The change in meaning is evident: the organic becomes disposable, an easily replaceable mechanism. Even so, the robot is identical in appearance to its employer; to the degree that Helena mistakes the robot Sulla for a real girl and the executives of R.U.R for robots. There is no way to distinguish the artificial being from the human since their appearance is exactly the same; therefore, device equals life, the boundaries between what is alive and what is a product of technology disappear. The human existence is threatened by the artificial.[35]

However, the ontological structure of the robot is essentially different from that of man, since it cannot reproduce or feel pain. Paradoxically, it is a sexed body with the generic differentiation between male and female. But this is a distinction made by the demand of the market. The robot's sexuality is inactive; to be more precise, it is a sexed being without sexuality. Nothing in it is spontaneous; it lacks the affections and impulses that make man an imperfect machine. From the modernist point of view, man is deficient.

Furthermore, while pain is, according to Le Breton, a sign of vital self-consciousness in humans, as far as the executives of R.U.R. are concerned it would be a technical perfection in a robot, 'an automatic protection against damage;'[36] yet another way to make their products more durable and efficient. And so the intuition of pain is mediatised, losing its original significance in the dominions of a technocratic society - it is no longer the foundation of self-preservation, but a necessary improvement in the operation of the anthropomorphic mechanism.

Subsequently, Doctor Gall, upon the request of Helena, perfects the Robots - he makes them conscious of their superiority and provides them with a 'soul,' as Helena asked. But what is supposed to be a utopia quickly becomes dystopia: the birthrate decreases significantly, and human reproduction disappears almost entirely. Production of robots means that 'people are becoming superfluous, unnecessary.'[37] Furthermore, the robots begin to organize themselves and demand rights; it seems as though they 'they've ceased to be machines.'[38] A new conscience reclaims the world for itself and repudiates man. It is terrifying that their hatred is rational and impassioned, a hatred that, up until recently, only man could feel: 'Nobody can hate man more than man.'[39]

The monstrosity of the R.U.R. robot is that he is not an individual but a multitude. He is not an outcast like Frankenstein's creature, nor an isolated case of a simulacrum like the automata or Hadaly. This artificial being coexists with humans, deriving strength in numbers and constituting a veritable army. This same social aspect, the very basis of what is human, makes the robot proclaim man his enemy. The ideal of progress has changed hands; products made by human that are able to keep up with the modern world and that ultimately relieve humanity of its command: the robots are convinced 'that they are more highly developed than man. That they are stronger and more intelligent. That man's their parasite.'[40]

The robots annihilate humanity, sparing only the shop chief Alquist, because he works with his hands, like a robot. But this new species is condemned to a short life in the world, since the manuscript that discloses the secret of their creation was destroyed. Man obtains a posthumous victory of sorts, bequeathing his creature the pride of progress but not the ability to reproduce. Sterile and without hope, they turn to the last man on Earth, begging him to reveal the secret of life and thereby solve their enigma of existence. They even force him to dissect robots, a task that disturbs Alquist, who is sure that he is killing a human being and therefore committing homicide. The total humanization of the robot is personified in the last robots designed by Doctor Gall, Primus and Helena; these have developed an emotion previously reserved for the human race: love. Alquist sees in them the hope for this new humanity. The artificial being pushes man further and further toward the margins of existence. As the robot questions its identity and criticizes the concept of what is human, it refuses to be a servile reflection of its creator. Its figure seems ghastly to us because it is in fact ours, yet separated entirely from our will.

C. Humanity on Trial

The distinction between being human and being artificial finally seems to break down in *Do Androids Dream of Electric Sheep?* (1968) by Philip K. Dick (1928-1982). Even in *R.U.R.* there was a differentiation between man and machine, genuine and artificial, model and copy. The artificial being was still the Other; the problem of human identity was threatened but could take shelter in the awareness that the artificial creature's otherness. In Dick's novel, however, the subject of the Other disappears; the android is a creature of autonomous design; that is, it looks like itself. Technological improvements allow the artificial to coexist with the biological, so androids' existence is closer than ever to naturally living beings. The story's main character, the bounty hunter Rick Deckard, is aware of this problem. He feels constant guilt that his sheep is a machine, and is afraid that his neighbours could discover the truth. He keeps the true condition of his pet as a secret because 'to say, 'Is your sheep genuine?' would be a worse breach of manners than to inquire whether a citizen's teeth, hair, or internal organs would test out authentic.'[41] In the dystopic future Deckard inhabits, plagued by a shortage of authentic animals, the yearning for the biologically real is even more acute. The technological simulacrum is amoral, because it endangers the very model that it serves to hide.

Deckard is ordered to 'retire' six androids that escaped to Earth, mingling with the human population. But these Nexus-6 models, superior in intelligence to their predecessors, are experts at going unnoticed; in fact, only the Voigt-Kampff test can discern them from humans. For all of their advancement, however, the androids lack empathy and do not develop feelings of like or dislike toward people or even other androids.

In spite of that, Dick's pseudo-humans are still more perfect than other artificial beings because they are equipped with a 'false memory,' a simulated past that they consider theirs. Unlike robots, that knew they were different from man, the android is unaware of its otherness. By virtue of its 'self-narrative' it fits into the historical spectrum of humanity.

> the *narrative* self - the self identified by a story told both to ourselves and others, and told both by ourselves and others.... The narrative self is a self-built out of our own and others' conceptions of our projects, capacities, possibilities, and potentials.[42]

The android has an identity because it is able to tell its own story. For example, when the young Rachael Rosen takes the Voigt-Kampff test and scores at an android level, she explains that her low degree of empathy is because she has never been to Earth. The Voigt-Kampff test, the last borderline between man and android, is thus exposed as insufficient; the solution for the dilemma between what is human and what is not is merely provisional.

In the novel, questions about identity are so ingrained that Deckard himself, in an interview with the presumed android Luba Luft, has to wonder about his humanity.

> 'An android,' he said, 'doesn't care what happens to another android. That's one of the indications we look for.'
> 'Then,' Miss Luft said, 'you must be an android.'
> That stopped him; he stared at her.
> 'Because,' she continued, 'your job is to kill them, isn't it? You're what they call' - she tried to remember.
> 'A bounty hunter,' Rick said. 'But I'm not an android.'
> 'This test you want to give me.' Her voice, now, had begun to return. 'Have you taken it?'
> 'Yes.' He nodded. 'A long, long time ago; when I first started with the department.'
> 'Maybe that's a false memory. Don't androids sometimes go around with false memories?'[43]

The android has been perfected to such a degree that it interrogates the human being; man is now the Other whose humanity is called into question. This artificial being criticises the concepts of genuine and natural, and retorts that such ideas are the premises to which humans cling to dismiss the suspicion that they too are a cultural device. The android is monstrous because he reveals that the human being is as artificial as any technological creature, that identity is a construction of cultural codes. Le Breton expressed this ontological question in the formulation: Am I a man? Am I a machine? [44]

The complete collapse of the subtle borders that still separated man from artificial occurs when Deckard returns home upon accomplishing his mission. On his way he comes across a frog and takes it with him, surprised that an authentic animal has survived. Once home, however, his wife discovers the tiny mechanism of the mechanical amphibian. The hope that something organic had persisted becomes disillusionment at the impossibility of distinguishing what is alive from a machine.

The literary dream of artificial beings is now a cultural reality. The entities discussed here are no longer exclusively an object of fiction; many consider them the predecessors of the cyborg, epitome of a post-humanism that rejects any limit between body and machine. The organic and spiritual vitalism of the human being becomes obsolete when confronted with a technological metaphysics that considers life as set of data, as mere information. We are no longer beings with meaning, who perceive and interpret our senses; what is human is reduced to neutral processes of transmission and reception of information. All of which bespeaks a crisis of human identity today.

The rejection of humanity begins with the body, as it is here where our precarious condition is most evident. The paradigm of identity and human unity is replaced: external and internal are no longer a stable continuum. The post-human being is constantly manipulated and is no longer stable or unique, and as such she/he is transformable and transformed.[45] These are the proclamations of what Le Breton has called *Contemporary Extreme*, phenomenon that includes the cyber-feminism announced by Donna Haraway, or Sarah Kember, or the cyber-control to which Norbert Wiener subjects the human being.

Through the literary examples quoted here we may begin to formulate a kind of *biopoetics*: the study of literary discourse whose object is life and what opposes or criticizes it. It also constitutes an approximation via literature to what Foucault called *biopolitics*. Doubtless the artificial being is a political monster. On one hand it is a control strategy that dissimulates the malaise of civilization, superimposing in technological creatures the idea of transcendence in the human being. On the other, it represents the possibility of overcoming gender differences and racial intolerance.

Humans remain suspicious of the ever-greater feats of artificial beings, but the distrust humanity projects onto its creatures are, ultimately, directed at humanity itself. The artificial being functions par excellence as a mirror: an exact replica of humanity, imitating it even in its expression of conscious independence. Like our reflection in a mirror, the image can, by habit, be avoided. But the fact that, for a moment, no distinction can be made between us and our reflection is disturbing.

Translated by: Benjamin Krueger

Notes

[1] E.T.A. Hoffman, *The Best Tales of Hoffmann*, Dover Publications, New York, 1967, p. 84.
[2] Ibid., p. 80.
[3] Ibid., p.81.
[4] Ibid.
[5] Ibid., p. 205.
[6] Ibid., p. 207.
[7] *The Works of Edgar Allan Poe, Internet Archive,* Viewed on 25 March 2009, <http://www.archive.org/details/worksofedgaralla04poeeuoft>, p. 227.
[8] Ibid.
[9] Ibid., p. 253.
[10] J. Baudrillard, *Simulacra and Simulation*, University of Michigan, Ann Arbor, Michigan, 1994, p. 3.
[11] M. Shelley, *Frankenstein: or, The Modern Prometheus*, Pocket Books, First Washington Square Press, New York, 1995, p. 48.
[12] Ibid., p. 54.
[13] R. Kearney, *Stranger, Gods, and Monsters: Ideas of Otherness*, Routledge, London, 2003, p. 115.
[14] Ibid., p. 117.
[15] R. Gubern, *Las mascaras de la ficción*. Anagrama, Barcelona, 2002, p. 37.
[16] Shelley, op. cit., p. 102.
[17] Ibid., p. 151.
[18] Ibid., p. 180.
[19] Ibid., p. 178.
[20] Ibid., p. 241.
[21] A. Villiers de L'Isle-Adam, *Tomorrow's Eve*, University of Illinois, Chicago, 2001, p. 31.
[22] Ibid., p. 39.
[23] Ibid., p. 64.
[24] Ibid., p. 65.
[25] Ibid., p. 69.
[26] Ibid., p. 68.
[27] Ibid., p. 59.
[28] Ibid., p. 65.
[29] Ibid., p. 192.
[30] Ibid.
[31] Ibid.
[32] K. Čapek, *R.U.R. and The Insect Play*, University of Oxford, Oxford, 1961, p. 14.
[33] Ibid., p. 7.

[34] Ibid., p. 9.
[35] D. Le Breton, *Adiós al cuerpo. Una teoría del cuerpo en el extremo contemporáneo*, La cifra Editorial, Mexico City, 2007, p. 151.
[36] Čapek, op. cit., p. 24.
[37] Ibid., p. 48.
[38] Ibid., p. 70.
[39] Ibid., pp. 72-73.
[40] Ibid., p. 59.
[41] P. Dick, *Do Androids Dream of Electric Sheep?* Ballantine Books, New York, 1996, p. 8.
[42] A. Clark, *Natural-Born Cyborgs: Minds, Technologies, and the Future of Human Intelligence*, Oxford University Press, New York, 2004, p. 132.
[43] Dick, op. cit., pp. 101-102.
[44] Le Breton, op. cit., p. 186.
[45] L. Sepúlveda, *La utopía de los seres posthumanos*, CONACULTA / Universidad Autónoma Benito Juárez de Oaxaca, Mexico City, 2004, p. 44.

Bibliography

Baudrillard, J., *Simulacra and Simulation*. trans. Glaser, S.F., University of Michigan, Ann Arbor, Michigan, 1994.

Čapek, J. & Čapek, K., *R.U.R. and The Insect Play*. trans. Selver, P., University of Oxford, Oxford, 1961.

Clark, A., *Natural-Born Cyborgs: Minds, Technologies, and the Future of Human Intelligence*. Oxford University Press, New York, 2004.

Dick, P.K., *Do Androids Dream of Electric Sheep?* Ballantine Books, New York, 1996.

Gubern, R., *Las mascaras de la ficción*. Anagrama, Barcelona, 2002.

Haraway, D., *Simians, Cyborgs and Women: The Reinvention of Nature*. Routledge, New York, 1991.

Hoffmann, E.T.A., *The Best Tales of Hoffmann*. Bleiler, E.E.F. (ed), Dover Publications, New York, 1967.

Kearney, R., *Strangers, Gods, and Monsters: Ideas of Otherness*. Routledge, London, 2003.

Kember, S. *Cyberfeminism and Artificial Life*. Routledge, London, 2003.

Le Breton, D., *Adiós al cuerpo,. Una teoría del cuerpo en el extremo contemporáneo*, trans. Flores, O., La cifra Editorial, Mexico City, 2007.

Poe, E. A., *The Works of Edgar Allan Poe*. Vol. 4. A. C. Armstrong & Son, New York, 1884.

Sepúlveda, L., *La utopía de los seres posthumanos*, CONACULTA /Universidad Autónoma Benito Juárez de Oaxaca, Mexico City, 2004.

Shelley, M., *Frankenstein: or, The Modern Prometheus*. Pocket Books, First Washington Square Press, New York, 1995.

Villiers de L' I.-A., *Tomorrow's Eve*. trans. Adams, R.M., University of Illinois, Chicago, 2001.

Notes on Contributors

JONATHAN A. ALLAN is a SSHRC-funded PhD Candidate at the Centre for Comparative Literature at the University of Toronto. He holds degrees in Spanish Literature from Queen's University (B.A. Honours, M.A.) and a degree in Comparative Literatures and Arts (M.A.) from Brock University. His dissertation, 'The Sexual Scripture: A Study of Male Virginity in Romance,' works to consider the poetics and politics of virginity in romance novels. Most recently he has researched the influence of Northrop Frye on Harold Bloom; in this study he works through a series of previously unpublished letters currently housed in the Northrop Frye Collection at the E. J. Pratt Library at Victoria University in the University of Toronto.

TRACY CROWE MOREY is an Assistant Professor at the Department of Modern Languages, Literatures, and Cultures at Brock University in Canada. Her current research and scholarship reflect an interest in the memory boom of alternate histories of the Spanish Civil War. She has presented at a number of national and international conferences on the Spanish *comedia nueva* and the early modern history play.

TAMARA EL-HOSS is an Assistant Professor in the department of Modern Languages, Literatures & Cultures at Brock University, in Canada, where she teaches francophone literature. Her research focuses on the representation of 'marginal' women in Maghrebian and Caribbean literatures in French. She has presented papers at numerous international and national conferences, and is the author of 'L'usage des italiques dans L'Amour, la fantasia d'Assia Djebar: une écriture hybride' and 'Veiling/Unveiling in Tahar Ben Jelloun's The Sand Child: Disguise and Deception of the Female Protagonist'. Her new field of research is 'Beur' literature.

PHIL FITZSIMMONS is a senior lecturer at the Centre for Research in Language and Literacy at the Faculty of Education, University of Wollongong, Australia. His long term research interests have been in the area of Monster Theory and children's and Adolescent literature. Other fields of interest include visual literacy and the metaphysical aspects of children's literature.

SHELLEY GALLIAH is a term instructor at Grant MacEwan College in Edmonton, Alberta, where she teaches various introductory level English courses. She received her MA at Dalhousie University, with her thesis on Raymond Carver's minimalist fiction. Her current interests are late nineteenth century science fiction and American Naturalism. She is an editor of the fifth edition of Forms of Writing, a composition textbook with readings, and will be working on the sixth revised edition.

ELIZABETH HOLLIS BERRY as a Social Sciences and Humanities Research Council of Canada post-doctoral fellow and she published a monograph on Anne Bronte's novels and poetry. Since then, in addition to completing a book-length manuscript on Delarivier Manley, her publications include articles on Renaissance, eighteenth-century and Victorian writers, on feminist literary theorists, and on the transatlantic slave-trade. Also included amongst her interests are women's writing, narrative theory, medieval and Renaissance drama, the history of the novel (particularly the contributions of early women novelists), and the cultural history of slavery. After teaching as an associate professor at a university in Ontario, she now teaches and writes in Edmonton.

JOANNA MADLOCH has a doctorate in Humanities from the University of Silesia, Poland. From the year 2004, as a Visiting Specialist she has taught Classical Mythology at Montclair State University, New Jersey. Her academic interests focus on the juncture of verbal and pictorial arts (with an emphasis of the connection between literature and photography.) She has published over twenty scholarly articles, as well as a book on the Russian-American writer, Joseph Brodsky.

JESÚS EDUARDO OLIVA ABARCA is a full-time student of the Ph. D. degree in Arts and Humanities at the Instituto de Comunicación, Artes y Humanidades de Monterrey in Mexico. His current interests are related to the research in studies about metafiction, and the relationship between literature, culture and mass-media. He has collaborated in various research projects with academic groups at the Facultad de Filosofía y Letras de la UANL, as logistic in academic activities, as symposia on literature at the institution where he is undertaking his Ph. D.

RUDY RAMOS is a graphic artist and painter who formally studied art in Ottawa and Toronto, Canada. He also spent a year at S. W. Hayter's Atelier 17, Paris, France in 1986 and holds a Master of Arts and teaches digital printing techniques in Toronto.

SAMANTHA MICHELE RILEY earned her B.A. at the University of Iowa in the department of Cinema and Comparative Literature. She also studied at the University of Freiburg, Germany. She is currently a Ph.D. candidate in the department of Comparative Literature at the University of North Carolina Chapel Hill, working on her dissertation topic 'The Performance of AIDS in the Global Queer Cinema'. She teaches first year German and English composition. Samantha recently published a biography of 19th German feminist Hedwig Dohm at the LiteraryEncyclopedia.com. She also works as co-editor of the Teachers Edition and developer of a first and second year German language textbook, *Auf gehts!* and *Weiter geht's*!

Notes on Contributors

FELIPE RUAN is an Assistant Professor of Spanish at Brock University, where he teaches in the Department of Modern Languages, Literatures and Cultures and in the Centre for Medieval and Renaissance Studies. His research centres on issues of individual and collective identity in the cultural material of the early modern Hispanic world. He has published articles on Cervantes's short prose fiction, on the concept of cultural taste in the works of Baltasar Gracián and on the influential sixteenth-century conduct treatise *Galateo español*.

CRISTINA RUIZ SERRANO is professor of Spanish and Spanish American Literature at Grant MacEwan College in Canada. Her current research is focused on the evolution of Magical Realism and other similar modes of representation in twentieth-century Spanish American and Russian Literatures, gender and literature, and the representation of feminine sexuality and female body in fictional texts. She has presented her research findings at international and national conferences and she has published articles on Magical Realism and the Fantastic, on Spanish Naturalism, and on Russian Literary theory.

CRISTINA SANTOS is an Associate Professor of Spanish at Brock University where she teaches in the Department of Modern Languages, Literatures and Cultures and Director of Studies in Comparative Literatures and Arts. Her current research and scholarship reflects an interest in investigating the monstrous depictions of women as aberrations of feminine nature vis-à-vis the socio-culturally proscribed norm. She has presented at various national and international conferences and serves on the Editorial Board for *The Journal of Monsters and the Monstrous* housed at Oxford University. She is the author of *Bending the Rules in the Quest for an Authentic Female Identity*; co-editor with Adriana Spahr of *Defiant Deviance: The Irreality of Reality in the Cultural Imaginary*; and co-editor with Laura K. Davis *The Monster Imagined: Humanity's Recreation of Monsters and Monstrosities*.

VERÓNICA SAUNERO-WARD, a native of La Paz, Bolivia, holds a Ph.D. in Latin American Literature from the Pennsylvania State University. Currently, Dr. Saunero-Ward is an Associate Professor of Spanish at New Mexico Highlands University. Her articles on contemporary literature written by women have been published in Bolivia, the United States, and Mexico. At present, Dr. Saunero-Ward is undertaking a book project on Giovanna Rivero's short stories. This work has been approved for publication by La Hoguera publishing company.

ADRIANA SPAHR is a professor at the Department of Humanities at Grant MacEwan University in Canada. Reflecting her long interest on the cultural, political and historical components in literary pieces her current research is focused on the use of the monstrous as element of control in Latin American society. She has participated in national and international conferences. She is the author of *La sonrisa de la amargura: 1973-1982 La historia argentina a través de tres novelas de Osvaldo Soriano* and co-editor with Cristina Santos of *Defiant Deviance: The Irreality of Reality in the Cultural Imaginary*.

ANNE URBANCIC received her Ph.D. from the University of Toronto where she is Senior Lecturer in the Department of Italian Studies. An award-winning instructor, she also coordinates and teaches in the Frye (Humanities) and Pearson (Social Sciences) Streams of the VIC ONE Program for First Year Students. As a researcher, she favours a transdisciplinary approach. She is a specialist in 19th/20th century Italian Literature and in foreign language pedagogy. She has published extensively in numerous academic journals in Europe and in North America. Together with G. Katz, she has also translated four contemporary Italian novels.